THE MARCUS W. JERNEGAN
ESSAYS IN AMERICAN
HISTORIOGRAPHY

MARCUS WILSON JERNEGAN

THE MARCUS W. JERNEGAN ESSAYS IN AMERICAN HISTORIOGRAPHY

*

BY HIS FORMER STUDENTS
AT THE UNIVERSITY OF CHICAGO

EDITED BY WILLIAM T. HUTCHINSON

NEW YORK · RUSSELL AND RUSSELL

The Library of Congress has cataloged
this book as follows:

The **Marcus W. Jernegan** essays in American historiography,
by his former students at the University of Chicago, edited
by William T. Hutchinson. ₍New York, Russell & Russell,
1958₎

x, 417 p.   port.   24 cm.

CONTENTS.—George Bancroft, by W. Stewart.—Richard Hildreth,
by A. H. Kelly.—Francis Parkman, by J. P. Smith.—Hermann Eduard
von Holst, by C. R. Wilson.—James Schouler, by L. E. Ellis.—Woodrow Wilson, by L. M. Sears.—John Bach McMaster, by W. T. Hutchinson.—John Fiske, by J. B. Sanders.—James Ford Rhodes, by R. C.
Miller.—Henry Adams, by H. S. Commager.—Alfred Thayer Mahan,
by J. W. Pratt.—Theodore Roosevelt, by H. J. Thornton.—Frederick
Jackson Turner, by A. Craven.—Herbert Levi Osgood, by E. C. O.

(Continued on next card)

58–12863

The **Marcus W. Jernegan** essays in American historiography
...   ₍1958₎   (Card 2)

CONTENTS—Continued.

Beatty.—Edward Channing, by R. R. Fahrney.—George Louis Beer,
by A. P. Scott.—Clarence Walworth Alvord, by M. Dargan, Jr.—
Claude Halstead Van Tyne, by P. G. Davidson.—Ulrich Bonnell
Phillips, by W. Gray.—Albert J. Beveridge, by T. E. Strevey.—Vernon
Louis Parrington, by W. T. Utter.

1. U. S.—Hist.—Historiography.   2. Historians, American.   3. Jernegan, Marcus Wilson, 1872–1949.   I. Hutchinson, William Thomas,
1895–   ed.

E175.45.M3   973.07   58–12863

Library of Congress

AS AN EXPRESSION OF THEIR FRIENDSHIP AND
ESTEEM, THE AUTHORS DEDICATE THESE ESSAYS TO

MARCUS WILSON JERNEGAN

AT THE TIME OF HIS RETIREMENT FROM THE
HISTORY FACULTY OF THE UNIVERSITY OF CHICAGO
AFTER NEARLY THIRTY YEARS OF FRUITFUL SERVICE

PREFACE

✷

ALITTLE over a century ago George Bancroft opened a new era of American historiography by publishing the first volume of his *History of the United States from the Discovery of the American Continent*. Thereafter, until our own day, the production record of scholars working in the field of United States history has been an impressive one. Each of their books, as it left the press, was obliged to run the reviewers' gauntlet; but there are few studies which examine the chief works of leading historians for the purpose of ascertaining their methods of research, the influences determining their outlook upon the past, and the reasons justifying their remembrance by students of American history.

Only within recent years, in fact, have courses in historiography been accorded a place in the curricula of graduate schools of history in this country. Among those teachers who have offered seminars in this subject with notable success is Professor Marcus Wilson Jernegan, of the University of Chicago.

At the suggestion of Professor Jennings B. Sanders, of the University of Tennessee, a number of Professor Jernegan's former students, wishing to give evidence of their appreciation for his guidance, prepared the essays in this volume. Its publication has been made possible by the cordial support of many of Professor Jernegan's friends.

These studies, taken together, do not pretend to furnish a comprehensive survey of American historiography. To achieve at least a semblance of unity, they all deal with scholars whose work is finished and who directed their research mainly toward United States history prior to the close of the Civil War. Nor do the authors wish to imply that each of the historians selected for consideration was without a peer even within his own field of specialization. The purpose has rather been to choose representatives of several of the leading types of historians; those who sought to write a detailed account of the nation's life from the time of Columbus or from the close of the American Revolution to their own day; those who made themselves masters of a briefer chronological period or of some important aspect of history; and those who confined their attention almost exclusively to the problems and development of one section of the United States.

Of the twenty-one chapters in this volume, two, somewhat modified in form, and a few paragraphs in three of the others, have already appeared in the *Mississippi Valley Historical Review* and are included here through the courtesy of Professor Arthur C. Cole, the editor of that quarterly.

More friends of Professor Jernegan volunteered to assist in the editing of this volume than could be accommodated with work. Professor Sanders and Mrs. Frank L. Esterquest have been especially helpful. The editor wishes also to acknowledge the generous aid given by his colleagues, Professors Bessie L. Pierce and Avery Craven, by Miss Esther Aphelin, and by Miss Mary Irwin and Miss Mary D. Alexander, of the University of Chicago Press.

THE EDITOR

August 5, 1937

CONTENTS

✳

ix

I

GEORGE BANCROFT

WATT STEWART

Oklahoma Agricultural and Mechanical College

EW Americans will seriously question the statement of the English scholar, George P. Gooch, that "American history came of age with Bancroft."[1] George Bancroft initiated a new era in American historiography and laid securely the foundations of American historical letters. His life, moreover, furnishes an instance of a phenomenon which is not too frequently encountered in the United States—that of an individual who was eminent both as a scholar and as a man of affairs.

The fundamentals of his character Bancroft drew in equal measure from his parents. His father, Aaron Bancroft, a Harvard graduate, was a liberal-minded Congregational divine. His interest in history is shown by his *Life of Washington* (1807), which enjoyed a degree of popularity in its day. He is said to have maintained "a steady, consistent attachment to freedom of conscience and of thought, the right of free inquiry, the right of private judgment."[2] His mother was Lucretia Chandler, who analyzed herself as follows: "I cair'd not for history, nor did I read much of Travels. . . . . I read novels to a wonderful extent, I took pleasure in a good play, and found delight in reading blank virce. . . . . I possessed a cheerful disposition. . . . . I was always ready for any amusement. . . . ."[3]

[1] G. P. Gooch, *History and Historians in the Nineteenth Century* (2d ed.; London, 1913), p. 403.

[2] M. A. DeWolfe Howe, *The Life and Letters of George Bancroft* (New York, 1908), I, 9.

[3] *Ibid.*, p. 13.

Throughout a long life George Bancroft practiced his father's strict ideas of morality and of independence; and the mother's imagination, excellent disposition, and delight in innocent amusement are evident in his work and in his life. One can readily accept the statement of a secretary of Mr. Bancroft that "things concerning God and country were his patrimony."[4]

After completing his preparatory work at Phillips Academy, Bancroft entered Harvard University, where, in 1817, at the age of seventeen, he was granted the Bachelor's degree. The following year the Harvard authorities awarded him a Göttingen University scholarship, and in June he sailed from Boston for Germany.

Bancroft's Harvard advisers desired him to prepare for the ministry. Accordingly, he devoted most of his time to the study of the ancient languages and oriental literature. But, happily realizing, as he said, "the impossibility of reconciling the acquisitions of a German University with the notions of Boston,"[5] he spent some time on courses in history, notably under Heeren, whose American translator he later became. As a reward for his assiduity the young student was granted in 1820 the degree of Doctor of Philosophy.

He did not at once return to the United States but spent the greater part of two more years in Europe, studying for brief periods at Heidelberg and Berlin, and traveling in France, England, Switzerland, and Italy.[6] At this period, as always throughout his life, Bancroft seized every opportunity to meet persons of interest and consequence. On one occasion while in Paris he attended a dinner at the home of Benjamin Constant, where he met Alexander von Humboldt and the Marquis de Lafayette.[7] Others whose acquaintance he made at this time were Goethe[8] and Lord

---

[4] Austin Scott's appreciation of Bancroft in *The Warner Library: The World's Best Literature* (University ed.; New York, 1917), III, 1433.

[5] Bancroft to E. Everett, Jan. 8, 1835, in Howe, I, 208.

[6] This period of Bancroft's life is interestingly covered in Howe, I, 24–154.

[7] *Ibid.*, pp. 104, 105.

[8] Very self-revealing is the note in Bancroft's diary written following his visit to Goethe: "I am only more and more astonished at the indecency and immorality of the latter

Byron. The four years in Europe left their imprint on him. While his intellectual powers were developing, his outlook broadened, his acquaintance with men and affairs of importance was extended, and something of the icy Puritanism of New England was, for the time at least, melted from him.[9]

The ten years immediately following his return from Europe were years of experiment, more or less of failure. He taught Greek at Harvard for a year, essaying meanwhile his father's vocation. However, his impatience with the system at Harvard, which he considered antiquated, prevented him from fitting smoothly into the regime there; and his sermons, pedantic and philosophical, failed to "take" with the people. Simultaneously, he attempted to woo the poetic muse, and published a volume of poems. His good sense enabled him to see that he was neither a preacher nor a poet. So, with Joseph Green Cogswell, formerly librarian and professor of mineralogy at Harvard, he founded the Round Hill School for boys. Eight years in a schoolmaster's vocation convinced him that it was not for him. Besides, he had about determined upon his great work; so he sold out to Cogswell and left the school in 1831.[10]

It was during the Round Hill period that Bancroft married his first wife, Miss Sarah H. Dwight, who died in 1837. In the fol-

[Goethe]. He appears to prefer to represent vice as lovely and exciting sympathy, than virtue, and would rather take for his heroine a prostitute or a profligate, than give birth to that purity of thought and loftiness of soul, which it is the peculiar duty of the poet to raise, by connecting his inventions with the actions of heroes, and embodying in verse the merits of the benefactors of mankind" (*ibid.*, p. 38).

9 The unfortunate "kissing incident" illustrates both the truth of this statement and the painful consequences that followed. In a letter written from Göttingen in 1820 to his good friend Andrews Norton at Harvard (August 19, Howe, I, 77) Bancroft had mentioned, as a warrant for calling the students "barbarians," their beards and their fashion of kissing, after a separation, "twice as lustily as Romeo ever kissed Juliet." But behold him, on his return to Boston two years later, administering resounding smacks to the cheeks of this same Norton! Norton never recovered from the shock; the friendship was broken, to Bancroft's great unhappiness. See John S. Bassett, *The Middle Group of American Historians* (New York, 1917), pp. 139–42.

10 Howe, I, 169–79.

lowing year he married Mrs. Elizabeth (Davis) Bliss, a woman of excellent attainments and family connections.[11]

The first Mrs. Bancroft was of a prominent Whig family. As Bancroft did not share her political views, she prevailed on him to forego politics of an active sort.[12] He had, however, a lively interest in government. His first public political utterance was a Fourth of July oration delivered at Northampton in 1826. Speaking at the time when Jefferson and John Adams were breathing their last, the young orator seemed to "catch the torch" as it fell from the former's hand. Jefferson himself might well have dictated some passages of that oration:

With the people the power resides, both theoretically and practically. The government is a democracy, a determined uncompromising democracy; administered immediately by the people, or by the people's responsible agents. . . . . The popular voice is all powerful with us; this is our oracle; this we acknowledge, is the voice of God.[13]

Here is an expression of Bancroft's fundamental political principle. Democracy was his native political bent, nurtured by travel and study. This precept colors with clear partiality many of the pages of his *History*. "Bancroft the politician and Bancroft the historian, were consistent exponents of the same democratic principle."[14]

Declarations such as that quoted above attracted the attention of the Bay State Republicans; and in 1830 Bancroft, without his foreknowledge, was elected to a seat in the legislature, which he did not accept. The next year he was requested to consent to the nomination for secretary of state of Massachusetts.[15] This also he declined.

His refusal, at his wife's request, to hold political office did not, however, prevent Bancroft from taking steps to make himself favorably known to the Jackson administration. His politi-

[11] *Ibid.*, pp. 183, 224. From the former union came four children, of whom two, both boys, lived to manhood. There were no children by the second Mrs. Bancroft.

[12] Wm. M. Sloane, "George Bancroft—in Society, in Politics, in Letters," *Century Illustrated Monthly Magazine*, XXXIII (N.S., IX; 1887), 479.

[13] Howe, I, 186.   [14] *Ibid.*, p. 187.   [15] Sloane, p. 479.

cal acumen is seen in a letter which in 1830 he wrote to Van
Buren, the Secretary of State. He inclosed a copy of an article
on the United States Bank which he had recently contributed to
the *North American Review*. With reference to it he wrote: "I intend in the course of the summer to prepare a further argument
in defence of the ground, generally taken by the Government in
this question. It would be eminently gratifying to me, if what I
have written should seem correctly argued."[16] Again, in 1834,
he wrote Van Buren, presenting a copy of the first volume of his
History. He mentioned the "excessive invectives" of the newspapers against himself and added, "My crime consisted in refusing to calumniate the present administration. . . . ."[17]

In Bancroft's announcement that he was opposed to the Bank,
Professor Bassett saw the turning-point in the career of the historian. The Federalists of New England concluded that he had
acted from selfish motives, but the Jackson men hailed the Bank
article with delight. They made him a political asset. He was
"too astute to refuse, and he followed the lead they opened to
him until at last he reached the highest places in the party."[18]
It is not claimed that Bancroft violated any principle of his own
in adopting the Jacksonian cause, but it was exceedingly convenient that his principles and his interests should so nicely coin-
cide. Harriet Martineau, after visiting in Bancroft's home in
1834, portrayed the situation well when she said that a Massachusetts man had little chance in public life unless he started as
a Federalist, and that he had no chance of rising above a certain
low point unless, when he reached that point, he made the transition into Democracy.[19] In 1834 Bancroft had already reached
that point and had made the transition.

By 1844 Bancroft had become the undisputed leader of the
Democrats in New England. He was active in the campaign of
that year, not only as a supporter of the Democratic presidential

[16] January 10, "Van Buren-Bancroft Correspondence," Massachusetts Historical Society, *Proceedings*, XLII (3d ser., II; 1909), 382.

[17] November 17, *ibid*., pp. 382–83.   [18] Bassett, p. 172.

[19] J. Clay Walker, *George Bancroft as Historian* (Heidelberg, 1914), p. 7.

nominee but as a candidate himself for governor of Massachu-setts. He had already gained some fame as a political speaker.[20] As a delegate to the national Democratic convention he support-ed Van Buren until it became evident that he could not be nomi-nated; then he shifted his support to Polk and, if his own account may be accepted, was himself directly responsible for Polk's nomination. Incidentally, it may be noted, he did not neglect to inform Polk of his services;[21] and, after Polk had been elected he wrote him, as he says, "a simple, quiet letter, designed to lead him *not* to think of me; and designed also to prevent persons quoting my name to him, as Anderson's was to me."[22]

Whatever one may think of this remarkable method of pre-venting the president-elect from thinking of him, especially in the light of his own defeat in Massachusetts, Polk duly did think of him, and offered him the post of Secretary of the Navy. Ban-croft promptly accepted, but his incumbency lasted only a year and a half. While in this office he wrote Charles Sumner, "I am glad you go for the good rule of dismissing wicked Whigs and putting in Democrats."[23] This statement, it may be well to ob-serve, was made as a preface to promising a job for Nathaniel Hawthorne. Though Bancroft was the only member of the Cabi-net who did not support Polk's war message of May, 1846, his subsequent course was "that of a faithful member of the official family."[24] Bancroft's most notable act as Secretary of the Navy was the founding of the Naval Academy at Annapolis. His pro-

[20] A Whig contemporary said that Bancroft "brought the rhetoric of his history to the platform. He was ornate, gilded, and occasionally flaming. Whatever he might be dis-cussing . . . . he seldom deigned to descend from his stilts. He had a favorite way of be-ginning these election harangues. He would look with an expression of astonishment at the audience, and exclaim, with the gesture of Hamlet at the sight of the ghost, 'This vast assemblage might well appall me.' This impressed those who had never heard it more than twice before, and it had the further effect of giving the audience aforesaid a good conceit of its own proportions" (quoted by Chas. O. Paullin in "New England Secretaries of the Navy," *New England Magazine*, N.S., XXXVII [1907-8], 657).

[21] Bancroft to Polk, July 6, 1844, in Howe, I, 251-54.

[22] Bancroft to Van Buren, "Van Buren–Bancroft Correspondence," p. 437.

[23] January 13, 1846 in Howe, I, 267.   [24] *Ibid.*, p. 291.

motion policy—merit, rather than rank, being the first consideration—caused friction between him and various members of the naval personnel, and it is possible that this was the main cause of his willingness to resign his office and go as minister to England.

The three-year sojourn in Europe was not of large political significance but was of the greatest value to his literary work. Some three months of each year he spent in Paris, meeting the leading men—Guizot, Thiers, Lamartine, and others—and searching the archives for material for his history.[25] The remainder of his time he devoted to similar activities in England.

Returning to the United States in the fall of 1849, Bancroft settled in New York, and until 1867 he was engaged mainly in writing additional volumes of his *History*. His life was varied a bit by other activities, such as delivering before Congress the memorial address on Lincoln and writing President Johnson's message to Congress of 1865.[26] A reward, probably, for the latter act was his appointment in 1867 as minister to the North German Confederation, shortly to become the German Empire. Bancroft remained in Berlin until 1874. As previously in England and France, he made use of his opportunities to meet eminent people and to carry on his researches in European archives. After his return to the United States, he took up his residence in Washington and spent there the remaining years of his life.

In this brief sketch of Bancroft's nonliterary activities, we see a scholar whom the shadows and the silence of the library did not unfit for the strenuous demands of public service. He was a practical man of affairs and a politician able to see the possibilities of a situation and realize them in action.

Bancroft, being a man of strong intellect, was also a man of strong convictions. Those convictions naturally find an echo in his writings. His philosophy of religion was the traditional Christian assumptions. He believed implicitly in the existence of an all-wise Providence, which directed the movements of the universe and controlled the most minute events. "Each page of

[25] *Ibid.*, II, 98.   [26] *Ibid.*, pp. 162–63.

history," he said, "may begin and end with Great is God and marvellous are his doings among the children of men."[27] In his oration on the "Progress of Mankind," delivered in 1854, he exclaimed: "The selfishness of evil defeats itself, and God rules in the affairs of men."[28] Similarly, references to the directing hand of Providence occur frequently in his works.[29] His political philosophy—supreme faith in democracy—has been sufficiently illustrated.[30] A corollary of this was his strong opposition to slavery.

Bancroft's concept of the nature of history is of some importance to an understanding of his work:

It is because God is visible in History that its office is the noblest except that of the poet. . . . . History, as she reclines in the lap of eternity, sees the mind of humanity itself engaged in formative efforts, constructing sciences, promulgating laws, organizing commonwealths and displaying its energies in the visible movement of its intelligence. Of all pursuits that require analysis, history, therefore, stands first. It is equal to philosophy; for as certainly as the actual bodies forth the ideal, so certainly does history contain philosophy. It is grander than the natural sciences; for its study is man, the last work of creation, and the most perfect in its relations with the Infinite.[31]

He thought of "history as a unit, its forces as constant and their manifestations as parts of an organized whole. Each individual must have his place in the picture, but the background is the history of the race."[32] He emphasized the idea of the continuity of history.[33] Stating the matter briefly, we may say that Bancroft considered each historical event as a separate manifestation of the will of Providence.

[27] Bancroft to Mrs. Bancroft, Dec. 31, 1847, in Howe, II, 77.

[28] Quoted in Gooch, p. 405.

[29] See Introduction to his *History of the United States from the Discovery of the Continent,* I (1834), 4; *ibid.,* p. 316; and IV (1883), 4, 6. (Unless otherwise identified, all citations to Bancroft's *History* will be understood to have been found in the six-volume edition, "The Author's Last Revision," of 1883–85.)

[30] See letter to Mrs. Bancroft, Jan. 17, 1832, in Howe, I, 199.

[31] Howe, II, 119, 120.   [32] Sloane, p. 484.   [33] Bancroft, *History,* II, 324.

There must be, he thought, the same conservation of energy in morals as in matter. "No tramp of a despot's foot ever trod out one idea. The world cannot retrograde."[34] Truth, morals, and justice have always been truth, morals, and justice, and are subject to no change; but man moves and acts with liberty and responsibility and develops better forms of knowledge and behavior. The evolution of society, therefore, produces a succession of states in each of which the principle of freedom is better established than in the antecedent. Tyranny and wrong lead inevitably to decay; freedom and right always prove resistless.[35] Reduced to its simplest expression, Bancroft's philosophy is the belief that "God rules in the affairs of men."

Bancroft is now known only through his *History of the United States of America*. That, it is true, is his chief work; but he gave some attention to other forms of literary composition. Our truest impression of the man is to be gained from his letters. Mark Anthony DeWolfe Howe has made what appears to be a judicious selection from the mass of these and has woven them skilfully into his *Life and Letters of George Bancroft*, the two volumes of which appeared in 1908.[36] To members of his family Bancroft wrote in much detail from day to day. Other letters to men in public life and in the literary world are interesting and informative. They are forceful in style, sometimes lively, though not often humorous in tone. One reviewer suspected that they were elaborately penned in the expectation that some day they would reach the eye of the public.[37]

Reference has already been made to Bancroft's venture in the field of poesy. His only metrical brain-child—a thin, lavender-bound volume of seventy-seven pages—saw the light in 1823. It attracted little attention and deserved none. The following lines

[34] From his oration on the "Progress of Mankind," quoted in Gooch, p. 405.

[35] Bancroft, *History*, VI, 7.

[36] For reviews of this work see the *American Historical Review*, XIV (1908–9), 150, and *Nation*, LXXXVI (1908), 446–47.

[37] *Nation*, LXXXVI (1908), 446.

are from the first poem, "Expectation," and the theme is that of the writer's departure for Europe in 1818:

> And fast away the tear he brushed,
> That down his cheeks too freely gushed,
> As swiftly from his native shore
> The vessel hurrying breezes bore.

It is said that later in his life Bancroft destroyed all of the copies of this little book of which he could get possession. So, respectful to the historian, we draw the curtain on the embryo poet.

While teaching at Round Hill School, Bancroft worked industriously. Among his productions at this period were Greek and Latin grammars, published respectively in 1824 and 1825. It was then, too, that he tried his hand at the business of translating— "an humble one," as he described it.[38] In 1824 appeared his translation of Heeren's *Reflections on the Politics of Ancient Greece*, and in 1829 followed a translation in two volumes of the same author's *History of the Political System of Europe and Its Colonies, from the Discovery of America to the Independence of the American Continent*.[39] In the years 1823 and 1824 he wrote numerous articles for the *North American Review* and a few for the *American Quarterly Review*.[40]

By 1828 history began to assume a leading place in Bancroft's interests. Early in the thirties, if not before, he turned to his great task of writing the *History of the United States*. The first volume came from the press in 1834. Succeeding volumes appeared at fairly regular intervals.[41] The original title was *His-*

[38] Translator's preface to A. H. L. Heeren, *A Sketch of the Political History of Ancient Greece*, p. vi.

[39] Howe, I, 180.

[40] *Ibid.*, p. 183. It was at this time that Jared Sparks, then editor of the *North American Review*, pointed out to Bancroft his "two grand mistakes: first to suffer yourself to be unduly excited about comparatively small things; and secondly, to have little respect for the judgment of others" (Howe, I, 183 n.). See also J. S. Bassett (ed.), "Correspondence of George Bancroft and Jared Sparks, 1823–1832," *Smith College Studies*, II, No. 2 (1917), 67–143.

[41] Howe, I, 225, 237; II, 102 n., 255; Bassett, *The Middle Group*, p. 202. Vol. II appeared in 1837; Vol. III, 1840; Vols. IV and V, 1852; Vol. VI, 1854; Vol. VII, 1858; Vol. VIII, 1860; Vol. IX, 1866; Vol. X, 1874; Vols. XI and XII, 1882. The longer intervals between Vols. III and IV and Vols. IX and X mark his active periods of public service.

tory of the United States from the Discovery of the American Continent; but in the "Centenary Edition" of 1876 it was altered to read *History of the United States of America, from the Discovery of the Continent,* in which form it has remained.

The work was divided, subdivided, and proportioned in this manner:

Part I. "Colonial History, 1492–1748," more than one-fourth of the work

Part II. "The American Revolution, 1748–1782," about two-thirds of the entire work

    a) "1748–1763, Overthrow of the European Colonial System"

    b) "1763–1774, How Great Britain Estranged America"

    c) "1774–1776, America Declares Itself Independent"

    d) "1776–1782, The Independence of America Is Acknowledged"

Part III. "The History of the Formation of the Constitution, 1782–1789," more than one-tenth of the work[42]

The volumes went through numerous editions. That printed in 1848 is designated "Fourteenth Edition." Changes were made, from time to time, by the author. The two most important revisions were the "Centenary Edition," as styled on the cover, or the "Thoroughly Revised Edition," as described on the title-page, which was printed in 1876, and "The Author's Last Revision," which appeared in the years 1883–85. In the first of these revisions, the ten original volumes, which brought the story to the end of the Revolution, were compressed into six volumes. The mechanics of the volumes are quite different from those of preceding editions, but the subject matter does not show striking changes. In "The Author's Last Revision" the content of the original twelve volumes was published in six volumes. In this edition the work was re-written, and important changes were made both in text and subject matter.

It is regrettable that Bancroft's swan song should have been

---

[42] The material of Part III was published originally as a separate work, but it is essentially a continuation of the *History* proper and was so included in "The Author's Last Revision."

the book entitled *Martin Van Buren to the End of His Public Career* (1889). Most of this work had been composed in 1844 at Van Buren's request,[43] to be printed and used as a campaign textbook. It was in the press when Van Buren was defeated for the nomination by Polk. Naturally, publication was suspended. Bancroft wrote Van Buren that "the suppressed epic" he intended "to make somewhat better by the opportunity of revision."[44] Bancroft's first "misprint," the *Poems*, marked the closing of one childhood; this marked the beginning of a second.

Whatever may be the present opinion of Bancroft's *History*, it was highly commended by his contemporaries. One student of the historian says that the first three volumes met with great success in America and "were reprinted in England and translated at once into Danish, Italian, German, and French."[45] Edward Everett wrote the author just after the appearance of the first volume, "I think you have written a Work which will last while the memory of America lasts."[46] Both by extent of sales and by the testimony of the writer's contemporaries, the *History* was an unqualified success. This "immediate and unbounded popularity and acceptance" came mainly, thinks Dr. Jameson, from the fact that the historian

caught, and with sincere and enthusiastic conviction repeated to the American people, the things which they were saying and thinking concerning themselves. . . . . Bancroft's first volume succeeded mainly because it was redolent of the ideas of the new Jacksonian democracy— its exuberant confidence, its uncritical self-laudation, its optimistic hopes.[47]

In respect to the manner in which Bancroft went about his task, his biographer says that, in preparing to write upon any period, the historian

devoted each page in a blank book of quarto size to a single day, and on that page noted every event belonging to it, together with thoughts of

[43] Van Buren to Bancroft, Feb. 25, 1844, in "Van Buren-Bancroft Correspondence," pp. 417, 418.

[44] *Ibid.*, p. 432   [45] Walker, p. 25.   [46] Howe, I, 206.

[47] J. Franklin Jameson, *The History of Historical Writing in America* (Boston and New York, 1891), pp. 103–4.

his own. quotations and allusions bearing upon these events. Even the phases of the moon were noted. This [meticulous procedure] gave him the daily sequence of historic events, and enabled his orderly mind to make an orderly presentation of his material.[48]

Bancroft's secretary, Austin Scott, adds that his employer "often struggled long with a thought for intellectual mastery":

In giving it expression, his habit was to dictate rapidly and with enthusiasm and at great length, but he usually selected the final form after repeated efforts. His first draft of a chapter was revised again and again and condensed. One of his early volumes in its first manuscript form was eight times as long as when finally published.[49]

Describing Bancroft's *History* as the completion of a "titanic task," Bassett makes an interesting comparison of his problem, its size, and the time used in completing it, with that of Rhodes, McMaster, and Hildreth. Bassett's conclusion is that Bancroft was, by comparison, a slow worker.[50]

Bancroft had a lively appreciation of the faults of previous writers on American history. And he had an explanation of them:

Many of the early writers in Europe were only careful to explain the physical qualities of the country; and the political institutions of dependent colonies were not thought worthy of exact inquiry. The early history was often written with a carelessness which seized on rumours and vague recollections as sufficient authority for an assertion which satisfied prejudice by wanton perversions, and which, where materials were not at hand, substituted the inferences of the writer for authenticated facts. These early books have ever since been cited as authorities, and the errors, sometimes repeated even by considerate writers, whose distrust was not excited, have almost acquired a prescriptive right to a place in the annals of America.[51]

[48] Howe, II, 104–5.

[49] *Warner's Library: The World's Best Literature*, III, 1436.

[50] *The Middle Group*, pp. 209–10 Bancroft's twelve volumes contain 1,700,000 words; time of preparation, fifty years. Rhodes' work, 1,410,000 words; time, sixteen years. McMaster's work, 2,208,000 words; time, thirty-five years and done while teaching. Hildreth's work 1,162,000 words; time, less than ten years.

[51] Preface to the original edition, I, vi.

Bancroft's method of insuring that his history should not have these faults was to derive his narrative "from writings and sources which were the contemporaries of the events that are [were] described."[52] He did, in fact, go to the sources. Throughout his life he was an avid hunter of source materials. In the preface to Volume VI Bancroft catalogues the manuscript materials which he used. The list includes records of the Public Record Office of Great Britain, records of the Treasury, proceedings in Parliament, manuscripts of the British Museum, various collections of private papers of English public men, the French archives, papers of the French Ministry of Marine and of War, selections of papers in Holland, some Spanish correspondence, papers of a number of the agents of the American colonies in London. He leaves the impression also that he had visted most of the original thirteen states and examined their archives.[53]

The extent of Bancroft's use of sources and the nature of them are revealed in his citations. Chapter ii, for instance, in Book IV, Volume VI (1883), pages 452–62, contains references to the following works:

	Times Cited
The *Federalist*	4
McRee's *Iredell*	3
Hamilton's *Works*	5
Independent Gazetteer	3
Penn-Packet	2
Jay's *Jay*	1
Thompson's *Long Island*	1
Elliot's *Debates*	3
Clinton MSS	1
Sparks (*Rev. Dipl. Corr.?*)	1
Moore's *North Carolina*	1

Of the 25 citations, 19 are from primary sources, 6 from secondary works. Of the primary source citations, 5 are from newspapers. In chapter iv, Volume VI (1852), pages 83–105 (in addition to 26 references to correspondence the source of which is not

[52] *Ibid.*, p. v.   [53] (1858 ed.), pp. v–viii.

indicated), there are 25 citations; of these, 17 are from primary sources. In chapter xv of the same volume, not counting 18 references to correspondence for which no source is given, there are 20 citations—9 from secondary works, 11 from primary sources.

These chapters are representative of others, in the parts of the work where authorities are cited. It is evident that Bancroft did, to a large extent, base his narrative on source material, both manuscript and printed, but that he did not scorn to employ secondary works which he found reliable. It appears that he did not use newspapers and periodicals as extensively as he might have done, though they were by no means wholly neglected. Of 21 references in chapter xiv ("South Carolina Founds the American Union, June–July, 1765") of Volume V (1858), 11 are to newspapers or periodicals; of 27 references in chapter xvi, 7 are to such sources, while in chapter xix the references of this nature are but 2 out of 22. References to English periodicals are few; and of American newspapers or periodicals, only those of the central and New England colonies are used. The newspaper most cited is the *Boston Gazette*.

Bancroft estimated that he had spent $50,000–$75,000 in obtaining source materials.[54] Public documents and obtainable private correspondence were, he thought, pretty well exhausted by him. While, as already observed, he might have made greater use of newspapers, it may be said that the faults of his *History* resulted not so much from neglect of available sources as from his interpretation of them.

The method of arrangement adopted by Bancroft was, in the main, chronological. Beginning with chapter xvii of Volume II (1883), every chapter of that volume and of the succeeding four volumes bears a date in addition to its main heading. The developments of a given period in England are usually presented in a chapter separate from that in which the developments in America of the same period are treated, though occasionally both are included in one chapter. The chronological treatment is emphasized by the use of marginal dates—at the side in early volumes

[54] Howe, II, 261.

and in the "Centenary Edition," and at the top in "The Author's Last Revision." This practice is also followed in that part of the work which covers the formation of the Constitution.

The types of subjects that predominate in the *History* are political-military and socio-religious. In Volume I (1883), chapter vi, "England Plants a New Nation in Virginia," scarcely a page is devoted to economic and social forces in England which led to the planting of Virginia. In nineteen chapters on the subject, "The English People Found a Nation in America," Part I, Volume I (1883), which carries the narrative to 1660, practically nothing is said of geographic conditions, and there is only an occasional brief mention of the economic motive. The chief interest is in the fields of politics and religion. There is a chapter on slavery in Virginia, emphasizing its social side. Much attention is also given to Puritanism. In the conclusion of chapter i, Volume V (1885), "Can the Thirteen United States Maintain Their Independence?" only a page and a quarter are devoted to Great Britain's chances of success and to the circumstances favoring the Americans. On the economic handicaps which confronted the latter the author is silent, and there is but a bare suggestion of the geographic difficulties with which the British had to contend. Bancroft's reviewers, almost with one voice, notice his predominant interest in political and military subjects and pay tribute to his ability to handle them.

Bancroft was sometimes guilty of complicating his work by bringing in extraneous materials. "At times," Howe declares, "the fact that he was writing a history of the United States seems to have suffered burial under the accumulation of knowledge on subjects but distantly related to the central theme."[55] In his criticism of Volume X, a writer in the *North American Review* says:

Mr. Bancroft's weak point, however, seems to be a certain vivacity or restlessness of mind which is apt to mislead his readers as to the relative importance of events. . . . . He devotes great care and excessive space to the subordinate but novel story of German and Russian diplo-

[55] *Ibid.*, p. 326.

macy, including more than thirty pages of pure German history, while the story of the negotiation for peace, the most important and the most brilliant effort of American diplomacy, occupies little more than forty pages.[56]

Similarly, in chapter viii, Volume I (1883),[57] a discussion of slavery—presumably in Virginia—is concerned chiefly with the history of slavery and the slave trade, the author harking back to the Middle Ages and the Venetian republic.

The interpretation which Bancroft placed upon any fact or group of facts was determined by his basic beliefs in association with an intense patriotism. His work has been described as "an epic of liberty." In 1830 the very air was charged with the new American consciousness of nationality, with the democratic idea incarnated in Andrew Jackson. These influences and the fact, as Howe says, that Bancroft's nature and training made him a theorist of radical tendencies[58] are responsible for the enthusiastic and somewhat rhapsodic quality of his work. Bancroft's love of democracy led him sometimes to see it, or a tendency toward it, where it did not exist. Thus he elevated Frederick the Great in the Seven Years' War to the post of champion of "Protestantism, philosophic freedom, and the nascent democracy, in their struggle with the conspiracy of European prejudice and legitimacy, of priestcraft and despotism."[59] He made the American democratic colonists the hope of the world.[60] It cannot be denied that Bancroft's equalitarian bent affected greatly his judgments of events and men.

Intense patriotism colored much that he wrote. Desiring to clear his country of the guilt of beginning the slave system in America, he stated that

the unjust, wasteful, and unhappy system was fastened upon the rising institutions of America, not by the consent of the corporation nor the desires of the emigrants; but as it was introduced by the mercantile

[56] CXX (1875), 427.
[57] Pp. 119–26.
[58] Howe, II, 320.
[59] *History*, II, 475.
[60] *Ibid.*, I, 612–13.

avarice of a foreign nation, so it was subsequently riveted by the policy of England, without regard to the interests or the wishes of the colony.[61]

To realize the one-sidedness here, it is necessary only to reflect that, if "mercantile avarice" sold, someone must have bought. To exalt the fatherland the purest motives are almost invariably attributed to the actors in the national drama. James Truslow Adams suggests that Bancroft wrote as if the history of the United States were that of the Kingdom of Heaven.[62]

Belief in an all-wise, ever-directing Providence greatly affected Bancroft's interpretation of events. He argued that Great Britain should have granted the colonies independence; for "why should man organize resistance to the grand design of Providence?"[63] Discussing the opposition in Boston to the Port Bill, he asserted:

The mechanics and merchants and laborers, altogether scarcely so many as thirty-five hundred able-bodied men, knew that they were acting not for a province of America, but for freedom itself. They were inspired by the thought that the Providence which rules the world demanded of them heroic self-denial as the champions of humanity, and they never doubted the fellow-feeling of the continent.[64]

Such instances might be multiplied. Allusions to Providence were fewer in the "Last Revision" than in the early editions; but despite this toning down, he did not forsake the belief that God rules in the affairs of men.

It is Bassett's testimony that Bancroft had no other "prejudice than his intense partiality for the American side of the revolutionary controversy."[65] Bancroft, quite naturally, thought himself impartial. He once wrote, "The historian like the judge must be superior to prepossession and to pride of opinion."[66] He cannot be believed to have been superior to either. Lack of detachment is evident throughout his *History*. He assumed that the United States was founded on a plan superior to that of other

[61] *History*, I (1834), 159. In Vol. I (1883) this passage is omitted; see pp. 119–26.

[62] "History and the Lower Criticism," *Atlantic Monthly*, CXXXII (1923), 310.

[63] *History*, IV, 4.   [65] *The Middle Group*, p. 188.

[64] *Ibid.*, pp. 5–6.   [66] To Chief Justice Waite, May 6, 1884, in Howe, II, 299.

nations, and that its growth justified his assumption. He glorified the struggle of the revolutionary fathers, and saw no good in the position taken by king and parliament. Bancroft did write with prejudice. If he had not felt it and permitted it to speak in his work, it is very doubtful that the *History* would have experienced pronounced success. However, measured by present standards, therein lies the greatest fault of his work.

"The main object has been the attainment of exact accuracy, so that, if possible, not even a partial error may escape correction." So wrote the author in his preface to the "Centenary Edition" of 1876.[67] Here his professed objective was certainly not realized. Lack of accuracy is to be found in matters of fact, in broad statements based on insufficient evidence, and in his treatment of quotations.

An interesting instance of aberration from the facts is Bancroft's statement relative to the first shot fired at Lexington. The text reads:

Pitcairn discharged a pistol, and with a loud voice cried, "Fire!" The order was followed by a few guns, which did no execution, and then by a close and deadly discharge of musketry.

In the disparity of numbers, Parker ordered his men to disperse. Then, and not till then, did a few of them, on their own impulse, return the British fire.[68]

On the same subject Professor Channing wrote: "In the early morning light, as they approached the green at Lexington, they saw some fifty armed men standing in military array. Suddenly a shot rang out; it was followed by a volley, and before the militiamen could escape, eight of them were killed and ten others were wounded."[69] Certainly the second statement is in conformity with the known facts while the first is not.

Bancroft's willingness to suppress unpleasant facts in order to gild the subjects of his *History* is amusingly illustrated in a letter

[67] I, v.

[68] *History*, IV, 155.

[69] Edward Channing, *History of the United States* (New York, 1918), III, 157-58.

that he wrote to a London firm ordering an engraving of Franklin, which he purposed to use as the frontispiece to Volume III.
"The warts on Franklin's face," he wrote, "I wish omitted."[70]
The stickler for historical accuracy will be glad to learn from the
portrait as actually reproduced that the copper-plate facial operation was not performed.

Numerous instances of very broad statements unsupported by
ascertainable facts—a form of inaccuracy to which Bancroft was
especially prone—are readily found. Speaking of the American
people in general at the time of the Revolution, he says: "They
were more sincerely religious, better educated, of serener minds,
and of purer morals than the men of any former republic."[71]
Again he writes: "The people of Massachusetts . . . . beyond
any other colony, ... loved the land of their ancestors."[72]

Bancroft is notorious for the inaccuracies of his quotations.
When he began writing, quotation marks had not attained that
odor of sanctity which they now possess. Comparison of numerous quotations in his *History* with the originals shows that he
indulged in such practices as changing tense or mood without indicating the changes,[73] transposing parts of a quotation,[74] sim-
plifying the language, putting together materials drawn from
different sources to make a single quotation,[75] and otherwise giv-

[70] Howe, I, 236.

[71] *History*, VI, 474.

[72] *Ibid.*, IV, 8.

[73] *Ibid.*, VI, 224: ". . . . that the power of the national judiciary should extend to all
cases of national revenue, impeachment of the national officers, and questions which involve the national peace or harmony." Reference is to Elliot's *Debates* (1901 ed.) I, 409,
which reads: "That the jurisdiction of the national judiciary shall extend to all cases of
national revenue, impeachment of national officers, and questions which involve the national peace and harmony."

[74] *History*, VI, 215: "Randolph offered a resolution, which Gouverneur Morris had formulated, 'that a national government ought to be established, consisting of a supreme
legislative, executive, and judiciary.' " Reference is to Elliot's *Debates*, I, 391, which
reads for the quotation: "That a national government ought to be established consisting of
a supreme judicial, legislative, and executive."

[75] *History*, V (1858), 383–95, contains Pitt's speech on the repeal of the Stamp Act made
in Parliament in January, 1766. In a note on p. 383 Bancroft says: "Besides many shorter accounts of this speech of Pitt, and the account in 'Political Debates,' and in Walpole, I have

ing a rather free rendition of the original. In the space of forty pages of Volume VI (1885), "The Formation of the Constitution," all the references to Elliot's *Debates*, Volume I, were tested and quotations, when such were used, compared. In not a single instance was a quotation absolutely accurate.

Such unorthodox practices are particularly misleading in a work based so largely, as was Bancroft's, on manuscript material. To make matters worse, the references are often not sufficiently definite to enable the reader to locate the sources, and—what is more—in Volume VII Bancroft discontinued altogether using notes and references. They are absent from Volume VIII as well, and were only partially restored in Volume IX. The last two volumes are fully documented. These faults exist even in "The Author's Last Revision," for in the first five volumes of this edition footnotes are almost entirely omitted.

As to Bancroft's literary style, much can be said; and in fact, much *has* been said. His most vitriolic reviewer wrote of it: "A more abominable style, for a historian, it would require the most perverse ingenuity to invent. Affected, stilted, pretentious, meretricious and hyperbolical, it sounds as if swaggering Thraso spoke it through a tragic mask."[76] "Vaporous phrases," "diffuseness," "want of precision," are expressions that have been used to describe his manner of writing. His rhetoric is high-flown and sometimes redundant. Describing the effect of the battles of Lexington and Concord, he wrote: "With one impulse, the colonies sprung to arms; with one spirit, they pledged themselves to each other 'to be ready for the extreme event.' With one heart, the continent cried: 'Liberty or Death.' "[77]

The style is picturesque, bright, and forward-moving, especially in the early editions. The last revision corrected some of the former exuberance of figure. Florid and occasional fantastic ex-

---

the Précis, preserved in the French Archives, and a pretty full report by Moffat of Rhode Island." Reference in uninterrupted quotation of the speech is to different ones of these sources—implicit evidence that the speech, as Bancroft records it, was composed from different sources.

[76] *Southern Review*, IV (1868), 225.   [77] *History*, IV, 168.

pressions were brought down to a more sober form of narration, to a style more in conformity with the ideas of the generation of writers and critics that dominated the last decades of the nineteenth century. To illustrate the style of both early and late editions and to indicate, as well, the elimination of extraneous or bombastic material, there is presented here the concluding paragraph of the chapter on the Pilgrims from the 1834 and the 1883 editions:

Through scenes of gloom and misery, the Pilgrims showed the way to an asylum for those who would go to the wilderness for the purity of religion or the liberty of conscience. Accustomed "in their native land to no more than a plain country life and the innocent trade of husbandry," they set the example of colonizing New England, and formed the mould for the civil and religious character of its institutions. Enduring every hardship themselves, they were the servants of posterity, the benefactors of succeeding generations. In the history of the world, many pages are devoted to commemorate the men who have besieged cities, subdued provinces, or overthrown empires. In the eye of reason and of truth, a colony is a better offering than a victory; the citizens of the United States should rather cherish the memory of those who founded a state on the basis of democratic liberty; the fathers of the country; the men who, as they first trod the soil of the New World, scattered seminal principles of republican freedom and national independence. They enjoyed, in anticipation, the thought of their extending influence, and the fame which their grateful successors would award to their virtues. "Out of small beginnings," said Bradford, "great things have been produced; and as one small candle may light a thousand, so the light here kindled hath shone to many, yea, in some sort to our whole nation,"—"Let it not be grievous to you,"—such was the consolation offered from England to the Pilgrims in the season of their greatest sufferings,—"let it not be grievous to you, that you have been instruments to break the ice for others. The honor shall be yours to the world's end."[78]

In the 1883 edition this paragraph reads:

It is as guides and pioneers that the fathers of the old colony merit gratitude. Through scenes of gloom and misery they showed the way

[78] I, 322–23.

to an asylum for those who would go to the wilderness for the liberty of conscience. Accustomed "in their native land to a plain country life and the innocent trade of husbandry," they set the example of colonizing New England with freeholders, and formed the mould for the civil and religious character of its institutions. They enjoyed, in anticipation, the fame which their successors would award to them. "Out of small beginnings," said Bradford, "great things have been produced; and, as one small candle may light a thousand, so the light here kindled hath shone to many, yea, in some sort to our whole nation." "Let it not be grievous to you"—such was the consolation offered from England to the pilgrims in the season of their greatest sufferings—"let it not be grievous to you that you have been instruments to break the ice for others. The honor shall be yours to the world's end." "Yea, the memory of the adventurers to this plantation shall never die."[79]

After one has made a comparison of these paragraphs, it is not difficult to agree with Howe that the final revision represents the progress of the years through which Bancroft lived, as well as the progress of the man himself. "The last revision gives proof that in his old age Bancroft was both teachable and taught."[80]

In summary it may be said that, though in the earlier editions Bancroft's work undoubtedly illustrates what Sir Henry Maine called "the nauseous grandiloquence of the American panegyrical historian,"[81] its faults were lessened in "The Author's Last Revision," by which it is only fair that his work be judged. In this edition a certain pomposity of style yet remained; and the quotation marks, so liberally strewn throughout the volumes, were just as unreliable as ever before. The value of his work for students of today is greatly lessened by his uncritical Americanism. It may be said, too, that Bancroft did not give the necessary time to keeping up with the developments in his field.

To criticize him in the light of present standards is an easy task; but such criticism should not blind one to his real virtues, his services to American history. He was a democrat; and his

[79] P. 214. For a further illustration see I (1834), 233–34, and I (1883), 152.

[80] Howe, II, 327.

[81] Quoted in Charles F. Adams, *Massachusetts: Its Historians and Its History* (Boston, 1893), p. 41, n. 1.

book, in Professor Bassett's opinion, "remains our great defense of the rise of American nationality, our most fervent great apology for the war of independence in all its untutored Americanism."[82] He showed the heroic epic values of American history. Add to this the fact that the scientific study of history in America may be said to have begun with Bancroft, and it is not difficult to agree with Von Holst's laudatory statement that "every historian of the United States must stand on Bancroft's shoulders."[83] His work greatly strengthened the popular devotion to the institutions of the republic. His ideas were the ideas of his time. His *History*, therefore, becomes a valuable document for our understanding of the national psychology in the first half of the nineteenth century.[84]

[82] *The Middle Group*, p. 203.

[83] Quoted in Walker, p. 56.

[84] Several paragraphs in the foregoing essay follow quite closely the author's "George Bancroft: Historian of the American Republic," *Mississippi Valley Historical Review*, XIX, No. 1 (June, 1932), 77–86. These are used by permission.

II

RICHARD HILDRETH

ALFRED H. KELLY
Wayne University

*

RICHARD HILDRETH may be numbered among those historians no longer read; his works are outmoded in style and thought, his place taken by other writers more acceptable to the ear and with a more sophisticated approach than his simple partisanship permitted. But he deserves consideration in any study of American historiography on two counts: first, he made important contributions to the modern philosophy of history; second, his influence upon the factual material and the ideas embodied in later histories was by no means negligible.

The future author of *The History of the United States* was born in 1805 in Deerfield, Massachusetts, of old and conservative New England lineage. His father, the Rev. Hosea Hildreth, was one of the last of the old-school Calvinists who finally deserted to the Unitarian position during the religious upheavals of the early nineteenth century. Richard received a secondary education at Exeter, then took a literary degree at Harvard in 1826, after which he studied law in a private office in Newburyport. Here he astounded his superiors with his extraordinary talent for long-continued concentration and his facile perception of detail. He was admitted to the bar in 1832, but his attention was already drifting elsewhere. During his law studies he had become a contributor to various New England periodicals and newspapers, and in 1832 he accepted the editorship of the *Boston*

25

Atlas. His articles on contemporary politics gave the sheet distinct pre-eminence in that field of journalism during its years under his charge. In 1837 he used its pages to attack southern statesmen who were encouraging recognition of Texan independence, and he was later credited with having been a pioneer in creating sentiment in New England against the annexation of the Lone Star republic to the Union. He was by this time a pronounced Whig and had developed the confirmed hatred of slavery that later was so much in evidence in his historical works. In 1836 he published *Archy Moore*,[1] the first of the anti-slavery novels of which *Uncle Tom's Cabin* was later the established prototype. It was without literary merit, but it was so cleverly attuned to the rising sentiment against slavery that it enjoyed an immense sale in the United States and was translated into several European languages. It was republished in 1852 in enlarged form under the title of *The White Slave*. In 1840 appeared his most able treatise upon slavery, *Despotism in America*.[2] It was a slashing attack in which the author revealed his characteristic vituperance and unwillingness to mince words about the issue. Every sentence was a declaration of war.

In 1840 he supported Harrison with a campaign biography, *The Contrast: Or William Henry Harrison versus Martin Van Buren*.[3] The same year he also published his *Banks, Banking, and Paper Currencies*,[4] in which he advocated with considerable foresight the system of free banking which later became common in New England and elsewhere. When his health failed shortly after this, he sought relief in British Guiana. While in South America he turned his attention to a projected series of philosophical essays. His *Theory of Morals*[5] and *Theory of Politics*[6] were the only

---

[1] R. Hildreth, *The Slave: Or Memoirs of Archy Moore* (New York, 1836).

[2] Hildreth, *Despotism in America* (Boston, 1840).

[3] Hildreth, *The Contrast: Or William Henry Harrison versus Martin Van Buren* (Boston, 1840).

[4] Hildreth, *Banks, Banking, and Paper Currencies* (Boston, 1840). For a bibliography of Hildreth's writings, see J. Sabin, *A Dictionary of Books Relating to America*, Vol. VIII.

[5] Hildreth, *Theory of Morals* (Boston, 1844).

[6] Hildreth, *Theory of Politics* (New York, 1853).

ones which ever appeared, though he sketched out works on
wealth, knowledge, taste, and education.

In 1847, after returning to this country, he took up once more
his *History of the United States,*[7] begun thirty years before during
his preparatory days at Exeter. The story was carried through
the American Revolution in the first three volumes, published in
1849; their reception was so encouraging that he continued to
write, and in 1852 completed his second series,[8] bringing the narrative to 1821. In the preface to the latter work he stated that
a third study would continue the narrative to his own day,
but he never realized this ambition. From 1855 to 1861 the historian served as a contributor to the *New York Tribune* and to
other newspapers and periodicals, to which he was now well
known as a political commentator and relentless enemy of slavery. At the same time he managed to wield a pen in New England politics, where he established a reputation as a powerful
friend and a bitter, uncompromising, and vehement foe of slavery. In 1861 President Lincoln appointed him consul at Trieste, a
position he held until his death at Florence in 1865.[9]

Hildreth made the purpose of his *History of the United States*
clear in the introduction to the first edition. There he struck
scornfully at history which seeks "to bask in the sunshine of national vanity," and proclaimed it as his goal to relate "plain
facts in plain English; . . . . with . . . . no aim but truth." He
would attempt "to set forth the personages of our colonial and
revolutionary history, such as they really were in their own day
and generation," with "their faults as well as their virtues, their

[7] Hildreth, *The History of the United States of America from the Discovery of the Continent to
the Organization of Government under the Federal Constitution, 1497–1789* (3 vols.; New York,
1849). Hereinafter referred to as *First Series.*

[8] Hildreth, *The History of the United States of America from the Adoption of the Federal Constitution to the End of the Sixteenth Congress, 1788–1821* (3 vols.; New York, 1851–52). Hereinafter referred to as *Second Series.*

[9] The best sketch of Hildreth's life is found in Evert A. and G. L. Duyckinck, *The Cyclopedia of American Literature* (rev. ed.; Philadelphia, 1875), II, 298–301. See also K. Murdock in *Dictionary of American Biography,* IX, 19–20; William T. Davis, *Professional and Industrial History of Suffolk County, Massachusetts* (3 vols., Boston, 1894), I, 164–65; F. L.
Mott, *A History of American Magazines, 1741–1850* (New York, 1930), p. 778.

weaknesses as well as their strength." He would endeavor to show "from what beginnings, by what influences, and through what changes the United States of America are what they are."[10]

It is apparent that Hildreth was highly resentful of contemporary historians who had capitalized upon the overinflated American sense of patriotism to achieve general popularity. He resented their idealization of the founders of the country, their distortion of the plain truth to suit the fictitious and absurd concept of a superheroic past. He set out to deflate American history and American patriots, and it must be put down to his credit that, for the colonial period at least, he succeeded very well. He was particularly impatient with that school of historians which had molded the heroic tradition of New England;[11] and in spite of the danger of falling upon that section and tearing it to pieces in the manner affected by later "debunkers," he was able to portray the history and leaders of that region without turning demigods into demons. It must be recalled that Hildreth wrote in the period when Bancroft was riding high on the sentiment of manifest destiny. The latter had fused the spirit of America into his narrative and was enjoying immense popularity; for his glamorous tale was exactly suited to a national temperament already convinced of the superiority of American culture. For Hildreth to challenge the pattern set by his more notable predecessor, a pattern accepted so enthusiastically by his prospective audience, required no small amount of courage. A man less pugnacious and direct than he might never have attempted it. Hildreth was convinced, however, as he tells us, that the cold truth concerning America's great men and achievements would have a solid appeal to the more dispassionate elements of the population; curi-

[10] Hildreth, *First Series*, I, iii–iv.

[11] In the introduction to the 1852 edition of his first series, Hildreth remarked: "The undress portraits I have presented of our colonial progenitors, though made up chiefly of traits delineated by themselves; my presumption in bursting the thin, shining bubble so assiduously blown up by so many windy mouths, of a colonial golden age of fabulous purity and virtue, have given very serious offense, especially in New England, region of set formality and hereditary grimace . . . ." (Hildreth, *History of the United States* [New York, 1852], I, x).

ously enough, he hoped that such an approach would have an especial interest for younger readers.[12]

The idea was both brave and intelligent; for it proclaimed that the purpose of history was simply the discovery and declaration of the unvarnished truth for the sake of that truth itself. It deprived history of any ulterior purpose of propaganda, argumentation, or glorification. Its intrinsic validity lay not in its literary quality, not in its possibilities as an instrument of conversion; instead it was a means to the truth; and the truth is completely self-sufficient—it is its own justification, and any historian who achieves it will find his reputation is secure. Few historians would challenge now the validity of this concept; few in Hildreth's day had realized it, either in the United States or elsewhere.

It is unfortunate that Hildreth did not maintain this position throughout his work. His first series is impartial enough, but in the second the temptation to write history for an ulterior purpose proved too much for him. He threw away deliberately the ideal of impartial truth-telling and set out, instead, to write the history of the United States from the Federalist point of view, with the result that he thoroughly destroyed whatever permanent historical value his work might have possessed. Even in his later volumes, however, Hildreth retains something of his clever faculty for setting forth details with accuracy and clarity. He seldom falls into minor errors of dates, names, or sequence, even when most carried away by prejudice or affection.[13] Instead, he achieves bias, where bias exists, by injudicious selection and argument rather than by factual distortion. This combination of strength and weakness is strongly reminiscent of his legal training. A good lawyer wins his case, not by distortion of facts through deceit, but through persuasive interpretation and a clever selection of emphasis. Hildreth, in his later works, is a shrewd and powerful advocate but a poor historian.

[12] *Ibid.*, p. xi.

[13] Hildreth does not give direct references for his statements in footnotes, but his accuracy was tested for this paper by checking two chapters of Vol. I against Osgood. Only one minor factual discrepancy was revealed.

Hildreth seems to have had a confused idea that the value of history lay, partly at least, in the explanation of the present by the past.[14] It was the idea which is so often offered today as the justification for historical production. Like many another historian, Hildreth forgot it completely when he began to write. With one or two exceptions he does not weave the events of history into an evolutionary pattern. His treatment is solely chronological—so much so that he does not even complete one line of development before he interrupts it with another. The narrative does not move in dynamic fashion toward Hildreth's own time and, with a few important exceptions, it is lacking in genetic quality. For instance, he spends some time discussing the early development of slavery and succeeds fairly well in explaining the legalistic foundations of the institution as he witnessed it in his own day.[15] He discusses the organization of colonial government in Massachusetts with something of an eye upon state and federal government in the national period.[16] But by and large, he is not concerned with ultimate implications of men and events; events occurred, men performed deeds, these things happened, therefore they are history and are to be ground out to an exceeding fineness in the historical mill.[17] Hildreth undoubtedly believed, like most historians after him, that the past has its own value regardless of its relevancy to present affairs and institutions. It is worth knowing for its own sake, not only as an interpretation of the future.

Far more serious than the failure of the past to explain the present is the failure of the past to explain itself. Hildreth's history lacks that synthetic quality which an adherence to a central theme, idea, or frame of reference would have imparted to it. There are, of course, a number of centers of interest; and within these narrative sequences an apparent causal chain is established,

[14] Hildreth, *First Series*, I, viii.

[15] *Ibid.*, pp. 518, 521, 563, 570-71; II, 177–81, 236–37, 271–75, 417–30.

[16] *Ibid.*, I, 186, 189.

[17] The generalization is less true of Vol. III. Here the development of the Revolution imparts something of an evolutionary character to the work.

but the separate centers of attention are not in turn correlated. Such history fails to present any general interpretation of the time or place under consideration. Lacking integration, it is atomistic without any imperative relationship between the events described. It is the old story of a number of facts strung together on a series of "meanwhiles."[18]

Perhaps the heart of the difficulty lay in the absence of any adequate philosophy to guide the historian in the selection of his facts. This is not to deny that there was a traditional body of material through which the historian was expected to range when Hildreth wrote. History was simply past politics. Hence the exhausting minutiae of legislative debate, inconsequential laws, dreary Indian wars, and the continuous squabbling between royal governors and colonial legislatures. All this body of political history—sometimes it was little more than anecdote —must be treated, regardless of its bearing upon any other portion of the narrative; and the historian never questioned whether he had fulfilled his function when he had rambled at length through all the remote avenues and byways of politics and wars.

Hildreth disposes of the economic development of New England in the seventeenth century in a page and a half.[19] The growth of the plantation system in the South receives but little more consideration. Even where he does touch upon social and economic subjects, he treats them in their legalistic and political aspects. For instance, he devotes almost no time to slavery as a social institution, but a great amount of space to the growth of the slave codes and their relationship to the English common law.[20] Again, he discusses the tariff of the early national period without reference to its economic significance. The causes of the war of 1812 include no references to land hunger or the price of grain; they are purely diplomatic.[21] There are exceptions to the

[18] The observation is less true of the Federalist period, when Hildreth's interest in the party struggles led him unconsciously to a better pattern of organization.

[19] Hildreth, *First Series*, II, 430–32.

[20] *Ibid.*, I, 521, 563, 570. See also the highly legalistic approach to the whole matter of colonial mores and social organization in Vol. II, chap. xxi.

[21] Hildreth, *Second Series*, III, 241–377.

rule; but for the most part the narrative runs along regardless of anything except the history of politics. When other centers of interest do crowd into the picture, they are consigned to isolated compartments with no effort made to integrate them. A historian trained in law and reflecting the force of political tradition should perhaps not be blamed for failing to do what his contemporaries did not even consider it worth while to attempt.[22]

It is also fair to remark that, when a historian's main attention centers on the narrative quality of his work, problems of organization and material become of less consequence. Hildreth's chief concern, in reality, was to tell a great story of a great past. It was worth telling for its own virtue, even though, as a conscientious scholar, he determined to avoid the follies of ancestor-worship. Viewed in this light, history is art rather than a science; and the relative importance of the men and events selected for treatment, even the cohesive quality of the history, are considerations of secondary importance. Hildreth is conscientious about telling the truth, but the truth may not explain anything. It has its own value. It is "good" to know the tale of our simple greatness, even though the past be stripped of the glamour in which pseudo history clothes it. The history may even become largely anecdotal; anecdotes play a significant role in this type of history because they are part of a tradition, because they are amusing, or simply because they contribute to the fulness of the narrative. In many places the narrative, lacking any other central point of organization, becomes a series of amusing or interesting little incidents presented for their intrinsic value but having no bearing on the story at all.

A reader approaching Hildreth's work through the early volumes might be inclined to observe that their author had written an extremely objective history. The word "objective" possibly has a double meaning: it may be taken to imply lack of interpretation, or it may imply lack of bias. The failure of Hildreth to look behind the facts or to give his work any analytical qual-

[22] About 40 per cent of Vols. I and II, *First Series*, deals with the legal enactments of various colonial legislatures.

ity certainly justifies the use of the word in that sense. The first series is also remarkably free from moral judgments, from pronounced prejudices against men, customs, or institutions. As already observed, it even achieves the unusual distinction of being free from spread-eagle patriotism. It betrays no affection or dislike for any early colonial power, colony, or section. One might almost conclude that here is a historian animated by hardly a sentiment of human bias or passion. Occasionally there are exceptions. He is unfriendly toward the narrow bigotry of seventeenth-century Protestantism and recoils before its "horror of toleration, an inherent and essential characteristic of every theocracy."[23] The conversion of the Indians is sarcastically referred to as achieved through war, which furnished "overwhelming proofs of Christian superiority."[24] Even the comparatively gentle Quaker doctrine of "the inner light" is labeled "but a whimsical, superstitious, ill-informed, passionate, narrow, ill-regulated reason; right, no doubt, upon many important points, but often exaggerated, unwilling or unable to justify itself by argument or fact."[25] Probably Hildreth's nineteenth-century liberalistic Unitarian background lies behind these sallies against religious bigotry.

Hildreth has one positive, deep-seated prejudice, mounting occasionally to evangelical passion—his hatred of slavery. Although he is unusually interested in the subject, he maintains the pretense of disinterested impartiality fairly well in the early series; and only an occasional satirical jibe betrays his animosity. He mourns the first introduction of slavery into Virginia and attacks the institution as a violation both of the charters and the common law.[26] He waxes indignant over the slave codes and observes that South Carolina had "the same bad pre-eminence on the subject of slave legislation which she still maintains."[27] In the national period the pretense of impartiality is completely swept aside, and Hildreth loses no opportunity for an open at-

[23] Hildreth, *First Series*, I, 329.

[24] *Ibid.*, p. 493.

[25] *Ibid.*, p. 402.

[26] *Ibid.*, pp. 119, 518, 521.

[27] *Ibid.*, II, 275.

tack upon slavery. He is a sturdy crusader for the destruction of an iniquitous institution.[28]

The most controversial topic which Hildreth treats is the American Revolution. In the middle of the last century the question of separation from England was still charged with bitterness for most Americans. It was a living issue of patriotism, not yet softened or pushed into the background by the struggle over slavery. Hildreth nevertheless succeeds in discussing the Revolution with the detachment of a scholar dissecting ancient history. There is hardly a spark of hatred toward England in the entire theme. He is sympathetic with the ideal of American liberty, but that is as far as his sense of fairness will allow him to proceed. The war, he conceives, was a war between gentlemen, precipitated by regrettable ignorance on the part of English statesmen and their monarch.[29] There is little patriotic fervor in the story of American revolutionary activity. The nonimportation agreements, for example, were sometimes enforced in a "partial, harsh and inquisitorial" manner.[30] Treatment of British troops in America before the war was often shameful.[31] The country was greatly divided on the question of independence;[32] the Tories were a large and respectable minority; yet they were exposed "to all sorts of personal indignities, in which private malice, ... had been too often gratified under the disguise of patriotism."[33] The story of the war itself is anything but a heroic epic in Hildreth's hands. There were confusion, jealousy, ill feeling, faulty strategy, and some downright cowardice under fire.[34] There is, to be sure, some doubt as to how much credit Hildreth deserves for so impartial a treatment of the Revolution. Friendship toward England harmonized well with his sympathies as a thoroughgoing Federalist. His liking for extreme New England Federalism is, of course, not apparent in the earlier

[28] In Hildreth, *Second Series*, I, 174–203, 385–88, is a lengthy discussion of the early debates in Congress on slavery. See also, *ibid.*, II, 182–85, 341, 499–506, 627–44; III, 682–98.

[29] Hildreth, *First Series*, Vol. III, chap. xxxi.

[30] *Ibid.*, II, 552.

[31] *Ibid.*, pp. 554–55.

[32] *Ibid.*, III, 133–34.

[33] *Ibid.*, p. 138.

[34] *Ibid.*, pp. 157, 199, 236.

volumes, but it is probable that it influenced his position. He could not denounce England for 1776 and then become completely pro-British in the political struggles of the early national period. One animus interfered with the other, and the pro–New England, pro-British, anti-Jeffersonian sentiment was the dominant one in his own mind. Hildreth was, before all else, the complete Federalist.

The strength of this emotion perhaps outweighs even his abhorrence of slavery. He hates slavery but loves nothing in return; he detests Jefferson with a withering scorn but loves Hamilton and all his works with an indiscriminate affection. In the introduction to the second three volumes of his study he remarks quite frankly that the national period is too near at hand for impartial treatment. He will, therefore, from now on express his own opinions with a freedom he has not hitherto permitted himself to exercise.[35] It is Hildreth's way of informing the reader that he is about to lapse into the spirit of a party politician writing "history" for campaign purposes, an occupation in which he had had some little experience.

He loses little time in making his revised approach clear. In discussing the adoption of the Constitution, he remarks that the "aristocracy of talents, wealth, and intelligence" supported it but "the democratic masses opposed or hesitated."[36] The inauguration of Washington gives him his first opportunity to present the heroes and villains he is about to unfold before us. His style loses something of the dulness noticeable in the earlier volumes and begins to flash with occasional witticisms, more often with sly thrusts of sarcasm. His narrative becomes more intensely personal. This is an age of battle between Olympian gods and deformed giants and ogres, and we are made to feel the vital part which they play in the struggle. Listen to the eulogy upon three principal figures of Federalist politics:

Hamilton possessed the same rare and lofty qualities, the same just balance of soul, with less, indeed, of Washington's severe simplicity and awe-inspiring presence, but with more of warmth, variety, orna-

[35] Hildreth, *Second Series*, I, pp. vii–viii.   [36] Hildreth, *First Series*, III, 537.

ment, and grace. If the Doric in architecture be taken as the symbol of Washington's character, Hamilton's belonged to the same grand style as developed in the Corinthian—if less impressive, more winning. If we add Jay for the Ionic, we have a trio not to be matched, in fact, not to be approached in our history, if indeed, in any other. Of earth-born Titans, as terrible as great, now angels, and now toads and serpents, there are every where enough. Of the serene and benign sons of the celestial gods, how few at any time have walked the earth![37]

It is not often that Hildreth permits himself the luxury of so flowery and eloquent a style. Only the unusual homage he felt obliged to pay the three men in question could inspire such a passage. He is more accustomed to the weapons of sarcasm and bitterness; he is more at home attacking Jefferson than in praising Federalists. He seldom attempts even to restrain his dislike for the Democratic leader. In political affairs, Hildreth asserts,

Jefferson was disposed to allow a controlling, indeed absolute authority to the popular judgment. The many he thought to be always more honest and disinterested, and in questions where the public interests were concerned, more wise than the few, who might always be suspected of having private purposes of their own to serve. Hence he was ever ready to allow even his most cherished theoretical principles to drop into silence the moment he found them in conflict with the popular current. To sympathize with popular passions seemed to be his test of patriotism; to sail before the wind as a popular favorite, the great object of his ambition; . . . .[38]

His imagination so far predominated over his reason as to lead him to see things, not as they were, but as he hoped, wished, suspected they might be; and, as is very apt to be the case with men of a fanatical turn of mind, there was nothing bad which he did not suspect of those who did not share in or subscribe to all his dogmas. Suspicion and facts he confounded together in one indistinguishable mass.[39]

The passage is not unique; it is typical. Hildreth never misses any opportunity to attack Jefferson's political ideals, policies, or his private life and character.[40] The vituperance spent upon the leader is not withheld from his followers. Gallatin was not of

---

[37] Hildreth, *Second Series*, II, 527. See also his eulogy of Adams in *ibid.*, I, 293.
[38] *Ibid.*, I, 292–93.   [39] *Ibid.*, pp. 340–41.   [40] *Ibid.*, pp. 361–70, 455–56.

Hamilton's high caliber as Secretary of Treasury.[41] Giles was a politician chiefly distinguished "for pertinacious virulence and total want of candor;"[42] Monroe was without sufficient honor to hold sacred, intimate secrets of a highly personal character.[43] And as for John Randolph, "he ever exhibited the familiar characteristics of that unhappy neutral sex sufficiently common in Eastern countries, though rare among us, but to which he was said to belong."[44]

It seems unnecessary to add, after these illustrations, that Hildreth is a conscientious apologist for all the Federalist policies of the national period. Hamilton receives the traditional eulogy for having set up confidence in business and credit and having restored the public honor by his banking and debt operations.[45] The Jeffersonian attitude toward assumption was contemptible, and Hildreth feels it quite natural that a group of men "who resisted so pertinaciously the payment of their own private debts .... should be inclined to look on the public creditors with equal disfavor."[46] The Federalist treatment of foreign affairs was of a high, impartial, and statesman-like quality from beginning to end; while the enemies of the administration were animated by a senseless and indiscriminate love of France and everything French. Ultimately, it was only Adams' noble sacrifice of himself and his party that saved us from a disastrous war with France.[47] The Alien and Sedition Laws were strong medicine, perhaps unwisely administered on occasions; but something of the sort was justified as an antidote to the poisonous and treasonable tactics constantly resorted to by the opposition.[48]

But it is the Jeffersonian administrations that offer Hildreth the golden opportunity for a complete synthesis of every sentiment of partisanship. Sectional prejudice merges naturally with party hatred, dislike of France, and vituperance against slavery.

[41] *Ibid.*, III, 107–8.
[42] *Ibid.*, I, 396–97.
[43] *Ibid.*, II, 104–19.
[44] *Ibid.*, p. 343.
[45] *Ibid.*, I, 274–76.
[46] *Ibid.*, p. 337.
[47] *Ibid.*, I, 531; II, 65, 288–89; III, 333–34.
[48] *Ibid.*, II, 230.

To attack Jefferson is to attack the South, that center of radical democracy, slavocracy, and Francophilism. To defend New England is to defend Federalism, to sympathize with England in her war upon autocracy. The war of 1812 brings all this feeling to a head: Hildreth here becomes the complete sectionalist, the complete Federalist, the complete Anglophile. And at last he thrusts aside even the restraints of patriotism and accepts openly the secessionist position of the Junto, which would have disrupted the Union in the interest of Federalist New England.[49]

Now, it is a curious fact that Hildreth's ardent sympathy for Federalism is not well supported by his social and economic philosophy. Like any other political group, the Federalist party had a well-rationalized body of social thought built upon the doctrine of the inequality of man, wealth as a measure of virtue and success, and government by the "rich, well-born and able." Some of these precepts Hildreth does accept—by implication, at least—although his history does not contain many generalizations of a philosophic nature. What few there are, are developed incidental to the party struggles of the Federalists and are usually in sympathy with the aristocratic concept. Hildreth preaches that political parties have their basis not so much in class lines as in divisions in the "natural aristocracy"; the great body of the people is an unleavened mass which distinguishes itself only by the occasional unanimity with which it rises to the support of one or the other upper-class group.[50] (This doctrine of the non-existence of class lines in political life has always been good conservative political philosophy in the United States, since it leaves the door open to apparent liberalism in any dispute.) He believes that merchants, large landowners, lawyers, ministers, and capitalists form a natural aristocracy in America, while the great body of small farmers form a natural democracy. Control rests with the aristocracy "in virtue of that inherent power which superior wealth, knowledge and social position every where carry with them, and which no formal declaration of equality can ever take away."[51] Revolution is anathema to him since it

[49] Ibid., III, 453 ff., 531 ff., 547 ff., 675–76, 711.   [50] Ibid., I, 348.   [51] Ibid., p. 347.

threatens the stability of this natural stratification of society. Thus he denounces the French Revolution at every turn as consisting "practically in nothing more or less than the seizure of absolute political authority by a few enthusiastic and audacious individuals . . . . constantly trampling, without scruple or hesitation, on those rights of man on which it professed to be founded."[52] All this is good Federalism, although the number of such generalizations remain rather few.

But in 1853 Hildreth published his *Theory of Politics*, in answer to the objections of those who asserted that his *History of the United States* was too barren of philosophy. It purports to contain the social and political thought of the author, developed as a result of his researches in history. Although the work, strictly speaking, is not history but political philosophy, it deserves consideration here since it throws considerable light on the social and political ideas of its author. In it he argues for wealth as the primary element of political power, able to maintain itself even in a degenerate aristocracy by the purchase of superior talent and military force.[53] The most important source of wealth in society is commerce. The power generated by these commercial profits leads to the destruction of democracy by creating property in government for a few families.[54] The unequal distribution of property is gross injustice; he accepts Paley's analogy of the ninety-nine pigeons who might spend all their time carrying food to the one most lazy, stupid, and weak of their lot as comparable to the present institution of private property.[55] In such a situation it is no wonder that the poor lose respect for the rights of property, "and are only kept under by the severest laws and a constant display of military power."[56] Under these circumstances, even the worst excesses of the French Revolution become an instrument of social justice.[57] Yet the democratic principle of government is valid in the long run: "The child catches many a fall, but learns at length not only to walk, but to run; and self-

---

[52] *Ibid.*, II, 103. See also I, 416.   [54] *Ibid.*, pp. 145–46.   [56] *Ibid.*, p. 155.
[53] Hildreth, *Theory of Politics*, p. 151.   [55] *Ibid.*, pp. 153–55.   [57] *Ibid.*, p. 209.

government is not, any more than walking, a thing to be learned in a day. . . . . ."[58]

These ideas make better social democracy than Federalism—it is little wonder that the *Athenaeum* in a contemporary review stated that Hildreth had a tendency toward socialism which he contrived to conceal even from himself.[59] The explanation probably lies in the nature of his loyalty to Federalism. His sentiment was largely traditional partisanship, inherited from his family background. It was mere political loyalty—a set of fixed attitudes toward the leaders and achievements of Federalism, undisturbed by any serious inquiry into the philosophic content of the faith or by a comparison of its principles with his own observations upon classes, property, or democracy. The kind of history Hildreth wrote does not readily penetrate the background of conflict between social groups and economic interests, between different concepts of social and political organization. Hence his traditional emotional attitude toward Federalism remained largely undisturbed by certain ultrademocratic ideas on the nature of political and economic power that crept in the side door of his brain. His mind was conveniently departmentalized.

Hildreth is no master of literary art or of fanciful flights of expression. Language is, for him, simply a vehicle of ideas. To achieve his purpose he seeks clarity, directness, and accuracy; there is never any doubt about the exact meaning of any of his passages. The lawyer speaks through the historian when Hildreth, with uncompromising accuracy, assembles the details of struggles over the Massachusetts charter or the intricacies of a revolutionary campaign. This ability to sort out and present with clarity the tangled jungle of a mass of detail has its uses, and Hildreth is at his best in writing military and legal history. The lawyer's brief, of course, is apt to be poor rhetoric. It never occurred to Hildreth that history might be a vehicle of beauty as well as a method of reaching the truth. Hildreth may be read profitably for information, rarely for analysis, and never for

[58] *Ibid.*, p. 225.   [59] *Athenaeum* (London), Nov. 12, 1853, p. 1354.

stimulation or enjoyment. Sparkling figures of speech and the artistic qualities of a well-turned composition had no attraction for him; he even prided himself on avoiding them. They were mere pitfalls into which the truth might stumble and be lost.

This is at once fortunate and unfortunate. His history is lacking entirely in literary appeal. It is dry as dust, grimly matter of fact, without life, and without color. Only when indignation stirs him to wrath or eulogy does it emerge from its monotonous recital. The work deserves no consideration in American literary history; it was probably not read except at the cost of much pain in his own day, and it certainly will not be read by anyone except special students in ours. On the other hand, history has more important objectives than pretty words; and when Hildreth wrote, those objectives were in particular need of attention. He knew, even though he could not achieve the goal, that the supreme objective of history is to tell the truth; and Hildreth's monotonous pages sometimes deal with a truth which he felt noble enough to stand alone. His style is a mere reflection of his ideal; and that ideal was a much-needed antidote for the American historiography of his own day, in danger of becoming the handmaiden of patriotic self-esteem and manifest destiny. In his dry, matter-of-fact attempts to tell the truth, in his emphatic rejection of the propagandistic quality of earlier and contemporary historians, he struck a healthy vein, which most subsequent scholars have ever since continued to develop.

It would be a mistake, moreover, to underestimate the influence of his content, and even his technique, upon the great school of colonial historians who came after him and who wrote of the period which he had developed. A comparison of the subject matter of Hildreth's early chapters with those of Osgood on the seventeenth century will confirm the suspicion that both in the facts related and in organization Osgood did not depart far from the traditional pattern which Hildreth followed. Certain chapters in Henry Adams' *History of the United States*, especially the ones on the purchase of Louisiana, follow closely the older treatment by Hildreth.[60] It is probable that in his Federalistic bias, his notions about the Constitution, and in his attitude toward slavery, von Holst was greatly influenced by Hildreth's work.[61] It is an old and obvious truism that the subject matter and organization of history change but slowly and uncertainly. As long as these later writers are credited with any influence on historical thought, Hildreth must be accorded a niche in American historiography. Certainly the whole validity of the historical approach rests upon the assumption that the bygone foundations of any institution warrant examination. Hildreth played his part in molding the future of history in this country; and some small measure of fame among historians should be granted him, even though his works are "dead."

[60] Cf. Hildreth, *Second Series*, Vol. II, chaps. xvi, xvii, with Henry Adams, *History of the United States*, Vol. I, chaps. xvi, xvii.

[61] The works of Hildreth used in the preparation of this paper were originally in the possession of H. von Holst, and are autographed, "H. von Holst, 1872." They are liberally underlined, especially in those portions dealing with Federalism, slavery, and the Constitution.

III

FRANCIS PARKMAN

JOE PATTERSON SMITH
Illinois College

*

ON SEPTEMBER 16, 1823, sixty years after the French
had been eliminated from the American continent as a
ruling power, Francis Parkman was born in a little
parsonage on Beacon Hill in Boston. Seventy years later, November 8, 1893, in his home at Jamaica Pond, near Boston, he
died. Fifty years of this life were expended in fighting maladies
and in discovering, gathering, evaluating, synthesizing, and portraying the records of a contest for a continent waged between
Catholic France and commercial England with the American Indian playing a lesser role. The monument, a dozen volumes collectively called *France and England in America*, resulting from this
half-century of labor has led enthusiastic commentators to style
Parkman "a genius," the "Herodotus of American history," and
"a Tacitus." Such characterizations are indeed brief and decidedly complimentary, but they give neither a satisfactory view of
Francis Parkman nor an estimation of the monumental work he
produced.

Francis Parkman was descended from a galaxy of Puritans,
prominent among whom had been John Cotton and Ebenezer
Parkman.[1] His grandfather, Samuel Parkman, was a Boston
merchant who had amassed a comfortable fortune while Boston
was still the center of American commercial activity and in the

[1] Charles H. Farnham, *A Life of Francis Parkman* (Boston, 1905), Genealogical Table,
p. 1, n. 1.

days before a high tariff had been invented to turn the thoughts of New Englanders away from ships and the sea. Samuel Parkman's son, a Unitarian minister, who had in his charge the new North Church in Boston, inherited this fortune. After somewhat reducing it by providing his family with a liberal education and by endowing certain charitable institutions, he bequeathed the balance of it to his children.[2] The competence which Francis Parkman inherited was sufficient to afford him the leisure for uninterrupted study and to finance many extensive projects which ultimately contributed to the making of *France and England in America*.

The boyhood of this last Francis Parkman was not unlike that of many other lads. He was educated in private schools, as befitted the son of an opulent clergyman of the day. He made youthful experiments in chemistry; participated in "two-penny" and "two-pin" dramas; hunted imaginary Indians; collected odd stones, skins, reptiles, and eggs of all sorts in Middlesex Fells, a wild woodland tract near his maternal grandfather's farm; and, though he was not physically able to share in strenuous sports, he enjoyed out-of-doors games to the limit of his strength. Over-zealous biographers of Parkman, in a previous generation, have made much of boyhood influences. He had, for example, already developed dramatic powers of moment. He had displayed a tenacity of purpose which was all-important to him later in carrying through the vast historical project he undertook. He had acquired a taste and a love for the out-of-doors which became an essential part of his equipment for studying the conquest of a continent. He had come to know that learning can be gained through careful observation. It would be unwise to overemphasize any of these tendencies either of character or intellect, but it seems safe to assert that the young man who went up to Harvard in the autumn of 1840 was better than the mine-run of college Freshmen—fun-loving and serious by turns.

The Harvard curriculum which the class of 1844 was expected to embrace offered little of real interest to Francis Parkman. He

[2] Henry D. Sedgwick, *Francis Parkman* (Boston, 1904), pp. 17–18.

cared neither for theology nor for most of the subjects kindred thereto. In his autobiographical fragment written November 28, 1868—in the third person to suppress the ego—he said,

.... he resolved to confine his homage to the Muse of History, ... At the age of eighteen the plan which he is still attempting to execute was, in its most essential features, formed. .... he entered upon a training tolerably well fitted to serve his purpose, slighted all college studies which could not promote it, and pursued with avidity such as had a bearing upon it, however indirect.[3]

He added, in a paper sent to Mr. Brimmer fifteen years later, "Before the end of the Sophomore year my various schemes had crystallized into a plan of writing the story of what was then known as the 'Old French War,'—that is, the war that ended in the conquest of Canada. ....."[4] Notwithstanding his dislike of the obligatory curriculum, Parkman was elected, upon his graduation, to Phi Beta Kappa, which fact may at least be a gauge that he was not a mediocre student. In the extracurricular life of the campus he was prominent, belonging to Chit Chat, and the Hasty Pudding Club.[5] There is ample evidence also that he enjoyed the tippling parties which have, since the beginning of college life, been a part thereof.[6]

Parkman spent his vacations in the woods and mountain fastnesses of northwestern New England and adjacent Canada. The day-by-day entries made in his notebooks at this time—a practice which he continued throughout life—are a heterogeneous mass of measurements of forts, jotted descriptions of battle sites, names and addresses of persons having letters and other data regarding the events of the French and Indian wars, and carefully recorded reminiscences of old men and women. Interspersed

[3] "Autobiography of Francis Parkman," Massachusetts Historical Society, *Proceedings*, 2d ser., VIII (1894), 351.

[4] *Ibid.*, p. 351 n.

[5] Farnham, p. 16.

[6] "We wanted you the other night. Joe got up one of his old-fashioned suppers on a scale of double magnificence, inviting thereunto every specimen of the class of '44 that lingered within an accessible distance. .... The spree was worthy of the entertainment. None got drunk, but all got jolly; and Joe's champagne disappeared first; then his Madeira; ....." (Parkman to Hale, Nov. 24, 1844, in Sedgwick, pp. 129–30).

among the observations pertinent to his study are many dealing with the customs of the peoples whom he visited. These last, students of early nineteenth-century social history cannot afford to overlook.[7]

In the autumn of 1843 Parkman suffered his first serious illness. He withdrew from Harvard and sailed for an extended tour of Italy, France, and England. In Italy he lived for a time in a Capuchin monastery of Passionists, hoping thereby to secure some insight into monkish practices, which knowledge he wished to transfer to an interpretation of the role played by monastic orders in the settlement of Canada.[8] In his diary of the period, scattered among the inconsequential comments which travelers usually make, are many pointed observations regarding the Jesuits—an order Parkman never tired of investigating.[9] He studied somewhat intensively the Roman Catholic church, an institution foreign to the Bostonian Unitarian milieu. Of it, he wrote:

> The Church of the Benedictines is the noblest edifice I have seen. This and others not unlike it have impressed me with new ideas of the Catholic religion. Not exactly, for I have reverenced it before as the religion of generations of brave and great men, but now I honor it for itself. They are mistaken who sneer at its ceremonies as a mere mechanical force; they have a powerful and salutary effect on the mind. Those who have witnessed the services in this Benedictine church, and deny what I say, must either be singularly stupid and insensible by nature, or rendered so by prejudice.[10]

He spent some days in Paris; but unless he did not confide to his diary his investigations for materials, he made none. The active Parkman surrendered to the lure of the Paris boulevards, and for

---

[7] Parkman's journal in *ibid.*, pp. 32–68.

[8] Parkman's journal in *ibid.*, pp. 96–103.

[9] In his diary he comments, "Priests with their black broad-brimmed hats and their long robes,—fat and good-looking men,—were the next numerous class. They draw life and sustenance from these dregs of humanity, just as tall pigweed flourishes on a dunghill" (*ibid.*, p. 76). Also, "A Virginian named St. Ives, lately converted to Catholicism, has been trying to convert me, along with some of the Jesuits here" (*ibid.*, p. 96).

[10] *Ibid.*, p. 80.

the moment sedentary pursuits went glimmering.[11] After a brief look at London and Edinburgh, he returned to Cambridge about June 20, 1844, in time to be graduated from Harvard with his class.[12] His health was much improved, and he wished to launch forth immediately upon further investigation of the old French wars. But his father desired that he enter Harvard Law School. Finally a compromise was agreed upon whereby Francis, after completing the law course, was to be permitted to make a trip to the western plains to observe first hand the habits of the Indians.

The last few months spent at law were not at all to Parkman's liking, and Blackstone was nothing more to him than a screen to hide from his curious fellows his more important nocturnal pursuits.[13] Henry Dwight Sedgwick says, basing his assertion on the records of the Harvard Library, that Parkman's studious efforts were confined to the broad reading of history and to the meticulous notation of accounts regarding the French, English, and Indians of early New England and Canada.

The seventh year of the "Fabulous Forties" was, probably, as important as any in Parkman's life. It witnessed his abandonment of law and a dignified scholar's robes for the more comely frontiersman's garb and accouterments. Clothed in these, he took up his abode among the Indians of the western plains, returning finally a wiser man but a physical, if not a mental, wreck. His sojourn among the Indians, Parkman recounted in *The Oregon Trail*, a tale which would scarcely be designated history but which leaves an impressive picture of the young Bostonian renegade, who had abandoned the ways of white-man's civilization to learn the customs and manners of another.[14] To be sure, he

[11] "I have been a fortnight in Paris, and seen it as well as it can be seen in a fortnight. Under peculiarly favorable circumstances, too; for it was the great season of balls and gayeties, and I had a guide, moreover, who knows Paris from top to bottom, within and without" (*ibid.*, p. 110).

[12] *Ibid.*, p. 116.

[13] Sedgwick, pp. 125, 132.

[14] Francis Parkman, *The Oregon Trail*. This narrative was first published in serial form in the *Knickerbocker Magazine* (New York) in 1847.

never lost the notion that the Indian was a savage—the exponent of customs repugnant to Americans—yet it is almost unbelievable that a person, reared as he had been, could adopt barbaric customs so completely as to revel in burned-dog feasts and all of the cruder practices of Indian life and then record them without a personal expression of disgust.[15] During the last few weeks of his stay among the Indians, Parkman was stricken with a malady, the cause and nature of which the medical science of his day was unable to fathom. The disease left him an invalid for life, with eyesight so gravely impaired that its use, as far as extensive reading was concerned, was gone forever, and with a mental condition which precluded concentration except for a few moments at a time.[16]

Parkman's life from this point on became a struggle, a struggle as unceasing as the one his pen was busily portraying. As he was re-creating the English war against the French, he was fighting an illness of mind and body which baffled the physicians of two continents.[17] Students who have theorized at great length and spun beautiful yarns about Parkman's conquest of untoward circumstances have overlooked the fact that in reality the condition which confronted him was as much a part of his personality as his wish to avoid thoughtless expressions of sympathy.[18] It is certain that his loss of eyesight meant less to him than to the subsequent delineators of his character and achievements. Parkman expressed his reaction to his partial blindness thus:

The eyes are nothing to the other infernal thing which now seems inclined to leave me alone, good riddance to it; so I contrive to dig slowly along by the aid of other people's eyes, doing the work more thoroughly no doubt, and adjusting my materials better than if I used my own.[19]

[15] Parkman's journal, in Sedgwick, pp. 177–80.

[16] George M. Wrong, "Francis Parkman," in *Canadian Historical Review*, IV (December, 1923), 292–93.

[17] "Autobiography of Francis Parkman," p. 358.

[18] Joseph Schafer, "Francis Parkman," *Mississippi Valley Historical Review*, X (March, 1924), 353.

[19] Parkman to Squier, Oct. 15, 1849, in Don C. Seitz (ed.,), *Letters from Francis Parkman to E. G. Squier* (Cedar Rapids, Iowa, 1911), p. 24.

His physical weakness, on the other hand, piqued him great-ly, for it forced the mere shell of the man that he was, to hold in leash his desire to be active. He was obliged to stand by as though he were a shadow, perceiving, perhaps, the movements all about him, yet impotent to share in them. He complained to Squier on May 13, 1849,

I hope you will find an opportunity to send me a line now and then, though I, poor devil, am compelled to lay disabled in port, while others are prosperously voyaging on the high seas. Damn the luck—perhaps my turn will come sometime.

Again on April 2, 1850,

I owe you a grudge, as it [your letter] kindled in me a burning desire to get among fevers and volcanoes, niggers, Indians and other outcasts of humanity, a restless fit which is apt to seize me at intervals and which you have unmercifully aggravated.[20]

Parkman did as many persons in similar circumstances have done—mastered the resources remaining to him and staked his all on the production of his story of the French and English in North America. Whenever he could summon sufficient physical energy, he expended it liberally in visiting the scenes he was de-scribing upon the pages of his copy.[21] The wealth he inherited was largely devoted to the purchase of documents; those which were beyond his means he interested others in procuring or in publishing. Every act, in short, was bent to his one obsession, that of historical writing. Even his venture in horticulture, which resulted in the *Lilium parkmanni*, was recreation designed to make him more fit in mind and body for his great task.[22] He was an aristocrat among aristocrats, hating the democracy which Bancroft was popularizing.[23] In religion he was what he styled a "reverent agnostic."[24] The scientific thought of the age, the rising industrialism, and the Civil War slipped past him almost

[20] *Ibid.*, pp. 22, 28.

[21] Parkman, *Montcalm and Wolfe* (Boston, 1905), I, ix.

[22] John Fiske, *A Century of Science* (Boston, 1899), pp. 257–58.

[23] Wrong, p. 297.   [24] Sedgwick, p. 142.

unnoticed. Unique spirit that he was, he had immersed himself in an epoch sixty years dead when he was born.

Francis Parkman's claim to be numbered among the illustrious American historians of the nineteenth century rests, first of all, upon his choice of a subject. His contemporary, Prescott, had achieved fame by portraying the conquests of Spain in the New World. Motley was popularizing the struggle of the Dutch for freedom. Parkman's task was more difficult than either of these. Prescott's work involved only the conflict between the civilized Spanish peoples and the nearly civilized Aztecs and Incas; Motley's, the struggle between the Dutch and their Spanish overlords. Parkman had to trace not only the conquest of the Indians by the French and English but also the rivalry of these people for the control and possession of the St. Lawrence and Ohio river valleys. His problem was further complicated by the fact that the materials upon which his narrative was founded were scattered in the archives of France, Great Britain, and the New World; while the materials which Prescott and Motley used were localized in the archives of Spain and the Netherlands. Time and again, the immense difficulties which he encountered in his search for, and use of, archival material are impressed upon the student of Parkman's volumes.

Even von Ranke could not have placed greater emphasis upon the use of primary sources than did Parkman. Though writing in an age before elaborately compiled and appended bibliographies had become the fashion, Parkman rarely left his reader in doubt as to the specific material he utilized.[25] His searches for documents commenced in 1841 and were completed only when the *Half Century of Conflict* appeared in 1892. He acknowledged his indebtedness to great collectors such as John Carter Brown, E. B. O'Callaghan, Jared Sparks, and Thomas Aspinwall, to say nothing of many others of lesser note and now forgotten.[26]

Parkman relied, as far as possible, upon printed primary sources and was instrumental in furthering the publication of one

[25] In the introduction of each work Parkman cites much of the material which he relied upon for his information, but he also refers to additional sources in the body of the text.

[26] Parkman, *Pioneers of France in the New World* (Boston, 1905), p. 185.

great collection and, undoubtedly, influenced the bringing-out of an English edition of another. Although the appearance in print of the La Salle papers meant that Parkman must re-write the entire volume of *La Salle and the Discovery of the Great West*, he unhesitatingly did so. Moreover, he deserves the major credit for securing the Congressional appropriation which made possible the publication of these documents.[27] Of what influence Parkman's work may have been in arousing a widespread interest in the activities of the monastic orders and the Catholic church in America, one can, at best, hazard only a guess. However, when the popularity of Parkman's work was at its height, in the late eighteen-nineties, a commercial publisher in Cleveland capitalized the current demand by issuing the magnificent French-English edition of *The Jesuit Relations and Other Allied Documents* under the editorship of Reuben Gold Thwaites. Many documents in remote public and private archives Parkman had transcribed by copyists. Late in life he presented the whole—some seventy folio volumes—along with his other notes and papers, to the Massachusetts Historical Society.

Geographers who have berated historians for paying little heed to the physiographic setting of historical events and movements have had no quarrel with the writings of Francis Parkman. Parkman was fortunate in that many of the places of conflict between the French and English, though in ruins, could be visited; and his notebooks abounded, as has been previously pointed out, with measurements and specifications of forts, descriptions of portages, and analyses of trails and routes. His depiction of these was masterful.

In his earlier volumes, however, his word-pictures were somewhat labored and confused. Thus, in describing the conditions the French encountered in their early attempts to colonize Florida, he wrote:

It was a paradise for the hunter and the naturalist. Earth, air, and water teemed with life, in endless varieties of beauty and ugliness. A half-tropical forest shadowed the low shores, where the palmetto and

---

[27] J. S. Bassett, "Letters of Francis Parkman to Pierre Margry," *Smith College Studies in History*, VIII (April, 1923), 119, 208. Also Sedgwick, pp. 289–91.

the cabbage palm mingled with the oak, the maple, the cypress, the liquid-ambar, the laurel, the myrtle, and the broad glistening leaves of the evergreen magnolia. Here was the haunt of bears, wildcats, lynxes, cougars, and the numberless deer of which they made their prey. In the sedges and the mud the alligator stretched his brutish length; turtles with outstretched necks basked on half-sunken logs; the rattlesnake sunned himself on the sandy bank, and the yet more dangerous moccason [sic] lurked under the water-lilies in inlets and sheltered coves. The air and the water were populous as the earth. The river swarmed with fish, from the fierce and restless gar, cased in his horny armor, to the lazy catfish in the muddy depths. There were the golden eagle and the white-headed eagle, the gray pelican and the white pelican, the blue heron and the white heron, the egret, the ibis, ducks of various sorts, the whooping crane, the black vulture, and the cormorant; and when at sunset the voyagers drew their boat upon the strand and built their camp-fire under the arches of the woods, the owls whooped around them all night long, and when morning came the sultry mists that wrapped the river were vocal with the clamor of wild turkeys.[28]

Such writing has led to the criticism, because of Parkman's excessive use of detail, that it is difficult to "see the forest for the trees." However, Parkman's literary style improved steadily as he told the story of France and England in America. Consequently, in the later volumes of his writings, descriptions were terse. The foregoing criticism cannot be applied to such passages as:

The Plains were a tract of grass, tolerably level in most parts, patched here and there with cornfields, studded with clumps of bushes, and forming a part of the high plateau at the eastern end of which Quebec stood. On the south it was bounded by the declivities along the St. Lawrence; on the north, by those along the St. Charles, or rather along the meadows through which that lazy stream crawled like a writhing snake. At the place that Wolfe chose for his battle-field the plateau was less than a mile wide.[29]

In the delineation of characters, Parkman was at his best. By means of the persons who played the important roles in French settlement and in French and English conflict in America, he

[28] Parkman, *Pioneers of France*, pp. 59-60.   [29] Parkman, *Montcalm and Wolfe*, II, 289.

carried forward his narrative. His method of portrayal consisted, for the most part, in letting the usually loquacious French and laconic English describe themselves and one another; and then, as his heroes passed out of the picture, Parkman summed up their virtues and vices, not forgetting the while to judge them by the norms of their own day.[30] Satire he used only sparingly, although some of his quips verge on the classical, making his actors more than marionettes.[31] His characterization of Wolfe, however, was not essentially different from the earlier treatment of the same character by Robert Wright. Eugene Guénin's interpretation of Montcalm agrees in all essentials with that by Parkman, although the French author undoubtedly based his study upon many sources which were not available to the New Englander. In the absence of an outstanding leader during the *Half-Century of Conflict*, he carried the narrative of the period by contrasting the two rival systems of colonization.[32] In this contrast, as well as in his comparisons of French and English leaders, Parkman displayed a degree of impartiality rarely equaled; for, although the French lost in the struggle for the possession of

[30] Parkman, *Count Frontenac and New France under Louis XIV* (Boston, 1906), pp. 458–59: "Frontenac's own acts and words best paint his character, and it is needless to enlarge upon it. What perhaps may be least forgiven him is the barbarity of the warfare that he waged, and the cruelties that he permitted. He had seen too many towns sacked to be much subject to the scruples of modern humanitarianism; yet he was no whit more ruthless than his times and his surroundings, and some of his contemporaries find fault with him for not allowing more Indian captives to be tortured. Many surpassed him in cruelty, none equalled him in capacity and vigor. When civilized enemies were once within his power, he treated them, according to their degree, with a chivalrous courtesy, or a generous kindness. If he was a hot and pertinacious foe, he was also a fast friend; and he excited love and hatred in about equal measure. His attitude towards public enemies was always proud and peremptory, yet his courage was guided by so clear a sagacity that he never was forced to recede from the position he had taken. Towards Indians, he was an admirable compound of sternness and conciliation. Of the immensity of his services to the colony there can be no doubt. He found it, under Denonville, in humiliation and terror; and he left it in honor, and almost in triumph."

[31] Parkman, *Montcalm and Wolfe*, I, 465; II, 213.

[32] Characters play only minor roles in this volume, though a case could be made out that Parkman still adhered to the biographical method in his treatment of this period. R. Wright, *The Life of Major-General James Wolfe* (London, 1864); Eugene Guénin, *Montcalm* (Paris, 1898).

North America, he neither belittled their characters nor enhanced the achievements of the British.[33]

The Indians of Parkman's volumes were neither the wooden figures standing before the cigar stores of a bygone generation nor the "painted cardboard warriors of 'The Leather Stocking Tales,'" but were savages, resisting with barbarity the encroachments of a civilization unsympathetic to their mode of life and which they did not understand. Investigators thus far have not criticized Parkman's picture of the redmen. With the present emphasis upon the comparative study of Indian tribes in North America it may be that some student will investigate his description of them. The close reader may at times wonder at his credulity in believing tales of not-too-trustworthy witnesses of the eighteenth century concerning the natives of the St. Lawrence and Illinois country. He accepted, with only slight misgiving, the story of an eighteenth-century traveler who claimed to have seen an Indian mounted on Braddock's charger nine years after Braddock's defeat.[34] As far as the present writer can determine, the Indians of the country east of the Great Plains used captured horses as provender rather than as beasts of burden. Likely enough, the observations made among the plains Indians in 1846 somewhat warped Parkman's interpretation of the eastern savages; for if men do adapt themselves to their environment, assuredly there were differences between the plains Indians of the nineteenth century and those who inhabited the wooded regions of the St. Lawrence in the seventeenth and eighteenth. A thorough estimate of Parkman's treatment of the Indians cannot be given here, because no scientific treatise is available which portrays the western Indians of the 1840's, among whom Parkman lived.[35] However, it suffices that Parkman permitted, for the

[33] After completing a volume by Parkman, the reader feels no inclination to pity or to hate, to eulogize or to denounce, either the English or the French. See particularly the latter chapters of *Montcalm and Wolfe*, II, 299 ff.

[34] Parkman, *The Conspiracy of Pontiac* (Boston, 1905), II, 189.

[35] Lucy E. Textor, *Official Relations between the United States and the Sioux Indians* ("Leland Stanford Junior University Publications," No. 2 [Palo Alto, Calif., 1896]), does not treat the habits, customs, etc., of the Sioux sufficiently to be of great value in such a study.

most part, the seventeenth- and eighteenth-century colonists to tell of their copper-colored combatants; that is, he accepted the scale of values used by contemporary white witnesses.

The genius for literary expression, the accurate portrayal of geographic scenes, the lively delineation of characters, the correlation of events into a coherent unity, and the vast use of primary documents may go far to describe Parkman's accomplishment but do not explain the spirit of critical analysis and impartiality—the warp and woof of historical writing—which pervades his works. Commentators are agreed that Parkman's detachment from the movements of the world accounted, in the main, for his great analytical powers. Indubitably, his training in law, with its rules of evidence closely akin to the principles of historical criticism, aided him in untangling conflicting statements, while his zeal to tell the truth lay at the base of his impartiality. Whatever the cause or the explanation of Parkman's gift for critical analysis, he upheld the practice of presenting both sides of mooted questions,[36] and qualified statements with "It is said, though on evidence of no weight, that . . . . ," and other similar comments.[37] But the correctness of quotation and citation which prevails throughout *France and England in America*, though probably inspired by Parkman, should be credited to his many amanuenses and publishers.[38] A random examination of direct quotations from available printed primary sources confirms the conviction, long established, of Parkman's accuracy.

Although forty-five years have elapsed since his task was completed, no other extended work treating the same epoch has appeared.[39] It is difficult, therefore, to gauge his undertaking as to proportion and emphasis of topics treated. Monographists, such as Reuben Gold Thwaites, have followed his chronological arrangement and depended to a remarkable extent upon his narratives for information. Thwaites treated in sixteen chapters of

[36] Parkman, *Montcalm and Wolfe*, I, 64–68, 90–127.   [37] *Ibid.*, p. 220.

[38] All commentators are agreed upon this accuracy; but, contrary to my opinion, they seem prone to credit it to Parkman.

[39] The nearest approach to an extended work is Wrong, *Conquest of New France* in the "Chronicles of America" series.

his *France in America* what Parkman considered in eleven volumes, and Channing dismissed the same epoch in three chapters of his *History of the United States*. Parkman's importance to these later writers is indicated, however, by the fact that in fifty pages of Thwaites's volume, Parkman's works are cited fifteen times against seventeen primary sources and eleven other secondary sources cited twenty-five times;[40] while Channing in thirty-five pages cited Parkman seven times, primary sources fourteen, and seven secondary works are referred to in the eleven other citations.[41] George M. Wrong, in his *Conquest of New France*, acknowledged Parkman to be the source of his information save where additional documentary evidence had appeared since Parkman's work was finished.

The Conspiracy of Pontiac, which is really an epilogue to the struggle of France and England in America, was the first of Parkman's historical writings to be published. John Fiske said that it was not well received. But when Parkman produced the second of the narratives, a decade and a half later, and when the other volumes followed this one from the presses in rapid succession, Parkman's reputation as a writer of moment and as a historian grew by leaps and bounds. His contemporaries were unstinted in their praise of his work.

The "Tribune" ventured to say to New Yorkers that in "vigor and pointedness of description, Mr. Parkman may be counted superior to Irving;" and the "Nation" said, "This book will add his name to the list of those historians who have done honor to American literature."[42]

Despite the laudation of the newspaper editors and literati of the day, Parkman stated (though to whom it was uttered cannot now be determined) that "some of the Catholics and some of the Puritans sputter at the book—others take it very kindly only regretting that the heretical author will probably be damned."[43]

[40] Reuben G. Thwaites, *France in America, 1497–1763* (New York, 1905), pp. 215–65.

[41] Edward Channing, *A History of the United States* (New York, 1924), II, 527–62.

[42] Sedgwick, pp. 247–48. This quotation is in praise of his *The Pioneers of France in the New World. The Conspiracy of Pontiac* was first published in 1851.

[43] Parkman to Squier, Oct. 24, 1867, in Seitz, p. 45. He was writing of his *The Jesuits in North America*.

Praise, however, was not confined to the press. Literary giants such as Henry James and James Russell Lowell greeted *Montcalm and Wolfe* with thoughtful commendation.[44]

The outstanding figures in the historical guild of that time hailed Parkman as a high priest of American historiography.[45] Henry Adams wrote him:

> Your two volumes on Montcalm and Wolfe deserve much more careful study than I am competent to give them, and so far as I can see, you have so thoroughly exhausted your sources as to leave little or nothing new to be said. The book puts you in the front rank of living English historians, and I regret only that the field is self-limited so that you can cultivate it no further. Your book is a model of thorough and impartial study and clear statement. Of its style and narrative the highest praise is that they are on a level with its thoroughness of study. Taken as a whole, your works are now dignified by proportions and completeness which can be hardly paralleled by the "literary baggage" of any other historical writer in the language known to me today. . . . .[46]

In 1923, the centenary of Parkman's birth, C. W. Alvord, writing in the *Nation*, criticized Parkman for his sins of omission and commission. He pointed out that Parkman had little grasp either of the constitutional problems involved or of the economic forces at play in the epoch he portrayed; that his treatment was episodical, dramatic, and romantic; and that he was partial to the English.[47] Such charges Alvord did not support with proof, and no other competent scholar has put himself on record as agreeing with his view. For me to attempt to defend Parkman against this criticism would be folly. It is fair, however, to give impressions of his work gathered during the pursuit of the present study.

Parkman's effort from the outset was to trace the causes which led France first to conquer a continent and then to be eliminated from it. He conceived the purpose of the historian to be that of narrating events in the spirit of the times in which they oc-

[44] Sedgwick, pp. 257–58. [45] E.g., G. Bancroft and J. Winsor. See *ibid.*, pp. 4, 258–61.

[46] Henry Adams to Parkman, Dec. 21, 1884, in *ibid.*, p. 255.

[47] C. W. Alvord, "Francis Parkman," in the *Nation*, CXVII (Oct. 10, 1923), 394–96.

curred.[48] Edward G. Bourne's estimate that Parkman made "as conscientious an effort as ever historian did by means of documents to understand and reclothe the past with the habiliments of life"[49] appears to be well warranted. A careful reading of the New Englander's works does not leave the impression, upon this writer at least, that he missed the economic forces which led to the rivalry between France and England.[50] In the period about which he was writing, only a few persons measured colonial development in terms of the aggregate trade in articles of commerce. Hence, if Parkman neither weighed the fish exported to Catholic France to the last fin nor measured the furs to the last hairy pelt, it may be largely because the documents from which his history was written did not do so. The author, furthermore, was writing about frontiersmen and frontier conditions for the most part, and backwoodsmen worried little about constitutional problems.

Parkman is dramatic, and his treatment of the epoch smacks of romance. Probably few would deny, however, that conflict between man and man and between man and nature, even on a small scale, possesses an element of romance and drama. It may be true that the events treated in *France and England in America* are merely episodes; such a charge can only be validated by a specialist in the particular field of Parkman's endeavor. Until such an expert has rendered a decision backed by fact, the judgment of Joseph Schafer, that Parkman's interpretation will be supported and not essentially altered as new data are discovered, seems to be a fair estimate of the New Englander's work. Parkman's impartiality has too long been acknowledged to need any comment.[51]

[48] "Faithfulness to the truth of history involves far more than a research, however patient and scrupulous, into special facts. Such facts may be detailed with the most minute exactness, and yet the narrative, taken as a whole, may be unmeaning or untrue. The narrator must seek to imbue himself with the life and spirit of the time. He must study events in their bearings near and remote; in the character, habits, and manners of those who took part in them. He must himself be, as it were, a sharer or a spectator of the action he describes" (Parkman, *Pioneers of France*, pp. xiv–xv).

[49] E. G. Bourne, *Essays in Historical Criticism* (New York, 1901), p. 287.

[50] References to economic matters are so scattered throughout the extensive work that one frequently loses sight of them.

[51] Parkman states: "The conclusions drawn from the facts may be a matter of opinion, but it will be remembered that the facts themselves can be overthrown only by overthrow-

Where Francis Parkman is ranked among American historians is largely, I believe, a matter of personal choice. Alvord, deprecating the dramatic and romantic strain running through *France and England in America*, assigned him to a place in the school of literary historians.[52] John Spencer Bassett, stressing Parkman's careful use of evidence and historical criticism, made him a member of the modern scientific group;[53] while Professors Bourne, Schafer, and Wrong, although not definitely stating their views, lead their readers to believe that the historian of the old French wars belongs in a position midway between the literary and strictly scientific practitioners of the art. Parkman, in their opinion, skilfully combined the modern technique with the verve of the leading mid–nineteenth-century historians.[54] From the many volumes of *France and England in America* each of these positions can be fortified with so many examples that it is difficult to choose one from among them.

Parkman's works influenced the later Frontier school of American historiography. It is truly a long jump from Parkman to Turner, but Roosevelt acknowledged that it was from Parkman that he obtained all of his inspiration for the *Winning of the West*.[55] It remains now for some student to trace the influence, if any, which Roosevelt's work had upon Turner. If such a relationship can be established, Parkman may be designated as the principal precursor of the historians of the West. Whatever may be the place which Parkman may rightfully be assigned among American historians, his works remain useful as a coherent treatment of the part that France played in the colonization of North America.

---

ing the evidence on which they rest, or bringing forward counter-evidence of equal or greater strength; and neither task will be found an easy one" (Francis Parkman, *The Old Regime in Canada* [Boston, 1874], p. ix).

[52] Alvord, "Francis Parkman," *loc. cit.*, pp. 394–96.

[53] Bassett, *The Middle Group of American Historians* (New York, 1917), p. ix; Bassett in *Cambridge History of American Literature* (New York, 1921), III, 188–91.

[54] *Supra*, nn. 16, 18, and 49.

[55] Roosevelt to Parkman, April 23, 1888, in Sedgwick, pp. 259–60.

IV

HERMANN EDUARD von HOLST

CHARLES R. WILSON
Colgate University

IN THE late nineteenth century, Hermann E. von Holst, author of a comprehensive study of American constitutional and political development, was one of the most celebrated of United States historians. Today he is regarded as outmoded, and his volumes stand as mute testimony to the fact that history is one of the most ephemeral types of literature. No pioneer endeavors on the physical frontier have been more fully engulfed by the advance of civilization than have his conclusions by the advance of critical scholarship. Chiefly important as a pioneer in writing a difficult portion of American history, he blazed a trail for others to follow and improve. Von Holst is significant, however, not merely for his earnest efforts on the intellectual frontier but because his career is one of the most remarkable in American historiography.

When he came to America in 1867, von Holst was a penniless immigrant. By the time of his death in 1904, he was internationally known in the world of scholarship. During the intervening years he had returned to Germany, to become a foreign authority on United States history of such repute that a great American university induced him to leave Europe and head its department of history. He had become recognized by the students of two continents as a teacher so compelling that they viewed his passing as a truly personal loss. As a writer he was so influential

60

that many instructors of his generation reflected in their teaching his moral interpretation of the causes for the American Civil War. His was the tale of an immigrant lad who climbed from rags to renown. But, orthodox as this story may have been in American industrial endeavor, it was quite unorthodox in American academic circles.

There was little, however, about von Holst's life which was orthodox. He was born on June 19, 1841, of German parentage, but under the sovereignty of the czar of Russia, in Fellin, a small town of Livonia (now Esthonia). His father, Valentin, and his mother, Marie Lenz, traced their descent from fourteenth-century German immigrants to the Baltic region, the frontier of its day. Hermann was the seventh of ten children struggling for existence on a Lutheran minister's income. While he was in the Gymnasium, his education was imperiled by his father's death; but, by rigid economies and a meager income from tutoring, he was able to complete it. Entering the University of Dorpat, in his native province, during the spring of 1860, he left it in 1863 to continue the study of modern history at Heidelberg, where he was awarded the Ph.D. degree in 1865. His dissertation, a study of Louis XIV's reign, based upon the archives at Paris, was entitled "Federzeichnungen aus der Geschichte des Despotismus."[1]

Von Holst had now attained his first objective in life. He was ready to teach, and secured a position in St. Petersburg in the summer of 1866.[2] His prospects for the future seemed bright. But, unknown to him, the privations he had endured in childhood and in adolescence had undermined his health[3] to such an extent that he was doomed, during his later and ripest years, to suffer the agonies of a stomach disorder which finally killed him.

[1] F. Schevill, "Hermann Eduard von Holst" (A. Johnson and D. Malone, eds.), *Dictionary of American Biography*, IX, 177–78; A. B. Hart, "Hermann von Holst," *Political Science Quarterly*, V, 677–78; "Hermann Eduard von Holst," *National Cyclopaedia of American Biography*, XI, 69; "Hermann Eduard von Holst" (J. G. Wilson and J. Fiske, eds.), *Appletons' Cyclopedia of American Biography*, III, 243; "Hermann Eduard von Holst," *Who's Who in America, 1899–1900;* "Professor von Holst," *Outlook*, LXXVI, 253.

[2] *National Cyclopaedia*, XI, 69.

[3] "Notes and News," *American Historical Review*, IX, 623; *Nation*, LXXVIII, 65.

Furthermore, Russian despotism soon intervened to alter his entire career, destroying the potentially brilliant future in French history for which he seemed destined. It was this circumstance, however, which eventually gave to von Holst his life's work and to the world his *Constitutional and Political History of the United States*.

In 1866 an attempt was made upon the life of Czar Alexander II. Von Holst was constrained to silence while a savage retribution was visited upon the culprit. During the following summer, however, when he was traveling in France, his pent-up resentment burst the bonds of discretion, and he penned a passionate indictment of the Russian government which was published in pamphlet form at Leipsic. An order for his arrest was issued in St. Petersburg, and exile to Siberia seemed a certainty if he returned to Russia. Von Holst therefore turned his back forever upon his native land and, in July of 1867, took a steerage passage for America, which, from his reading of Laboulaye, he idealized as the perfect haven of liberty.[4]

If ever a man started at the bottom of the ladder to climb to fame, it was von Holst when he landed in New York. He lacked everything—money, home, friends, objective—everything except his education and the energy of desperation. Taking a single room with three laboring men, he started out as merely another immigrant day-laborer. Too poor to afford heat in their room, he and his fellow-sufferers frequently found it necessary to go to bed in order to keep warm.[5] The privations von Holst thus endured during this first winter in America undermined still further his delicate constitution.[6]

It was not long, however, before his education saved him from a more extended slum existence. He managed to secure a tutor-

[4] Schevill, p. 177; *Amer. Hist. Rev.*, IX, 623; *Natl. Cyclopaedia*, XI, 69; Hermann E. von Holst, *The Constitutional and Political History of the United States* (7 vols.; Washington, D.C., 1876–92), I, Preface, ix.

[5] Lucie Hammond, "Hermann von Holst, the Historian," *Review of Reviews*, XXIX, 321; "Von Holst," *School Review*, XII, 264; "An International Historical Scholar," *World's Work*, VII, 4513.

[6] Schevill, p. 178.

ship in modern languages at a small private school for children. His income was not large, but it was regular; and he was able to augment it somewhat by acting as a New York correspondent for the *Kölnische Zeitung*. In the fall of 1869, he was fortunate enough to be named assistant editor, under Alexander J. Schem, of the *Deutsch-Amerikanisches Konversations-Lexicon*. The work was exacting and the pay was small; but he continued, and even expanded, his newspaper endeavors. Now not only did he correspond for the *Kölnische Zeitung;* he became a contributor to several American papers, among them the *Nation*.[7] He also threw himself actively into American politics as an opponent of Tammany Hall and as a Republican campaign orator in 1868.

In the meantime von Holst had maintained his personal contacts in Germany, particularly those with Heinrich von Sybel, professor in the University of Bonn, who, like himself, was a student of French history. This relationship soon proved to be the agency whereby von Holst was enabled once again to resume his connection with his favorite subject.

Shortly after the formation of the North German Confederation in 1867, a group of Bremen merchants sought a capable publicist to prepare an account of the workings of popular suffrage and government in America which might be helpful in educating the new electorate in Germany. They turned for advice to Friedrich Kapp, who had returned to Germany after his abortive effort in behalf of General Frémont in 1864. Kapp seems to have referred the matter to von Sybel.[8] Knowing from von Holst's political activities that he had thoroughly acclimated himself in America, von Sybel unhesitatingly recommended him for the task.[9] Von Holst received the commission.

He started to work immediately, but he soon discovered that he had embarked upon a project so extensive that a lifetime could hardly encompass it. He therefore announced to his patrons that in time he could write a constitutional history of the

---

[7] "Hermann Eduard von Holst," *The Encyclopedia Americana*, XIV, 324; *Nat'l Cyclopaedia*, XI, 70; *Amer. Hist. Rev.*, IX, 623; Schevill, p. 178.

[8] *Amer. Hist. Rev.*, IX, 623.   [9] Hammond, p. 321.

United States, but that the smaller work demanded of him was an impossibility.[10] He thus failed to become a propagandist, but the preliminary survey he had made fascinated him so much that he fairly burned with the desire to delve deeper into American political history. Von Holst had found the subject for his *magnum opus*.[11]

The close of the Franco-Prussian War marked a new epoch in von Holst's life. With the transfer of Alsace to Germany, the University of Strassburg, which had been suppressed during the French Revolution because of its pro-German sympathies, was revived. The world was combed for a faculty at once respectable and acceptable under the circumstances. Von Holst's dissertation on French history had appeared in Leipsic during 1868,[12] making him somewhat *persona grata* in Alsace and at the same time proving him to be a sound scholar. Furthermore, his Russian birth and his American experience, together with his earlier European travels, lent him a desirable cosmopolitanism. Yet his German extraction and training gave assurance that he was a relatively safe appointee. Consequently, he was offered a position as assistant professor extraordinarius of American history and constitutional law at a salary of one thousand thalers. He accepted eagerly, tarrying in the United States only long enough to marry Miss Annie Isabelle Hatt, a girl "of old New England stock" and a graduate of Vassar. Von Holst later said that the Strassburg period marked the happiest years of his life.[13]

The year after von Holst accepted the call to Strassburg, the first volume of his *Constitutional and Political History of the United States* appeared.[14] This publication brought him, in 1874, an in-

[10] *Nation*, LXXVIII, 65.

[11] Von Holst, *Const. and Pol. Hist.*, I, Preface, x; Schevill, p. 178.

[12] *Appleton's*, III, 243.

[13] *Nation*, LXXVIII, 65; Schevill, p. 178; *Natl. Cyclopaedia*, XI, 70.

[14] The German title of von Holst's first volume was *Verfassung und Demokratie der Vereinigten Staaten von America*. This was freely translated into "The Constitutional and Political History," etc. Subsequent volumes in German were published under the title: *Verfassungsgeschichte der Vereinigten Staaten seit der Administration Jacksons*, but in the translation the original title was retained.

vitation to the University of Freiburg as a full professor of modern history. Here he came completely into his own and dominated the academic scene for a period of nearly twenty years.[15] Despite his heavy duties in other fields, he was able to continue his research in American history.[16] In the meantime he was unconsciously shaping his career so that its last active phase would be spent in America.

In 1878, upon the appearance in Germany of the second volume of the *Constitutional and Political History*, von Holst was designated by the Royal Prussian Academy of Sciences as a fellow to make further investigations into the history of the United States and to gather additional material for his great work. Taking a year's leave from Freiburg, he spent it all in America. On this visit he crossed the Mason-Dixon line for the first time and also had his earliest glimpse of the trans-Mississippi West. But of greater significance for the future were his lectures at Johns Hopkins and at Cornell universities.[17] Not until 1883 did he visit the United States again. This time it was as one of thirty distinguished foreign guests of the Northern Pacific Railroad Company invited to witness the opening of its transcontinental line. Although his stay was short, he had an opportunity to broaden his contacts and enhance his reputation still further, for he lectured at Harvard and in a number of cities.[18]

Between these visits to the United States, von Holst was active in German politics. As tutor of the eldest son of the Grand Duke of Baden he had gained the friendship of that influential noble. Attracted by von Holst's keen interest in politics, his knowledge of political history, and his experience in America, the duke appointed him, in 1881, to membership in the Herrenhaus, the upper chamber of the Baden Landtag. For the next three terms he was elected by the University, serving as vice-

[15] *Amer. Hist. Rev.*, IX, 623.

[16] *Hart*, p. 679.

[17] Von Holst, *Const. and Pol. Hist.*, III, Translator's Note, iii; *Amer. Hist. Rev.*, IX, 624; *World's Work*, VII, 4514; *Natl. Cyclopaedia*, XI, 70.

[18] Hammond, p. 321; *Appleton's*, III, 243; *Natl. Cyclopaedia*, XI, 70.

president during the last two of them. In 1890, however, impetuously coming out in opposition to the Bismarckian policies, he was defeated.[19]

Busy as these years were with other matters, von Holst continued his scholarly production. The second volume of the *Constitutional and Political History*, which had appeared in 1878, was followed by two more volumes in the eighties and a fifth in 1891. The entire work was published in an English translation, of seven volumes and an index, between 1876 and 1892.[20] In 1882, *John C. Calhoun*, written in English, appeared as one of the "American Statesmen" series, while *Das Staatsrecht der Vereinigten Staaten*, one of the Marquardsen series of monographs on public law, was published in 1885 (tr. 1887), and *John Brown* in 1888 (tr. 1889).[21]

In consequence of these varied activities, von Holst was better known in America than most of her native historians. His prestige there was enormous. It was not without reason, then, that he received invitations, from time to time, to join the faculties of Johns Hopkins, Cornell, and Clark universities. The University of Chicago rightfully felt it had executed a real *coup* when in 1892, as a feature of its rebirth, it presuaded him to accept the chairmanship of its department of history.[22]

Von Holst was ill when he came to Chicago. Since 1881, at least, he had suffered the tortures of the damned, and "the greater part of his intellectual work was done in such a physical condition that many men would have gone to the hospital and comfortably given up the ghost."[23] But in spite of severe attacks which periodically forced him to his bed and broke the con-

[19] *Nation*, LXXVIII, 65; *Natl. Cyclopaedia*, XI, 70.

[20] Vol. I, *State Sovereignty and Slavery, 1750–1832;* Vol. II, *Jackson's Administration—Annexation of Texas, 1828–1846;* Vol. III, *Annexation of Texas—Compromise of 1850, 1846–1850;* Vol. IV, *Compromise of 1850—Kansas-Nebraska Bill, 1850–1854;* Vol. V, *Kansas-Nebraska Bill—Buchanan's Election, 1854–1856;* Vol. VI, *Buchanan's Election—End of 35th Congress, 1856–1859;* Vol. VII, *Harper's Ferry—Lincoln's Inauguration, 1859–1861.*

[21] Schevill, p. 178.

[22] *Outlook*, LXXVI, 253; *School Review*, XII, 264; Hammond, p. 321; *Natl. Cyclopaedia*, XI, 70.

[23] *Nation*, LXXVIII, 65.

tinuity of his work, he carried on. Throwing himself into his teaching with amazing vitality, he exercised a power over his students which is legendary. A vigorous lecturer, he used no notes whatsoever, depending entirely upon his marvelous memory for the most minute facts. He pounded his points home with the fervency of a crusader. Colleagues might have their doubts, and wish for the certainty about anything which he evinced about everything; but his students, swept along by the verve and gusto of his attack, became his blind partisans. Crowded classrooms, knots of casual listeners in the hallways, and outbursts of applause at the end of the hour attested to his masterly teaching.[24]

In spite of illness and the elaborate preparation he made for his classes, von Holst did not give up his research. In 1894 he was invited to deliver a series of twelve lectures on the French Revolution at Lowell Institute. He planned a fresh attack on the subject and drew his material largely from the sources. These lectures were later expanded and published, with notes, in two volumes as *The French Revolution Tested by Mirabeau's Career*.[25]

While von Holst had been sensationally successful at Chicago, he was not entirely happy. He had never quite been able to adjust himself to the peculiarities of the American university system. He was the registrar's *bête noire*. Furthermore, his health grew worse instead of better, and he was homesick for Germany. In an effort to keep him relatively well satisfied, the University granted him a "sick leave" in 1896–97 which permitted him to go abroad again. Journeying to Freiburg almost immediately, he spent the year there, lecturing on the French Revolution, Germany since the Reformation, the Napoleonic period, and Europe since 1815. He rounded out this exceedingly active vacation by directing seminar work.[26]

With the conclusion of his leave, von Holst returned to Chicago, highly appreciative of the esteem in which he was held.

---

[24] Charles D. Warner (ed.), *Library of the World's Best Literature*, XIX, 7497; Hammond, p. 322.

[25] Schevill, p. 178.   [26] *Natl. Cyclopaedia*, XI, 70.

But it was the beginning of the end. He found it increasingly difficult to meet his classes and fulfil his academic obligations. Feeling that he was becoming a dead weight to the University and that rest and travel might restore his shattered health, he tendered his resignation. The University officials refused to accept it, but retired him upon a pension in 1899.[27] It was a deserved tribute to a man who had done a difficult job well.

Leaving Chicago, von Holst sought the congenial climate of Italy in his effort to regain his health; but he was fighting a losing battle and knew it. When he perceived that the end was not far off, he returned to Germany, going finally to Freiburg, where he could die among scenes and friends he loved. On January 20, 1904, he passed on.[28] The historical fraternity had lost not merely a distinguished scholar but a personality which would have been outstanding in any profession.

Von Holst's death was, strangely enough, the occasion for a vicious attack upon his work by the *American Bookman*. Unquestionably, a number of the criticisms were justified; but, just as certainly, the article as a whole gave vent to an amazing amount of spleen, particularly out of place under the circumstances. To the *Bookman*, the *Constitutional and Political History* was "one of the most disappointing works that ever have been written." It was nothing more than a "doctor's thesis multiplied to the dimensions of an encyclopedia." "Ponderous, but largely futile and unbalanced," it suffered even in style, with its "involved sentences," "monotonous movement," and "tawdry grotesqueness of rhetorical display." Von Holst was "always trying to be emphatic; with the result that he reminds you of a sullen convict doggedly breaking stones in a prison quarry." Nor was the man himself worthy of respect, for at Chicago "he sweated pessimism and snarled at our institutions until his health broke down and he returned to Europe."[29]

---

[27] *Amer. Hist. Rev.*, IX, 624.

[28] Schevill, p. 178.   [29] "Professor H. E. von Holst," *Bookman*, XIX, 18.

Unreasonably extreme as the *Bookman*'s position was, it nevertheless pointed in the direction, at least, of subsequent opinion. Von Holst's history has withstood the test of time and critical scholarship perhaps less successfully than that of any of his major contemporaries—Schouler, Henry Adams, or McMaster. Now generally regarded as historic rather than historical, it is something to be explained rather than accepted. The reason for this is hardly to be found in any serious disadvantage under which he, as a foreigner, labored in writing a history of the United States. For that very reason, in fact, he was in many respects better qualified to do his work than were his American-born contemporaries.[30] Even he realized this at the outset of his task.[31] The faults of his history largely resulted from defects in the writer himself.

Close study of von Holst's work seems to indicate that his major shortcomings were preconceptions and dogmatism. The nature of his particular preconceptions is perhaps to be explained by the *tempora* and mores in which he lived. Because he permitted their existence to influence his findings, and then endeavored to drive these conclusions home with a sort of pontifical finality, the value of his work is almost completely vitiated as history. It was not, therefore, without reason that the *Bookman* asserted that von Holst "went about his task very much as a German student goes about the writing of a doctoral dissertation. He lays down some kind of a thesis, and then he ransacks heaven and earth for the material that will, when ingeniously manipulated, prove his thesis true."[32] The *Bookman*'s critic was not the only one to recognize this fault.[33]

Stripped of all its ramifications, von Holst's thesis is a comparatively simple one. The pre–Civil War history of the United

[30] *Library of the World's Best Literature*, XIX, 7496.

[31] Von Holst, *Const. and Pol. Hist.*, I, Preface (written by the author in English), viii. Later, however, von Holst came to doubt this seriously. See his "An Open Letter to Heinrich von Sybel. (In lieu of the Preface)," *ibid.*, VII, iv–v.

[32] *Bookman*, XIX, 17.

[33] "The Close of von Holst's Work" *Atlantic Monthly*, LXX, 840.

States, it maintains, consisted essentially of a titanic struggle between the forces of light and darkness,[34] culminating in a smashing victory for the rightful cause with the inauguration of Lincoln in 1861. In setting forth this positive doctrine, von Holst found it necessary to lay down two basic postulates, both of them at least questionable: the first is that the American Union was older than the states; that at the beginning of the national existence there had been no such thing as state sovereignty.

Throughout the Revolutionary War, according to von Holst, Congress "was recognized by all the colonies as *de jure* and *de facto* the national government, and . . . . came in contact with foreign powers and entered into engagements, the binding force of which on the people has never been called in question. The individual colonies . . . . did not take a single step which could have placed them before the mother country or the world in the light of *de facto* sovereign states." But weak-kneed compromises on the part of nationalistic leaders had resulted in the recognition of state sovereignty in the Articles of Confederation. Similar weakness had prevented the nationalist principle from being written clearly into even the Constitution. At Philadelphia, he maintained, the advocates both of state sovereignty and of nationality were required, in order to come to any agreement at all, to make "mutual sacrifices . . . . not only in principles, but in theories." The product was an unsatisfactory compromise which achieved merely "the prevention of the dissolution of the Union and the creation of a federal power with the character of a federal government to such an extent that by it the possibility of the growth of the members of the federation into one consistent whole was secured."[35]

With the very inauguration of the new government, "the conflict between the opposing tendencies broke out anew," both sides pretending to be the defenders of the Constitution and both

[34] G. P. Gooch, *History and Historians in the Nineteenth Century* (2d. ed., New York, 1913), p. 410; Schevill, p. 178; *Library of the World's Best Literature*, XIX, 7497; Hart, p. 686.

[35] Von Holst, *Const. and Pol. Hist.*, I, 5, 20, 76.

sides, on occasion, threatening dissolution of the Union. As time went on, however, and the sectionalism between the North and the South intensified, "the ambiguous nature of the constitution became apparent in an equal degree." The North, which not only was "the more populous and wealthy" portion of the Union but was also "morally and intellectually, the more highly developed," gradually espoused the point of view which the facts of the past proved to be legally sound. Carrying the implications of this view to their logical conclusion, it finally succeeded, by an appeal to the sword, in deciding, once and for all, "the one great question . . . . to which, from the terms of the constitution, no certain answer had ever before been given."[36] To von Holst there was no doubt whatever but that the proponents of state sovereignty were both historically and legally in error.

The second postulate in the von Holst thesis is that slavery, the great moral wrong of the age, was "the keynote to the whole development of American constitutional doctrine; that it held the clue to every labyrinth and maze of American public life; and that its existence was alone sufficient to explain the history of our country from 1783" to the Civil War.[37] He first revealed his hand in discussing the attitude of the southern congressmen toward the famed Philadelphia Quaker petition of 1790 requesting that the slave trade be prohibited by law. He stated,

The *noli me tangere* was thrown back at the north in tones as emphatic and haughty as it was subsequently by Calhoun or Toombs. Here we have the whole struggle of seventy years in a nutshell. All subsequent events were only the variations of the themes of these debates, the logical development of the principles here laid down, and their practical application to concrete questions.[38]

According to von Holst, the slavery problem, which was eventually to threaten both democracy and the Union, might have been solved before it became serious had it not been for the unfortunate disposition of antislavery men to follow the example

[36] *Ibid.*, pp. 77–79.

[37] *Bookman*, XIX, 17.   [38] Von Holst, *Const. and Pol. Hist.*, I, 90.

of the nationalists and compromise. The most important of the slavery compromises were also in the Constitutional Convention, where "for the first time, the veil was rent which had hitherto made a clear conception of the true state of the slavery question impossible. The rents were wide enough to let it be seen that behind them lay a world of war, of war to the knife, although they did not show how this war would develop and how it would end."[39]

Thus, because the Constitution recognized slavery indirectly, stated von Holst, "a mighty pillar of support was thrust under the rotten structure." In this instance, as was true likewise in the state-sovereignty dispute, the northern delegates submitted to the demands of the South in order to insure the adoption of the Constitution. But "principle had been bargained away" for the sake of a Union which would be endangered in the future by the very fact that slavery had been given a new lease on life. Already the slavocracy had emerged in the United States, and "every new demand dictated to the slavocracy by the impulse of self-preservation presented to the north the alternative of yielding and therewith taking a farther step away from the right principle or of endangering the Union." Thus the first links in the chain of events which led inexorably to the Civil War had been forged; for the South, now having cast the die in favor of slavery, must force its expansion or lose out in the struggle for existence. But if slavery "struck deeper root and spread wider, then human rights, free labor and all freedom, political, religious and moral, would perforce ever bow lower under the yoke of the slavocracy, as long as men would neither sacrifice the Union nor venture to fight for the Union."[40]

To von Holst those who maintained and defended slavery were as completely the victims of egregious error as were those who advocated the doctrine of state sovereignty. To give logical completeness to his pattern of American history, therefore, it was necessary for him to associate in the same persons, the same political party, and the same section these fundamental legal and

[39] *Ibid.*, pp. 288–89.   [40] *Ibid.*, pp. 299–301.

moral errors. This he did definitely, forcibly, and as early as possible. "It was not mere chance," he stated in Volume I, that state sovereignty "revealed itself in combination with the question which afterwards imparted such magnitude to it."[41] What was more logical than that the spirit of darkness with regard to a moral question should utilize an erroneous constitutional theory in an effort to protect its vulnerable flanks? Von Holst gave himself away in the subtitle to his first volume: "State Sovereignty and Slavery." The implication is clear. The twin evils of American history were predestined for consolidation from the very beginning. Once merged, they threatened democracy as well as the Union, until the inauguration of Lincoln presented the opportunity for their complete extirpation.

All of von Holst's writings on American history fit into this general pattern. His minor works were merely centrifugal offthrowings of his *magnum opus*. Thus his *Das Staatsrecht der Vereinigten Staaten*, while purporting to be a treatise on constitutional law, is really little more than a sketch of the principles of American government embracing a refinement of the constitutional thread in his large history. In both instances, Joseph Story was his guiding star.

Likewise, his *Calhoun* is largely a telescoped version of the main work. It is not a biography in the ordinary sense of the word. It is an intellectual analysis rather than a personal assessment. Calhoun's philosophy afforded von Holst an opportunity to restate his own main thesis, and the succeeding clash in opinion between subject and author lent the book somewhat the atmosphere of a debate. To von Holst, Calhoun was a sincere, able man, who, through the force of circumstances, became the fanatical spokesman in his generation for the hosts of error.[42] Personifying the combination of slavery defense and state sovereignty, he endeavored at the same time to remain a unionist.[43] The consequent dilemma made a doctrinaire of him and finally enmeshed him hopelessly in the subtleties of his own fallacious

[41] *Ibid.*, p. 89.
[42] Von Holst, *John C. Calhoun*, pp. 1, 95.   [43] *Ibid.*, pp. 95, 125, 143, 303.

logic.[44] He was not the statesman of disunion; he was the keen-eyed prophet who foresaw it and endeavored to avert it but, in so doing, actually hastened it.[45] He it was who enabled the slavocracy to maintain supremacy over the democracy of the nation as long as it did.[46] His failure was a result of destiny.

Von Holst's *John Brown*, really merely an interpretative essay, also is very closely connected with the large history. Once more the struggle between light and darkness—truth against error, morality against unmorality, democracy against slavocracy—is the unifying thread. Brown personifies the rightful cause as Calhoun does the wrongful. Emerging "at the call of the Lord of hosts to fight out a life-and-death struggle with slavery—'the sum of all iniquities,'" he was as "tender and soft as a girl who nestles in her mother's lap, and yet every inch a man." It was "the treason against Kansas committed by the weak-kneed, the self-seeking, and the corrupt politicians" which roused Brown to action.[47] Yet, according to von Holst, he had no direct connection with the Pottawatomie massacre,[48] and did not, indeed, take the offensive until after his trip east in 1857. His Harper's Ferry project was "a piece of insanity in the literal sense of the word," so much so that "it was an unseemly piece of pleasantry on the part of the Attorney General to accuse Brown later of high treason and on the part of the jury to declare him guilty." Nevertheless, because of certain incidents connected with the raid, von Holst admitted that from the politico-legal standpoint justice was done Brown "in the main." The man's spirit, however, said von Holst, is not to be assessed by the verdict passed upon him. It is "the motives which actuated him" which "must furnish the ground on which to judge his character."[49] There is

---

[44] *Ibid.*, pp. 127–28, 143–44, 168–69.

[45] *Ibid.*, pp. 122, 128–31, 142, 300.   [46] *Ibid.*, p. 350.

[47] Von Holst, *John Brown*, pp. 73, 76, 87.

[48] *Ibid.*, p. 91. Von Holst later was forced to abandon this view. See his *Const. and Pol. Hist.*, V, 310, and especially VII, 20 n.

[49] Von Holst, *John Brown*, pp. 102, 111, 154.

little variation here from the thread running through the *Constitutional and Political History*.

It is easy to trace the origin of von Holst's preconceptions. His European education naturally disposed him to reject human slavery, and his religious background caused him to view it as a moral matter over which there could be no argument. Before he came to America, his Russian experience had brought into full bloom his hatred for political despotism of the type he believed the "slavocracy" represented. His historical training under Haeusser, von Sybel, and Treitschke, leaders of the so-called Prussian or Unitarian school in Germany,[50] disposed him to favor a centralization of power in the United States. His faith in the unitarian principle was crystallized by his own observation of the contrast between the inefficiency of the German Confederation and the extraordinary efficiency of the new German Empire.

Coming to America at the close of the Civil War, he settled in Horace Greeley's and Henry Ward Beecher's North. Here he found ready-made an interpretation of American history which struck him as quite plausible because its implications squared perfectly with his own predilections. Northern publicists and politicians, speaking for the victorious faction in a bitter struggle for supremacy in the government, emphatically viewed the Civil War as the climax of a great moral and constitutional struggle which had begun almost with the independence of the colonies. The causes for the war, they insisted, were therefore to be found in peculiar southern heresies which had been thrust forward in a spirit of rule or ruin. Dreadful as the bloodshed had been, certain immeasurably great benefits had resulted, namely, the destruction of slavery, the scotching of state sovereignty, and the triumph of the right.

To von Holst, the lover of liberty and the proponent of centralization, all this made capital sense. Prior to 1879, no visit to the South marred his complacency. Also from the very nature of his situation, the sources from which he drew the inspiration for his writings were preponderantly northern. He would, therefore,

[50] Schevill, p. 178.

have been more than human, if, considering his natural predis-
position, the period, the environment, and his sources he had
written anything other than a history of the United States from
the Federalist-Whig-Republican and antislavery, northern point
of view. Completely convinced in his own mind that he had hit
upon the truly unifying thread of American history, he permitted
his fervent nature free rein and drove his points home in his char-
acteristically lusty fashion. His indefatigable labors deserved a
better fate.

Particular criticisms of von Holst's work in most cases find
their roots in his thesis. It was his effort to square everything
by the rigid standard of his preconception which led him into
his major pitfalls. Thus his evaluation of historical materials is
decidedly faulty. He went to the sources and used them liberally;
he even used some of southern origin. His innumerable citations
to the documents and to the memoirs of the contemporary statesmen give an air of complete authority to his presentation. This
in reality does not exist, for von Holst picked and chose most
carefully. He appears to have accepted at face value any document which furthered his thesis, but to have made short shrift
of the materials which disproved it. His parade of authorities
consisted of Hamilton, John Adams, Marshall, John Quincy
Adams, Webster, Story, Curtis, Henry Wilson, the *New York
Tribune*, and the *Independent*.[51] Jefferson, Calhoun, Davis, and
Douglas are quoted for the purpose of refuting them.[52] Southern
and "doughface" newspapers ordinarily were cited only to indicate the enormity of their error. Occasionally an "admission"
is elicited from them, but rarely a valid argument.

[51] Other sources of information von Holst drew upon were: F. Kapp, *Geschichte der
Sklaverei in den Vereinigten Staaten von Amerika;* E. B. Hunt, *Union Foundations: A Study of
American Nationality as a Fact of Science;* J. R. Giddings, *History of the Rebellion;* T. S. Goodwin, *The Natural History of Secession, or Despotism and Democracy at Necessary, Eternal, Exter-
minating War;* H. Wilson, *The Rise and Fall of the Slave Power in America; Annual Reports*
of the American Anti-slavery Society; and J. G. Fee, *An Anti-slavery Manual.*

[52] He thus comments on Jefferson Davis' *Rise and Fall of the Confederate Government:* "In
his two large volumes he has indeed shown himself a master in the art of keeping silent on
what is most important in order to dwell, at dreary length, on the doctrine of state sovereignty" (von Holst, *Const. and Pol. Hist.*, VII, 120 n.).

Another criticism of von Holst, for which the thesis is largely responsible, is that his history is incomplete, unbalanced, and poorly proportioned.[53] Volume I is, in many respects, little else than a series of more or less connected essays. It is certainly not consecutive history.[54] The succeeding volumes, while better integrated, leave much to be desired. They suffer not so much from gaps as from a lack of social and economic background for the general political development and a complete subordination of all other matters to the slavery question. The faulty apportionment of space in his major work is evident from the fact that the first three volumes cover the period 1750–1850, while the last four are devoted to the years 1850–61. His thesis being what it was, von Holst felt justified in exercising the right of selection to exclude or merely mention those matters which did not bear upon the development of the slavery contest. Furthermore, he saw no objection, as the struggle over slavery became more intense, to devoting an increasingly larger amount of space to a progressively shorter period of time.

A third criticism of von Holst is that he viewed the Civil War as an end in itself rather than as an important link in a long chain of events which was destined to transform the nation.[55] The reason for this is partly the lack of perspective; a handicap to be anticipated by one writing so soon after the event. But even more is it to be found in his thesis. That being what it was, the Civil War had to be an end—the happy denouement in a tense, thrilling, moral drama.

This same factor is responsible for von Holst's inability to appreciate the statesmanship involved in compromise. To him a principle was something to die for. To bargain over a question like slavery was prima facie evidence of abject weakness or worse. Compromise solved nothing; it merely postponed. Northern "doughfaces," therefore, were contemptible. Von Holst was

[53] *Bookman*, XIX, 18; Hart, p. 682.

[54] Hart, p. 680; Schevill, p. 178.

[55] A. C. McLaughlin, "American History and American Democracy," *Amer. Hist. Rev.*, XX, 259–60.

completely incapable of seeing that time, if gained, frequently takes the solution of questions out of the hands of government. Likewise he failed to understand that the "Northern men with Southern principles," whom he despised so heartily, were willing to concede somewhat in order to preserve a Union which to them was more important than the freedom of the slaves.[56]

Von Holst's thesis is also responsible for specific mistakes of interpretation. For example, he was unable to see that there was any basis other than slavery for the unlikeness of North and South.[57] Consequently, he was led into another error. He admitted that there was little nationalism in the country even prior to 1820.[58] Since slavery was sectional in its nature, he believed, no real nationalism was possible as long as it existed. This, in turn, led him to an erroneous interpretation of American expansion. The acquisition of Louisiana and Florida to him was chiefly important as a stimulus to long constitutional debate because of the significance of these areas to the future of slavery.[59] The annexation of Texas was the product of a slaveholder's conspiracy;[60] the Mexican War and its aftermath were clearly consequences of the whip-cracking policy of the slavocracy at Washington.[61] The Kansas-Nebraska Act was an obvious sell-out to the South,[62] while the Dred Scott decision was a moral and political atrocity embodying judicial prostitution.[63]

[56] "Von Holst's Constitutional History of the United States," *Atlantic Monthly*, XLIX, 278.

[57] Hart, pp. 686–87.   [58] *Atlantic Monthly*, XLIX, 278.   [59] McLaughlin, p. 259.

[60] Speaking of Calhoun's agency in the annexation of Texas, von Holst stated: "The horrible craving for land which devoured the entrails of the slavocracy, drove the greatest of the slavocrats, for the sake of obtaining this land, to ignore entirely, and without any compunction, all the underlying principles of his political doctrines" (Von Holst, *Const. and Pol. Hist.*, II, 702–3).

[61] "The shameless spirit of party hurried the chariot of legislation on with loose rein over stocks and stones, and with every forward step the whip cracked louder and more triumphantly" (*ibid.*, III, 242).

[62] "A thick coating in several layers, which the slightest analysis would have shown to be a noxious product of political manufacture, was made to surround the bitter pill, in order to induce the north to swallow it" (*ibid.*, IV, 339).

[63] "How could the opposition fail to look upon the judgment, legally as an invalid usurpation and as a perversion of the law, never to be recognized, politically as an absurd

In view of these errors in interpretation, von Holst was certain to be unfair in his judgment of men. With him the acid test of a man's quality was his attitude on state sovereignty and slavery, and "he traversed the past like a belated nemesis dealing out to our departed statesmen the retribution which he thought their sins deserved"[64] if they failed to measure up to his standard. Owing to his antipathy for compromisers, Henry Clay is a pigmy in his pages,[65] while the once godlike Daniel Webster becomes a fallen angel.[66] He could appreciate, if not sympathize, with sincere error, but he hated hypocrisy and lack of principle. Therefore the villain in his story is not Calhoun, whom he slyly admired in spite of that worthy's "obvious" fallacies, but Douglas, whom he believed to be an unprincipled demagogue willing to barter his soul for political advancement.[67] He is unjustifiably hard on Polk, Pierce, and Buchanan;[68] and he clearly never understood either Jefferson, whom he suspected of wishing to disrupt the Union, or Jackson, whom he considered an irresponsible dictator.[69] Von Holst required his heroes to have a decided moral flavor. Therefore, John Brown stands out boldly even in the large history, while Lincoln is recognized as the statesman par excellence, a product of ninety years of development.[70]

---

and bold assumption, and morally as an unparalleled prostitution of the judicial ermine? . . . . what appeared in the garb of a judicial decree was, in reality, only a campaign document" (ibid., VI, 46).

[64] Library of the World's Best Literature, XIX, 7496.

[65] "An idealist who wasted the best part of his creative power in impracticable projects, and a politician who was an unsurpassable master of the art of solving great and unavoidable problems by little expedients,—these are the most notable traits in Clay's political character. . . . . His other qualities and achievements did not lift him above the level of ordinary politicians" (von Holst, Const. and Pol. Hist., I, 414–15).

[66] Von Holst did not believe, however, that Webster's seventh of March speech was solely motivated by his wish to gain the presidency (ibid., III, 502–7).

[67] "Douglas was not only by profession, but also by nature and inclination, a demagogue . . . . " (ibid., p. 410). "Whoever desires the end must also desire the means—such was his moral code" (ibid., V, 278).

[68] Ibid., III, 273; V, 246, 352–53; VI, 3, 5; Hart, p. 685.

[69] Von Holst, Const. and Pol. Hist., I, 158–60; II, 29–31; McLaughlin, p. 259.

[70] Von Holst, Const. and Pol. Hist., VI, 285–86; VII, 18–20.

Of the minor criticisms of von Holst, the chief, perhaps, is that he cherished a theory of progress. His thesis led him to identify progress solely with northern beliefs and policies. To him history was purposive.[71] It consisted of a struggle between good and evil; and the good, in the long run, won out. Whatever the temporary setbacks a rightful cause might have, its eventual victory was inevitable. To hold such a positive theory is unquestionably a weakness in a historian. Von Holst's forthrightness was probably due in large degree to his German training. "It is the domination of this philosophical background which defines the author's great work as essentially a product of German historiography."[72]

Other criticisms of von Holst are perhaps not so valid. He was frequently assailed for his style, and there can be no doubt that the *Constitutional and Political History* is not light reading.[73] But von Holst can hardly be blamed entirely for this. It is true that his profusion of metaphors becomes wearying at times and that he did violence to continuity by interrupting the sequence of events to analyze the motives of statesmen.[74] But these are relatively minor defects. It is the turgid nature of the writing which is the chief occasion for comment. The natural complexity of German sentence structure, however, is always bewildering to Americans. Furthermore, it cannot be doubted that certain idiomatic expressions, quite clear in German, could be translated into English only with difficulty. Finally, von Holst was unfortunate in his translators.[75] Soon after the work appeared, critics complained that the Lalor translation left much to be desired.[76] It is significant that his *Calhoun*, which he wrote in English, is generally regarded as his best book, in style as well as in analysis.

Critics have also made a point of the fact that the *Constitutional and Political History* contains much material that is not of a strict-

---

[71] Schevill, p. 178. See von Holst, *Const. and Pol. Hist.*, I, Preface, x–xi.

[72] Schevill, p. 178.   [73] *Bookman*, XIX, 17.   [74] Hart, pp. 682–83.

[75] *Library of the World's Best Literature*, XIX, 7497; *Atlantic Monthly*, XLIX, 278; Schevill, p. 178.

[76] The major translator was John J. Lalor, although Alfred B. Mason collaborated on Vol. I and aided on Vol. III, while Paul Shorey collaborated on Vol. III.

ly constitutional nature. It is more nearly a legislative history with particular emphasis on slavery.[77] In so far as the use of the title *Constitutional and Political History* is concerned, not the author, but his publisher, was responsible. Von Holst had originally used the expression "Verfassung und Demokratie," which was almost disregarded when the work was given its English title. Nevertheless, it cannot be denied that he was guilty of writing a historical treatise on state sovereignty and slavery under a title which, even in German, little suggested the actual contents of the book.

It is sometimes stated that von Holst despised American institutions and took every occasion in his writings to belittle them.[78] This is hardly a tenable stricture. He unquestionably was critical, but he was critical in an intelligent fashion. Certainly he had good grounds for many of the unpleasant judgments he gave. It is highly probable that the resentment of his reviewers arose from an American sensitivity to any disapproval from abroad. Von Holst's background disposed him to treat sympathetically basic American institutions, and his very approach to his subject precluded any positive unfriendliness. His attitude is more one of disillusionment than of contempt.[79]

In view of these criticisms von Holst can hardly be included among those historians in the "scientific" school.[80] Nevertheless, he was worthy of emulation in some respects, and he made a few real contributions. No one can deny the man's industry. He was a pioneer in comprehensively presenting, after much labor, the latter part of the period covered by his major work; and he ransacked libraries wherever possible in order to run down obscure items for his history.[81] He apologized because he had delved into printed sources only,[82] but, as a matter of fact, writ-

[77] *Atlantic Monthly*, LXX, 839; *Bookman*, XIX, 17; Hart, p. 683.

[78] *Bookman*, XIX, 17; von Holst, *Const. and Pol. Hist.*, I, Preface, ix.

[79] Von Holst, *Const. and Pol. Hist.*, I, Preface, ix–x.

[80] *Amer. Hist. Rev.*, IX, 624.

[81] Hart, pp. 680, 682; Eric Goldman, "Hermann Eduard Von Holst," *Mississippi Valley Historical Review*, XXIII, No. 4 (March, 1937), 528–29.

[82] Von Holst, *Const. and Pol. Hist.*, I, Preface, vii.

ing at a time before manuscripts were as available and as much stressed as they are today, no humble apology was necessary. There was need of much spade work in the printed sources, and he did it. Using biographies, reminiscences, and especially the neglected *Congressional Globe* and other government publications, he waded through a sea of material hitherto practically untouched.[83] He was one of the first historians in the United States to use newspapers systematically.[84] Unquestionably, he brought to the attention of scholars, through his footnotes, innumerable "forgotten pamphlets, memoirs and political discussions."

Again, no one can doubt von Holst's sincerity. The worst that can be said of him is that he told the truth as he saw it. He expressed a point of view,[85] which reveals at least that he had thought his subject through to some sort of a conclusion. If von Holst's opinion and conclusions have been superseded by later research, his zeal and fervor nonetheless stimulated others into studying intensively the subjects he covered in survey fashion. His work marked a point of departure for future scholars in the field. Furthermore, von Holst's accuracy within the scope of his thesis is unassailable. Systematic and methodical, he footnoted profusely; and his references have a high degree of reliability. He was not guilty of the careless little errors so common in the writings of many historians.

Likewise, when his vision was unobscured by his prejudice, he was capable of keen analysis. Thus he understood clearly that American history, if the proper perspective were to be maintained, must be viewed broadly as a part of the general history of Western civilization. He understood also that the American

[83] Hart, p. 680.

[84] James Ford Rhodes, "Concerning the Writing of History," American Historical Association, *Annual Report*, I (1900), 53.

[85] Speaking of the effort to write without a point of view—"as a reasoning machine without any feeling whatever"—he stated: "There are historians and political philosophers who pretend that this is the only correct way to treat historical and political problems. They may be good chroniclers and quite fit statesmen for some commonwealth in the clouds, but they will never be able to write a history or to make us understand the nature and the working of the government of an actual state" (von Holst, *Const. and Pol. Hist.*, I, Preface, viii–ix).

Revolution could not properly be portrayed as a nationalistic movement. Furthermore, his entire history is an impressive argument to the effect that forces influence men in history rather than the reverse.[86]

Finally, von Holst was a master of synthesis, organization, and generalization. His power of synthesis is strikingly revealed in his treatment of the Constitutional Convention, which represents an excellent digest, from a particular point of view, of a mass of material which might easily have overwhelmed the average writer. His organization is best revealed by the relentless way in which he followed his thesis throughout his seven volumes. The foundation is laid in Volume I, and each successive episode in the later volumes is a brick which fits easily into the superstructure he was building. Close reasoning, frequently too close; inferential tie-ups, often unjustifiable; and the positive, philosophical overtone, which was his trade-mark, weld the entire history into a well-articulated whole. His powers of generalization are best revealed in his discussion of the Lecompton constitution and of the Mormons.[87] He had few peers in his ability to abstract a debate and express the salient points in concise fashion.

Von Holst's significance for the present-day student lies in the factual material he presented, in his bibliographical suggestions, in his example of industry, sincerity, and accuracy within his conceptual limitations, and in the thorough digestion of the material he wished to present. But he must be used with care. His persuasive special pleading, his zealous assurance, and his tendency to suppress contrary evidence are likely to mislead the unwary. That he was a significant historian cannot be doubted. His influence was undoubtedly large. That he was a definitive historian cannot be conceded. His works have not withstood the test of time. That he was or was not a great historian depends upon whether greatness be measured in terms of immediate or future influence.

[86] *Ibid.*, I, Preface, x, 18–19; IV, Preface, iii.
[87] *Ibid.*, VI, 132 ff., 235 ff.

V

JAMES SCHOULER[1]

LEWIS ETHAN ELLIS

Rutgers University

*

JAMES SCHOULER bore the name of his grandfather, a lowland Scot of Kilbarchan near Glasgow. This ancestor changed his habitat abruptly from Scotland to America, altering his name gradually from the Scottish "Scouler" through "Schooler" to "Schouler." The reasons for the latter changes are not in the record; those for the former are not obscure. In 1815 he attended a meeting at which plans savoring of treason were discussed. He left in haste; but news of the plot came to the authorities, who, after dealing with the conspirators, sought young Scouler as a government witness. Smuggling himself out of the country, he settled in West Cambridge (later Arlington), Massachusetts, and gained a competence as a printer of calico cloth.[2]

His son William, more intellectual but less steadfast, drifted from his father's trade into newspaper work, becoming editor

[1] This paper, somewhat abbreviated, originally appeared in the *Mississippi Valley Historical Review*, Vol. XVI, No. 2 (September, 1929). It is used here, by permission.

[2] Principal sources of biographical material are three: sketch of James Schouler by John H. Latané in *Dictionary of American Biography*, XVI (New York, 1935), 459–60; Edward Stanwood, "Memoir of James Schouler," Massachusetts Historical Society, *Proceedings*, LIV, 283–88 (cited hereafter as "Memoir"); "Biography of James Schouler." This last work, by an unnamed author, is inserted at the close of Schouler's volume, *Historical Briefs* (New York, 1896), pp. 169–310 (cited hereafter as "Biography"). It contains many passages evidently from Schouler's own pen, bearing out the statement that it was written from materials furnished by him.

and co-proprietor of the *Boston Atlas*, a leading New England Whig journal. The failure of the party in 1852 ruined his paper and deprived him of the seat which he had held for many years in the state legislature. An interlude as clerk of that body in 1853 preceded a family move to Cincinnati in 1854, the year before James's matriculation at Harvard. Four years in Ohio saw the elder Schouler unsuccessful in paying the debts of the *Cincinnati Gazette*, in which he had bought an interest, a failure in a commission business thanks to a faithless partner, a convert to the Free Soil movement, a delegate to the Republican convention of 1856, and a salaried editor of the *Ohio State Journal*. The Republican connection brought him back to Massachusetts and to an editorship which helped to launch the party in that state, but left him still so impoverished that his son was unable to secure his diploma promptly upon graduation because the father had been unable to meet the necessary bills. In 1860 he became adjutant general of the state, serving until 1866. A convivial, likeable, and improvident soul, his contacts in newspaper and political work were to stand both himself and his son in good stead.[3]

To this amiable gentleman and his wife, Frances Eliza Warren, was born the subject of this sketch, March 20, 1839. His flattering contemporary biographer depicts him as a precocious and home-loving child whose health was early threatened by too much bending over books. A physical breakdown was averted by three months with his grandparents, daily shower baths, and copious doses of bitter sarsaparilla. He soon reverted to his omnivorous reading of Dickens, Shakespeare, Scott, and Macaulay; and in 1850, at the ripe age of eleven, began issuing the *Family Visitor and Home Journal*, a hand-written occasional for home consumption. The only number preserved to his biographer contained: chapter vii of a temperance tale, "It Is All for the Best"; an instalment on Alfred the Great in a series, "Lives of Celebrated Men"; and a poem, "New England." An early talent for music was cultivated until increasing deafness shut off this av-

3 "Biography," pp. 189–246.

enue of expression. At eleven he began piano lessons; at fourteen he became organist and director of an adult choir; and by the time he entered college, he had written out a collection of a hundred tunes, some of which were of his own arrangement. At Harvard he became a member and secretary of the first glee club.[4]

Parental poverty in the Ohio days forced him to eke out his living by borrowing from relatives, by teaching during the school year, and by serving as organist. His first college year was spent with a private family some distance from the campus, which fact combined with his scanty means and natural shyness to leave him rather out of the current of Harvard life. Presently he found a congenial roommate in the college Yard and became progressively more active in undergraduate affairs. He also seems to have profited more than some of his fellows by the educational opportunities afforded by the Harvard of his day. In addition to his musical outlet, he gave promise of his future lines of activity by gaining some reputation as a speaker and by becoming, in his Senior year, editor of the *Harvard Magazine*, for which he did considerable writing. He graduated just within the top quarter of his class of about one hundred.[5]

He originally leaned toward teaching and spent his first year after graduation in that work at St. Paul's School, Concord, New Hampshire. After his hope of an appointment to the chair of English literature at Trinity College was not realized, this would-be pedagogue became a lawyer. Entering an office late in 1860, he emerged a member of the bar two years later, at the age of twenty-three. Prior to his active legal career, an enlistment of nine months in the army (1862–63) afforded the future author a firsthand view of a very minor portion of the scene which was later to engage his pen—a view whose breadth was magnified in its beholder's mind before he dipped his pen into the inkpot. Moreover, a touch of army fever aggravated an ear trouble which had first bothered him at Harvard and which was later to make him quite deaf. This condition, coupled with the failure of a publishing venture, was undoubtedly a factor of influence in

4 *Ibid.*, pp. 202–19.   5 *Ibid.*, pp. 221–30.

turning him gradually from the active practice of law to the writing of legal textbooks and of history.[6]

Returning from the war, he took to himself a partner and launched into practice. The firm reversed the traditional experience of young practitioners—it prospered. The senior Schouler was then adjutant general and in active touch with troops and troop movements. The short-term enlistments of the Civil War left many former soldiers with claims to prosecute against the government. So many of these cases found their way into the offices of the junior Schouler that one is permitted to look askance at the statement of his biographer, who asserts that "an inevitable swarm of soldier claimants sought him from the State House which his scrupulous father avoided all agency in directing."[7] Presently, the father, being supplanted in his post, entered a profitable quasi partnership with the son, thus forming a union of practical knowledge of the needs and status of the returned soldier with a technical knowledge of the law. Their combined talents were applied to pressing the claims of veterans before the newly formed court of claims—an opportunity to make money which was congenial both to the father's experience and to the son's ability before the courts. Thus many soldiers, first from Massachusetts and later from other states, were drawn to the firm's offices, for business expanded to such an extent as to justify the opening, in 1869, of a branch in Washington in addition to the Boston office, which remained in charge of the father and the partner.[8] This profitable business allowed the father to retire on an annuity in 1872, contributed to the son's financial independence, and doubtless aided the germination in the latter's mind of a determination to try the pen as an avocation. At Washington the young man touched the heart of affairs in the midst of the Reconstruction crisis. These contacts, which focused his life, temporarily, upon the capital city, also helped

[6] *Ibid.*, pp. 248–57; "Memoir," pp. 284–85.

[7] "Biography," pp. 248–52; "Memoir," pp. 284.

[8] "Biography," pp. 268–72; "Memoir," p. 285. An outgrowth of this practice was the case of *Hosmer* v. *The United States*, 9 Wall 432 (1870), which was "the only soldiers' test case arising out of the war in which the Executive department was positively overruled."

to center permanently the point of view of his historical writings.[9]

Here, in 1870, appeared the first in his series of eight legal textbooks, written in response to the promise of Little, Brown and Company to publish anything he might write on a suitable subject. The production of these volumes occupied much of his time until 1887.[10] Here, too, was born in 1871 the quarterly *United States Jurist*, issued by a law publishing firm but backed by Schouler, who wished "to supply a magazine for the American bar of a national cast, an exponent of the best thought and intelligence for diffusion among the legal profession of the whole country."[11] The same year witnessed the rapid aggravation of his deafness, which now reached the point where he was unable to hear the ticking of a watch with either ear. This affliction tended to make court appearances difficult; and in 1873 or 1874 he returned to Boston, where he engaged largely in probate work in the intervals of the writing which came to occupy more and more of his attention.[12]

As has been suggested above, Schouler had felt the urge to authorship. During the war he had submitted an essay on the governorship of Sir Henry Vane to the *Atlantic Monthly*, which had rejected it. This disappointment led him to confide to his diary during November, 1864, "I shall now betake myself in earnest to my historical studies, with a view of writing in time some book on our constitutional history,—an idea which I have secretly cherished a twelvemonth or more."[13] Two years later the *North American Review* published his paper on "Our Diplomacy during the Rebellion."[14] This encouraged him to further efforts and he conceived the plan of taking up where Bancroft had left off. He would thus link the American Revolution with the Civil War. In 1870 he wrote the first draft of an introductory

[9] "Biography," pp. 273–78; "Memoir," p. 286.

[10] They enjoyed some vogue and ran into several editions; the scope of the present study, however, does not include their consideration.

[11] "Biography," p. 276. This journal languished and died for want of support after its sponsor's return to Boston.

[12] *Ibid.*, pp. 282–85.   [13] *Ibid.*, p. 288.   [14] CII, 446–73.

chapter of such a work. This was sidetracked for a time by his experiment with the *United States Jurist* and was further discouraged by the fact that Little, Brown and Company, his textbook publishers, also handled Bancroft's works, and being uncertain of the latter's plans, were unwilling to commit themselves to Schouler's venture. He persevered, however; and in 1880 appeared the first volume of his great monument, *The History of the United States of America, under the Constitution*, a work in seven volumes covering the years 1783–1877.[15] Five volumes were published between 1880 and 1891, the sixth in 1899, and the last in 1913. Other important works from the pen of the author are: *Thomas Jefferson* (New York, 1893); *Historical Briefs* (New York, 1896); *Constitutional Studies, State and Federal* (New York, 1897); *Alexander Hamilton* (Boston, 1901); *Eighty Years of Union, Being a Short History of the United States, 1783–1865* (New York, 1903); *Americans of 1776* (New York, 1906); and *Ideals of the Republic* (Boston, 1908).[16]

His writing soon brought him recognition from the teaching profession, and he was in 1883 made a professor in the Boston University Law School and in 1886 chosen to a similar position in the National University Law School in Washington, which position his annual winter sojourns in that city made it possible for him to fill for a few weeks each season. In 1890 he became lecturer in constitutional history at the Johns Hopkins University, a post which he held for seventeen years. With these varied activities added to his legal work, his life was a busy one during the winter seasons. His economic status, assured since his excursion into the war-claims business and made doubly secure by numerous other sources of income, was firmly established by

---

[15] Publication was begun in Washington; but the firm of W. H. Morrison, which had been doing the work, experienced financial difficulties before it was completed. After two volumes had appeared, Little, Brown & Co. told Schouler that it was free to go ahead; but the Morrisons, though unable to push the work properly, clung to their contract rights until the appearance of Vol. IV. Thereupon, in 1890, they gave up and Dodd, Mead and Company took over ("Biography," pp. 289–90).

[16] "Memoir," p. 286; "Biography," pp. 281–89. This catalogue does not include contributions to legal journals or periodicals, save that several in the latter are reprinted in *Historical Briefs*.

a considerable inheritance from a maternal uncle. His summers were spent at Intervale, near North Conway, New Hampshire, where "Kilbarchan" was one of the first of a colony of summer homes. Here he expended considerable energy and thought in the building-up of the rural community, being senior warden of Christ Church, donor of the lot and building of the North Conway Public Library Association, and evidently something of a benevolent despot in the affairs of these institutions. In North Conway, too, his life came to a close on April 16, 1920, after an illness contracted during a trip up from Boston during the Easter season of that year.[17]

Schouler's use of sources shows clearly the bent toward the political which characterized all of his work except for a temporary excursion into the realm of social and intellectual history in his *Americans of 1776* (1906). Beyond the formal printed page he drew largely upon his personal knowledge, real or assumed, of persons, places, and events. In Boston he had access to the Public Library and the Boston Athenaeum. The Library of Congress furnished him with printed and manuscript material; in several cases he was the first to make use of the latter. Thus, he was the initial exploiter of the manuscripts of four presidents—Monroe, Jackson, Van Buren, and Polk—and the first to employ constructively the papers of Andrew Johnson and the diary of Gideon Welles.[18]

In order to arrive at a quantitative and qualitative estimate of the nature and extent of his sources, the footnotes of Volumes I and VII of the *History of the United States* have been examined with care, and the results are indicated in the footnote below.[19] The significance of these figures is lessened by the extent to which the author drew upon his own experience and observation and by the fact that a considerable proportion of his pages are un-

[17] "Biography," pp. 293–309; Ellen H. Mason, "The Late James Schouler, LL.D.," *Granite Monthly*, LII, 290–92.

[18] *History of the United States*, I, vii; VII, iii–v.

[19] Analysis of sources of Vols. I and VII:

(Footnote continued on facing page)

documented. With these qualifications Table 1 in footnote 19
warrants certain conclusions. The author's material is very
largely official, semi-official, and legal. It concerns the writings
and doings of men who were at the center of affairs of state and

---

TABLE 1

ANALYSIS OF SOURCES OF VOL. I, 1783–1801

A. TYPES OF SOURCES*

	Number
Biographical	21
Personal papers	15
Official documents, government publications, etc.	15
General and special historical works	15
Newspapers (used but slightly)	10
Travel accounts (used but slightly)	7
Miscellaneous	19
	99

B. USE MADE OF VARIOUS SOURCES†

	Times Quoted From
U.S. Statutes at Large	123
Hamilton's Works	53
Jefferson's Works	47
Annals of Congress	46
John Adams' Works	46
Hildreth, United States	44
Madison's Works	30
Washington's Writings	28
J. C. Hamilton, Republic	25
Bancroft, United States	23
Fisher Ames's Works	21
Elliot's Debates	11
Madison's Debates	3
The Federalist	1

    * Of these, 43 were cited but once.

    † This listing gives the author's own designation of his sources.

TABLE 2

ANALYSIS OF SOURCES OF VOL. VII, 1865–77

A. TYPES OF SOURCES

	Number
Biographical	12
Periodicals—especially the Nation and Harper's Magazine	7
Official documents, government publications, etc.	4
Newspapers cited by name (frequently cited vaguely, as "newspapers of the day")	3
Travel accounts	3
Personal papers	2
	31

(Footnote 19 continued on following page)

the documents which record the results of their activity. Matters economic, industrial, or social are pushed to the periphery or ignored entirely.[20] Even in the political realm the emphasis is unevenly distributed. Today, only a rash writer on the period of the Constitutional Convention would venture to place Elliot's *Debates*, Madison's *Notes*, and the *Federalist* at the bottom of his list of authorities. Analysis of the source references in the seventh volume shows a change. Premier place is given to a secondary work, James Ford Rhodes's *History of the United States*. Periodicals and newspapers, more numerous and available for the period treated, are more relied upon. Statutes are frequently cited; the debates which produced the statutes being used but seldom. The emphasis remains, as at first, primarily political.

Schouler has left a fairly complete statement of his own rules and methods of historical writing and of the ends to be sought by such writing. These are found in occasional essays read before the American Historical Association and collected in the volume *Historical Briefs*, where they may be examined briefly and then tested in the laboratory of his own works.[21] "History," he wrote, "is the record of consecutive events,— of consecutive

---

B. USE MADE OF VARIOUS SOURCES

	Times Cited
Rhodes, *History of U.S.*, Vols. V–VII	235
Welles, *Diary*	53
U.S. Statutes at Large	43
N.Y. Nation	40
Johnson manuscripts	30
Harper's Magazine	29
Century Magazine	20
McCulloch, *Men and Measures*	20
Congressional Globe	13
Supreme Court Decisions	9
N.Y. Tribune	3
N.Y. Times	2
Boston Herald	1

[20] In order to check on this matter the tables of contents of Vols. V and VII were examined and the total number of pages devoted to the foregoing types of material, as distinguished from the purely political and diplomatic, was ascertained. In Vol. V, 22 out of 517 pages, and in Vol. VII, 29 out of 360 pages, were so filled, an average of less than 6 per cent.

[21] The titles of the most important essays, with page references, are given herewith: "Historical Grouping," pp. 16–21; "Spirit of Research," pp. 22–33; "Historical Industries," pp. 34–47; "Historical Monographs," pp. 48–59; "Historical Testimony," pp. 60–70; "Historical Style," pp. 71–84.

public events."[22] This at once explains and limits his point of view. He advised the aspiring writer first to select and circumscribe a rather narrow field, and then to familiarize himself with every phase of the life of the period—its military, political, social, industrial, and religious aspects.[23] Knowing the facts, he held the next duty to be to secure a proper relationship between the less and the more important, and to treat the whole with a due perspective and in the light of its own day.[24] He placed considerable emphasis on the need of careful planning on the part of the writer of history, likening him to the architect who lays out all the proportions and details of his edifice meticulously in advance.[25] In fact, one of the principal impressions to be received from reading his essays on historiography is his stress on methodical procedure.

He distinguished clearly between the primary and secondary source and carefully evaluated their comparative merits.[26] After stating his personal preference for an original source, he continued: ". . . . but secondary sources of knowledge I have largely accepted as a labor-saving means, where I could bring my own accumulated knowledge and habits of verification to bear upon them, so as to judge fairly of their comparative worth."[27] He realized both the desirability and the difficulty of securing an unbiased attitude, but avowedly preferred to err on the side of bias than fail to teach the lessons which he believed that history held for the intelligent investigator.[28]

[22] *Historical Briefs*, p. 23.

[23] *Ibid.*, pp. 25–29.

[24] ". . . . every epoch is best read and explained by its own light, by its own contemporaneous record; and every other record ought to be held but secondary and subservient in comparison" (*ibid.*, p. 21).

[25] *Ibid.*, p. 27.   [26] *Ibid.*, pp. 66–68.   [27] *Ibid.*, p. 42.

[28] "Let us, however, have earnestness; for the writer, historian, or biographer to be most distrusted, is he, in my opinion, who gains no earnestness at all from his subject, but remains wholly neutral, negative, and external,—critical, quizzical or cynical, as the mood may move him,—or extending the arm of judicial patronage, like some self-chosen Rhadamanthus who practices before the looking glass" (*ibid.*, pp. 62–65). "And while retracing thus the footprints of the past, we shall do well if we deduce the right moral . . . ." (*ibid.*, p. 33), "Whatever the historian may print and publish for the edification of the public, let him endeavor to make the result apparent for which he prospected; let him tell the tale, unfold the particulars, and inculcate the lesson . . . ." (*ibid.*, p. 47).

In the concluding essays of his *Ideals of the Republic* (1908) the reader is given something of a crystallization of the author's general attitude toward life and things which may be worth summarizing before passing to a more detailed criticism of his historical technique.[29] These show him to be a mild conservative, not averse to the *status quo*, with a somewhat careful solicitude for the preservation of wealth so long as it does not become predatory or exhibitionist, and a firm belief that God's in His Heaven even if all's not right with the world. Opportunity in America was still to be spelled with a capital "O," despite some premonitions that the future might produce problems in the field of labor-capital relations. Particularly was he impatient with, and apprehensive of, some of the innovations of American inventive genius. Of the automobile, for example, he wrote:

Of all recent inventions for the pleasure of the rich, nothing at all, it seems to me, widens so impressively class jealousies among us as the automobile. This costly toy . . . . is the symbol and epitome of obtrusive arrogance towards the multitude, offset only by the danger it brings to those themselves who use it. . . . .[30]

He stressed, however, the goal of truth above everything else, writing that

the deductions, the moral lessons of history, one should hold subordinate to a candid, conscientious and courageous exploration for the truth and the whole truth; all hypotheses should be kept under curb; the writer's imagination ought to be like that of a painter whose model is kept before his eyes. . . . .[31]

Schouler had no use whatever for the "comprehensive methods" of a "literary bureau," as employed by Hubert H. Bancroft, and launched a diatribe against those who hired work done to save themselves labor. He alleged that such workers were only mercenaries who lacked discrimination, judgment, insight, and the eye for the kernel of a situation.[32] This did not mean that he would use no help for the purely mechanical processes of

[29] Pp. 259 ff.
[30] *Ibid.*, p. 277.
[31] *Historical Briefs*, p. 60.
[32] *Ibid.*, pp. 37 ff.

scholarship—extracting, indexing, reading proof, and gathering statistics—"but for art, for scholarship, for literature and religion . . . . I would keep the freest play possible to the individual and to individual effort."[33] He deprecated the tendency toward large-scale and collective enterprises which he saw growing up in his later years; and while he realized that this was inevitable in business, he made the foregoing plea for individualism in other spheres. He stated his own practice in investigation rather fully:

Whether it be from an innate distrust of hired subworkers, or for economy's sake, or from the pride of responsible authorship, or because of habits which I early formed in life of concentrating and warming into interest wherever I personally investigated . . . . I never employed literary assistance of any sort, except . . . . for copying out my rough drafts in a neat hand for my own revision, and for transcribing passages from other books which I had first selected. . . . . In fine, every real research, where I have published, and every page of composition, has been my own. . . . . I have shown my manuscript to no one at all for criticism or approval, nor have I received suggestions, in any volume, even as to literary style and expression, except upon printed sheets from the casual proof-reader, as the book went finally through the press.[34]

This refusal to send his manuscript for criticism to friends, made him an easy victim of reviewers, who condemned his lack of style in no uncertain terms. His answer was a rather lame defense in the essay on "Historical Style":

First of all, an author's style should be the image of himself, and if it exposes him instead as the copyist of other minds, it must fail of impressiveness. . . . . Next, to borrow the advice of our admirable Prescott . . . . one should chiefly "be engrossed with the thought and not with the fashion of expressing it." For the chief thing after all in effective writing is to put clearly the idea intended.[35]

For perfecting one's style before beginning to write, he suggested reading other authors; but he warned his hearers to rely wholly upon themselves when actually composing.[36]

[33] *Ibid.*, p. 38.   [35] *Ibid.*, pp. 73–74.
[34] *Ibid.*, pp. 40–41.   [36] *Ibid.*, pp. 77–79.

His writing routine was varied to conform with the type of volume which he had under preparation. In his textbook writing he turned out, according to his boast, some six thousand pages of material, in which "with rare exceptions in certain paragraphs, [I] sent regularly my first and only draft to the printer as written out with the running pen, keeping the general proportion and plan of each volume well in view. . . . . "[37] Historical composition, on the other hand, demanded different treatment. Here it was his practice to hand a day's production to the amanuensis for copying, with wide spaces left between the lines. This was laid aside for several weeks or months and then revised by interlineations, after which it went, without transcribing, to the printers. He advocated plenty of recreation, while writing, and an occasional change of scene, and suggested that each day's routine should be varied, with never more than three or four hours being given to actual composition. The remainder of the time should be devoted to the more mechanical processes of scholarship—reading proof, collecting materials, and arranging them—or attending to business and correspondence.[38] A schedule, be it observed, ideal enough to be beyond attainment by most practitioners of his craft.

The *History of the United States* best illustrates Schouler's method of arranging his compositions. It is primarily chronological with topical subdivisions. The number of chapters is comparatively small, but the later volumes are divided into sections which correspond to the usual chapters. The presidential administration and the congressional term are the underlying time units treated in the earlier volumes. Thus, Volume I disposes of "The Thirteen Confederate States," "The Constitutional Convention," and "The More Perfect Union" in the introductory chapter and is then subdivided as follows:

Chap. ii. First Administration of George Washington
          A. Period of First Congress
          B. Period of Second Congress

---

[37] *Ibid.*, p. 80.   [38] *Ibid.*, pp. 83–84.

This is the basic treatment throughout, with occasional digressions to cover particular topics which do not fit the general scheme. Examples are the chapter in Volume II on "The United States in 1809" and the chapter in Volume V on "The Mexican War." Military, diplomatic, and biographical chapters in the two concluding volumes work havoc with this design, and the administration-Congress method of treatment becomes little more than a convenient device for holding the former together.

This plan of organization inevitably results in a choppy and somewhat disconnected narrative, as is illustrated in Volume V, where the following topics are treated successively on pages 274–80: Marcy as Secretary of State; black-coat circular; the Koszta affair; World's Fair in New York City; New York State politics; pride of American citizenship; state elections; assembly of Congress; Russian war; a satisfactory message; delusion of international tranquillity; disposition to please slavery; and the Kansas-Nebraska Bill, the new generator of discontent. It has the merit, however, of acquainting the student with just what happened during any brief period of history.

An attempt to evaluate the author's work presents certain pros and many cons which may be summarized and illustrated. Less favorable observations include faulty style, bias, poor citations of sources, inaccuracies of text, and omissions of material. On the credit side may be noted good proportioning of space, effective use of the personalities of prominent leaders in the narrative, opening-up of new collections of source material, and pioneering in a hitherto largely unworked field of American history.

Despite the practice gained in turning out six thousand pages of legal textbooks and several hundred pages in the field of history, Schouler's style never attained a pleasant smoothness. His sentences, often crisp enough in their content, are frequently unduly long. They are, moreover, sometimes the vehicle of widely variant ideas. To Schouler the all-embracing binder was the comma, varied by an occasional semicolon. The result was a harshness easily noticeable. An illustration is in point:

The White House, as Lincoln occupied it, was that, to all intents, which it still remains, though less cramped in its natural surroundings. In its upper chambers, both for home and office life, dwelt Lincoln, like most of his predecessors; and his only summer variation was in using, with his family, a modest cottage at the Soldiers' Home on the northern suburb, towards which, by the main road, he might be seen riding in a barouche from the White House, on a bright September afternoon, with a few mounted cavalry for his escort.[39]

As has been already noted, he not only admitted bias but frequently displayed it. This was both positive and negative. Of Lincoln, he wrote: "The farther we recede from the era of our great civil strife, the more colossal stands out the figure of Abraham Lincoln upon the dim perspective."[40] He tried hard to demonstrate Johnson's sobriety, but was compelled to admit that the latter's own letters show that he was intoxicated when inducted into the vice-presidency.[41] His whole treatment of Johnson is designed to "vindicate" a much-maligned man—who, in truth it should be noted, was sadly in need of a just appraisal when Schouler's volume appeared.

On the other hand, he was outspoken in his insistence that southerners were responsible for the Civil War. Of Mexican filibusters and expeditions into Cuba, he said: ". . . . the sanguine friends of slavery encouraged new conquests to the southward. This to disunion dreamers promised stability and strength to the future Southern confederacy. . . . ."[42] Of Calhoun he was unable to speak temperately. Late in life, according to Schouler, Calhoun was . . . . perversely bent upon destruction. Misrepresenting

[39] *Hist. of U.S.*, VI, 324. Reviews commenting on this point: *Nation*, LXIII, 387; LXV, 423; *Amer. Hist. Rev.*, III, 379 ff.

[40] *Hist. of U.S.*, VI, 1.   [41] *Ibid.*, VII, 8.   [42] *Ibid.*, V, 211.

the free section as all the while the aggressor, and warning his fellow-slaveholders that they would soon be forced to choose between abolition and secession, he set himself to breaking cord after cord which bound the slave States to the Union, so as to bring in the latter alternative by way of anticipation.

And in 1861: "The philosophy of Southern statesmanship was, in truth, poisoned and vitiated . . . . by the sophistries of the great Calhoun. . . . ."[43] Speaking of vacancies in the civil and military establishments after secession, he said that many resigned, "while viperous incumbents still coiled tightly to strike unseen at the hand that fed them.[44] Of the Confederate constitution, he remarked: "When we examine the flag and the written charter of this aspirant to the family of nations, we are at once impressed by the infringement of copyright. Here, surely, was shown a poverty of ideas in the art of government. . . . ."[45] However, he supported the Jeffersonian embargo and condemned the Hartford Convention in no uncertain terms.[46]

His work falls far short of later standards of precision in the citation of authorities.[47] His statements of fact will not always bear the test of truth. Of the Civil War, he says; "It is a memorable fact . . . . that the circumference of rebellion was bounded by the slaveholding States, and that not a single Commonwealth where freedom was the condition had the slightest inclination to be drawn into its toils."[48] In the earlier editions errors in spelling and in proper names are too frequent and con-

---

[43] *Ibid.*, pp. 153, 504.　　　[45] *Ibid.*, pp. 54–55.

[44] *Ibid.*, VI, 19.　　　[46] *Ibid.*, II, 181, 197, 474–76.

[47] A few examples chosen at random from the opening and concluding volumes of the *Hist. of U.S.* are illustrative:

	Page	Citation
Vol. I	169	4 Hildreth
	182	*Life of Timothy Pickering* (1790)
	185	John Adams's *Works*
	273	*Congressional Documents*
	399	See *Centinel* and other newspapers, May–July, 1798.
Vol. VII	13	*New York Tribune* and other newspapers of the day (this is a very frequent type)
	61	Newspapers
	185	Newspapers; author's recollections (another type frequently found in this volume)

[48] *Ibid.*, VI, 61.

sistent to be laid to the typesetter, and these are not entirely corrected in later editions.[49]

Further criticism is due his work because of neglect or omission of prominent subjects and sources of information. In his treatment of the Civil War the administration policy of arbitrary arrests goes almost unmentioned. His volume on Reconstruction makes slight use of the growing mass of monographic material and overlooks entirely Professor William A. Dunning's studies in that field. In his biography of Jefferson he gives no inkling of the manipulations by which the Democratic phalanx was organized and prepared for the assault on the stronghold of Federalism. Nor, in discussing in the same volume the Louisiana Purchase, does he throw any light on the constitutional and party questions raised by that excursion into diplomacy.[50]

A final criticism from the point of view of later scholarship is his overemphasis of the political, legal, and constitutional aspects of history. He made conscientious efforts to overcome this tendency, but his training in the law and his acquaintance with political affairs at the national capital were too much for him. In fairness it should be remembered, however, that he was merely writing history as it was being written in his day. Nevertheless, in comparison with his contemporaries, it would seem that his first volumes did achieve an unusual degree of success in reaching beyond the purely political. Early critics note with pleasure his detailed excursions into "the social and economic life of the people; their recreations; their habits of thought and action; their municipal arrangements; the character and influence of the immigration. . . . ."[51] But the excursions were excursions only, and to the end he remained primarily a political and constitutional historian who continued to produce in this vein after the tide had turned in other directions.[52]

[49] See the review of Vol. IV in the *Nation*, XLIX, 57, which cites various specific instances of this. Also *ibid.*, LXV, 424; *Amer. Hist. Rev.*, XIX, 667.

[50] *Amer. Hist. Rev.*, V, 774; XIX, 666.

[51] *Nation*, XXXIV, 41, reviewing Vol. I.

[52] A qualification should perhaps be added by referring again to his *Americans of 1776* (1906), which was an attempt at socio-economic history. It was his only real essay in this direction.

On the credit side is to be noted his sense of proportion. Having chosen the political field for development, he was judicious in the allotment of emphasis to events within that field.[53] He succeeded in weaving into the narrative pleasing and effective studies of the leading individuals of the period described.[54] A third contribution which he made to historical literature was the initial exploitation of several of the important manuscript collections, as noted above.

A summary estimate of his place in historiography would include the following: Training and association made him a historian of politics, diplomacy, and battles—a fact which, in his own day, was not such a drawback as in a later one. It was perhaps his misfortune that he continued to live and compose in a time when a wider range of subject was demanded by those who write book reviews and dabble in the mysteries of historiography. Inheritance and mental bent gave him a bias on various subjects which was accentuated by the fact that he lived close to, or during, certain highly provocative phases of our national life. This was bound to color any attempt he might make to write of the events in which he participated or of which he was a witness. Lastly, and particularly important in his own day, which really ended before doctoral requirements and administrative pressure made every pedagogue an author, his great contribution was that he, first among historians, succeeded in bridging with a continuous narrative the period from the beginnings of the nation to the end of Reconstruction.

[53] *Nation*, XLIX, 55 ff.; *Amer. Hist. Rev.*, V, 771; XIX, 665.

[54] *Nation*, XLIX, 57. Another reviewer, however, accuses him of letting his bias outweigh his skill in this regard (*Amer. Hist. Rev.*, V, 773).

VI

WOODROW WILSON

LOUIS MARTIN SEARS
Purdue University

✳

OODROW WILSON did not found a school of historical interpretation. In the field of history his writings were not voluminous or especially important. By neither of the two usual measures of a historian's significance—originality of interpretation and productive erudition —did Woodrow Wilson establish a valid claim to a first place among American historians. Yet few would doubt the propriety of including him among the twenty-one who are treated here. The explanation is not simple. Nothing that touched Wilson is ever truly simple. He defies analysis as a person, as a politician, or as a statesman. Even in his relatively minor roles of historian, political scientist, and publicist, he did not conform to type. In a word, he was *sui generis*. But to say this merely begs the question. What was there about him, then, that entitles him to a place among the important historians of the United States?

Even a modest attempt to answer this question must presuppose a basic unity of personality. Wilson the historian can never be divorced entirely from Wilson the far greater maker of history. Seldom does it happen that a professional scholar and writer of history is swept from cloister into maelstrom. When an acknowledged student of the past, not pre-eminent, perhaps, but competent beyond a question, is translated to the very vortex of events, and aids in shaping the destinies of nations and of races,

102

all eyes are turned to the equipment which he brings to his new task. His training and accomplishments as scholar and historian become the objects of a world-wide curiosity. What did the shaper of events have previously to say about the nature of events themselves and man's relation to the forces which encompass him? From this viewpoint Woodrow Wilson as historian assumes a fresh importance. What was the technical equipment, the professional point of view, the formal utterance, of the not undistinguished writer of history who so suddenly became its maker?

Such an inquiry seems the more pertinent because of the widely held conviction of mankind that history affords genuine lessons, which, if only comprehended by wise and humane leaders, should avert in the future the calamities which history itself records. The past ought to be a guide to the present and possibly to the future. So it seems from a priori reasoning, though in sober fact the past affords but slight illumination. Logic encounters a hiatus, of which the world, despite its a priori reasoning, is all too sadly conscious. The world would really like to learn the proper lesson from the past. Where could it study this lesson with better prospect of success than in the reactions of the historian, Woodrow Wilson, to the living issues of his tremendous day?

It is not necessary to phrase this issue quite so formally to realize that Woodrow Wilson as historian is a subject of more than common interest to mankind. No sooner is the subject posited than one seeks in history, or in Wilson's view of history, the explanation for the heart and kernel of his political philosophy, namely, his firm adherence to the right of self-determination. For, just as "legitimacy" was the key word of the Congress of Vienna, called to liquidate the Napoleonic wars, so "self-determination" was the key word of the Peace Conference at Versailles, called to liquidate the World War. And even as "legitimacy" will be forever associated with Prince Metternich, so "self-determination" will be equally associated with Woodrow Wilson. It was the very heart and essence of his political philosophy as expressed on the world-stage. And his effort to translate conviction into action at the Peace Conference of Versailles was, beyond all question, Wilson's own endeavor to apply in the realm of politics, the major lesson he had learned as a historian. The historian had turned statesman. He would convert his lesson to practical account.

The lesson was undoubtedly the outgrowth of Wilson's observations as a youth in post-war Georgia, where the devastations of the Civil War led him to an obvious conclusion; that had Horace Greeley had his way and the South enjoyed the self-determination she so ardently desired, the waste and horror of the war need never have occurred. Sherman's march was history. The lesson echoed at Versailles. Woodrow Wilson was the historian who linked the past and present.

If Paris was the climax and the culmination, the roots lay back in boyhood, in a Presbyterian manse where living was not exactly plain but thinking was unquestionably high. The Bible was the dominating cultural influence within that home. Its powerful appeal as history was assuredly not lost upon so strong and sensitive a spirit. The Bible, as taught him by a cultured and strong-minded father, was a living influence in the thought of Wilson the historian. But, like so many imponderables of the spirit, that influence may be assumed more readily than weighed.

Not that formal testimony is lacking. It was impressively set forth in Wilson's address on "The Bible and Progress," delivered at Denver on May 7, 1911, in recognition of the tercentenary of the King James translation of the Bible.[1] Nor is this the only testimony. The Bible was a living force in Wilson's thinking.

Well grounded at home in the essentials of Anglo-Saxon culture, Wilson brought to his career in college unusual maturity of background. It was natural enough that he should early devote himself to problems in biography and history. With remarkable facility he turned out a series of brief historical biographies— Prince Bismarck, the Earl of Chatham, John Bright, William E. Gladstone, characters the most dissimilar—essays remarkable for

[1] R. S. Baker and W. E. Dodd (eds.), *The Public Papers of Woodrow Wilson* (New York and London, 1925–27), II, 291–302.

precocity rather than profundity, but which lie completely beyond the competence of the average college student. Nor are they merely *Probstücke*. Even the earliest have purple patches of originality and power, as will appear in some quotations chosen almost at random. Wilson from the first gave promise of that rare facility of epigram and trenchant phrase which lent to all his utterance its chief and best distinction. Already there was evidence, moreover, of that capacity for sweeping generalization which often leads the historian astray but without which no historian can possibly be great. It is these brilliant asides, as it were, occurring throughout his earliest and his latest work, that mark Wilson as one who, had he clung to history alone, to the neglect of other opportunities and interests, might have been in his own right a historian of truly major import. But Nature was too lavish in her gifts to let him sacrifice himself that way.

Returning more specifically to the thought and content of the biographical studies, was it perhaps a whim of Fate that Woodrow Wilson's first published article should be upon a German theme and should concern Prince Bismarck? Written at the age of twenty, while Wilson was a Sophomore at Princeton, it appeared in the *Nassau Literary Magazine* for November, 1877. Its subject was, of course, at the height of his achievement. The analysis of a living statesman is in some respects more difficult than a retrospect upon the dead. There are fewer guides and precedents and greater opportunities for prejudice and passion. That Wilson's was a creditable performance is an evidence of his early maturity of judgment. That he had already established critical bases for comparison would appear from the single quotation which our space permits. Young Wilson wrote:

In Bismarck are united the moral force of Cromwell and the political shrewdness of Richelieu; the comprehensive intellect of Burke, without his learning, and the diplomatic ability of Talleyrand, without his coldness. In haughtiness, a rival of Chatham; in devotion to his country's interests, a peer of Hampden; in boldness of speech and action, an equal of Brougham, Bismarck's qualities are in most unique combination.[2]

[2] *Ibid.*, I, 6–7.

In the same college magazine, for October, 1878, appeared Wilson's prize essay on "William Earl Chatham." Like its predecessor, it was composed with evident awareness of the value of antithesis, in somewhat the Macaulayan tradition which has influenced so many younger writers. It offers interesting evidence of a growing historical and literary mastery. Limiting ourselves once more to a single quotation, we may find much to admire in the estimate that William Pitt

harmonized with his age in nothing but in affectation, and even his affectation had an earnestness and frankness about it which did not belong to the all-pervading affectation of the society around him. He was in everything enthusiastically earnest, and his age laughed at earnestness; he was vehement, and his age affected coldness and indifference; he was sternly virtuous, scorning corruption, and his age was skeptical of virtue, nursing corruption; he had eager, burning beliefs and was actuated by a warm love for principle, and his age delighted in doubtings and questionings, was guided by no principle save that of expediency; he was constantly and confidently to appeal to the higher, brighter, purer instincts of human nature, and his age doubted the existence of any such instincts, nay, even argued from its own experience that all human nature was low and pulseless.[3]

Wilson's next contribution as a historian (there had been an intervening article on "Cabinet Government in the United States") was offered in March, 1880, when, as a law student at the University of Virginia, he published an essay on John Bright, remarkable for the intellectual detachment of its southern-born author who had abundant reason to recall the Englishman's antagonism toward the Confederate cause, and equally noteworthy for its courage in presenting such views to the post-war generation of the South, at that time in the colleges.[4]

In William E. Gladstone, the young historian and critic found a subject even more congenial. He seems aware of an affinity of spirit. The subjective element is decidedly noticeable. Wilson, in describing Gladstone, appears at times to be portraying the character that he envisions for himself. This is possibly an exaggeration, but the reader is invited to peruse the Gladstone essay

[3] Ibid., p. 12.   [4] Ibid., pp. 43–59.

with that point of view in mind. There is antithesis, as usual, and it is very well developed. There is, besides, an eager championship of a character which has frequently been charged with inconsistency. Wilson looks beyond apparent inconsistencies to an essential unity. There is here no slight foreshadowing of the defense some later scholar might need to make for him. Among the characters who stirred his interest up to the age of twenty-four, Gladstone was the most fervently admired. The English liberal was a pattern to the American.[5]

So far Wilson had been writing for the magazines, in work demanding an even level of accomplishment. For even Homer sometimes nods in books, but seldom in the periodicals. Already the young scholar, whose brief excursions were of a quality so excellent, was turning to the more elaborate, but in some respects less taxing, field of producing books in covers. The first of Wilson's formal printed works was *Congressional Government*. A treatise in political science, it bore the stamp of creative originality, in no way revealing by its contents that it was a doctoral dissertation and that its author was a young man of twenty-nine, a graduate student at the Johns Hopkins University.

In some respects it surpassed any of his later works upon related subjects. It was daring writing for the time, and it foreshadowed important crises in the life of the author himself and in the development of the nation. What a modern bearing is conveyed, for example, by the assertion that "indeed it is quite evident that if federal power be not altogether irresponsible, it is the federal judiciary which is the only effectual balance wheel of the whole system"![6] How prophetic, too, the declaration that "the power of the courts is safe only during seasons of political peace, when parties are not aroused to passion or tempted by the command of irresistible majorities."[7] Startlingly suggestive of years to come was the forecast, buttressed by several historical examples, that "in no event would the control of the patronage by the Senate have unbalanced the federal system more seriously than

5 *Ibid.*, pp. 63–88.

6 Woodrow Wilson, *Congressional Government* (Boston, 1885), p. 34.   7 *Ibid.*, p. 40.

it may some day be unbalanced by an irresponsible exertion of that body's semi-executive powers in regard to the foreign policy of the government."[8]

If these selected thoughts seem clairvoyant, others were, in a more restricted sense, historical. Wilson attributed the presence of a distinguished group of constitutional lawyers in the Senate of the middle nineteenth century to the circumstance that national problems were legalistic and called for precisely their endowments as trained lawyers. Many historical allusions enrich the book throughout, but its chief claim to recognition as history lies in its thoughtful and elaborate "Introductory," pages 1–57.

Congressional Government represented a very high level of achievement. To maintain that plane during all of an average lifetime devoted to writing would spell certain greatness. To do even better work upon reaching full maturity would carry one to most exalted heights. To A. Maurice Low, a critic whose competence cannot be doubted, the book appeared to be a classic.[9]

Congressional Government decidedly surpassed *The State*, which followed it in 1889 and which conformed too meticulously to textbook format and textbook limitations to have much weight outside the classroom. William Allen White condemned it as no more than an essay which might have been produced by any bright young political scientist who, having fallen under Darwinian influences, attempted to interpret politics by the new light of biology.[10] But White was hard to please. Certainly *The State* met the hearty approbation of so able an English critic as Oscar Browning, who regarded the work as intelligent pioneering in a branch of sociology essential to the happiness and good government of the human race.[11]

A textbook like its predecessors, and like them a more or less inevitable residuum of college teaching, *Division and Reunion*,

[8] *Ibid.*, p. 49.

[9] A. Maurice Low, *Woodrow Wilson, an Interpretation* (Boston, 1918), p. 60.

[10] William Allen White, *Woodrow Wilson, the Man, His Times and His Task* (Boston and New York, 1924), pp. 121–22.

[11] H. Wilson Harris, *President Wilson, His Problems and His Policy: An English View* (New York, 1917), p. 28.

published in 1893 in the "Epochs of American History" series under the editorship of Albert Bushnell Hart, was the political scientist's first prolonged adventure in the domain of history. Suffering the limitations imposed by textbook format, notably in its extreme compression, the work is none the less enriched by generalizations of sweeping import and frequently of marked originality. A few examples must suffice.

Of John Quincy Adams, not a favorite of his, Wilson wrote: "His ideas of public duty were the old tonic, with the addition of a little acid."[12] He found in the Jacksonian doctrine that a majority popular vote entitled a candidate to the presidency, even when the Constitution did not so state, "the rise of a democratic theory very far advanced beyond that of Jefferson's party, and destined again and again to assert itself as against strict constitutional principle."[13] Again, of the Webster-Hayne debate, Wilson cogently remarked:

The North was now beginning to insist upon a national government; the South was continuing to insist upon the original understanding of the Constitution: that was all. The right upon which Hayne insisted, indeed, was not the right of his State to secede from the Union, but the singular right to declare a law of the United States null and void by Act of her own Legislature, and remain in the Union while denying the validity of its statutes.[14]

Even more sweeping is the summarizing statement regarding nullification: "What is most striking in the whole affair for the student of institutions is, that it gave to the practical politics of an English people a theoretical cast such as the politics of no English community had ever worn before."[15]

The author contributed nothing of note in his treatment of the Mexican War, but upon its consequences he was more illuminating:

The issue [in 1848] was not yet the existence of slavery within the States, but the admission of slavery into the Territories. The object of the extreme southern men was to gain territory for slavery; the object

---

[12] Woodrow Wilson, *Division and Reunion* (New York, ed. of 1921), p. 10.

[13] *Ibid.*, p. 18.   [14] *Ibid.*, p. 47.   [15] *Ibid.*, pp. 67–68.

of the men now drawing together into new parties in the North was to exclude slavery altogether from the new national domain in the West.[16]

That is a fair enough statement, even if not strikingly original.

Wilson introduced into his text a brilliant summary of the ingredients which went to fashion the Republican party;[17] he discoursed with an enlightening simplicity upon the organic character of constitutions;[18] and he attained a distinguished level of historical interpretation when, awarding the South the sounder constitutional argument in the Civil War, he asserted:

She had stood still while the rest of the country had undergone profound changes; and, standing still, she retained the old principles which had once been universal. Both she and her principles, it turned out, had been caught at last in the great national drift, and were to be overwhelmed. Her slender economic resources were no match for the mighty strength of the nation with which she had fallen out of sympathy.[19]

Toward Lincoln, he was sympathetic. Even Grant, who might have been anathema, was generously interpreted.[20]

Division and Reunion was a substantial textbook. It is accurate and within its range even scholarly, although not based upon extensive original research. It covers too much in too small a compass to be entertaining. Only at irregular intervals does felicity of phrase or originality of interpretation captivate the reader, but it excels most textbooks in its literary appeal. Its highest claim to merit, in the opinion of a critic not too friendly to its author, is the detachment of its point of view.[21] The young southerner allowed no post-war bitterness to vitiate his work.

George Washington, which in 1896 followed these textbooks, was Wilson's most elaborate essay in formal biography. Among his works it is distinctly an exotic. It has a style and manner all its own, almost unrelated to the other Wilson, or better, possibly, the other Wilsons. The opening chapter, entitled "In Wash-

[16] *Ibid.*, p. 167.
[17] *Ibid.*, p. 188.
[18] *Ibid.*, p. 211.

[19] *Ibid.*, p. 212.
[20] *Ibid.*, pp. 276–77.
[21] White, p. 122.

ington's Day," devotes thirty-eight out of a total of three hundred and fourteen text pages to a discussion of Virginian and colonial society. It is good popular stuff, but the space might better have been allotted to Washington himself. The hero emerges eventually in "A Virginia Breeding," which carries through his reception at Fort Le Boeuf and his return to Williamsburg, January, 1754. It is a bit casual and discursive, but suitable for the nontechnical reader. Nothing at all exceptional, it is run-of-the-mill writing, in a style peculiar to this book; for the work is marred by a pedantry of simplicity. " 'Twas," for example, is employed *ad nauseam*. " 'Twould" is merely an unpleasant variant. "Spite of sickness and short rations" is in the same pseudo-colloquial vein. "Broad and fertile acres at Mount Vernon" is not only trite but false. The Philipse romance, mostly fictitious, is stressed, whereas that with Sally Cary Fairfax is virtually ignored. There is an emphasis on Washington's magnificence and love of dress which has been adversely noticed by William Allen White. "No man," he claims, "who wrote that gala story of the wax-work Washington, the story with its paper frills and social furbelows, could honestly be said to have put aside the things of this world."[22]

The proportions of the book are most eccentric. The Jumonville episode, for example, is dismissed with a paragraph (p. 74). Even the Revolution requires only thirty pages, while in this truncated version there is room for an anecdote of sixty-six words on what Washington's landlady's granddaughter, sitting on his knee, thought of redcoats versus bluecoats, with Washington's reply. Five pages suffice for his years in retirement.

There is, of course, much good writing in this book. Characters in the Continental Congress are well described. Military movements march before us swiftly. Chapter viii, "The Stress of Victory," is very good indeed; whereas the pages on Washington's acceptance of the presidency are conventional, emotional, and unimportant.[23]

[22] *Ibid.*, p. 124.
[23] Woodrow Wilson, *George Washington* (New York and London, ed. 1903), pp. 265 ff.

Good in spots, the book is mediocre as a whole; and its eccentricities of style render it at times absurd. It represented nothing on which to build its author's fame. As one of Wilson's friendly biographers has remarked, "He only added to the steel-engraving status of the Father of his Country."[24] A less well-disposed critic dismisses the book as "rather fourth-rate stuff."[25]

Drawn to an elaborate scale, and culminating Wilson's work as a historian per se, was *A History of the American People*, published in 1902 in five volumes by the Messrs. Harper. Pleasantly free from the vagaries of the *Washington*, the *History* is an agreeably composed, if not exactly novel, interpretation of the national development. As its author years afterward humorously observed, "At one time I tried to write history. I did not know enough to write it, but I knew from experience how hard it was to find an historian out, and I trusted I would not be found out."[26]

Apart from its simple, agreeable, and perspicuous style, and the temperate and judicious estimates of characters both North and South, which could have been anticipated from the author of *Division and Reunion*, the outstanding feature of this considerable literary venture is its format. There is an amazing wealth of illustrations, most happily selected; and three of the volumes are followed by supplements admirably chosen to include such items as the "Articles of Confederation of the New England Colonies, 1643"; "Penn's Plan of Union—1697"; "Franklin's Plan of Union—1754"; the "Articles of Confederation—1777"—to recite the contents of Volume II alone. Where could one look more advantageously, in fact, for a comparison of the constitutions of the United States and of the Confederate States, paragraph by paragraph and in parallel columns, than in Volume IV of this same work?

It is the penalty for popular writing that, although the au-

[24] William E. Dodd, *Woodrow Wilson and His Work* (New York, 1920), p. 29.

[25] White, p. 124.

[26] Address of President Wilson at the Y.M.C.A. celebration, Pittsburgh, Oct. 24, 1914, in *Addresses: Wilson—March 4—Sept. 25, 1913–1916*, p. 7. See also his *Robert E. Lee, an Interpretation* (Chapel Hill, N.C., 1924), pp. 22–23.

thor enhances his reputation among the populace, he does not deepen it among his fellow-craftsmen. The *History* suffers this disadvantage: it is not the most serious measure of its author's intellect or of his power to fertilize ideas. Within its limits, self-imposed, it was, however, excellent. The conclusion of the work is an admirable example of Wilson's capacity for generalization. His summary of the forces manifest already at the *fin de siècle* was indeed prophetic of that new era, perhaps of that "New Deal,"of which the author was in no small sense the pioneer. Wilson concluded:

Parties were turning to the new days to come and to the common efforts of peace. Statesmen knew that it was to be their task to release the energies of the country for the great day of trade and of manufacture which was to change the face of the world: to ease the processes of labor, govern capital in the interest of those who were its indispensable servants in pushing the great industries of the country to their final value and perfection, and make law the instrument, not of justice merely, but also of social progress.[27]

Reverting to the textbook style—and wisely, it would seem, reverting also to the narrower domain of political science, which held for Wilson a more abiding interest than history—he delivered the George Blumenthal Foundation Lectures at Columbia University in 1907, on "Constitutional Government in the United States." The subject afforded ample scope for historical allusions. Magna Carta, the Golden Bull, and the government of the early Germans were among the large historical topics; Queen Elizabeth, Frederick the Great, John Marshall, and Andrew Jackson were among the personages assessed. In the field of constitutional government, one of Wilson's most pregnant and arresting thoughts established a comparison between the Whig theory of political dynamic and the Newtonian theory of the universe. The division of powers—executive, legislative, and judicial—so dear to Whig politicians, affirmed the speaker, was comparable to the Newtonian conception of checks and balances within the universe itself. Nevertheless, the Darwinian hypothe-

[27] Woodrow Wilson, *A History of the American People* (5 vols.; New York and London, 1902), V, 300.

sis that followed Newton's stressed organic unity and the necessity for an untrammeled head. The Americans who made and first interpreted the Constitution took over Newton's concepts bodily by way of Montesquieu. Consequently, their successors faced a reconstruction of their Constitution into something "Darwinian in structure and in practice."[28]

Here was an idea of utmost profundity. Had it been original, it would have marked a really first-rate mind; for to such a mind alone is insight of such depth reserved. But the idea was not new, as Wilson himself admitted in 1912 at the annual banquet of the Economic Club of New York City, when he generously assigned the credit to a distinguished Scotsman who in the period of Wilson's presidency had been his guest at Princeton. If he did not originate the idea, he made it his own by adoption. In the alembic of his own mind, he rendered it intelligible to others, advising his hearers to think over the proposition

that what we have been witnessing for the past hundred years is the transformation of a Newtonian constitution into a Darwinian constitution. (*Applause.*) The place where the strongest will is present will be the seat of sovereignty. . . . . There are no checks and balances in the mechanical sense in the constitution; historical circumstances have determined the character of our government.[29]

Almost verbatim, Woodrow Wilson provided President F. D. Roosevelt with his comment on the N.R.A. decision of the Supreme Court when Wilson declared, in his chapter on "The Courts," that "the Constitution was not meant to hold the government back to the time of horses and wagons, the time when postboys carried every communication that passed from merchant to merchant, when trade had few long routes within the nation and did not venture in bulk beyond neighborhood transactions."[30] Further elaboration of this thought reveals Wilson

[28] Woodrow Wilson, *Constitutional Government in the United States* (New York, 1908), pp. 54–57.

[29] Woodrow Wilson, "Government in Relation to Business," address delivered at the annual banquet of the Economic Club of New York at the Hotel Astor, May 23, 1912. See also his address at the Suffrage Convention, Atlantic City, N.J., Sept. 8, 1916.

[30] Woodrow Wilson, *Constitutional Government in the United States* (New York, 1907), p. 169; also p. 178.

as a distinct forerunner of the "New Deal," but space precludes quotation more extended.

At the same time Wilson recognized the dangers inherent in centralization. He traced these centralizing tendencies to the failure of nullification in South Carolina—again, it may be said, a sweeping generalization. Thereafter vested with power to determine economic opportunities within the several states, the federal government "was suffered to become a general providence."[31] Within this growing sovereignty—for Wilson believed Congress, not the president, to be the ultimate authority in this post-Newtonian, or, in other words, Darwinian, Constitution—public opinion would afford the only check upon congressional extravagance and absurdity.[32]

Other pertinent reflections in this important work foretold an extension of the president's authority and usefulness in the field of foreign affairs,[33] and the subordination of the states to regional authority.[34]

Much else there is of moment in this product of a ripened scholarship. Not primarily historical, the work does credit to Wilson as historian, for without historical references, and these in abundance and variety, it would lose its flavor. Description and prediction alike would no longer be convincing.

One more book in covers, and we may turn to the scattered allusions in Wilson's voluminous addresses, certain prefaces, and other miscellaneous writings. The volume in question, *The New Freedom*, is a compendium of addresses delivered in the campaign of 1912 and transcribed with but scant attempt at editing. It is important for the study of Wilson the politician, statesman, and world-leader. It is, however, of little significance for our present essay. Perhaps its only strictly historical reference is to those conservatives who do not see that history should teach the living influence of past events rather than embalm events themselves in a ritual of genuflections at the expense of living truth. As Wilson put the case, "Some citizens of this country have never got beyond the Declaration of Independence, signed in Philadelphia,

---

[31] *Ibid.*, pp. 175–76.　　　[33] *Ibid.*, p. 59.
[32] *Ibid.*, p. 179.　　　[34] *Ibid.*, p. 180.

July 4, 1776. Their bosoms swell against George III, but they have no consciousness of the war for freedom that is going on to-day."[35] Again historical, but of less general import, was the payment of respects to Alexander Hamilton, founding-father of that political party against which Wilson never ceased to battle. Of Hamilton, he said: "A great man, but, in my judgment, not a great American. He did not think in terms of American life."[36] True, he did not think in Jeffersonian terms; but "American" is an elastic word, as Wilson should have known—did know, in fact, for he himself once declared that "no man can boast that he understands America."[37]

A student who seeks to evaluate Wilson's work in history must search his well-nigh innumerable published addresses for pertinent, although fugitive, material. The critic of his books alone will gain but an imperfect concept of Wilson the historian. One of the best of Wilson's own interpretations of the historian's task may be found in an address, entitled "The Course of American History," made to the local historical society of Newark, New Jersey, on May 16, 1895. This essay is remarkable. It shows a knowledge both of traditional views and of views more recently accepted. In addition, it is strikingly original. Tribute is paid to local history, with a proper warning against the dullness which so often mars it. "The history of a nation," said the speaker, "is only the history of its villages written large." The trained historian will not confine himself to lists of county clerks. He will rediscover the life these clerks once led.[38]

Wilson was naturally aware of the popular belief that much of American history was the resultant of a long conflict for predominance between New England and the South. This interpretation he deemed utterly inadequate. It ignored the middle

[35] Woodrow Wilson, *The New Freedom* (New York, 1913), p. 48.

[36] *Ibid.*, p. 55.

[37] "Address of President Wilson at the Celebration of the Rededication of Congress Hall, Philadelphia, Pa., October 25, 1913," *Addresses: Wilson—March 4—Sept. 25, 1913–1916*, p. 5.

[38] Woodrow Wilson, "The Course of American History," *Collections of the New Jersey Historical Society* (Newark, 1900), p. 183.

states—New York, New Jersey, Pennsylvania—which, by their composite early origins, presaged complex America. Again Wilson was naturally aware of the interesting idea that the march of western Europeans eastward into central and eastern Europe was the counterpart of the westward march of civilization across the continent of North America. But here likewise he showed his independence of thought. The earlier European migrant carried eastward his own low cultural level; whereas the western pioneer, bearing the high culture of seventeenth-century Europe, crossed a pathless sea to confront the hardships of a wilderness frontier. It was a contrast in migrations, the latter calling for the higher courage. By 1895, when he was speaking, the last frontier had scarcely gone. As Wilson epitomized the situation,

The Westerner, in some day soon to come, will pass out of our life, as he so long ago passed out of the life of the Old World. Then a new epoch will open for us. Perhaps it has opened already. Slowly we shall grow old, compact our people, study the delicate adjustments of an intricate society, and ponder the niceties, as we have hitherto pondered the bulks and structural framework, of government. Have we not, indeed, already come to these things?[39]

Such thought in 1937 would be intelligent but fairly obvious and conventional. In 1895 it was notably original.

This essay furnished Wilson with an occasion to amplify James Russell Lowell's portrait of Abraham Lincoln, "New birth of our new soil, the first American." Wilson's was a prose version but withal a very noble one. Lincoln, according to his successor in democracy, was a deep nationalist. He was of the West, but he understood an East that never understood him. For the East was sectional, and not American in any sense like Lincoln.[40] This single essay would give warrant for calling its author a good historian. It dealt in large ideas; yet never failed to shed new light upon existing concepts.

Lincoln was always a subject dear to Wilson. Both were democrats of the small *d*. Southerner that Wilson was, he could appreciate the common sense of Lincoln in contrast with the frenzy

[39] *Ibid.*, pp. 195–96.   [40] *Ibid.*, pp. 204–5.

of "hot, impracticable Abolitionists" like William Lloyd Garrison.[41] Thus the address which Wilson delivered at the dedication of the Lincoln Memorial at Hodgenville, Kentucky, was obviously a work of love. The theme was heartening. Lincoln was the supreme vindication of Wilson's own ideas upon democracy.

> This little hut [proclaimed the speaker] was the cradle of one of the great sons of men, a man of singular, delightful, vital genius who presently emerged upon the great stage of the nation's history, gaunt, shy, ungainly, but dominant and majestic, a natural leader of men, himself inevitably the central figure of the great plot. No man can explain this, but every man can see how it demonstrates the vigor of democracy, where every door is open, in every hamlet and countryside, in city and wilderness alike, for the ruler to emerge when he will and claim his leadership in the free life. Such are the authentic proofs of the validity and vitality of democracy.[42]

In treating Lincoln, the historian stuck closer to his subject than when he handled Lee. Despite some southern predilections, Lincoln was the more congenial theme. Lee was but the text for a rather rambling sermon, which stressed at length the democratic contribution of the medieval church and attributed to ecclesiastics drawn from plebeian stock the ability which alone could save "a sterile aristocratic polity." For, said Wilson, "an aristocratic polity goes to seed."[43] Just how this bears on Lee, the reader may himself determine.

In this sermon of 1909, Wilson also sounded a solemn warning against the centralizing tendencies in American political life. He insisted:

> There is one lesson that the peoples of the world have learned so often that they ought to esteem themselves contemptible if they have to learn it again, and that is that if you concentrate the management of a people's affairs in a single central government and carry that concen-

---

[41] Woodrow Wilson, *On Being Human* (New York, 1897), reprint of an article in the *Atlantic Monthly*, 1897, pp. 47–48.

[42] Woodrow Wilson, "Abraham Lincoln," in *Democracy To-Day*, ed. Christian Gauss (Chicago, 1917), p. 97.

[43] Woodrow Wilson, *Robert E. Lee, an Interpretation* (Chapel Hill, N.C., 1924; reprint of an address before the University of North Carolina, May, 1909), p. 21.

tration beyond a certain point of oversight and regulation, you will certainly provoke again those revolutionary processes by which individual liberty was asserted.[44]

If Wilson was a bit out of touch with Lee, he was even less at home with Franklin. An edition of the *Autobiography* in 1901 carried a fourteen-page preface by Wilson. It was clever and in some measure original. Hard on Franklin, it most assuredly was. Franklin's common sense, his cool detachment, his eighteenth-century outlook, failed to match Wilsonian idealism. Franklin was depicted—with some degree of subtlety, one must concede —as too cool-headed a materialist to appeal to a thinker who was already groping after cosmic change. The Introduction is not unfair, but it somewhat predisposes the reader against the author of the autobiography.[45] Wilson was not the man to sympathize with Franklin. Editorially, he was an unhappy choice.

Scarcely more felicitous was an address, on "John Wesley's Place in History," delivered at Wesleyan University on the occasion of the Wesley bicentennial. It was a piece for an occasion— competent, full of examples, historical, and wholly uninspired. Like the Franklin Introduction, it reveals a slightly narrow Wilson, this time in a manner less easily defined. Quite possibly, a true Calvinist like Wilson could never fully grasp the Methodist approach.[46] That Calvinism did explain no small part of his thinking is affirmed by Sir Thomas Barclay, who found in Wilson a capacity, like that of Immanuel Kant, to extract philosophy from his own inner depths.[47]

Whether touched with sympathy for certain characters in history or repelled instinctively by others, one must acquit Wilson of any conscious lack of fairness. He had read extensively and thought deeply. Again, and yet again, he shed new light upon

[44] *Ibid.*, p. 30.

[45] *The Autobiography of Benjamin Franklin: with an Introduction by Woodrow Wilson* ("Century Classics") (New York, 1901), pp. v–xix.

[46] Woodrow Wilson, *John Wesley's Place in History* (New York and Cincinnati, 1916), pp. 3–48.

[47] Sir Thomas Barclay, *Le Président Wilson et l'évolution de la politique étrangère des Etats-Unis*, Préface de M. Paul Painlevé (Paris, 1918), pp. 161–62.

some phase of history, perhaps already hackneyed. We may properly conclude the present survey with certain large deductions that Wilson drew from the life of the past.

Thus, in a notable preface to *Harper's Encyclopaedia of United States History from 458 A.D. to 1902*, Wilson advocated the comparative study of European history and British and American institutions in the interest of a sane philosophy of politics "which shall forever put out of school the thin and sentimental theories of the disciples of Rousseau."[48] The eighteenth century was not a favorite with Wilson. Its ideals were too Newtonian for his Darwinian tastes.

In his Mobile address of October 27, 1913, famous in diplomacy for its attempt to conciliate the Latin-Americans, Wilson indulged in important historical generalizations when he pointed to the shift in Europe's orientation wrought by the voyages of Columbus. After Great Britain supplanted the Mediterranean as Europe's pivot, the eye of that continent looked due west. Wilson believed that, as Columbus turned the ·march of civilization westward, so the Panama Canal would bend it toward the south. "I feel that these gentleman honoring us with their presence today will presently find that some part, at any rate, of the center of gravity of the world has shifted."[49]

Geography inspired the Mobile thesis. But to Wilson's mental temper, geography was less congenial than philosophy. Out of his ripeness of experience as a statesman and a scholar he could say to the Press Club of New York City, on June 30, 1916: "I have not read history without observing that the greatest forces in the world and the only permanent forces are the moral forces."[50]

Philosophy, in turn, yielded to religion in one of Wilson's final writings, *The Road Away from Revolution*, published in 1923, when

[48] *Harper's Encyclopaedia of United States History from 458 A.D. to 1902*, Preface by Woodrow Wilson (New York and London, 1902), p. xxix.

[49] Woodrow Wilson, *Address at Mobile, Alabama, October 27, 1913*, p. 6.

[50] James B. Scott (ed.), *President Wilson's Foreign Policy: Messages, Addresses, Papers* (New York, 1918), p. xii.

the storm of life was nearly past. Through this valedictory runs
a note of religious ecstasy:

The sum of the whole matter is this, that our civilization cannot survive materially unless it be redeemed spiritually. It can be saved only
by becoming permeated with the spirit of Christ and being made free
and happy by the practices which spring out of that spirit. Only thus
can discontent be driven out and all the shadows lifted from the road
ahead.[51]

Here we may leave him. History, philosophy, experience, have
culminated in religion. A final judgment must await on History's
own verdict. Supremely great or only great will be determined
by the rising or the falling curve of influence of Wilson's ideals
as a statesman. As historian, one may conclude that greatness
lay within his grasp but that he never fully seized it. His nature
was too rich to be so circumscribed.

[51] Woodrow Wilson, *The Road Away from Revolution* (Boston, 1923), pp. 12–13.

VII

JOHN BACH McMASTER

WILLIAM T. HUTCHINSON
University of Chicago

*

WHEN John Bach McMaster was born in Brooklyn, New York, on June 29, 1852, his parents, Julia Anna Matilda Bach and James McMaster, were enjoying a comfortable income from trade in Mexico, a bank in New Orleans, and a sugar plantation in Louisiana.[1] A few years later, however, their modest fortune was largely swept away by Confederate confiscations and a costly speculation in the stock of an oil company. Their children would be obliged to earn their own living.

Waving flags, marching soldiers, and impassioned oratory were among John McMaster's earliest memories. Both at home and in public school during the Civil War the boy heard almost daily about blue-clad heroes on land and sea. These oft-repeated lessons in patriotism were not to be easily forgotten.

McMaster graduated from the College of the City of New York in June, 1872. He was then the president of his class, a member of the Phi Beta Kappa society, and known about the campus for his skill in freehand drawing and debate. A fellowship in English, with the teaching of a course in grammar as its necessary accompaniment, enabled him by the following summer to earn a Master's degree.[2] The death of his father thereupon

[1] McMaster's maternal grandfather and grandmother were of English and Irish descent, respectively. His father, of Scottish forbears, was a native of New York State.

[2] McMaster's familiarity with the works of the leading English and American poets and novelists is often reflected in his historical writings.

122

left McMaster with the duty of contributing even more money than before to the support of his family.

If his memory of these days served him well over a half-century later, he devoted many hours while in college to the works of Macaulay, Parkman, Bancroft, and Hildreth. Using Macaulay's masterpiece as his model, he was impressed by the inadequacies of American histories dealing with the years after 1783. He browsed endlessly among the old newspapers and pamphlets in the Astor Library and dreamed of re-creating America's story with his own pen. However this may be, there is no doubt of his early enthusiasm for history and his practice of making careful notes on what he read.[3]

McMaster's appointment in 1873 as the civil assistant of Major George L. Gillespie, U.S.A., who was directing a topographical survey of the Shenandoah Valley battlefields, was in harmony with the young man's interest in the Civil War; but it turned his attention from written history to map-making and interviewing eye witnesses of Sheridan's campaigns.[4] This valuable experience may account for McMaster's later emphasis upon the importance of historical geography, although it bade fair to lead him into engineering as his life's work. When this assignment was completed in the spring of 1874, he divided his time for the next two years between tutoring children of the James Roosevelt and Abram S. Hewitt families and preparing a map of New York State. This training, together with a degree in civil engineering received from his alma mater in 1875 and the publication of his two little books on bridge-, tunnel-, and dam-build-

[3] *Dictionary of American Biography* (New York, 1928–36), XII, 140–42; *The Booklover's Reading Club Hand-Book To Accompany the Reading Course Entitled "American Foundation History, Course XXI"* (Philadelphia, 1901), p. 47.

[4] P. H. Sheridan, *Personal Memoirs* (2 vols.; New York, 1888), II, 117. For facts relating to McMaster's early life I am much indebted to E. P. Oberholtzer, "John Bach McMaster, 1852–1932," in the *Pennsylvania Magazine of History and Biography*, LVII, No. 1 (January, 1933), 1–31, and to a typed "summary of a biographical talk which McMaster gave on one of the few occasions he appeared in public after his retirement," kindly sent to me by Professor Roy F. Nichols, of the University of Pennsylvania. These references will hereafter be cited as *Oberholtzer* and *Nichols' Notes* respectively.

ing, gained him an instructorship in geodesy in the new John C. Green School of Science of Princeton College.

Here, between 1877 and 1883, McMaster increased his reputation among those of his own profession by contributing articles to scientific periodicals.[5] His interest in the trans-Mississippi country, first aroused by reading of the western origins of the Civil War,[6] was quickened by a summer spent in Utah and Wyoming territories as a member of a Princeton field expedition. Except for this excursion, McMaster devoted the long college vacations to historical research and writing. Of the many volumes which challenged his attention during these years at Princeton, Henry T. Buckle's *History of Civilization* perhaps most deeply impressed him.[7]

McMaster gave new evidence of his versatility in 1883 by publishing a book of over six hundred pages dealing with the six years following the close of the American Revolution. Because of this volume—the first of eight appearing during the next thirty years under the title, *A History of the People of the United States*—McMaster "burst into the historiographical firmament as a star of the first magnitude."[8]

The University of Pennsylvania hastened to call McMaster to its newly established chair in American history, one of three then existing in the United States. He honored it until his retirement as professor emeritus in 1920. During his long tenure he

[5] For the titles of McMaster's chief scientific works and articles, see W. T. Hutchinson, "John Bach McMaster, Historian of the American People," *Mississippi Valley Historical Review* (Cedar Rapids, Iowa), XVI, No. 1 (June, 1929), 25 and n. (hereafter cited as *Hutchinson*).

[6] *Nichols' Notes.*

[7] *Oberholtzer*, p. 8. At this time McMaster wrote an essay entitled, "The Struggle of Men with Nature," but was unable to find a publisher for it. The influence of McMaster's training as an engineer is evident in his account of the Johnstown (Pennsylvania) flood of 1889, written shortly after the disaster. Following the author's death, portions of this manuscript were published, with a foreword by Professor Oberholtzer, in the *Pennsylvania Magazine of History and Biography*, LVII (1933), 209–43; 316–54.

[8] W. A. Dunning, "A Generation of American Historiography," American Historical Association *Annual Report* for 1917 (Washington, 1920), p. 349; J. B. McMaster, *A History of the People of the United States from the Revolution to the Civil War* (8 vols.; New York, 1883–1913). Hereafter cited as "McMaster, *History*."

influenced the thought of not a few graduate students who were later to be leaders in the field of history.[9] Former undergraduates in his survey courses still express amazement at his unusual memory for the factual details of his subject; but, as a teacher, he was at his best in the informality of the seminar room.[10]

Although the literary style, general arrangement, and content of McMaster's maiden volume in history were exhaustively commented upon by its many reviewers, its title was probably more discussed than any other feature of the book. Some critics, apparently to the author's surprise, asserted that it echoed John Richard Green's *A Short History of the English People*, published nine years before.[11] McMaster's title signified that the United States for the first time had a social historian. It struck a new note in American historiography, suggesting the growth of democracy and the importance of the common man. Many other students were soon to follow his lead into the rich domain of social history.[12]

[9] Among the historians who studied under him were, E. C. Barker, H. E. Bolton, E. P. Cheyney, E. S. Corwin, W. E. Lingelbach, A. C. Myers, E. P. Oberholtzer, F. L. Paxson, W. T. Root, W. R. Shepherd, W. W. Sweet, and C. H. Van Tyne.

[10] Although the social and economic aspects of American life chiefly attracted him as subjects for research, he also offered courses in constitutional history. With Frederick D. Stone, McMaster compiled a large volume entitled, *Pennsylvania and the Federal Constitution, 1787–1788* (Lancaster, Pennsylvania, 1888). Jay Monaghan, who, as an undergraduate, was one of McMaster's students, has kindly permitted me to quote the following from his unpublished essay entitled, "John Bach McMaster, Pioneer," p. 1: "Here was a frail little man weighing less than a hundred pounds, a self-effacing little man whose modest voice was extremely difficult to hear. . . . . In the lecture room he reminded his students of one of the professional guides who escort tourists through the Forum at Rome, reciting a well learned piece, which if interrupted, must be started again at the beginning. . . . . It is doubtful whether any of his undergraduate students took anything away from the classroom except a mental picture of a very pale little person with delicate hands and an unusually large, bald head that looked very white against the blackboard. He appeared as cold and impersonal as a piece of chalk. His eyes looked out through large round glasses, like an owl unused to the light." For a quite different characterization, see *Oberholtzer*, pp. 13–15, 17–18, 21–24, 31.

[11] *Ibid.*, pp. 26–27. According to Oberholtzer, McMaster was not aware that he had been influenced by Green. For a summary of leading reviews of McMaster, *History*, see *Hutchinson*, pp. 27 ff.

[12] J. F. Jameson, J. B. McMaster, and E. Channing, *The Present State of Historical Writing in America* (Worcester, Massachusetts, 1910), p. 21 (hereafter cited as "Jameson, McMaster, and Channing").

McMaster believed that the state and its activities were not alone important in the lives of its citizens, and that it was possible to differentiate between a history of the United States as a political entity and a history of its people. Unlike earlier American historians, he determined to make the latter the theme of his story. Centennial celebrations of the outstanding occurrences of the Revolution were the order of the day about 1880, and Americans were thus made more aware than ever before of their glorious heritage. According to McMaster, the time was ripe to remind them that, although their rise as a nation was "the distinguishing event, the really great event" of world-history during the nineteenth century, their past was not merely a tale of "wars, conspiracies, ... rebellions" and debates in Congress, but was, above all else, the unexampled social, economic, and moral development of a "highly favored people" from primitive beginnings to an enlightened and happier present.[13] Richard Hildreth had been the partisan of a political party; McMaster would be the partisan of the people. Nor would he yield to George Bancroft on the score of patriotism and pride in race. These virtues, however, inspired him to treat of the "sociological" aspects of history which the New Englander had neglected in his writings.[14]

Although McMaster wrote often and much about democracy, he never paused to define it. At times he seemed to identify it with individual rights and liberty; at others with equality of men under law; occasionally he emphasized the "humane spirit"

[13] McMaster, *History*, I, 1–2. See also his remarks on offering the toast, "History, Like Charity, Begins at Home," in the *Pennsylvania Magazine of History and Biography*, XXIV (1910), 300. That he did not wholly achieve his ideal in his *History* is evident from the fact that almost all of its sixth volume, and well over half of its eighth, deal with political subjects.

[14] "Jameson, McMaster, and Channing," p. 17. McMaster also criticized Bancroft's "tone of exaltation" but added that he was the "first great American historian." Francis Parkman, according to McMaster, was the best of the "literary and dramatic school"; but he, Motley, and Prescott were too much absorbed in "royalty and heroes," overlooking the "great masses of toiling men" and the "silent revolutions by which nations pass from barbarism to civilization." See also, McMaster, *History*, I, 18–19. Partiality for everything Anglo-Saxon was a characteristic of most English and American historians about 1880, perhaps reflecting the influence of Edward A. Freeman.

animating men and women as the chief evidence of the existence of democracy; but as a rule it apparently held for him the political connotation stressed by Lincoln—a government of and for the people.[15] That popularly elected officials might be more responsive to the will of minority pressure groups than to a mandate from a majority of the people is not suggested in his writings.

Although the meaning of democracy to McMaster was somewhat indistinct, he left his readers in no doubt concerning his concept of "progress." The increase of democracy was a chief component of progress, but its reality was also amply demonstrated by the fact that both the rich and poor in the United States were more intelligent, tolerant, liberal, moral, humane, and happy in the early twentieth century than they had been in 1789. This improvement was in no small measure a result of the amazing series of inventions which had widened the opportunities for remunerative employment and increased the material comforts and leisure time available to all. In short, "every art, every science, every branch of human industry has been enormously developed by us. . . . . In the face of these facts it is wicked to talk of degeneration and decay."[16]

McMaster's belief in America's progress and democracy, his stress upon the life of her common folk, his determination to explode the myth that her "old times" were as "good times" as those of his own day, and his optimistic faith in the beneficence of the Industrial Revolution help to explain why the many purchasers of his early volumes were so well satisfied.[17] These ever

[15] *History*, I, 1–2; III, 146, 151–53. From "equality" he took pains to exclude an equal distribution of wealth. See, *ibid.*, I, 442, and his *The Acquisition of Political, Social and Industrial Rights of Man in America* (Cleveland, Ohio, 1903), p. 90 (hereafter cited as *Rights of Man*).

[16] McMaster, "Old Standards of Public Morals," *American Historical Association Annual Report* for 1905 (Washington, 1906), I, 58 (hereafter cited as "Public Morals"). McMaster, *With the Fathers. Studies in the History of the United States* (New York, 1896), pp. 313–21 (hereafter cited as *With the Fathers*). McMaster, *History*, I, 98 ff.; II, 159.

[17] *History*, I, 32: "In the general advance of society from ignorance toward knowledge, the whole line was going forward. The tail was constantly coming up to where the head had been. . . . . Yet the distance between the head and the tail was as great as ever."

recurring themes flattered the pride, bolstered the patriotism, and squared with the dominant ethics of his contemporaries. His pages were eminently "safe," even for young readers.[18] But his loyalty to the way of life of his own generation and his eagerness to portray the great advance made during the nineteenth century sometimes led him to exaggerate the evils of the past.[19] By showing how much improvement had been made through a rapid but peaceful evolution under the rule of the people, he hoped that his *History* would be "full of instruction" to the social agitators of the 1880's and furnish Europe with such an object lesson on the benefits of democratic government "as will not be in vain." Thus, in the achievement of his didactic purpose, he seemed to encourage revolution abroad but was conservatively opposed to any sudden change at home. McMaster could be counted upon to defend the established law and order in the United States.[20]

He spoke for an intelligent and humane democracy, proud of its accomplishments, marching surely with the aid of science toward an even better future, ruled by a simple and dignified government, responsive to the infallible popular will, jealous of its honor, and conscious of its superiority over the monarchies beyond the seas. Democracy to him represented the ultimate goal toward which all governments and social life evolved. Its future, therefore, was secure. He never questioned that America was a democracy or that democracy and the Industrial Revolution were entirely compatible. The importance of the struggle between labor and capital entirely escaped him, and the wage-

---

[18] McMaster had great difficulty in finding a publisher for the first volume of his *History*. Mr. D. Appleton apparently decided to bring out the work after learning that the manuscript pleased his wife and children (*Oberholtzer*, p. 11).

[19] See especially, McMaster, *History*, I, 78, 98–102, 133 ff.; V, chap. xlix; VII, 199–201; *With the Fathers*, pp. 107, 238 ff. His wholly unfavorable picture of the educational situation in the South in the eighteenth century (*History*, I, 26–27) brought him a sharp rebuke from E. McCrady in his chapter entitled "Education in South Carolina Prior to and during the Revolution" in C. Meriwether (ed.), *History of Higher Education in South Carolina* (Washington, 1889), pp. 211–35.

[20] *With the Fathers*, p. 320; *History*, II, 616. McMaster championed freedom of speech and press as long as they were not used to incite forcible resistance to duly constituted authorities.

earner received scant attention in the eight volumes of his *History*. Time and again he pointed out the injustice of imprisonment for debt, but nothing more exasperated him than the advocacy of paper money by men burdened with financial obligations.[21]

Ever a gentleman in his outlook upon the past; occasionally prudish, or at least Victorian, in his ethical points of view; impatient with ignorance and irreverence for holy things, McMaster's democracy was not broad enough to include the Shaysites, the leaders of the French Revolution, the disorderly mobs of President Jackson's day, and the exercise of the suffrage privilege by ignorant foreigners.[22] Although he upheld the right of all men in America to share in their government, he admitted that democracy had adversely affected their art and literature.[23]

McMaster's faith in the ultimate rightfulness of the people was also qualified by his insistence that education was both the chief deterrent of crime and the essential cornerstone of any stable democracy.[24] In his view, courses in United States history should have a prominent place in the curriculum of every secondary school. The memorization of facts about America's past and a knowledge of the "fundamental principles" of her democracy would aid in making good citizens of the foreign-born and enable all young people better to understand the problems of their

[21] *History*, VI, 102. "Another movement [Mormonism] destined in our day to rise to an importance as serious as the struggle between capital and labor was by this time well under way in the West" (in *ibid.*, Vol. I, chap. i, of 102 pages, giving an overview of the United States in 1783, only three pages deal with the artisan class "concerning which our information is most imperfect" [p. 95]). But see *ibid.*, V, 82–88, 121–22. For his interest in prisoners for debt, see *ibid.*, IV, 535, and *Rights of Man*, pp. 49–51, 63–66. His dislike of paper money is evident in his *History*, I, 203, 281–95, 572–73; IV, 280 ff.; V, 161 ff.; "Wildcat Banking in the Teens," *Atlantic Monthly*, LXXII (September, 1893), 331–43; "Public Morals," pp. 58–60, 63–64.

[22] He also opposed both rum and lotteries. See his *History*, IV, 522–29.

[23] In his opinion, public officeholders were not more dishonest after the coming of universal manhood suffrage. In *ibid.*, IV, 580, he writes of "the Hall of the House of Representatives in the south building, the chamber now given up to the most hideous collection of statues ever gathered together in any land. . . . ."

[24] *Ibid.*, I, 351; IV, 539; V, 268, 287; VII, 157, 199–201.

own day.[25] To further the attainment of these goals, McMaster published, between 1897 and 1907, three textbooks for students of history in the primary, grammar, and high schools of the land. Their widespread and long-continued use attested their popularity. Except for the pages devoted to America's participation in the World War, which were added in the author's several later revisions, these volumes were written with commendable objectivity. In the high-school textbook McMaster attempted to cons gn "many things of secondary consequence" to long footnotes in order to reserve the narrative for "essentials." Barring this unique feature, the volume closely resembled its many competitors.[26]

Because McMaster was so partial to his own times, he was free from a too favorable bias toward the men and measures of the late eighteenth century, the period of all others in American history which "good" citizens held to be beyond reproach. Hildreth had pointed out a generation before, and McMaster also emphasized, that "the delegates to Annapolis and later to Philadelphia were brought together in response to the demands of the business men of the country, not to form an ideal plan of government but such a practical plan as would meet the business needs of the people."[27] Thus McMaster, like Hildreth, was a forerunner of the economic school of historians. The framers of the Constitution, however, were a "most remarkable assemblage of men, to whom, under God, we owe our liberty, our prosperity, our high place among the nations."[28] In McMaster's opinion,

[25] Remarks by McMaster in the American Historical Association *Annual Report* for 1896, I (Washington, 1896), 260–63; *American Historical Review*, X (New York, 1905), 497.

[26] See the Preface of McMaster, *A Brief History of the United States* (New York, 1907). See also his *A School History of the United States* (New York, 1897); *A Primary History of the United States* (New York, 1901); *Compendio de historia de los Estados Unidos tr. y. adaptación por Marcos Moré del Solar* (New York, 1902); *A Brief History of the United States, Adapted for Use in the California Schools* ("California State Series") (Sacramento, 1909); *New Grammar School History of the United States, Compiled by the State Text-Book Committee and Approved by the State Board of Education* (Sacramento, 1903).

[27] *Rights of Man*, p. 27; McMaster, *History*, III, 496.

[28] *History*, I, 399, 438, 533; III, 496; *With the Fathers*, pp. 181, 185, 238; McMaster, *The Life and Times of Stephen Girard, Mariner and Merchant* (2 vols.; Philadelphia, 1918), I, 94 (cited hereafter as *Stephen Girard*).

they dreamed of a society wherein all men should be equal, enjoying their inalienable rights. Although they provided a government suitable for such a utopia, they were wise enough to realize that the people of their own day were not ready for, and could not be given, complete liberty and equality. Since that time, however, Americans had been true to the vision of the Fathers.[29] Realistic in his assessment of the need for the federal convention, idealistic in his estimate of the intent and results of its labors, McMaster's work here, as so often, resembles a bridge between the old and the new in American historiography.

In 1883, when the first volume of the *History* appeared, a few critics noted, and rightfully so, that Thomas B. Macaulay's *A History of England from the Accession of James the Second* had strongly influenced McMaster's style and his conception of the duty of a historian.[30] Significantly enough, when he found occasion several years later to discuss Macaulay's shortcomings, he in effect also pointed out some of his own chief weaknesses.[31] In McMaster's opinion, Macaulay challenged attention by "the astonishing amount of information he could pour out on matters of even trivial importance." "We look in vain for the faintest approach to a philosophical or analytical treatment." Macaulay's "characters . . . . are mere pegs on which to hang a splendid historical picture of the times in which these people lived." McMaster might also have added that the distinguished Englishman had a high regard for newspapers as sources and often contrasted the "then" and the "now" in order to show progress. McMaster brought materials, hitherto but little used, to the writing of American history; and he gave new emphases to the story of his

[29] *Rights of Man*, pp. 14, 40–41, 122–23. "Public Morals," pp. 58, 66: "The preaching, as it should always be, was above the practice. The moral standard, as it should always be, was far in advance of the times. To the credit of the fathers many of them soon overtook it." In his *History*, I, 484, he states: "That the work [the *Federalist*] is a true statement of what the framers of that instrument [the Constitution] meant it to be cannot be doubted."

[30] *Hutchinson*, pp. 26–27 and 26 n.

[31] McMaster, "Thomas Babington Macaulay," in J. W. Cunliffe and A. H. Thorndike (eds.), *The World's Best Literature* (New York, 1917), XVI, 9381–86. This essay was first published in 1899.

country's past, but his originality in these respects was largely derivative.

McMaster seldom ventured to assign specific causes for particular events in history or to discuss their effects upon the future. Occasionally he pointed out that "accidents" were important, as when he asserted that "one gun from Sumter [in aid of the "Star of the West" on January 10, 1861] would have changed the current of events."[32] His usual method of presentation suggests, however, that he believed the duty of a historian to be discharged when he had re-created for his readers the "atmosphere" or general setting in which an event took place. At times the occurrence remains indistinct amid the preponderating shadow of its environment.[33] He hesitated to point his vast store of facts toward a conclusion. He was an assiduous accumulator of the material from which the past may be reconstructed, but he rarely summarized.

For this reason, McMaster's *History* is lacking in dynamic quality. Its long chapters often belie their titles and are a series of essays upon diverse subjects cemented together by a few words of transition into a superficial, rather than an essential, unity. Although the reader is furnished with successive cross-sections or horizontal views of the past, he finds no vertical thrust to carry him upward through the years. McMaster skilfully regiments his facts upon parade, but they do not march. This seems the more strange when it is remembered that he believed strongly in the reality of progress.

McMaster might have provided his *History* with unity and vitality if he had been willing to arrange his materials upon a framework of interpretation. That American society had evolved toward a higher civilization he firmly maintained; but this conviction was merely a point of view, not a thesis or philosophy

---

[32] McMaster, *History*, VIII, 508. On the other hand, he occasionally minimized the importance of "accidents." See his *The Life, Memoirs, Military Career, and Death of General U. S. Grant, with War Anecdotes and Freely Drawn Extracts from His Autobiography* (Philadelphia, 1884 [this date should surely be 1885]), p. 70 (cited hereafter as *U. S. Grant*).

[33] McMaster, *History*, Vol. II, chap. ix, almost loses the Jay Treaty in the lavishness of its setting.

sufficiently clear cut and commodious to serve as a mold into which to pour a detailed description of the complex life of half a continent. But McMaster held that the writing of critical essays was not the function of a historian.[34] In his view, "interpretations" distorted the past; they created a false unity out of a very real diversity and made the people of a century ago conform in their lives to "trends" of which they were not aware. McMaster was interested only in viewing the American scene from their own level, hedged in by their own limited horizon and unconscious of their place in the flowing pattern of life. Unlike most historians, he refused to subordinate the past to the present. Until historians can agree upon what is true, what is important, and what is the only proper way to write history, the rightfulness or wrongfulness of McMaster's method must be left for some future omniscience to judge.

One of McMaster's chief contributions to American historiography was his extensive use of newspapers as sources of great value. No later student could afford to neglect them after he had revealed the richness of their store. McMaster's dependence upon them largely determined his method of presentation and adversely affected his literary style. Without doubt, the morning journal has vitality; but its life is largely extinct as soon as the evening edition is ready for sale. Bizarre and exceptional events receive too much attention in the daily press, but the routine and really important aspects of the life of a community are usually given little space. When the newspapers made clear that the people were momentarily interested in some fad, fashion, or phenomenon, McMaster allotted more pages to it in his narrative than to those subjects, arousing little contemporary discussion, which were destined to be of primary significance in the years to come. As soon as the latter "made the news," they were noted in his *History;* but often without mention of the silent and slow development which alone could render them understandable.

Because of his wish to present all of the topics of current dis-

---

[34] *Oberholtzer*, pp. 24–25, 29–30.

cussion during a particular year in history and to keep in step dissimilar events occurring simultaneously, McMaster often jumped from one incompleted subject to another in order that each might reach its conclusion in its proper time relationship with the others. To pattern a chapter of history after the disparate items found in the press results in a mosaic of miscellaneous episodes with only their synchronous occurrence to serve as a cohesive force. McMaster's paragraphs are frequently either a compound of diverse views upon a single topic taken from a half-dozen journals or a paraphrase of one editor's comments upon a subject of current interest. His "on the one hand"—"on the other hand" method of presentation, followed by no conclusion of his own, makes for impartiality at the expense of interest and variety. By quoting so much, he was unable to avoid some repetitions of thought and facts. McMaster the compiler and editor not infrequently crowded out McMaster the author and historian.[35]

The newspapers of the Old South and Southwest were not used extensively by McMaster until the subject of his study was the twenty years before the Civil War. At all times he slighted the press of the Old Northwest. The journals of Montreal, London, and Paris were levied upon when occasion required. Although McMaster so stated but once in his footnotes, there is little doubt that he cited newspapers which he knew only from extracts published in other journals. To classify geographically all of the newspapers referred to by him would be a most tedious task because he abbreviated their titles and did not indicate their places of publication.

The accompanying table, giving an analysis of the source materials used by McMaster in his *History*, suggests that it is possible to exaggerate the extent of his reliance upon the press. His footnotes do not pass muster when gauged by the rigid standards of today, and most likely they fail to record all of the titles that he

[35] This is most evident in his *Stephen Girard*. That McMaster could write tersely is shown by his three chapters in Vol. VII of A. W. Ward, G. W. Prothero, and S. Leathes (eds.), *The Cambridge Modern History* (14 vols., London, 1902–11).

consulted in preparing his work.[36] McMaster elsewhere paid tribute to the writers of monographs, but he infrequently referred to them as sources of his own information.[37] Bancroft is

ANALYSIS OF J. B. McMASTER'S

History of the People of the United States*

Volume	Year of Publication	Period Covered	No. of Chapters	Pages of Text	Lines of Footnotes	MSS Collections	Printed Documents of National and State Governments	News-papers	Pamphlets	Magazines	Other Printed Sources	Second-ary Works	Totals
I.......	1883	1783–89	6	604	2,320	1	23	49	61	12	61	98	305
II......	1885	1789–1803	7	635	2,947	4	29	98	115	12	37	48	343
III.....	1892	1803–12	10	560	1,249	9	35	39	43	0	25	31	182
IV.....	1895	1812–21	16	601	807	3	29	33	18	2	12	17	114
V......	1900	1821–30	14	556	1,882	1	65	56	18	11	31	29	211
VI.....	1906	1830–42	17	637	1,497	5	48	88	20	3	12	27	203
VII....	1910	1841–50	15	614	1,549	6	85	134	18	7	43	20	313
VIII....	1913	1850–61	12	521	2,218	8	76	141	15	6	27	40	313
8......	30	78	97	4,728	14,469	37	390	638	308	53	248	310	1,984

* In this analysis each volume of the *History* is considered as a unit; and each separate newspaper, pamphlet, etc., is counted but once, no matter how many times it may be cited by the author throughout the volume. "Jackson Papers," "Poinsett Papers," "War Department Archives," are examples of a "MSS Collection" as the term is used in this analysis. It is evident that McMaster worked, or had copyists work, in the Library of Congress, in the archives of the executive departments in Washington, Ottawa, London, Paris, and Madrid, and in the collections of the Historical Society of Pennsylvania, the Astor and Lenox libraries (now New York Public Library), the New York Historical Society, the Buffalo Historical Society, the American Antiquarian Society, and the New Hampshire Historical Society.

McMaster, *History*, I, 35, 37, 39: "It is from this source [letters] alone that a just and accurate knowledge is to be obtained of many great events and many stirring times." In view of the sources used by McMaster in preparing his first volume he is here bearing witness against himself. But in *ibid.*, II, 57–58, he writes: "While the newspapers of that day [1790's] were as powerful in guiding public opinion as in our own, they were a much surer index to the state of the public mind" because they were "made up of contributions which came directly from the people or were copied from other gazettes." McMaster urged historians to go to documents for their materials (*Benjamin Franklin as a Man of Letters* [Boston, 1887], pp. 267–71). Here McMaster criticizes Temple Franklin for changing the language of some of his father's letters before publishing them. He adds that it is equally censurable to print all the trivialities a great man has written. McMaster, however, sometimes failed to quote accurately in his own works. Cf. *History*, V, 480, with *Register of Debates in Congress*, V (1828–29), 128, and *ibid.*, pp. 134–37, with *History*, V, 481–82. Also cf. *ibid.*, V, 500–501, with *Register of Debates in Congress*, II, Part II (1825–26), 1955–58. Strangely enough, McMaster in "A Pioneer in Historical Literature," *Atlantic Monthly*, LXXIII (April, 1894), 563, after stating that Washington in his old age altered some of the letters of his youth, added: "That [Jared] Sparks has followed these [alterations] does not matter in the slightest. The language, the spelling, the felicity of expression, are nothing. The facts and the information the letters contain are everything; and these things the work of Sparks has made accessible to us all."

[36] McMaster's footnotes are often so spaced that it is not clear how many pages of text are served by any one of them. See his *History*, Vol. III, chap. xvi. An amusing oversight by a proofreader will be found in a footnote on p. 374 of his *A History of the People of the United States during Lincoln's Administration* (New York, 1927), where the "Pickwick Papers," instead of the "Pickett Papers," are cited (this volume will be referred to hereafter as *Lincoln's Administration*).

[37] "Jameson, McMaster, and Channing," p. 21. In his *History*, V, 367 n., he calls S. B. Weeks, "The Beginnings of the Common School System in the South," in *Report* of the U.S. Commissioner of Education, 1896–97, "a model monograph of its kind."

said to have cautioned him not to throw too generous a largess to fellow-historians by disclosing the mines from which he was digging his gold.[38]

Because McMaster was accustomed to present the leading arguments on all sides of a controversial question without revealing his own views, his writings leave a general impression of impartiality. The following paragraphs, which summarize his opinions of particular institutions, sections, and individuals, do apparent violence to this conclusion; but they have been drawn from the several thousand pages of his works. They are conspicuous here because they are concentrated within a brief space; they stand out prominently in the original only because they are exceptional. McMaster was sometimes unable to hold his feelings in leash, letting "the most," "the greatest," "shameful," and other words similarly expressing a judgment, slip from his pen. If challenged, he would have been hard-driven to make a convincing defense of these terse, unqualified characterizations. The superlatives in one volume of his *History* occasionally contradict those used in another.[39]

Of the three branches of the central government, McMaster preferred that the legislature should be dominant. In his view, the chief executive should have no veto, the electoral college should be abolished, and the judiciary should be made elective.[40]

[38] *Oberholtzer,* p. 25.

[39] See his scathing remarks about the Fugitive Slave Law of 1793, the Sedition Act of 1798, and the Embargo Enforcement Act of 1808, in his *History,* II, 356, 397; III, 326; *Stephen Girard,* I, 397; and in his *Daniel Webster* (New York, 1902), p. 58. John Fiske and he were the authors of *Modern Development of the New World,* which is Vol. XXIII of *A History of All Nations* (Philadelphia, 1906). Of this volume, McMaster, according to a footnote on p. 366, wrote only the last 24 pages. In fact, on p. 267 Fiske calls himself "the author of the present work." The point of view throughout the volume is that of a conservative, antislavery, antitariff, anti-imperialistic, antisilver Democrat. Although McMaster's name appears on the title-page, the text, in its praise of free trade (pp. 44–45, 149), the Albany Regency (p. 79), John Tyler (pp. 86–87), the electoral college (p. 240), and an appointive judiciary (p. 22), contradicts his opinions as expressed in his *History.* On the relationship between McMaster and Fiske as historians, see *Oberholtzer,* p. 26, and *post,* pp. 150 n., 155.

[40] McMaster, *History,* III, 152. McMaster, "The Election of the President," *Atlantic Monthly,* LXXVIII (September, 1896), 336–37. He disliked the English cabinet type of government, unicameral legislatures, the spoils system, courts-martial, and frequent constitutional amendment.

He condemned the cloture rule of the House of Representatives because it denied to the minority the fullest opportunity to be heard. Congress should be a deliberative body and not merely an instrument for "registering the decrees of the majority."[41] As a broad constructionist and a nationalist, McMaster supported the First National Bank, protective tariffs, and internal improvements at the expense of the central government. He had no kind word for the newly formed Democratic Party of the 1790's when it was out of power, but severely criticized the Federalists for their factious opposition during President Jefferson's first administration.[42]

Men of genius, according to McMaster, were not needed in the White House, although to be sure the time had gone by when a president of the United States, no matter how able he might be, could overturn the democratic institutions of his country. "The average man is good enough [for President]," McMaster wrote, "and for him two terms are ample. We want a strong government of the people by the people, not the government of the people by a strong man, and we ought not to tolerate anything which has even a semblance of heredity."[43] "In this country," he continued later, "all questions of great importance are finally settled not by Presidents, nor by Congresses, nor by the legislatures of the States, but by the hard common sense of the people, who in their own good time and way have heretofore adjusted all difficulties wisely."[44] McMaster had no patience with "the idle pomp, the foolish waste of time and money, which now make memorable each inauguration day."[45]

Although he criticized early historians for emphasizing battles in their writings, he gave much space in his own *History* to the

[41] McMaster, *History*, III, 398; *With the Fathers*, p. 209.

[42] McMaster, *History*, II, 629; III, 197. But, as exceptions to this generalization, he condemned the Jeffersonians for repealing the Judiciary Act of 1801 and for their unjust handling of Pickering's impeachment (*ibid.*, II, 607; III, 173).

[43] *With the Fathers*, pp. 69–70. McMaster, *History*, V, 522: "No leader in our country can debase the people. He is exactly what the will of the people enables him to be, and the moment he ceases to execute that will he ceases to be a leader."

[44] *With the Fathers*, pp. 72, 252.   [45] McMaster, *History*, III, 336.

wars of 1812 and 1846 and wrote one large volume on the Civil War[46] and two on the World War.[47] The exploits of the American navy especially appealed to his interest and patriotism. They furnished a continuing bond of friendship between him and Theodore Roosevelt, whom he had first known when he was tutoring the children of Roosevelt's uncle.[48] McMaster was amazed at President Wilson's long-sustained patience from 1914 to 1917 in the face of repeated proofs of German atrocities and untrustworthiness.[49] No pacifist, the little professor, so fragile in appearance, had shot a mountain lion, hung the walls of his office with western scenes by Frederic Remington, and believed that "the evils of war [are] succeeded by the fruits of genius." There is, he asserted,

a great truth with which the history of every people is replete with examples, the truth that periods of national commotion, disorder, and contention are invariably followed by periods of intellectual activity. Whatever can turn the minds of men from the channels in which they have long been running, and stir them to their inmost depths, has never yet failed to produce most salutary and lasting results.[50]

McMaster was the first national historian to appreciate the importance of the West and to give it a significant place in the story of the United States. At a time when the "noble red man" was idealized by novelists and poets, McMaster wrote of him with a full awareness of his vices as well as his virtues. He

[46] McMaster, in his *Lincoln's Administration*, apparently used little documentary material except for his treatment of naval operations, blockade-running, and foreign affairs. Indeed, the chapters on these subjects are the chief contributions made by the volume to the general topic of the Civil War.

[47] McMaster, *The United States in the World War* (2 vols.; New York, 1918–20). This study mainly deals with war work in the United States. In view of McMaster's nearness to the events described, his task was a difficult one and was most creditably carried to completion. He, however, apparently believed that the Germans were the only propagandists.

[48] McMaster, *History*, IV, 70–120, 254. He here illustrated his accounts of the ship duels of the War of 1812 with some of the sketches which first appeared in Roosevelt's *Naval History of the War of 1812*. See also, *History*, II, 323, 388; III, 208, 507–48.

[49] McMaster, *The United States in the World War*, I, 35, 264–65, 330, 393.

[50] McMaster's encounter with the cougar was kindly called to my attention by Jay Monaghan (see *supra*, n. 10), who found the episode described in Roosevelt, *The Wilderness Hunter* (New York, 1910), III, 160–61. See also, *ibid.*, II, 132. For the quotation in the text, see McMaster, *History*, I, 77.

viewed the frontier realistically as a region where democracy was at home, although he did not anticipate the conclusions of Frederick Jackson Turner.[51] The farmer and his problems, except for his "perverse" desire to pay his debts with paper money, rarely appear in the forty-seven hundred pages which McMaster devoted to the life of a society predominantly rural in its attitudes and occupations. This omission is the most conspicuous "blind spot" in the entire *History*.

The middle states are usually the regional focus of this work. McMaster declined to retraverse ground already made familiar by his predecessors; and they, in his opinion, had accorded too much emphasis in their writings to the colonial period, the American Revolution, and New England. To McMaster, the ante bellum South was a backward region of plantations. Slavery, a "blot" on the fair name of America, was the all important basis and explanation of the civilization below Mason and Dixon's line. "Toil was the only thing," wrote McMaster, "from which the rich planter [of the 1780's] abstained. Horse-racing by day and deer-hunting by night, duelling and gambling, made up, with the social festivities of the class to which he belonged, his sole occupation and pleasure." This too-simple thesis, and this prejudice, denied him an understanding of the complex life of the South; but at least he was the first historian of northern birth to give that section as much space as New England in his writings.[52] Like Edward Channing, McMaster gained tolerance

[51] *Ibid.*, I, 5–8, 140, 159; II, 145, 285–86, 573 ff.; III, 146–52; V, 151–59; VII, 206. His description of a Methodist circuit rider (V, 159–60) represents McMaster at his best. F. J. Turner, "Recent Studies in American History," *Atlantic Monthly*, LXXVII (June, 1896), 840. McMaster's interest in the West is also shown by his editorship of *Trail Makers* (10 vols.; New York, 1904) and *History of the Expedition under the Command of Captains Lewis and Clark—With an Account of the Louisiana Purchase by J. B. McMaster* (New York, 1922), and by his articles, "The Struggle for the West," *Lippincott's Monthly Magazine*, XLIX (1892), 758–71, and "The Delivery of Louisiana to the United States," *Independent*, LV (1903), 2987–92.

[52] McMaster, *History*, I, 26–27, 70–74; II, 13–19; V, 184 ff.; VII, 228 ff. In *ibid.*, II, 15, he writes: "If the infamy of holding slaves belongs to the South, the greater infamy of supplying slaves must be shared by England and the North." McMaster strongly favored granting equal civil and political rights to the freedmen. He seemed to be unaware of the problem of the "color line" (W. E. Dodd, "Profitable Fields of Investigation in American History, 1815–1860," *American Historical Review*, XVIII, No. 3 [April, 1913], 535).

with age. His *History of the People of the United States during Lincoln's Administration*, published in 1927 and destined to be his valedictory, was accorded a cold reception by reviewers, who felt that the old master had not kept in touch with the improved methods of the new social historians. The volume, nevertheless, is praiseworthy for its almost complete lack of bias.[53]

Society interested McMaster more than its leaders, and the eight volumes of his *History* have no hero. He often, however, sat in judgment upon the men whom he was so reluctant to bring into his story. In general, the *History* is not the place to seek a judicious appraisal of any noteworthy figure of America's past. The author was ever more prone to criticize an individual than to praise him, and usually dismissed him from the narrative with a label of unqualified approval or censure for his share in only one episode of his whole career. Of thirty-five men taken at random from the pages of the *History*, only ten fare well in the author's hands. Washington, Jefferson, Madison, and Monroe certainly receive less than justice.[54] William Penn, Benjamin Franklin, Samuel Adams, and Daniel Webster were apparently McMaster's only favorites among the better-known leaders in American history up to the Civil War.[55] Perhaps his tendency to belittle prominent men reflected his own modesty and dislike of conceit.

In spite of the subordination of personalities in his major work, McMaster wrote four biographies. These vary widely in merit and represent the author both at his worst and at his best. His study of Ulysses S. Grant, published at the time of the general's death, does credit neither to the subject nor to the biographer. Doubtless this paper-bound volume was written under

[53] In this volume McMaster attributes the defeat of the Confederacy chiefly to the blockade and to the breakdown of morale after the Battle of Gettysburg and the fall of Vicksburg.

[54] Patrick Henry, John Hancock, Tom Paine, John Randolph, and Roger B. Taney were other leaders who found no favor in McMaster's sight. See *History*, I, 150, 490, 565; II, 336, 457–59, 517; III, 180–81, 399, 559; IV, 240. On Washington, see *ibid.*, II, 212, 415, 453; V, 28, 293–94 (here is a brief and belated eulogy, possibly in deference to the criticisms by McMaster's reviewers). On Jefferson, see *ibid.*, II, 51, 53, 103, 114, 159, 338, 419, 517, 603, 627; III, 69, 197, 219, 282, 303, 318; V, 366; VI, 30.

[55] *Ibid.*, I, 233, 422; IV, 213–14, 540–41; VII, 270.

forced draft—a hundred-page compilation of anecdotes, long quotations, and ill-considered eulogy thrown together at the behest of an impatient Philadelphia publisher. Taking McMaster at his word, he believed Grant to be the most illustrious American since the Revolution, a better general than Lee or Washington, and the man "to whom under God, we owe the salvation of the Republic."[56] The Mexican War, Presidents Tyler and Johnson, and General Halleck are sharply criticized. Lincoln hovers dimly in the background as "Grant's friend" who "would have been deposed and a dictator . . . . placed in his stead" if Vicksburg had not fallen.[57] Grant's "grave error," according to McMaster, was "to accept the presidency"; and his veto of the Inflation Bill was "the great act of his administration." "His fate was the fate of every deliverer, and the men who shouted 'Hosannah' one day cried 'Crucify' the next." Thus, in this biography McMaster indulged in the emotional bombast which he elsewhere so sharply condemned when used either by an orator or an author.[58] Judging from the degree to which this book reflects the "old history" and the antisouthern point of view of Reconstruction days, it was fortunate for McMaster's later reputation that his volumes on the years 1850–65 were still far in the future in 1885.[59]

Amid all that McMaster wrote, his *Benjamin Franklin as a Man of Letters* is outstanding for its compelling interest and pleasing style. The biography is not a eulogy. Franklin's irreverence, lax personal life, nepotism, and support of paper money overstrained the author's limited sense of humor and his stern in-

---

[56] *U. S. Grant*, pp. 28, 36, 71–72.

[57] *Ibid.*, pp. 19–20, 24, 28–30, 40–41, 73. Lincoln fares but little better in McMaster's *Lincoln's Administration*. Here (pp. 19, 529, 592) McMaster commends the president's kindness, magnanimity, and second inaugural address but devotes more attention to G. B. McClellan and J. P. Benjamin.

[58] *U. S. Grant*, pp. 35, 70, 73. *Benjamin Franklin*, pp. 54, 267: "He [Franklin] indulges in no silly flights of imagination; he assumes no air of learning; he uses no figures of speech save those the most ignorant of mankind are constantly using unconsciously; he is free from everything that commonly defaces the writings of young men." See also, *History*, II, 536.

[59] *U. S. Grant*, pp. 28–30. As late as 1927, McMaster was unable to conceal his dislike for President Johnson. See *Lincoln's Administration*, p. 592.

sistence upon the proprieties. In this volume, as in all others that bear McMaster's name, there are sweeping, inaccurate generalizations and long digressions. But the book well achieves its limited purpose and includes an excellent account of the eventful history of the famous *Autobiography* and of other Franklin manuscripts.[60]

After paying this tribute to the founder of the University which he served, McMaster then turned to Daniel Webster, whom he so much emphasized in his courses on constitutional history. As in the case of his study of Grant, the subject obliged the author to develop a theme which was at variance with the "essence" of history as defined by him in the opening pages of his major work. Although he there pointed out the basic importance of social and economic forces in history, he failed to use them to explain the career of the Massachusetts statesman. Webster's brilliant oratory in defense of the Constitution and the Union is the focus of the biography. The early partisan, states-rights Webster; and the aged, "behind-the-times" Webster of the seventh of March speech, are used as foils to enhance the glorious years of his life between 1830 and 1850. The volume merits little praise, and its earlier chapters appear to have been written for juvenile readers.[61]

One of the first scholarly biographies in United States business history appeared in 1907 from the pen of Ellis P. Oberholtzer, a former student of McMaster and for long his colleague at the University of Pennsylvania.[62] About a decade later, McMaster contributed a two-volume study of Stephen Girard to this new field of research. From its pages, so heavy with long quotations, much can be learned about the policies and problems of a leading merchant-shipowner in the early years of the Republic; but the man Girard remains submerged under his letters, his ledgers,

[60] *Benjamin Franklin*, pp. 45–48, 58, 63, 87–89, 158, 278. See also McMaster, "Franklin in France," *Atlantic Monthly*, LX (September, 1887), 318–26. McMaster's conception of the duty of a biographer is perhaps suggested in his *History*, V, 297, where he calls Thomas R. Lounsbury's *James Fenimore Cooper* (New York, 1883) "a model biography."

[61] *Daniel Webster*, pp. 64–65, 300, 324.

[62] Oberholtzer, *Jay Cooke, Financier of the Civil War* (2 vols.; Philadelphia, 1907).

and the cargo lists of his ships. This biography, nevertheless, is the most valuable of the four written by McMaster. Its preparation was doubtless a congenial task for a loyal Philadelphian, the son of a banker with an unflagging interest in money affairs and the sea.[63]

Yielding little to criticism and refusing to review the works of other historians, McMaster, with almost no change of method or technique, kept steadily at his task for over fifty years.[64] During the last quarter of the nineteenth century he was a pioneer, uncovering hitherto unused source materials, emphasizing new values in American history, and portraying long-forgotten episodes in the nation's story. Social and economic life, the West, the newspaper and pamphlet, and a picture of the past as it appeared to the people of the past are the terms which suggest McMaster's chief contributions to American historiography. Many of the new generation of scholars advanced along the path he first blazed, and a few of them found richer land than he was privileged to discover. But as the trail-maker, McMaster had the more arduous task. He was the first scholar to attune the written history of the United States to the spirit of her plain folk. Well has he been called the "Walt Whitman of American historiography."[65]

[63] K. W. Porter, "Trends in American Business Biography, " *Journal of Economic and Business History*, IV (August, 1932), 598–601.

[64] McMaster's death occurred at Darien, Connecticut, on May 24, 1932.

[65] R. F. Nichols, "An Appraisal of the 'History of American Life' series by a Political Historian," a paper read at the Providence meeting of the American Historical Association, on December 30, 1936.

VIII

JOHN FISKE

JENNINGS B. SANDERS
University of Tennessee

✳

EDMUND FISK GREEN (John Fiske)[1] was born at Hartford, Connecticut, March 30, 1842, the son of Edmund Brewster Green and Mary Fisk Bound Green. His father was a Whig editor and journalist and for a time was secretary to Henry Clay. Descended from Quaker and Puritan stock, the future philosopher-historian was reared in a typical New England home, neither rich nor poor, where the doctrines of Calvin and Jonathan Edwards were still taught and emphasized. He received his early education at private schools where chapel exercises and prayers were a part of the daily routine, and as a mere lad joined the Congregational church in Middletown, Connecticut. Much of his youth was spent in this town, where his musical bent found him a place in the choir of the North Church. He once taught a Sunday-school class there.[2]

All that we know about Fiske's early life indicates that he was very precocious. At the age of seven he was conning Caesar and

[1] In 1855, when his widowed mother married Edwin Wallace Stoughton, young Green had his name changed to "John Fisk," which name was legalized by the Superior Court of Connecticut. In 1860 he began spelling his name with an *e*. There had been several John Fisks in the family; Fiske's great-grandfather was of that name (John Spencer Clark, *The Life and Letters of John Fiske* [Boston and New York, 1917], I, 9–12, 55–56). Fiske dedicated his *The Dutch and Quaker Colonies in America* (Boston and New York, 1899) "To My Old Friend, John Spencer Clark."

[2] T. S. Perry, *John Fiske* (Boston, 1906), p. 4; Clark, I, 1, 3–8, 21–22, 37, 65–66, 79–80, 85.

had already read Charles Rollin's *Ancient History* and Oliver Goldsmith's *Grecian History*. Before he was eight he had been through the whole of Shakespeare and a good part of Milton, Bunyan, and Pope. At nine he began the study of Greek; and by eleven had read Gibbon, James C. Robertson, Prescott, and most of Froissart. At eleven he wrote from memory a chronological table from 1000 B.C. to 1820, filling a quarto blankbook of sixty pages; and at thirteen he had read the whole of Virgil, Horace, Tacitus, Sallust, and Suetonius and much of Livy, Cicero, Ovid, Catullus, and Juvenal. Moreover, he had gone through Euclid, plane and spherical trigonometry, surveying, navigation, and analytic geometry, as well as into differential calculus. At fifteen he completed his studies at Betts Academy, Stamford, with the highest record ever attained there. By this time he could translate Plato and Herodotus at sight and had begun German; and he had written essays on such topics as the ancient Romans, the Augustan era, and the Crimean War. When he was sixteen he kept his diary in Spanish and was reading French, Italian, and Portuguese. These three languages, as well as German, he learned without the aid of a teacher. The next year he began the study of Hebrew; and a year later, Sanskrit.[3]

Such was the equipment of the stripling who, at seventeen and eighteen, began to entertain some doubts as to the soundness of the orthodox Christianity in which he had been reared. He rejected the Congregational dogma; and in an age when the foundations of Christian faith were being tested, he refused to accept the Bible as the divinely inspired source of authority. Relatives and friends, as well as the pastor of the North Church, labored to win him from his "backsliding," but all to no avail. His minister, who apparently had difficulty in meeting Fiske's arguments, gave him up for lost and proceeded to damn him publicly. Religiously and socially the young intellectual was ostracized. The budding Unitarian became the "infidel of the North Church."[4]

[3] Clark, I, 63, 67, 69–70; Perry, pp. 8–9; "A Well-equipped Historian," *Critic*, O.S. XXVI, 310.

[4] Clark, I, 88–102, 115–17, 119–28.

This fact seems to have had an important bearing upon Fiske's choice of a college in which to continue his education. All along, he had thought of going to Yale, and to that end passed the Freshman entrance examination there. Having done so, it appears that he concluded Harvard had the more difficult curriculum and the more liberal atmosphere, and in consequence he determined to attend the Cambridge institution. In 1860, after some special preparatory work at Cambridge, Fiske entered Harvard as a Sophomore, and was graduated three years later.[5]

At Harvard, Fiske continued his linguistic pursuits, adding Icelandic, Gothic, Danish, Swedish, Dutch, Rumanian, and a smattering of Russian. In addition, he began to study philosophy and comparative philology and to gain some knowledge of science from textbooks. He wrote essays on Darwinism and related subjects, an interest that was to culminate some years later in his *Outlines of Cosmic Philosophy*.[6]

By the time Fiske reached the Junior year, he was already known as a Darwinian and as a disciple of Ralph Waldo Emerson and Theodore Parker. The Harvard faculty thereupon kept a watchful eye on the young man; and when he was observed reading Comte during divine service, a thing Harvard students are said to have done for years, he was brought before the faculty and severely admonished. He was accused of insulting the Christian faith; and so bitter were the president and some of the professors toward him, that only an apology by Fiske and a strong defense by liberal friends on the faculty kept him from being dismissed from the college.[7]

The department of history at Harvard, during Fiske's student days there, appears not to have been a strong one. Professor Henry W. Torrey and one assistant were in charge of instruction, and this was limited to Freshmen and Seniors. Professor Torrey was unprepared for his work and seems to have dropped into history "in a friendly sort of way." "Better historic instruction," says one biographer of Fiske, "is now given in the public high schools."[8]

[5] *Ibid.*, pp. 71–77, 85–87, 145; Perry, p. 19.
[6] Perry, pp. 8–13, 24. [7] Clark, I, 231–35. [8] *Ibid.*, pp. 154–55.

The Civil War seems not to have interested Fiske much at first; he was too deeply engrossed in his studies and in the current philosophic stirrings to be diverted. But by 1862 he was aroused by the great conflict, though not sufficiently to compel him to abandon his books and to enter the ranks. He followed the campaigns closely and became a warm defender of Lincoln's administration. He called slavery a "fiendish institution" and wished the war to result in its abolition. Having no sympathy for opponents of the war, he once wrote that he thought it would be well if Lincoln hanged the Democratic leaders and ousted McClellan from the army.[9]

After his graduation from the college in 1863, Fiske entered the Harvard Law School, and received the LL.B. degree two years later. Meanwhile, in 1864, he was admitted to the Boston bar and was married to Abby Morgan Brooks. By the next year, being convinced that the law was not his calling, he looked about for other employment.[10] Fortunately for him, the liberals at Harvard gained the upper hand, and Charles W. Eliot was elected president. Fiske was then made a lecturer on philosophy, and, for one brief period, an acting professor of history. His tenure was short. Harvard was still too orthodox to tolerate an exponent of Darwinism; and the Board of Overseers dismissed him, charging that he was an atheist, a positivist, and a materialist.[11] But in 1872 he was given an appointment at Harvard in which, presumably, he could not be dangerous; this was the position of assistant librarian at a salary of $2,500, which place he held until 1879.[12]

While the library post offered Fiske an opportunity to read widely in history and other subjects, it did not permit him to

[9] *Ibid.*, pp. 236–39, 241.

[10] *Ibid.*, pp. 268, 283, 299, 304; Perry, p. 19.

[11] *Dictionary of American Biography* (New York, 1931), VI, 421. Fiske moved to Cambridge in 1867, where he engaged in the writing of essays and reviews. His nomination as acting professor of history for the spring term, 1870, was confirmed by a bare majority. Clark, I, 328, 373–74; Perry, p. 26.

[12] Perry, p. 28; Clark, I, 399. Fiske was for long a member of the Harvard Board of Overseers. See the "Biographical Sketch" in Fiske, *The War of Independence* (Boston and New York, 1889), p. viii.

accomplish much in the way of writing. A grant of $1,000 from a friend and a year's leave of absence in 1873 enabled him to go to England; and there, in "beloved London," his *Outlines of Cosmic Philosophy* appeared in 1874. In 1878 his friends hoped he would be appointed to the chair of history resigned by Henry Adams, but in this they were disappointed.[13] Nevertheless, Fiske was then on the threshold of a new and important period in his career.

One biographer has said about Fiske: "He wrote on various subjects as circumstances suggested, and found himself gradually drifting towards History."[14] Although it was not until after 1886 that most of his writings in this field were published, he appeared definitely in the role of a historical lecturer in 1879, when, employed by Mrs. Mary Hemenway, a wealthy lady of Boston, he delivered a series of addresses on American history in the Old South Church. These were enthusiastically received. After his second appearance, Fiske wrote to his mother: "I had a sort of sense that I was fascinating the people and it was delicious beyond expression." With the stamp of Boston's approval upon him, the young lecturer was now on the road to success. Arrangements were made for him to give the lectures at University College, London, in 1879; and his success there far exceeded his fondest expectations.[15] In 1881 he lectured at Washington University, St. Louis, and three years later was appointed its nonresident professor of history.[16]

Desirous at first of producing a work in American history similar to Green's *Short History of the English People*, Fiske entered into an agreement with Harper's in 1881 to write a two-or three-volume account of the United States from the earliest days

---

[13] J. Fiske, *Essays Historical and Literary* (2 vols. in 1; New York, 1925), II, 204; Clark, II, 69–70.

[14] Perry, p. 37.

[15] Clark, II, 109–11; Perry, pp. 39–42.

[16] Perry, p. 47. In 1889 Fiske referred to his position at the St. Louis institution as that of "University Professor of American History." Fiske, *The Beginnings of New England: Or the Puritan Theocracy in its Relation to Civil and Religious Liberty* (Boston and New York, 1889), p. v.

to the inauguration of Garfield. Six years later, however, the agreement was annulled. According to one biographer, Fiske had become convinced that he could not compress his materials within the narrow limits set for him by the company, and he was unwilling to undertake the publication of a larger work. However this may have been, it is of some interest that Fiske, late in life, made use of the materials assembled for the Harper's work in writing a three-volume survey of American history for "A History of All Nations" series. Shortly after the annulment of his agreement with Harper's, he made a contract with Houghton Mifflin and Company, providing for cash advances to him and permitting him to lecture three months each year.[17] For these reasons, the question arises: Did Fiske fear that a three-volume survey of American History, coming out in 1888 or thereabouts, would militate against his writing more books in that field and reduce interest in his historical lectures by making known the gist of his thoughts?

With publication assured, Fiske became a prolific writer, covering no less than the history of America from the earliest times to approximately the year 1900, although his major work was contained in the eleven volumes treating the period prior to 1789. The seven studies in this series were: *The Discovery of America with Some Account of Ancient America and the Spanish Conquest* (2 vols.), *The Beginnings of New England: Or the Puritan Theocracy in Its Relation to Civil and Religious Liberty* (1 vol.), *Old Virginia and Her Neighbors* (2 vols.), *The Dutch and Quaker Colonies* (2 vols.), *New France and New England* (1 vol.), *The American Revolution* (2 vols.), and *The Critical Period of American History, 1783–1789* (1 vol.).[18] For *A History of All Nations*, Fiske wrote a three-volume series on the history of the Americas: *Colonization*

---

[17] Clark, II, 338-39, 376, 395-98. In the *Atlantic Monthly*, a Houghton Mifflin Co. publication, appeared articles by Fiske in 1886 on themes treated later in his *The American Revolution* (Boston, 1891) and his *The Critical Period of American History, 1783–1789* (Boston and New York, 1888). See the *Atlantic Monthly*, LVII, 46–66; LVIII, 77–78, 376–85, 648–66.

[18] These eleven volumes were published by the Houghton Mifflin Co. between 1888 and 1902.

of the New World; Independence of the New World; and *Modern Development of the New World.*[19] Miscellaneous works include *American Political Ideas Viewed from the Standpoint of Universal History, Three Lectures Delivered at the Royal Institution of Great Britain in May, 1880; The War of Independence* (in "Riverside Literature" series); *The Mississippi Valley in the Civil War;*[20] and *Essays Historical and Literary* (2 vols.).[21] He wrote the text books *Civil Government in the United States* and *A History of the United States for Schools.*[22] Interlarded with these twenty-one volumes of history were books and articles on philosophical and other subjects. And in the midst of the extensive labors necessary for so large a production, Fiske found time to deliver hundreds of lectures in different parts of the country.[23]

Considering his works, not in the order of their publication

[19] *A History of All Nations,* Vols. XXI–XXIII (Philadelphia and New York, 1905–6). The first two volumes in this series bear the name of Fiske as the author; the third volume bears the names of Fiske and John Bach McMaster as joint authors. This last point is of some interest; for on p. 366 of this last volume there is a note stating that Fiske wrote the account down to that point—through the Treaty of Paris, concluding the Spanish-American War—and that McMaster wrote the remaining pages, twenty-four in number, carrying the narrative down to Theodore Roosevelt's accession to the presidency. Again, the prefatory statement in the first volume raises some questions. According to it, the editor compiled the tables of contents for the three volumes and added some pages to the third volume. But as has been seen, McMaster wrote the additional pages for the third volume. Query: What, if anything, had McMaster to do with the first two volumes and the first three hundred and sixty-six pages of the third volume?

[20] These three volumes were published in 1885, 1889, and 1900, respectively.

[21] Two vols. in one; New York, 1925 (original edition, New York, 1902). This work contains sketches and estimates of the careers of Thomas Hutchinson, Charles Lee, Alexander Hamilton, Thomas Jefferson, James Madison, Andrew Jackson, and Daniel Webster, and also has an essay on the Harrison-Tyler ascendancy. Four additional essays are entitled: "Old and New Ways of Treating History," "The Fall of New France," "Connecticut's Influence on the Federal Constitution," "The Deeper Significance of the Boston Tea Party." Fiske previously had written biographical sketches of Charles Lee, Jefferson, Madison, Jackson, and Webster, for *Appleton's Cyclopedia of American Biography* (6 vols.; New York, 1888–89), edited by Fiske and James Grant Wilson. See Fiske, *Essays Historical and Literary,* I, vii.

[22] The first of these texts appeared in 1890; the other in 1894 and in several later editions.

[23] From 1888 to 1893 Fiske delivered five hundred and twenty-seven lectures on historical subjects, fourteen on philosophy, and six on music. Perry, pp. 47–48. Fiske had some ability in music as a pianist, critic, and composer (Fiske, *The War of Independence,* pp. xiii–xiv).

but in the order of the chronological periods treated by them, *The Discovery of America* comes first to attention. Perhaps the best of all his histories, this study was "the outcome of two lines of study pursued, with more or less interruption from other studies, for about thirty years." When the speed with which he produced his other volumes is borne in mind, this statement appears to be significant. Another prefatory remark is of even greater interest: "The present book is in all its parts written from the original sources of information."[24] And while this assertion doubtless is not to be taken literally, the notes in the book do cite and make reference to a vast amount of source material. Fiske's unusual command of languages served him to good purpose in the preparation of this particular study; he cites works in French, German, Greek, Latin, Spanish, Italian, Portuguese, Icelandic, and in the Scandinavian languages.

Developing the two themes which he had chosen for the work, namely, aboriginal America and the discovery of America, Fiske gave one hundred and forty-seven pages to the first topic, and over nine hundred and fifty to the second. He interpreted "the discovery of America" as being something more than what was accomplished by the well-known voyages of discovery; it was made to embrace the history of Spanish rule in the Indies, of the conquest of Mexico and Peru, of exploration in what are now the southern and southwestern portions of the United States, of the circumnavigation of the globe by Magellan and Drake, of French discovery and exploration in the St. Lawrence and Mississippi valleys and in the West, and of the work of Davis, Frobisher, and Bering. Naturally enough, the role of Spain in discovery and conquest receives the most attention in this book; and, believing in the right of civilized men to conquer the less civilized, Fiske, while not condoning much that the Spaniards did, finds full justification for their main accomplishment. If Spaniards are to be condemned, reasoned Fiske, so must our own forefathers, who conquered and dispossessed the Indians. They would have justified themselves by saying that "they were founding Christian

[24] *Discovery of America*, I, v, x.

states and diffusing the blessings of a higher civilization; and such, in spite of much alloy in the motives and imperfection in the performance, was certainly the case." And as for the Spaniards, they doubtless "did introduce a better state of society into Mexico than they found there."[25]

His *The Beginnings of New England*, tracing the history of that region to 1689, contained "the substance" of lectures given at Washington University. Moreover, the author had just read *The Emancipation of Massachusetts*, by Brooks Adams, his "former pupil," and had found himself "often agreeing" with "the specific conclusions" of that book. Except for a forty-nine-page chapter on "The Roman Idea and the English Idea," tracing the oriental, Roman, and English methods of nation-building and showing the importance of the fusion of the Teutonic idea of representation and the Greek idea of federation, there is nothing striking about the book. The usual facts are set forth in a lucid manner, and the account of controversies that rent New England society in the seventeenth century appears singularly fair. The book has few footnotes, but it does have an annotated bibliography of certain source materials and secondary works.[26]

Fiske's next book in this important series was *Old Virginia and Her Neighbors*, running to over seven hundred pages and dealing with the southern region to 1753. The author stated in the Preface that "more than five years" had elapsed since the appearance of his *Discovery of America* but that he hoped his next book would appear "after a much shorter interval." The succeeding work, *The Dutch and Quaker Colonies in America*, "already in preparation" when the foregoing preface was written, actually left the press only two years later. Of these two books, the first is decidedly the better. Neither has a bibliography, although there are scattered footnotes, some of which make reference to sources. It is the manner of telling the story, not the story itself—for that

---

[25] *Ibid.*, II, 291–92. Fiske here rather contradicts a statement made in his *The Dutch and Quaker Colonies in America*, I, 136: "Not a rood of ground was taken by the settlers of New England without paying for it, except in the single instance where the Pequots rashly began a war and were exterminated."

[26] *Beginnings of New England*, pp. v–vi, 279–87.

was already well known—that makes these two accounts of interest.

Much the same judgment must be given regarding his *New France and New England*, a work which resumes the colonial story where it had been dropped in his earlier books, and traces the history of the intercolonial wars through the Quebec campaign of 1759. The book was published posthumously, "only the first two chapters" having been revised by the author for the press; however, "the text of all the chapters" was printed "as it left his hand."[27] Interested in intellectual history, Fiske here dealt at relatively great length with the witchcraft delusion and the "Great Awakening." In handling both topics, he apparently sought to be fair.[28] Despite his early reputation as an irreligious man—a charge which perhaps can best be refuted by his own writings—Fiske could say that the Great Awakening "certainly did much to heighten and deepen the religious life in New England."[29]

In *The American Revolution* certain features are outstanding: (1) the bulk of the discussion of the Revolution on its causal side has to do with the northern colonies, especially New England; (2) the internal revolution—social, economic, and political—is overlooked by the author; (3) the Revolution is made to appear as having been a decorous, conservative movement in which English, as well as American, liberty was at stake; (4) discussions of political conditions in England during the Revolutionary epoch are written with remarkable clarity, and accounts of military campaigns in America are interesting and suggestive.

Since it is a theme that recurs from time to time in Fiske's writings, particular attention must be directed to his conception of the movement in this country that resulted in the independence of the United States. The assertion that labor disturbances of his own day, such as the railroad strikes, "accompanied with

[27] *New France and New England*, pp. vi–vii.

[28] Thomas Fisk, a forbear of John Fiske, was foreman of a jury that condemned a witch (*ibid.*, pp. 174–75).

[29] *Ibid.*, pp. 222, 232.

savage attempts at boycotting," were not different in principle
from the Boston Tea Party drew from Fiske a stout rejoinder.
The nature of the upheaval in Boston in 1765, he insisted, must
not be confused with that of the famous episode of 1773. The
mob's destruction of Thomas Hutchinson's house in 1765 was
"an event in the history of crime, and belongs among such incidents as fill the Newgate Calendar." It was, he says, condemned
by the Massachusetts people. The Boston Tea Party, however,
was an event in which figured some of the most prominent and
wealthy of Boston's citizens; and, although illegal, as was the
Stamp Act Riot of 1765, it "will always remain a typical instance
of what is majestic and sublime."[30] Moreover, in writing of the
"Boston Massacre," Fiske asserted that by then our forefathers
had "reached a point where any manifestation of brute force in
the course of a political dispute was exceedingly disgusting . . . .
to them."[31]

Fiske could not bring himself to admit that revolutions as a
rule are not polite affairs; nor could he regard the tarring and
feathering, the assaults upon private property, and the occasional
assertiveness of the unenfranchised as properly a part of the Revolution. And yet to view that movement chiefly as an event in the
history of political metaphysics would seem, at best, naïve.

In his opinion the patriots fought for English, as well as
American, freedom;[32] but if we may use his writings elsewhere as
an authority, this aspect was unappreciated by the rank and file
in England. After Saratoga, says he, "while the great majority
of the British nation believed that America must be retained at
whatever cost, a majority of this majority believed that it must
be conquered before it could be conciliated or reasoned with;
. . . ."[33] To his way of thinking, the ascendancy of the younger
Pitt marked the failure of George III's despotic system, a system
which he had sought to fasten upon America the better to enable

[30] Fiske, *Essays Historical and Literary*, II, 164, 173, 195.

[31] Fiske, *The American Revolution*, I, 71.

[32] Fiske, *The Critical Period*, pp. 1–2, 48–49.   [33] *The American Revolution*, II, 7.

him to fasten it upon England.[34] Thus, all unawares to the majority of Englishmen, Americans saved England from the shackles of tyranny, and won their own independence in the bargain! Our Revolution was not for the purpose of securing new freedom so much as for retaining the old; it was "in no respect destructive" but, on the contrary, "was the most conservative revolution known to history, ..."[35]

In *The Critical Period of American History, 1783–1789*, Fiske dealt with the treaty concluding the Revolutionary War, with the trials and tribulations of the Confederation and the states, and with the framing and ratification of the Constitution. Clearly told, the story seems to contain but few, if any, topics that cannot be found treated in greater detail in works already published at that time, especially the first volume of John Bach McMaster's *A History of the People of the United States*. Indeed, in his bibliographical annotations, Fiske wrote: "I take pleasure in acknowledging my indebtedness to Professor McMaster for several interesting illustrative details."[36]

Of Fiske's miscellaneous writings, *The Mississippi Valley in the Civil War* is especially useful. It appears to have been based upon lectures first given in St. Louis "in aid of a fund for erecting a monument to General Grant." During much of the war, Fiske had followed the campaigns with interest, using large maps and marking the movements of the armies with red- and blue-headed pins. By way of preparation for the book under consideration, he said that he "had due recourse to the abundant printed sources of information" and had had personal association with many of the actors in the great drama. Moreover, he was for thirty years intimately acquainted with John Codman Ropes.[37] The book is

[34] John Fiske, "Political Consequences in England of Cornwallis's Surrender at Yorktown," *Atlantic Monthly*, LVII, 66.

[35] *The Critical Period*, pp. 64, 88–90.

[36] *Ibid.*, p. 352. In the preface to the first edition of this book Fiske stated that his work made "no pretensions to completeness" but that he had tried to group facts "in such a way as to bring out and emphasize their causal sequence, ..." (*ibid.*, p. v). See also E. P. Oberholtzer, in the *Pennsylvania Magazine of History and Biography*, LVII, 26.

[37] *The Mississippi Valley in the Civil War*, pp. v, vi, viii.

especially well written and is illustrated with excellent maps designed by the author. While he expresses his opinions freely, even on purely military matters (General Sherman presided at the St. Louis lectures!), he held them, according to his preface, subject to revision.[38]

Not peculiar to any particular book, but running through Fiske's histories in general, are certain dominant views, theories, and prejudices. One of these was the question of the currency, and in his discussion of it the author made some of his most caustic and extravagant statements. Regardless of the period he was describing, he lost no opportunity to condemn currency inflation or any other policy which, to his way of thinking, looked toward the establishment of an "unsound" monetary system.

In describing the powers of the Virginia council of 1607, Fiske observed that they included the right to coin money "for circulation in the colony only—a kind of currency with which Americans of divers generations seem to have been very much in love, inasmuch as from time to time we have seen political parties cite it as the crowning merit of a currency that nobody can take it out of the country, which is very much like praising spring-water by saying that it refuses to flow."[39] Moreover, Massachusetts in 1690 issued bills of credit, a "curse" with which "the colony was plagued for more than forty years."[40] One of the meritorious traits of Thomas Hutchinson's character was revealed by his opposition to the Massachusetts Land Bank.[41] And our foreign relations during the Confederation period, troublous as they were, "were less alarming than the universal demoralization attendant upon the disturbances of trade

[38] "In treating such a subject as the present one, the difficulties in ensuring complete accuracy of statement and perfect soundness of judgment are manifold. If my opinions are sometimes strongly expressed, they are always held subject to revision" (*ibid.*, p. ix).

[39] Fiske, *Colonization of the New World*, p. 244.

[40] Fiske, *Independence of the New World*, p. 29.

[41] Fiske, *Essays Historical and Literary*, I, 13–15, 22. "Pretty much the same nonsense was talked in 1737 as afterward in 1786, and yet again in 1873." According to Fiske, it was largely due to Hutchinson that Massachusetts was financially able to enter upon the Revolution. But did not Rhode Island also enter upon the Revolution, despite "the poverty-stricken condition" of that colony resulting from paper money issues?

caused by an unsound paper currency." The years 1783–87 were "a true Bryanite paradise." Fiske repeatedly said that "the soundest ideas about money" were held by people of the coastal region, "while the wildest delusions prevailed among the inland farmers." The leader of the famous rebellion of 1786 in Massachusetts "was a rather feeble creature named Daniel Shays. . . . ."[42]

It was "the opinion of the convention" of 1787 that congressional issues of inconvertible paper currency were contrary to the public welfare and should be prohibited. However, some of the Fathers thought that in time of war the federal government should have the power. "Out of deference to these short-sighted objectors, the prohibition was not extended to the United States."[43] It was due to this weakness on the part of the framers of the Constitution that "the way was left open for that frightful calamity, the legal-tender act of 1862, in comparison with which all the other evils wrought by our civil war count almost as nothing."[44] This act was in "flagrant violation of the Constitution." Those men of 1787 who opposed federal paper-money issues would have insisted upon an express prohibition could they "have foreseen the possibility of such extraordinary judgments as have lately emanated from the Supreme Court of the United States. . . . ."[45]

In harmony with these views, Fiske regarded Grant's veto of the Inflation Bill of 1874 as one of the two cardinal events of his time, the other one being the settlement of the Alabama Claims. Grant's veto, says Fiske, was "a service to his country for which he deserves as much credit as for any of his victories in the field."[46]

Approaching the silver phase of the money question, Fiske as-

[42] Fiske, *Independence of the New World*, pp. 297–99.

[43] *Ibid.*, p. 312; Fiske, *The Critical Period*, p. 275.

[44] Fiske, *Independence of the New World*, p. 312.

[45] Fiske, *The Critical Period*, pp. 275–76. Fiske here apparently was referring to the case of *Juilliard* v. *Greenman*, 1884, upholding the constitutionality of the greenbacks' legal tender quality.

[46] Fiske, in Fiske and McMaster, *Modern Development of the New World*, p. 218.

serted that the agricultural sections of the country, particularly those of the South and West, knew little of monetary theory or practice. His explanation of the "Crime of 1873" reveals his own lack of understanding of the background of that measure.

In 1873 Congress passed an act demonetizing silver. Previous to that time, both gold and silver had been legal tender; and no harm was done, so long as the old ratio between their values remained steady, so that a silver dollar was really equivalent to a gold one. But with the increased output of silver-mines, as well as from other causes, silver presently began to decline and the old ratio was permanently disturbed. *Then* Congress proceeded to do the right thing when it took away the legal-tender character of silver and converted it into token-money.[47]

Equally unsatisfactory is his discussion of the Bland-Allison Act of 1878, which, he says, "provided that the Secretary of the Treasury should purchase sufficient bullion to coin the minimum amount of $2,000,000 a month in silver dollars . . . . ."[48] If Tilden had been president instead of Hayes, the Democratic House probably would never have passed this measure; but if it had done so, "it would *surely* not have passed it over the President's veto, for Tilden had his party well under control." Hence it was that "that silver incubus" was fastened upon the country. With the same air of omniscience Fiske wrote that Cleveland would have vetoed the Sherman Silver Purchase Act had he been president at the time of its passage.[49]

The presidential campaign of 1896 evidently was nauseating to our philosopher-historian. The Democratic party "chose for its candidate one William Jennings Bryan, of Nebraska, a Populist who had scarcely been heard of outside of his own neighborhood." The "National" or "Gold" Democrats, however, possessed "sound principles" and nominated John McCauley Palmer, of Illinois, who "was beyond all comparison the ablest and strongest of the candidates nominated that year for the chief office." This last group of Democrats stood for the gold standard, for the separation of government from banking, for currency reform, and for the "repeal of our abominable navigation laws."

47 *Ibid.*, p. 232 (italics mine).   48 *Ibid.*, p. 233.   49 *Ibid.*, pp. 234, 246 (italics mine).

They also opposed protectionism. Fiske seems to have regarded the Silverites as ignorant, dishonest, and even blasphemous. "What can be expected from people who can read the legend on one of our so-called silver dollars and not be struck with the blasphemy of declaring our trust in God upon a piece of metal which embodies the falsehood that forty is equal to a hundred?"[50]

If currency inflation was one of Fiske's pet aversions, no less so was a protective tariff, a subject for which he reserved some of his choicest invective. In his lecture "Manifest Destiny," delivered at the Royal Institution of Great Britain in 1880, he spoke of "our shameful tariff—falsely called 'protective'. . . . ." "Born of crass ignorance and self-defeating greed, it cannot bear the light." It was a "curse to American labour—scarcely less blighting than the curse of negro slavery—. . . . ."[51]

These convictions as to the tariff appear to have grown with the years, and in a later work Fiske unburdened himself without limit upon the "iniquitous" policy. "But it is characteristic of the tariff habit, as of the alcohol habit, that the more you get, the more you crave." Moreover, he added, protective tariffs "are infractions of the Constitution which never gave to Congress any power to levy taxes for any other object than revenue. . . . ." They "are really legalized robbery, since no power on earth has any moral right to make me pay twice the normal price for my coat in order to benefit some woolen-manufacturer; . . . ." To Fiske, the protectionist policy was "an engine of corruption as insidious and poisonous as the spoils system."[52]

Opposition to protectionism was but a phase of Fiske's general dislike of all governmental policies that smacked of paternalism.[53] Condoning Hamilton's economic program because of the

[50] *Ibid.*, pp. 251–52.

[51] John Fiske, *American Political Ideas Viewed from the Standpoint of Universal History*, p. 149.

[52] Fiske, in Fiske and McMaster, pp. 242, 245.

[53] Fiske wrote of "the barbarous superstitions of the Middle Ages concerning trade between nations" and noted how they persisted into the late eighteenth century (*The Critical Period*, p. 134).

extraordinary emergency of his day, he felt, nevertheless, that those Americans of 1789–91 who feared that control by the rich would result from the shrewd Secretary of the Treasury's schemes had good reason to be alarmed; "for now after the lapse of a hundred years the gravest danger that threatens us is precisely such a plutocracy!" The Hamiltonian alliance with financiers and manufacturers prepared the way for more and more paternalism on the part of the federal government, until in the administration of John Quincy Adams "there was fast growing up a tendency toward the mollycoddling, old granny theory of government, according to which the ruling powers are to take care of the people, build their roads for them, ... rob Peter to pay Paul for carrying on a losing business, and tinker and bemuddle things generally." It was Jackson, says Fiske, who checked this tendency; and "Old Hickory's" instincts usually led him aright in government. But neither the General nor his successors were able completely to arrest the evil, and in Fiske's own time the menace of those seeking governmental favors still was great. Said he, "our political freedom and our social welfare are to-day in infinitely greater peril from Pennsylvania's iron-masters and the owners of silver mines in Nevada than from all the ignorant foreigners that have flocked to us from Europe. Our legacy of danger for this generation was bequeathed to us by Hamilton, not by Jefferson."[54]

Another theme that runs through Fiske's historical writings is the superiority of the civilization of English-speaking peoples and the desirability of uniting them more closely. Beginning in 1873, he visited England several times, and counted among his acquaintances there Spencer, Huxley, Darwin, Green, Freeman, and other men of almost equal prominence.[55] As has been noted already, his book *Outlines of Cosmic Philosophy* was written in London. He felt that he had much in common with English

[54] Fiske, *Essays Historical and Literary*, I, 130, 174, 179, 310–11, 324; II, 158–59. Fiske saw a direct connection between the experience of the Connecticut towns under "The Fundamental Orders" and the federal-national arrangement adopted at the Philadelphia Convention of 1787. He condemned Clay's American System as economically unsound.

[55] *Ibid.*, II, 204, 218, 248. Fiske was last in England in 1883. Clark, I, 456–92.

gentlemen, and perhaps his "sound" money views and his free-trade bias were attributable in some degree to his Anglophilism.

While Fiske looked forward to the time when wars would be no more, he believed in the righteousness of an armed conflict waged by a superior people against a backward race in the cause of order. It was by such wars that imperial Rome advanced civilization. "This was a murderous work, and in doing it the Romans became excessively cruel, but it had to be done by some one before you could expect to have great and peaceful civilizations like our own." How the theory that American history "descends in unbroken continuity from the days when stout Arminius in the forests of northern Germany successfully defied the might of imperial Rome"[56] was to be reconciled with this view, Fiske did not undertake to say.

Fiske was convinced of "the common mission" of Englishmen and Americans: "of establishing throughout the larger part of the earth a higher civilization and more permanent political order than any that has gone before. . . . ." Imperialism and pacifism were ingeniously blended; English-speaking peoples were the peace-loving portion of humankind, and therefore the cause of world-peace would be promoted by the transference of the preponderance of physical power to them—"into the hands of the dollar-hunters, if you please, but out of the hands of the scalp-hunters."[57] Our own war with Spain exemplified the "mission theory" thus expounded; for that war, while having its sordid side in its inception, was due to Spain's failure in the Western Hemisphere. "She who had so persistently misused her opportunity must have it taken away, and this was doing God's work."[58]

The United States, reasoned Fiske, might ultimately support a population of 1,500,000,000; and estimating that by 1980, a population of 600,000,000 would exist here, 150,000,000 in Australia and New Zealand, "to say nothing of the increase of

[56] Fiske, *American Political Ideas Viewed from the Standpoint of Universal History*, pp, 7, 110.

[57] *Ibid.*, pp. 8, 130, 151.   [58] Fiske, in Fiske and McMaster, p. 353.

power in other parts of the English-speaking world," European states now important would decline to the level of small powers. This, he prophesied, would compel European states to federate just as the American states were compelled to unite after the Revolution.[59] Meanwhile, the English-speaking peoples, "the moral influence" of whose combination was demonstrated in 1823, would have gained the upper hand; and with the United States pursuing a policy of free trade, Americans would be able so to invade European markets and cut down profits from manufacturing there that a reduction of armaments would inevitably result![60]

But this was not all. Fiske envisaged a day "when all communities of English race and speech may be united in a bond which allows perfect freedom to each community, but shall require all questions of international concern to be adjusted peaceably in accordance with general principles respected by all alike."[61] Thus it appears that his ideal world was to be one dominated by English-speaking peoples living under a federal system of intercontinental proportions—a kind of grandiose United States. Weaker peoples, as already observed, would be compelled to federate, so that eventually the principle of federalism would become universal; but men of English race and speech, wiser in the ways of government than the rest of mankind, and better able than they to interpret the designs of Providence, would by that time have acquired a world-wide hegemony and would also have established peace on earth, if not good will among men. Bolstered by free trade, which they then could pursue without fear, and by a "sound" currency, these elect men of the earth could inaugurate an era of business enterprise and order, and the destiny of mankind could thus be brought nearer to its fulfilment.

That Fiske once dreamed of a consolidation of even more extensive proportions is clear. In an encomium on William Pitt he wrote of a solidarity not merely of English-speaking peoples but

[59] Fiske, *American Political Ideas Viewed from the Standpoint of Universal History*, pp. 130–31, 145.

[60] Fiske, *Independence of the New World*, p. 400.   [61] *Ibid.*, p. 156.

of the "Teutonic race." Of the wisdom of Pitt's policy in the Seven Years' War, "we now [1891] see the fruits in that renovated German Empire which has come to be the strongest power on the continent of Europe, which is daily establishing fresh bonds of sympathy with the United States, and whose political interests are daily growing more and more visibly identical with those of Great Britain." The "vast conception" which embraced the possibilities of this solidarity would become more and more apparent with advancing years, and "the figure of Chatham in the annals of the Teutonic race will appear no less great and commanding than the figure of Charlemagne a thousand years before."[62]

Thus, despite the violence done his political theories, militaristic and autocratic Germany was brought by Fiske within the scope of his grand design for the world. It may be a point of some significance that in his lectures in England in 1880 on "American Political Ideas" he spoke merely of an English-speaking, rather than of a Teutonic, solidarity; and that the latter idea, set forth apparently for the first time in 1891, does not reappear in his discussions of the same general theme eight to ten years afterwards. Would it not seem that the growing rivalry of England and Germany, 1890–1900, and the attitude assumed toward the United States by Germany during the Spanish-American War caused Fiske to alter his view and to exclude that power from his charmed circle?

Closely related to his Anglo-American prejudices was Fiske's belief in the superiority as a civilizing force of Protestantism over Catholicism. To him, the triumph of the English over their Latin enemies from time to time represented not only a victory of political individualism but of religious individualism as well. The decline and fall of the French and Spanish colonial empires and the rise of imperial systems dominated by English-speaking peoples in their stead were used to prove this thesis. Liberal in his religious views so long as only Protestant religions were under consideration, Fiske was intolerant whenever Catholicism

[62] Fiske, *The American Revolution*, II, 20.

was brought into the discussion. Rather than an evil, he regarded "variety in religious beliefs" as "a positive benefit to a civilized community"; but he thought "uniformity in belief should be dreaded as tending toward Chinese narrowness and stagnation." Hence it was that Protestantism "has done so much to save the world from torpor and paralysis."[63]

When he discussed the results of the Treaty of 1763, he made no pretense of objectivity. The settlement meant that England "was destined to become the revered mother of many free and enlightened nations, all speaking the matchless language which the English Bible has forever consecrated, ..." It signified also "that the guidance of the world was henceforth to be, not in the hands of imperial bureaus or papal conclaves, but in the hands of the representatives of honest labour and the preachers of righteousness, unhampered by ritual or dogma." The history of the United States was but the first great example of these truths.

In days to come, the lesson will be taken up and reiterated by other great communities planted by England, in Africa, in Australia, and the islands of the Pacific, until barbarous sacerdotalism and despotic privilege shall have vanished from the earth, and the principles of Protestantism, rightly understood, and of English self-government, shall have become forever the undisputed possession of all mankind.[64]

As for a philosophy of history, aside from the foregoing, Fiske rejected Freeman's narrow political view and agreed with Green that history should be an all-inclusive record of the past. Nor did he accept Buckle's theory that the past of men was determined by their environment.[65] At the age of twenty-five, and long before he had gained any recognition as a historian, Fiske wrote: "That there is a causal sequence, which must sooner or

[63] Fiske, *The Discovery of America*, II, 564–69. For a somewhat calmer statement, see Fiske, *The Beginnings of New England*, pp. 37–39. Cf. John Fiske, *Excursions of an Evolutionist* (Boston and New York, 1883), pp. 266–67, 291–93.

[64] Fiske, *Essays Historical and Literary*, II, 121–22.

[65] *Ibid.*, p. 24. Nor did he subscribe to the "great-man theory" of history (*ibid.*, p. 278; Fiske, *Excursions of an Evolutionist*, pp. 198–200).

later admit of being formulated, in the tangled and devious course of human affairs, we not only readily grant, but we also steadfastly maintain." Again, "historical laws cannot, like physical laws, be obtained from the inspection of a few crucial instances."[66] More than a quarter-century later he wrote that facts should be grouped so as to make clear cause and effect, and referred to "the charm that is felt upon seeing an event emerge naturally from its causes; . . . ."[67]

While Fiske apparently did not at any time in his career attempt to formulate any "laws" of history, he seems always to have believed in their existence. Thus he wrote

that since general tendencies are manifested only in the thoughts and actions of men, it is these that the historian must study, and that as causal agencies a Cromwell or a Luther may count for more than a million ordinary men; but after all, our ultimate source of enlightenment still lies in the study of the general conditions under which the activity of our Cromwell or Luther was brought forth.

It was by "tracing the silent operation of common and familiar facts," not by seizing upon the "unusual or catastrophic," that both physical science and the study of history had progressed. Lessons could be found in a study of the past, but care must be exercised lest false analogies be drawn. One thing was clear: "It is proved beyond a doubt that the institutions of civilized society are descended from institutions like those now to be observed in savage society."[68] Fiske never wearied of showing how English and American political institutions evolved from ancient forms.

Essentially a philosophic historian, Fiske could not be satisfied with a mere recording of *what* happened; he must show *why* it happened and to what it has led or to what it is likely to lead. With much boldness he essayed the difficult task of establishing

[66] John Fiske, "Considerations on University Reform," *Atlantic Monthly*, XIX, 457.

[67] John Fiske, *A History of the United States for Schools*, p. iv.

[68] Fiske, *Essays Historical and Literary*, II, 24–25, 31 (cf. Fiske, *Outlines of Cosmic Philosophy*, II, 191–224).

definite connections between events separated by long years or even by centuries: Simon de Montfort's Parliament of 1265, and the Stamp Act Congress of 1765; the days of Arminius and Civilis, "and the days of Jefferson and Franklin"; the year 1689 and the year 1776.[69]

In view of the numerous subjects upon which Fiske revealed his prejudices, his own remarks on the matter of bias are well-nigh incredible. "History must not harbour prejudices, because the spirit proper for history is the spirit proper for science. The two are identical." The function of the historian is to inquire into the past of the race "in order to arrive at general views that are correct," views that may serve as lessons for the future. The historian must be dispassionate, but this does not mean that he cannot express his moral judgment; indeed, "he will expose stupidity and denounce wickedness, wherever he encounters them, ..."[70]

As for American historians, Fiske found Bancroft's work faulty. "Its grasp upon historical facts, ... is feeble and its style sophomorical, while it abounds in vapid declamation." Parkman, on the other hand, a distant relative of Fiske, "must be called the greatest of our historians and among the greatest of all times."[71] In an entirely different connection, Fiske, in alluding to Parkman, noted his picturesqueness, his thoroughness, and his accuracy. He then added: "The presence of a sound political philosophy, ... is felt in all his works."[72] This "sound political philosophy" was embodied in Parkman's conclusion that England succeeded better than France in colonization because of the "historical training of her people in habits of reflection, industry, and self-reliance, ..." And perhaps even

---

[69] Fiske, *The Beginnings of New England*, pp. 24, 32, 278.

[70] Fiske, *Essays Historical and Literary*, II, 6–7, 22–23. "The old-fashioned historian," wrote Fiske, "was usually satisfied with copying his predecessors, and thus an error once started became perpetuated; but in our own day no history written in such a way would command the respect of scholars." The modern historian must ransack the records of the past with the zeal "of a detective officer seeking the hidden evidences of crime."

[71] Fiske, in Fiske and McMaster, p. 273; Clark, I, 13.

[72] Fiske, *The Discovery of America*, II, 530 n.

more to the point: "The Germanic race, and especially the Anglo-Saxon branch of it, is peculiarly masculine, and, therefore, peculiarly fitted for self-government."[73]

In writings as voluminous and hastily prepared as those of Fiske, major and minor errors of fact, half-truths, exaggerations, and platitudes inevitably crept into his pages. Even with the high critical standards of the present day, a short monograph completely free from imperfections remains still to be written. After making due allowance, however, for Fiske and for the public for whom he wrote, he is still deserving of much criticism. He tells us that the American loyalists set themselves against "the inborn love of self-government"; that in the 1830's, "any one who chose could buy" public lands "at the fixed price of $1.25 per acre"; that from the Battle of New Orleans "until the Civil War" Jackson "occupied the most prominent place in the popular mind"; that throughout Jackson's career "he had been devoutly religious"; that before Jackson's presidency the civil service was conducted "with ability and purity";[74] that the Democratic candidate for the presidency in 1844 was James K. Polk "of North Carolina";[75] and that in 1876 it was a "shabby trick that kept" Tilden "out of the place to which he had been chosen, ..."[76]

We read, too, that General George H. Thomas "was one of the noblest figures in American history"; that Andrew Johnson "remained to the last a coarse and ignorant man, swelling with self-importance, and so rude that he could hardly do a right thing without making it seem wrong";[77] that Joseph E. Johnston was

[73] Francis Parkman, *The Old Régime in Canada* (revised, with additions; Boston, 1901), pp. 446–48.

[74] Fiske, *Essays Historical and Literary*, I, 5, 252, 287, 308, 345. Fiske wrote that the Scotch-Irish small farmers of the South Carolina uplands were Whigs to a man during the Revolution (*The American Revolution*, II, 165). Fiske's Whig father was disappointed in his efforts to secure a federal appointment for himself, 1849–1850 (Clark, *op. cit.*, I, 6, 7).

[75] Fiske, in Fiske and McMaster, p. 114. Polk was born in North Carolina but had for long been a resident of Tennessee.

[76] Fiske, *Essays Historical and Literary*, I, 175.

[77] Fiske, in Fiske and McMaster, pp. 165, 211–12.

"one of the noblest Romans of all"; that Francis P. Blair, Jr., "was endowed with a lofty and unselfish public spirit, a weight of character that impressed itself upon every one, and a courage that nothing could daunt"; that General C. F. Smith was "one of the truest men and finest officers in the Federal service"; that "in the naval annals of the English race" Admiral Farragut "will take rank second to none unless it be Nelson";[78] that Francis Drake was "destined to take the highest rank among the naval heroes of all ages, with the possible exception of Nelson";[79] and that "from the seizure of Camp Jackson [in Missouri] in 1861 down to the appearance of Sherman's army in the rear of Virginia in 1865, there may be traced an unbroken chain of causation."[80]

Moreover, expressions such as "simply silly," "this was too silly," and "Let me here pause for a moment, dear reader," do not inspire confidence in the minds of present-day readers. So intolerant was Fiske of views that conflicted with his own, that at times he exhibited the utmost contempt for the people who held them. For example, one may learn from him that in addition to the Democratic and Republican tickets in the campaign of 1892 "there were two or three other tickets embodying the views of cranks of various complexions."[81] And yet, paradoxical as it may seem, Fiske once wrote that "it is the duty of the historian to learn how to limit and qualify his words of blame or approval; . . . ."[82]

[78] Fiske, *The Mississippi Valley in the Civil War*, pp. vii, 9, 62, 115.

[79] Fiske, *Colonization of the New World*, p. 234.

[80] Fiske, *The Mississippi Valley in the Civil War*, p. 7. A philosophic historian, Fiske could not resist the temptation to speculate and prophesy as to what Jefferson's attitude would "unquestionably" have been had he attended the Virginia Convention of 1788; as to what Hamilton's later political views would have been had he not lost his life in the famous duel with Burr; and as to what the results would have been had the Stuarts triumphed in England in the Civil War (Fiske, *Essays Historical and Literary*, I, 141–42, 169; *Beginnings of New England*, pp. 168–69).

[81] Fiske, *Essays Historical and Literary*, I, 5, 15; Fiske, in Fiske and McMaster, pp. 158, 246.

[82] Fiske, *Beginnings of New England*, p. 38. Fiske had a way of softening judgments of historical characters of whom he approved. For example: "It is unquestionable that Grant

Fiske drove himself at a terrific rate. From 1888 until his death in 1901, a period during which his chief attention was given to history, he averaged more than one volume a year; at the same time he delivered numerous lectures and wrote to some extent on subjects other than history. Coming of a family of comfortable means, and marrying into one of like character, he had a standard of living that could be maintained for himself, his wife, and his six children only at great expense. His prodigious industry seems to have been inspired in no inconsiderable part by his need for money.[83]

In addition to his enormous literary labors, there was a constantly growing correspondence demanding his attention. In the preface to one of his works he wrote in 1891: "If I were to answer all the letters which arrive by every mail, I should never be able to do another day's work." He added that it was "becoming impossible even to *read* them all; and there is scarcely time for giving due attention to one in ten."[84]

Fiske, as a historian, admirably supports the generalization that soundness of scholarship and critical judgment do not always accompany brilliancy of intellect and stylistic skill. It may have been distrust of his scholarship that kept him from an appointment to a Harvard professorship. For the most part, he wrote on old and familiar topics, usually with much zest and clarity. There is perhaps but very little in his books that could not readily have been found in print elsewhere at the time he wrote them. Bancroft, Hildreth, Doyle, Palfrey, Parkman, Winsor, McMaster, and others had covered the ground before him; and this fact rendered the contribution made to knowledge by Fiske's books as negligible as that of present-day school or col-

---

shared with Daniel Webster, and many other men of strong and massive natures, a somewhat overweening fondness for John Barleycorn" (*The Mississippi Valley in the Civil War*, p. 68).

[83] *Dictionary of American Biography*, VI, 422. "It has always seemed to us," wrote George L. Beer, "that if Fiske had not been forced to earn his livelihood by writing he never would have ventured into the field of history" (*Critic*, XXXIX, 118).

[84] Fiske, *The Discovery of America*, I, xvii–xviii. According to J. S. Clark (I, v), "Fiske was not a voluminous correspondent; . . . ."

lege texts. His contribution was in the organization and attractive presentation of facts long known.[85] The range of his interests was so wide that he was unable to specialize in anything. In consequence he ultimately gained the unenviable reputation of possessing no originality either in science or in history.[86] His unusual talents were turned into a channel so broad that the resulting stream of books, impressive as it was, was much too shallow to float any bark of scholarship save one of the lightest draft. For the student of history, his career is at once an inspiration and a warning: his learning was extensive, his stylistic ability remarkable, his industry well-nigh phenomenal; but his writings were so prolific that rarely in the whole range of them may one detect the sure hand of a master.

[85] Professor A. B. Hart concludes that Fiske's chief merit was as an interpreter of the "dull and confused," and as one who brought home to the "average man wholesome truths about our ancestors" ("The Historical Services of John Fiske," *International Monthly*, IV, 566–68). James Schouler, on the other hand, regarded Fiske "as the chief of our native historians, living or dead." Fiske could "enlist a hundred readers where ten had read before." Further, he could "get at the why of things" ("Tribute to Fiske," Massachusetts Historical Society, *Proceedings*, 2d ser., XV, 194). See also Lyman Abbott, "John Fiske's Histories," *Outlook*, LXIX, 711. For a statement as to the relationship between Fiske's evolutionary philosophy and his historical writings, see S. S. Green, "Reminiscences of John Fiske," American Antiquarian Society, *Proceedings*, N.S. XIV, 423.

Although the present essay is largely a new study, the writer's earlier article on Fiske ("John Fiske," *Mississippi Valley Historical Review*, XVII, No. 2 [September, 1930], 264–77) has been used somewhat in its preparation.

[86] *Dictionary of American Biography*, VI, 422–23.

IX

JAMES FORD RHODES[1]

RAYMOND CURTIS MILLER
Wayne University

J AMES FORD RHODES was born in Cleveland, Ohio, May 1, 1848. The place and date must be recorded because they account for the formation of early and almost indestructible impressions on the mind of the future historian. Rhodes came from New England stock, from those hardy emigrants who left the rocks of the East for the more fertile soil of the Connecticut Reserve but who carried with them to the West the New England conscience, the New England wilful provincialism, the New England stubbornness in holding fixed ideas, which they cherished till long after old New England had become tolerant and even liberal. In the happy years of prosperity, when the tariff sun shone on the hills of Massachusetts and Connecticut and brought to full blossom the shops and mills and factories, when the trade of New England was growing with the expansion of her industries and her markets, her cold austerity and uncompromising righteousness melted perceptibly in the warm glow of physical contentment and financial profits. The second generation of industrial leaders became accustomed to their broadcloth and to the directors' green table and could read with sympathetic approval Webster's seventh of March appeal for peace and prosperity.

But if the East was ready to accept the business man's peace,

[1] This paper was first printed in the *Mississippi Valley Historical Review*, Vol. XV, No. 4 (March, 1929), and is here reprinted, by permission, substantially as it there appeared.

and in the interests of Union and markets to stone her abolitionists, the sons of that region in the West were of another mind and
stood ready to prove themselves more New England than New
England. This was the region in which abolition societies did
more than talk. They organized the underground railroad, they
rescued slaves from their captors, they defied all the powers of
state and nation in the name of the higher law, and—supreme
offense—they elected abolitionists to Congress to carry the battle to the South in the halls of Washington. This part of the
West idealized the negro, though they did not love him; hated
the aristocratic master, though they did not know him; accepted
the worst exaggerations of the abolitionists; and carried their
belief into political action. Through petitions, agitations, riots,
elections, and congressional absurdities, they concentrated the
attention of the nation on the problem of slavery, supported the
Wilmot Proviso, misrepresented the Kansas-Nebraska Bill, created the Republican party, and triumphed in the peaceful revolution of 1860. The Western Reserve and the little city of Cleveland
were heart and soul in the antislavery cause.

It was in this atmosphere of exaggeration and confusion that
the small son of the Rhodes family received his first political impressions. From the lips of the principal of his high school he
heard the news of the war, as printed in the northern papers and
as explained by a northern pedagogue. It was this partisan and
necessarily incomplete portrayal which first awakened Rhodes's
interest in politics and history.

There was nothing in his formal schooling to correct or modify
this early impression. Because of a deficiency in mathematics and
classical languages, he was unable to pass the entrance examinations, and so entered the College of the City of New York in
1865 as a special student. Here his interest in history deepened
and led him to read widely in the field. The following year, at
the old University of Chicago, was devoted chiefly to the study
of philosophy. With this meager training his formal education
ended. In the summer of 1867 he sailed for France, and for three
years thereafter he studied and traveled in Europe. Rhodes found

time to attend a course of lectures at the University of Paris[2] and
to do a little newspaper work, but his chief interest was the more
prosaic iron industries of Germany and Scotland. In 1870 he
joined his father in the iron business, and four years later was
made a partner in the firm of Rhodes and Company.[3]

But the business world, remunerative though it proved for
him, did not satisfy him, and he resolved to abandon it at the
first possible moment. By 1885 Rhodes had reached that comfortable economic standing which enabled him to close his office
desk and give his whole time to the profession which he called
the rich-man's pastime. At the age of thirty-seven he began the
serious study of history.

Conscious of his lack of preparation, the prospective historian
devoted the next three years to intensive study and wide reading.
It should be noted that Rhodes, according to his own statement,
read slowly and with effort. He chose to study the one best
work of an author rather than to read more hastily his whole production; in other words, he was seeking historical method rather
than historical information and perspective.[4] Following the
publication of the seventh volume of his *History*, which closes
with the Reconstruction era, he felt the need of special preparation before undertaking to write about the new issues of the post-
war period. For several years he studied eighteenth- and nineteenth-century Europe, because he wisely concluded that many
of her problems resembled those which were uppermost in the
United States of his own day.[5]

The result of this self-directed study was an uneven preparation for his task. He had an extensive and accurate knowledge
of antiquity and English history but a surprising unfamiliarity

[2] Lectures by Edouard Laboulaye on "Montesquieu's *L'Esprit des lois*."

[3] The facts of his early life are given in the *National Cyclopedia of American Biography*,
VII, 92, and by Dumas Malone in *Dictionary of American Biography*, XV, 531–33. Rhodes's
own sketch of his life, on which Dr. Frederic Bancroft based his article in *Harper's Weekly*,
XXXVI, No. 1878 (Dec. 17, 1892), pp. 1218–19, is printed by M. A. DeWolfe Howe in
James Ford Rhodes, American Historian (1929), pp. 17–29.

[4] Rhodes, *Historical Essays* (New York, 1909), p. 68.

[5] Rhodes, *A History of the United States* (New York, 1919), VI, vi.

with some phases of American development. On the other hand, his active participation in industry and his close association with business companions after he retired (Mark Hanna was his brother-in-law) gave him both information and a point of view which, to say the least, were far different from those possessed by a college professor. Rhodes sampled the world of his day and found it good; his own personal experiences convinced him that contemporary economic organization deserved very little criticism, and he did not understand or sympathize with the aspirations of labor, either in the factory or on the farm.

It was a peculiar training, but Rhodes did not consider it a handicap. On several occasions he contrasted business with the cloister as a preparation for writing history. Although he held no brief for the active career, there certainly never is evident any belief that it was inferior.[6]

In 1891, just before the publication of his first two volumes, Rhodes left the West for the classic confines of Cambridge, and later removed to Boston. But he did not shake all the dust of business from his feet. He is perhaps the only important historian of recent America who could give such an address in *Who's Who in America* as "In care of the Second National Bank, Boston."

This choice of residence is significant. M. DeWolfe Howe, his biographer, suggests the almost pitiful eagerness with which Rhodes sought admission to the charmed inner circle of Boston intellectuals. Slowly it opened to receive him, though his acceptance seemed rapid to those born to entrance; and his pleasure in these social contacts and in the English friendships which New England was able to give him was freely expressed. On the title-page of his third volume (published 1895) he placed below his name, as the sole honor worth mentioning, "member of the Massachusetts Historical Society"; it was the only association to which he gave any attention. His friends there were follow-

---

[6] Rhodes, *Essays*, pp. 66, 79; Rhodes's tribute to Samuel Rawson Gardiner, in Massachusetts Historical Society, *Proceedings*, 2d ser., XVI, 6.

ers of the belated and rather sterile "liberalism" of the seventies and of the *Nation*, "mugwumps" or their sympathizers, lost in an unreal intellectualism. Rhodes was not of New England birth; but he was, by eager adoption, one of the school of New England historians.[7]

When Rhodes began his work in 1887, he was unable to find some of the sources of historical information upon which students customarily relied. Government publications were abundant, but there was little available correspondence or biography to aid him in opening up the new field. This fact, as in the case of McMaster earlier, drove him to the newspapers. Rhodes used these valuable sources both as a register of public opinion and as a guide in the molding of opinion. He insisted that the newspaper was a safe guide, though it ought to be subjected to the same criticism as any document and employed only with the knowledge of the bias, hopes, and information of the editor.[8] Rhodes made wise use of newspapers from all parts of the nation, but the South and West are less represented than the East. Although many extracts from western and southern journals came to his hands only when quoted in the eastern press, he did not follow them back to their source.

There is a serious lack of creditable information about the South, especially in Rhodes's early volumes; and much of it is unfair. To characterize Fanny Kemble as an impartial witness for the plantation and slavery system is certainly open to doubt; for she was the unhappy actress-wife of a none-too-successful planter on an isolated and depleted plantation, and her experiences were hardly typical.[9] This absence of material on the South is easily explained, for it did not exist in the North when he wrote; and his firsthand knowledge of the South was slight indeed. Whatever the cause, a lack of balance mars his work. No one who knew the South at all and had Rhodes's earnest de-

---

[7] Howe, *James Ford Rhodes*, pp. 82, 288. The sentiment runs clearly through the letters quoted throughout the book.

[8] Rhodes, *Essays*, pp. 83 ff.   [9] Rhodes, *History*, I, 305.

sire to serve truth could have written the famous slavery chapter in Volume I.[10] His treatment of the West is open to about the same criticism.

It may be agreed that Rhodes's early volumes show a lack of balance because of faulty sources. But in 1913 the author published a book of lectures on the Civil War, and in 1917 a history of that war, both of which were announced as complete re-examinations of the whole topic. In 1920 an entirely new edition of the *History*, with the addition of a Volume VIII, was presented as "thoroughly revised." In view of the fact that Rhodes was soon to issue a whole volume on a new field, it must be assumed that he had both time and strength to make this revision, and it is certain that material was available on which to base it.

In truth, he did not make such a revision. If he had read the more recent literature on the origin of the Civil War, he paid small attention to its effect upon his earlier conclusions. In general, except for a few footnotes, there was no recognition of the enormous body of source material and monographs which had become available in the thirty years since he had begun his work. On no fundamental point on which his findings had been challenged by the work of subsequent students had Rhodes modified his position in the least.

Rhodes, then, brought from his early life and his business associations some attitudes and preconceptions which affected his historical work. The scarcity of available sources was another of his handicaps and made it difficult for him to obtain the proper perspective of the period which he was depicting. Of equal importance with these factors in shaping his work were his ideas of history. No discussion of his volumes would be either fair or complete which did not mention his fundamental conceptions of the nature and bounds of the task upon which he was engaged or which did not set forth the ideal which he held before himself. Some of the limitations in scope, content, and method, for which he has since been criticized, were deliberately chosen.

[10] *Ibid.*, chap. iv

Rhodes took the classic historians as his model, and attempted to discover the secret of their success:

. . . . Thucydides and Tacitus are superior to the historians who have written in our century, because by long reflection and studious method they have better digested their materials and compressed their narratives. Unity in narration has been adhered to more rigidly. They stick closer to their subject. They are not allured into the fascinating by-paths of narration, which are so tempting to men who have accumulated a mass of facts, incidents, and opinion.[11]

Rhodes resolved to make his history a unit, a synthetic whole, in which less attention should be given to the facts than to the sweep of movement and to the dramatic quality of the whole work. It was for this reason that he chose the particular period of American history in which he worked; for he found in the rise and fall of the slave power, in the clash and glamour of the Civil War and its warlike aftermath, in the titanic dimensions of the struggle, that "epic" quality which lent itself to such treatment. "This period, the brief space of a generation, was an era big with fate for our country, and for the American must remain fraught with the same interest that the war of the Peloponnesus had for the ancient Greek, or the struggle between the Cavalier and the Puritan has for their descendants."[12] The strength and weakness of this method of presentation is revealed in the work of Rhodes. Unity could be attained only by the omission of material which seemed irrelevant, and emphasis upon a central theme is occasionally so pronounced that it approaches distortion. As Professor Turner put it, the result is a history of the slavery struggle and not a history of the American people or of the United States.[13]

Rhodes was openly and frankly subjective in his work; no one could have the slightest doubt as to where his sympathies lay, or why. His method was deliberately chosen. In reviewing a volume by J. B. McMaster before any of his own important works

[11] Rhodes, "History," American Historical Association, *Report, 1899*, I, 58.

[12] Rhodes, *History*, I, 1.

[13] F. J. Turner's review of Rhodes's *History of the United States*, in *Political Science Quarterly*, XI, 167.

appeared, Rhodes commended highly his use of newspapers and concluded: "The author either gives positively his own notion or allows plainly to be seen what is his own idea on controverted points. This is the proper way to write history."[14] Rhodes himself frankly avowed his antislavery sympathy and even added, ". . . . it seems clear that he [who has this sympathy] can most truly write the story."[15] Rhodes could be judicial; but he followed the practice of the law court, where evidence is presented and weighed in order that judgment may be pronounced.

The sympathies which Rhodes displayed were not those of conscious preconception but were, in his opinion, the result of a very impartial investigation of the facts. Error, he felt, was the result either of deliberate misrepresentation or neglect, and neither of these faults could be charged to him. "It may well enough be true that the designedly untruthful historian, like the undevout astronomer, is an anomaly."[16] Although he earnestly desired to tell the truth, he gave no heed to the more subtle psychological factors of importance in every human action. Mere labor, and an honest determination to be truthful, seemed to him an adequate protection from bias. Rhodes did try to guard himself against the influences of personal friendship and expressed the opinion that history ought to deal with a time long past in order to avoid such prejudices.[17] Although this was his ideal, he did violence to it by writing of men and events well known to him.

Rhodes had no ambition to be a "popularizer." "The proper mental attitude of the general historian is to take no thought of

[14] Rhodes's review of McMaster's *History of the People of the United States*, in *Magazine of Western History*, II, 464.

[15] Rhodes, *History*, I, 152. Speaking of Carl Schurz, Rhodes said in 1892: "For I have tried to write in the same spirit in which he wrote H. Clay—a spirit of impartiality which, however, does not go so far as to emasculate the judgment and which prompts one to speak plainly when plain-speaking is necessary" (Howe, p. 72).

[16] Rhodes's tribute to Gardiner, p. 3. See *supra*, n. 6.

[17] Rhodes's review of Samuel S. Cox's *Three Decades of Federal Legislation*, in *Mag. of West. Hist.*, III, 358–59. This is in contradiction to a later statement that one virtue of the classical historians was the fact that they wrote of their contemporaries. Rhodes, "History," p. 59.

popularity. . . . . The audience which the general historian should have in mind is that of historical experts—men who are devoting their lives to the study of history."[18] Only the type of reader for whom he wrote would justify the flood of citations on his pages or understand his assertion that footnotes "which give authority for the statements in the text can never be in excess."[19]

Rhodes was extraordinarily frank in stating and defending the prepossessions and principles which conditioned his craftsmanship. "If, like Thucydides and Tacitus," he wrote, "the American historian chooses the history of his own country as his field he may infuse his patriotism into his narrative."[20] This fervor is less noticeable in his major work than in his earlier writings; but it does shape his conclusions even there, especially in dealing with foreign relations. His patriotism colored his whole understanding of the Revolution and the constitutional struggle, of which he seems to have made little direct study, so that some of his later comparisons, especially in constitutional interpretation, are grossly unfair. In his later volumes this feeling became fused with his defense of the economic *status quo* with especially unfortunate results, and made him handle opponents of his own social philosophy and critics of American institutions with scant courtesy. "We had united the highest civilization to a government of the people by the people, and to a well-being of the masses."[21] To attribute the well-being of American labor solely to the government is an absurdity; but the whole quotation, with its juxtaposition of highest civilization, government, and prosperity, is a summary of Rhodes's confusion which defies comment.

These very definite ideas of what is good history, together with his social attitudes and the thought patterns fixed by his experience in business, exerted a powerful influence in molding

[18] Rhodes, *Essays*, p. 44.

[19] *Ibid.*, p. 33.

[20] Rhodes, "History," p. 62.

[21] Rhodes, "Some Lessons of History," *Mag. of West. Hist.*, II, 149.

the author's interpretation. The questions of detail, which follow from these more general factors, can probably best be discussed in connection with his major work, to which, for convenience, will be added *The McKinley and Roosevelt Administrations*.[22] When Rhodes began his research, he planned only a history of the rise of the Republican party, 1850–58; but in his hands the project expanded to include the whole period of war and reconstruction, a monumental seven-volume study closing with 1876. Long after the completion of the seventh volume, Rhodes added an eighth to his *History*, and soon thereafter a book on the next two administrations.[23] This time division and the great difference in the quality between his earlier and this later work make it desirable to discuss his writings in two parts, divided by the disputed election of 1876.

For the introductory chapter of Volume I of his *History*, Rhodes depended on secondary material, chiefly von Holst, and consequently made mistakes which the slightest search of primary materials would have avoided. As the historian approached his own period, these factual errors became rarer; and the criticisms must be directed to his choice of materials and his interpretation of them.

In the period before the war, when the West figured in politics as it has at no other time in our history, Rhodes completely ignored the region as a distinct section and confused and misrepresented its ideals and aspirations. Perhaps the most charitable explanation of this omission is that his thesis—the slavery struggle—was a limited one. Even if this is so, the story of slavery and the approach of the armed conflict is shot through and

[22] The publishers in 1922 gave this distinctive title to his last work, but Rhodes, in *History*, VIII, 358, 443, made specific forward reference to a subsequent book on Roosevelt. A personal letter of Jan. 15, 1929, from the Macmillan Company, states that "it was Mr. Rhodes' intention always that his volume on the McKinley and Roosevelt administrations should be ultimately added to his *History of the United States*."

[23] Between Vols. VII and VIII of the *History* elapsed a period of thirteen years, only one less than that occupied by the publication of the entire first seven volumes. The issuing of several volumes of history, lectures, and essays in the interval emphasizes the division into two parts. Rhodes is confusing and contradictory in his later statements of his original plans.

through with the West and its problems. The Wilmot Proviso, the Kansas struggle—these are certainly problems vital to the slavery controversy and to the coming of the Civil War. Professor Shippee illustrated the point when he said that Rhodes's discussion of Texas and the Mexican War without Robert J. Walker is "like a de-Hamletized *Hamlet*."[24]

This neglect of the West was deliberate; for, when he began his task, the pioneer studies of Professor F. J. Turner were in print; and by the time Volume III was prepared (it was published in 1895), the whole historical world was talking of the significance of the West in American history. In spite of the work of Turner and his many followers, there is, neither in Rhodes's first edition nor in its revision, more than a few lines about the struggle for public lands, internal improvements, the trading and logrolling by railroads for land grants, or the effects of these issues upon the political fortunes of the men in whose words and votes Rhodes took delight. There is only the barest mention of the demand for the Homestead Law or of its passage;[25] and in complete ignorance of it and of all other similar factors, Rhodes could write: "If ever a political party fought a campaign for pure unadulterated principle, the Republicans did in 1860."[26]

In similarly incomprehensible fashion Rhodes entirely overlooked all economic and social forces in the development of the nation. This is especially surprising, since almost his first published work was a history of the coal and iron industries of Cleveland.[27] He sharply criticized Samuel S. Cox for leaving out of his legislative memoirs such facts as the development of steel rails, the Bessemer process, cheap transportation, the fall of agricultural prices, the change of manners, the improvement of cooking in public hostelries, the decline of the lecture, the development of the theater.[28] Perhaps Rhodes, like some modern critics

[24] Lester B. Shippee, "Rhodes's *History of the United States*," *Miss. Valley Hist. Rev.*, VIII, 137.

[25] Rhodes, *History*, II, 352, 359–60; IV, 58.

[26] Rhodes's review of Cox, *loc. cit.*, p. 360.

[27] Rhodes, "The Coal and Iron Industry of Cleveland," *Mag. of West. Hist.*, II, 337.

[28] Rhodes's review of Cox, pp. 356–57.

of the historians' craft, found it easier to teach than to follow his own instructions; but one can search his nine lengthy volumes in vain for a sign of real understanding of these and other similar factors in their relation to the flow of historical events. They are mentioned, but the reader is well justified in doubting whether the author could give a plausible reason for introducing them to his narrative at just the places where they are now found.

Perhaps a single illustration, pointed out by C. F. Adams, will serve to demonstrate the unfortunate consequences of this blindness to economic forces. Rhodes repeatedly expressed surprise that the South should have dared face the war, overwhelmed, as it was, in numbers and economic resources.[29] Mr. Adams insisted that the South did not expect to win by arms; cotton was king, and, because its supply would be cut off from Europe by the war, the Confederates confidently expected an intervention from abroad to bring them the victory. So strong was this hope that they talked, before the blockade was effective, of an embargo on cotton exports, to hasten the inevitable action by England and France.[30] Giving no place to this plan, Rhodes missed the meaning of the diplomatic struggle abroad, especially in England, and failed to appreciate the importance of the northern navy in the war.

If, as some competent military critics insist, the South collapsed because of a breakdown of economic life at home and the consequent shattering of civilian morale, rather than as a result of military defeat or loss of man-power, the story of the war should be written mainly from the angle of the supply of essential materials and a slow southern starvation. Mr. Rhodes has reduced the account of the navy almost to the vanishing-point; Mr. Adams calculated that one-sixth of 1 per cent of the entire space of Volume V was devoted to its operations.[31] The author failed to see, in the series of operations on the sea and

[29] E.g., *ibid.*, p. 359.

[30] Charles F. Adams' review of Rhodes's *History of the United States*, Vol. V, in Massachusetts Historical Society *Proceedings*, 2d ser., XIX, 328 ff.; William H. Russell, *My Diary North and South* (New York, 1863), chap. xiii.

[31] Adams, p. 326.

the southern coast, prime factors in the outcome of the war, and wrote that the work of the navy was "unrelieved by prospects of brilliant exploits." Modern wars are not won by medieval feats of individual daring.

The interpretation which Rhodes gave to events was, almost without exception, political, both in causation and results; and at no place does this method show its limitations more than in the discussion of Reconstruction. He was aware of the bitter struggle of the South against its difficulties, and of the injustice which the legislation of the victors imposed; but the historian of today, taking account of the economic and social disturbances of the Reconstruction period, would refuse to attribute its horrors solely to the measures of the congressional radicals. No plan, however wise or merciful, could have removed the social, moral, and economic consequences of a four-year war, fought almost exclusively on the soil of the South and entailing, through the blockade, an almost complete stoppage of normal economic life. Rhodes, with his eye solely on politics, attributed to legislation results which came from far deeper and more fundamental causes.

Reviewers of the various volumes of Rhodes's *History* which deal with the war differ widely in their opinion of the value of his analysis of the campaigns of the armies. Professor Lester B. Shippee, who is not a military expert, praises these sections highly: "Of all the work no portion is better constructed, more delicately balanced, than those portions of volumes 3, 4, and 5 in which the military side of the history from 1861 to 1865 is so attractively portrayed. . . . . If there is any one portion of the story covered by his work which little needs retelling it is the military side of the war."[32] Thomas Robson Hay, an engineer with a penchant for military history, has recently worked over the materials with results which must seriously modify Rhodes's conclusions about the western theater of the war.[33] Perhaps

[32] Shippee, p. 141.

[33] Thomas Robson Hay, "The Davis-Hood-Johnston Controversy of 1864," *Miss. Valley Hist. Rev.*, XI, 54 ff.; Hay, "Confederate Leadership at Vicksburg," *ibid.*, pp. 543 ff.

the most competent student of military affairs who has expressed an opinion of this section is Charles Francis Adams. In his review of Volume V, Adams concentrated attention on the campaign of 1864, and shows, in a manner which almost defies dispute, that Rhodes completely missed the whole purpose of the strategy, that his descriptions of it are consequently inaccurate and meaningless, that the responsibility for the costly failure must rest upon Butler rather than on Grant, but that it was Grant, and not Lincoln, who kept that incompetent civilian in his important post.[34] This sample gains in significance, of course, if it is a true index of the value of Rhodes as a military historian.

Rhodes was at his best in the handling of personalities, and in his assessment of men and their motives he made his outstanding contribution as a historian. Politics was to him a clash between leaders. Because he ignored other factors, he overemphasized the effect of individuals upon political movements. How else was it possible for him to assume that Lincoln, whose policy President Johnson closely followed in Reconstruction, "could have brought us through the trying times safely and wisely"?[35]

In the large number of men whom he portrays, it seems unfair to single out those sketches which are at best only caricatures, and ignore those which are well done. Let this be the apology, then, for the comment on his presentation of Andrew Johnson, John Brown, and Stephen Douglas. In the first case, the author followed the judgment of the dominating senatorial cabal, whose measures, indeed, he deplored but whose characterization of its chief enemy he accepted. Perhaps about the same can be said of his picture of Buchanan.

John Brown was an ignorant bigot, whose misguided enthusiasm seriously embarrassed the Free State leaders of Kansas and whose unjustifiable crimes at Ossawatomie and Harper's Ferry

[34] Adams, pp. 342 ff. Attention should be called to Rhodes's response to this review, which is similar in tone to his answer to other criticisms and is perhaps an explanation of his failure to make a thorough revision. His letter to Adams is a good-tempered and moderate, but firm and resolute, defense of his original findings. Howe, p. 148.

[35] Rhodes's review of Cox, p. 365. See also his suggestion that Webster's arguments created national unity and so a war, *History*, I, 142.

jeopardized the cause of freedom as much as did the attack on Charles Sumner that of the South. But Rhodes belonged to what Professor J. W. Burgess called the "John Brown cult," and spent pages in a futile attempt to distinguish between the man and his insane action.[36] Rhodes was forced to recognize the nature of Brown's acts but was unable to change his preconceived opinions of the man in defiance of the thought of his day.

But a more serious charge than a mere refusal to revise his judgment must be made in the case of his treatment of Douglas. Rhodes, with his inability to understand the West and with his neglect of economic factors, could not comprehend the importance of railroads to that distant section. His interest in politics was restricted to the national theater, and he found no place in his pages for such important intrastate conflicts as the Benton-Atchison feud in Missouri. These shortcomings blinded him to the fundamentals of the Kansas-Nebraska Bill, and the dust stirred up by the Free Soil party and its successor hid the real Douglas in a murky cloud.[37] But even these considerations do not account for the bitterness with which Rhodes assailed Douglas or for the almost vindictive manner in which the Illinois statesman was made to play the role of the black-mustached villain in the drama of slavery.

Professor Frank H. Hodder has presented what he thinks to be Rhodes's motive.[38] Certainly a lawsuit, as a result of which the historian was compelled to pay to the defrauded heirs of Douglas a considerable sum of money, might create a frame of mind in which historical perspective could be retained with difficulty. This treatment of Douglas by Rhodes is the most serious historical offense with which he has been charged. Both because of the

[36] J. W. Burgess' review of Rhodes's *History of the United States*, Vols. I and II, in *Pol. Sci. Quart.*, VIII, 342.

[37] Rhodes, *History*, I, 428. Rhodes completely neglected the fact that, to win the South, Douglas had only to refuse to act at all on the railroads; if the repeal of the Missouri Compromise were a bid for the South, he would not have waited to have his hand forced by Senator Dixon, F. H. Hodder, "Propaganda as a Source of American History," *Miss. Valley Hist. Rev.*, IX, 10 ff.

[38] Hodder, pp. 10 ff.

distortion of the facts and the apparent motive for this misrepresentation, it is one of the unhappiest incidents of recent historical writing.

In the last two volumes of the *History*, covering the period 1877–1909, similar faults and omissions appear, but unfortunately without many of the attendant virtues. These volumes were afterthoughts. They fall outside the period of history which Rhodes had made his own, and deal with years when his own recollections and experiences were at once an asset and a weakness. Any comparison with the first seven volumes is difficult because these books are far below the standard previously set. Volume VII covers a time-space almost equal in length to the total embraced by all the volumes which preceded it. This dilution of material makes these last volumes thin indeed.

Rhodes found the focus of his early work in the slave struggle; but after 1876, when the close of Reconstruction removed slavery as the dominant issue, he was lost. Today we see that the dominant pattern of the period is the economic, commercial, and industrial developments, with their resulting social, legal, and administrative problems. Rhodes, however, was not concerned with nonpolitical facts and was aware of no unity more significant than simple chronology.

Even the coherence given by a single author was lacking, for in at least nine of the twenty chapters of the final volume Rhodes depended upon assistants, whose choice of material and method of procedure, however excellent, were bound to differ from his own. The result is a series of essays on the administrations of the presidents, interspersed with rather superficial studies of striking and spectacular phenomena. Several chapters were published as separate articles in 1910 and 1911.

This exclusively political treatment resulted in an odd distribution of time and space between events related, and in some curious omissions. The Fourteenth Amendment has no meaning except in relation to judicial cases involving negroes. The story of the organization of the Tariff Commission is complete, so far as the political fate of the bill is concerned; but there is no glimpse behind the curtain into the social implications, or of the forces leading to the failure of the measure.[39] Even the fact that the chairman of the Commission was a spokesman for the Wool Growers' Association caused Rhodes no surprise. The Sherman Antitrust Act is dismissed with a brief paragraph; the Interstate Commerce Law receives three pages, as do Grant's unfortunate business ventures. Two pages are given to the reversal of the income-tax decision, but there is nothing fundamental in the discussion. All this, in spite of the fact that the average space devoted to the problem of the selection of the president's cabinet is over five pages and that eleven pages are accorded to the nomination of Harrison.

No complaint can be fairly made of the space allotted to labor troubles, but it does not follow that the treatment is satisfactory. Charles A. Beard, in his review of Volume VIII, was scathing in his comments on this section of the work: "Is it just to give nearly a hundred pages to disorders (real or alleged) ascribed to labor and scarcely a line to labor organization, programs, constructive efforts and unendurable labor conditions? . . . . In short, more than a fifth of the book is devoted to labor troubles, giving one the impression that labor lives for disorder alone."[40] The Knights of Labor are mentioned as trouble-makers, but their program seemed unworthy of notice. The rise of the American Federation apparently escaped the author's attention. Certainly there is no sympathy expressed for labor in either its difficulties or its aspirations. The judicial decision in the case of the Chicago anarchist riots is accepted without question as "legally just"; and—wonder of wonders—the author cites Judge Gary as the authority for his statement.

In these volumes the West counted no more than in the earlier section of the work. The idea that there is any relationship between increasing labor difficulties and the passing of free lands probably never occurred to the author. There is no systematic treatment of the economic problems of agricultural America.

[39] Rhodes, *History*, VIII, 168–78.
[40] C. A. Beard in *New Republic*, Dec. 17, 1919, p. 82.

Isolated bits can be pieced together, by one who is familiar with the problems involved, into a sadly incomplete and confusing whole; but the casual reader will find nothing in the two volumes to explain why the East and the West should not have been reversed in position on the money question, or to account for the distribution of the vote in 1896. The rise of the Farmer's Alliance gets hardly a phrase; in the year when the farmers of Kansas were burning corn for fuel, Rhodes cited Malthus to prove that there could be no overproduction of foodstuffs.[41]

On the whole currency problem Rhodes showed no comprehension of money theory, or the bimetallic argument, or of the Populist financial program, which embraced far more than inflation by paper alone. Nowhere in the work is there a suggestion why the farmers' complaints ended in the late 1890's or why there was thereafter a temporary lull in the political storms which had convulsed the West since the close of the Civil War.

Certainly Rhodes was not intentionally unfair in handling labor and agricultural problems. But equally certain it is that he did not—probably could not—penetrate the causes behind these issues. "One feels that Mr. Rhodes would have been glad to know why people could act in such an insane manner, but one cannot admit that he had any essential realization of the case."[42]

These two volumes cover the years through which Rhodes had lived, and involve many men whom he personally knew and admired. He was in profound sympathy with the social philosophy of the leaders who directed affairs in the last third of the century, and could not find it in his heart to subject them to the criticism he well knew how to use. Bryan was perhaps the only man with whom Rhodes was at all severe in these volumes, but when his criticism of the Boy Orator is contrasted with his treatment of Douglas, it pales into insignificance. Even such a notorious affair as the "embalmed-beef" scandal is hardly recognizable in the hands of the friendly and genial historian.

Rhodes's sources of information are much the same as in his

---

[41] See quotation from an earlier article given in *History*, VIII, 237.

[42] Shippee, p. 140.

earlier works, but their use is not guarded with quite the same critical spirit. The *Nation* continued to be his chief reliance, though it declined in value as the period advanced. Rhodes carefully read the ever increasing flood of biographies and autobiographies, apparently without even a suspicion of the reason for these special pleadings before the bar of succeeding generations. Just at the close of the World War, Rhodes used documents written by Roosevelt in 1906 and 1916, in which the statesman recorded what he remembered of an event in 1902 discreditable to the Germans.[43] Rhodes's apologies hardly excuse him for basing his account of the event upon such untrustworthy evidence.

So much of the information and interpretation is based upon the memory of the historian that Professor Frederic L. Paxson's evaluation has much to justify it. "Where this volume ceases to be tested history it often becomes retrospect, and the author passes judgment upon facts of his own experience. It is worth while to have preserved for historical use an 'Annals of the Eighties' by one of the greatest historians of the decade, even though the 'Annals' is of subsequent writing."[44]

A summary of these criticisms and a discussion of the place which Rhodes merits among American historians would be as difficult as it is unnecessary. Rhodes's history is not analytical. He was a storyteller rather than a philosopher; and his simple tale of what happened, with slight interest in cause or result, was in accord with the best standards of his day. Historical fashions have changed, and it would be most unfair to minimize the work of Rhodes because he failed to anticipate this revolution in method and content.

Perhaps it should be emphasized again that most of the limitations about which the present-day critic complains were deliberately chosen by Rhodes. Centering his interest on the single theme that most people in 1890 accepted as the central thread of American history, he rigidly excluded all extraneous material.

[43] Rhodes, *The McKinley and Roosevelt Administrations, 1897–1909* (New York, 1922), pp. 249–53.

[44] F. L. Paxson's review of Rhodes's *History*, Vol. VIII, in *Amer. Hist. Rev.*, XXV, 526.

His narrative seems superficial today only because the modern standards of historical criticism are so different from those known to Rhodes, and because a host of individual workers, delving in obscure corners of the period, have unearthed material of which he was completely ignorant.

Given the age in which Rhodes wrote, the materials which were then available, and the background from which he came, his fairness on most issues is deserving of much praise. As a rule, he made a determined effort to be impartial, and his large measure of success is a tribute to his integrity and sterling resolution. Perhaps the most noteworthy evidence of his openness of mind was his confession that, as a mature man and a successful iron-manufacturer, he was converted to free trade by the editorials of the *Nation*.[45] Lacking technical preparation, he brought to his task honesty, patience, and simple common sense. As a historian, he set a standard which is high indeed.

Rhodes opened up a new field of research; and for his pioneer work, with all its toil and discouragements, the historical craft owes him much. Perhaps the highest tribute which has been paid to the real value of his output is the fact that, fifty years after he began his labors, students still make his volumes the point of departure for their research, and sometimes ungraciously preface their own conclusions with a quotation from Rhodes in order to show the magnitude of his error. Even if Rhodes's work has served in no other way than as a straw man to be demolished, it merits attention from the student of historiography, and historians owe a debt to its author.

[45] Rhodes, *Essays*, p. 282.

X

HENRY ADAMS

HENRY STEELE COMMAGER
New York University

*

IT WOULD be fun to send you some of my examination papers," wrote Professor Adams to his friend Charles Milnes
Gaskell. "My rule in making them up is to ask questions
which I can't myself answer."[1] It was a report and a prophecy.
All his life Henry Adams made it a rule to ask questions which
he couldn't answer—questions which were, perhaps, quite un-
answerable. In the beginning, when Adams was merely a teacher, there was something whimsical about it, and faintly perverse. Later on, it became part of a literary technique, an in-
verse method of stating a fact or suggesting an idea. In the end,
it was a serious business, a desperately serious business. In the
end he asked questions because he wanted answers—because,
indeed, "a historical formula that should satisfy the conditions
of the stellar universe weighed heavily on his mind."[2] But his
true function was to ask questions, not to answer them; his true
function was to provoke speculation, not to satisfy it.

What Adams did, then, was relatively unimportant; but what
he signified was immensely important. At Harvard the teacher
was more interesting than the subject; in his Washington study
the author was more interesting than the books. In the end
Adams abandoned the effort to eliminate the personal equation

[1] Worthington C. Ford (ed.), *Letters of Henry Adams, 1858–1891* (Boston, 1930), p. 211.

[2] H. Adams, *The Education of Henry Adams: An Autobiography* (Boston, 1930), p. 376. The
first edition of this work appeared in 1918.

and recognized that, in so far as he was concerned, in so far as his generation was concerned, the Education of Henry Adams was the crucial question. He recognized that no questions which Adams could ask were quite as interesting as the questions which he inspired, that no facts summoned from the historical past were quite as illuminating as the facts of his own intellectual history. He recognized, quite impersonally, that if the historian expected to find a formula that would explain American character, if he expected to find a formula that would reduce history to a science, if he expected to find a formula that would satisfy the conditions of a stellar universe, he must find a formula to explain Henry Adams.

Obviously, then, it is not as a teacher or as a historian, or even as a philosopher, that Adams is chiefly significant, but as a symbol. Adams himself regarded his teaching experience as a failure, his historical work as negligible, and his philosophical speculations as suggestive rather than final; and Adams' critical acumen was so sharp, his judgment so sound, and his sincerity so unimpeachable that it would be insolent to differ with him. And Adams was very positive about this matter. Lodge and Laughlin and Taylor and half a dozen others might recall that he was the most inspiring of teachers, that his learning was prodigious and his interpretation profound; but he himself "was content neither with what he had taught nor with the way he had taught it"; and he was sure that Harvard University, "as far as it was represented by Henry Adams—produced at great waste of time and money results not worth reaching."[3] Nor was he less dogmatic about the value of his books—he who was so rarely dogmatic. Adams "had even published a dozen volumes of American history," he confessed,

for no other purpose than to satisfy himself whether, by the severest process of stating, with the least possible comment, such facts as seemed sure, in such order as seemed rigorously consequent, he could fix for a familiar moment a necessary sequence of human movement. The result had satisfied him as little as at Harvard College. Where he saw se-

[3] *Ibid.*, p. 304.

quence, other men saw something quite different, and no one saw the same unit of measure.[4]

Nor was this the perversity of old age or an effort to outwit criticism. Even as he was publishing the stately volumes of his *History*, he wrote to Elizabeth Cameron:

There are not nine pages in the nine volumes that now express anything of my interests or feelings; unless perhaps some of my disillusionments. So you must not blame me if I feel, or seem to feel, morbid on the subject of the history. I care more for one chapter, or any dozen pages of *Esther* than for the whole history;[5]

and to Dr. J. F. Jameson he confessed: "I would much rather wipe out all I have ever said than go on with more."[6] And as for the dynamic theory of history, the rule of phase applied to history, the law of entropy, and the law of acceleration, Adams was too good a historian not to see the fallacy of analogies from science to society, too good a scientist not to know that the science of today is the superstition of tomorrow. He was concerned indeed—the conclusion seems inescapable—with urging the necessity of formulating some philosophy of history, some science of society; he was concerned with asking questions and pointing to the consequences of all conceivable answers.[7]

Adams dismissed his own historical labors in a paragraph, and it would perhaps be discourteous for us to insist that they deserve more than this inattention. But even if we should agree that Adams' teaching was futile and his historical writing irrelevant, we would still be eager to discover the cause of that futility, the meaning of that irrelevancy; we would still be inclined to ask questions. Here are the volumes, standing soberly on our shelves, eloquent witnesses to the unwilling conformity of an Adams: *The Writings of Albert Gallatin*,[8] *The Life of Albert Gallatin*,[9] *John Randolph*,[10] *The History of the United States of America during the*

---

[4] *Ibid.*, p. 382.   [5] *Letters of Henry Adams*, Feb. 13, 1891, p. 468.

[6] *American Historical Review*, XXVI, p. 9. See also *The Education of Henry Adams*, p. 325.

[7] *The Education of Henry Adams*, pp. 474–98.

[8] 3 vols.; Philadelphia, 1879.

[9] Philadelphia, 1880.   [10] Boston, 1882.

Administrations of Jefferson and Madison.[11] Why, it may be asked, did Adams write these books? Why did he write them in conventional, what he called "old-school," form? Why, having written them, did he profess to think them worthless? Adams himself could not answer these questions in any satisfactory way, and it is not to be supposed that we can do better than he was able to do. We could say that he wrote them because he could think of nothing better to do, but that would be to adopt consciously the paradox that is pointless if deliberate. We could say that he wrote them to satisfy his own curiosity about the Adams family and the role it played in the evolution of the American nation; and Adams, who was never unconscious of his family, would readily accept this explanation. Certainly he felt that the history of the Adams family was central to the history of the American people, and that the problem presented by the victory of Jefferson over John Adams and of Jackson over John Quincy Adams was as fascinating as any problem in history. We could say that he wrote them in order to clarify in his own mind the meaning of American history, in order to prepare the way for the formulation of historical laws. He observed:

The scientific interest of American history centered in national character, and in the workings of a society destined to become vast, in which individuals were important chiefly as types. Although this kind of interest was different from that of European history, it was at least as important to the world. Should history ever become a true science, it must expect to establish its laws, not from the complicated story of rival European nationalities, but from the economical evolution of a great democracy. North America was the most favorable field on the globe for the spread of a society so large, uniform, and isolated as to answer the purposes of science. . . . . The interest of such a subject exceeded that of any other branch of science, for it brought mankind within sight of its own end.[12]

These histories and biographies conformed to a pattern, and the pattern was not without either beauty or symmetry. They satisfied certain requirements both of form and of substance; they

[11] 9 vols.; New York, 1889–91.

[12] Adams, *History* (edition of 1930), Book IX, pp. 222, 225.

were thorough, accurate, scholarly, critical, impartial; they were distinguished in thought and in style. It is not an exaggeration, indeed, to insist that the *Gallatin* is the best political biography, the *Administrations of Jefferson and Madison* the finest piece of historical writing, in our literature. They stated "such facts as seemed sure, in such order as seemed rigorously consequent"; they "fixed for a familiar moment" a sequence of human movement. But the result, we must remember, satisfied Adams as little as had teaching. The history was good history—better history had not been written. Everyone agreed that it was good history; but no one, least of all Adams, knew what it was good for. It was good for facts, of course; but Adams himself confessed that "I never loved or taught facts, if I could help it, having that antipathy to facts which only idiots and philosophers attain."[13] It was good for what it told of American character, for what it prophesied of American democracy; but the character changed and the prophecies were invalid, for Adams' ideal ploughboy was less likely in 1900 than in 1800 to "figure out in quaternions the relations of his furrows." It was good for the purposes of philosophy, in so far as it "fixed a sequence of human movement"; but Adams came to doubt that it was a necessary sequence and was satisfied that "the sequence of men led to nothing, and that the sequence of their society could lead no further, while the mere sequence of time was artificial, and the sequence of thought was chaos."[14]

But if, by his own valuation, Adams' historical labors contributed nothing to history, we can turn perhaps to his philosophy with hope of more satisfactory results. It is something to say that Adams is the only American historian who has ever seriously attempted to formulate a philosophy of history. He was not unaware of the difficulties; but no Adams had ever been frightened by difficulties, and Henry Adams, certainly, had nothing to lose. So in 1894, three years after he had published the

[13] Letter from H. Adams to H. O. Taylor in 1915, quoted by J. T. Adams on pp. 340, 348, of his *The Adams Family* (New York, 1930). *The Education of Henry Adams*, pp. 37, 301-2.

[14] *The Education of Henry Adams*, p. 382.

last volume of that history which he regarded with such indifference, he addressed a letter to his colleagues in the American Historical Association on the tendency of history to become a science:

That the effort to make history a science may fail is possible, and perhaps probable; but that it should cease, unless for reasons that would cause all science to cease, is not within the range of experience. Historians will not, and even if they would they can not, abandon the attempt. Science itself would admit its own failure if it admitted that man, the most important of all its subjects, could not be brought within its range.[15]

But alas, the generation of Comte and Buckle was past, and historians did not even undertake the attempt which Adams had announced as inevitable.

But, however derelict his professional colleagues, Adams would not be derelict. Years earlier, in drawing the brilliant Mrs. Lightfoot Lee, he had written sympathetically of the intellectual curiosity that looked for first causes:

Here, then, was the explanation of her restlessness, discontent, ambition,—call it what you will. It was the feeling of a passenger on an ocean steamer whose mind will not give him rest until he has been in the engine-room and talked with the engineer. She wanted to see with her own eyes the action of primary forces; to touch with her own hand the massive machinery of society; to measure with her own mind the capacity of the motive power.[16]

Adams experienced the same discontent, the same restlessness in the face of the riddles of history. "To the tired student, the idea that he must give it up seemed sheer senility. . . . . Every man with self-respect enough to become effective, if only as a machine, has had to account to himself for himself somehow, and to invent a formula of his own for his own universe, if the standard formulas fail."[17] That the standard formulas had failed, none would deny; and Adams invented one of his own.

[15] "The Tendency of History," American Historical Association *Annual Report, 1894* (Washington, 1895), p. 18.

[16] H. Adams, *Democracy, an American Novel* (New York, 1880), p. 10.

[17] *The Education of Henry Adams*, p. 472.

The result of Adams' speculations can be read in the concluding chapters of the *Education*, in the "Letter to American Teachers of History"[18] and in the essay on the "Rule of Phase Applied to History." "If history ever meant to correct the errors she made in detail," he had written, "she must agree on a scale for the whole";[19] and these essays constituted an attempt to formulate a scale for the whole. The scale was to be large enough to be inclusive. The problem was to bring human history in harmony with the organic laws of the universe, and the formula that Adams hit upon was the Law of the Dissipation of Energy.

The formula had many ramifications and was supported by an impressive array of scientific data; for from those early years, when he had hobnobbed with Sir Charles Lyell and with the *Pteraspis*, Adams had prided himself on his knowledge of science. Those who will, can read the evidence and ponder the conclusions; the argument, for all its bewildering mathematical formulas, is simple enough. The Second Law of Thermodynamics announced that energy was constantly being expended without being replaced. The idea of progress, therefore, was a delusion; and the evidence customarily adduced to substantiate the idea sustained, instead, a very different conclusion. Civilization itself had been brought about by the operation of the Law of Entropy—the law of the dissipation of energy by the constant degradation of its vital power, rather than the reverse. Society, as an organism, is subject to the law of degradation precisely like any other organism, and faces therefore the prospect of running down indefinitely until at last total stagnation is reached. And the period of stagnation, Adams continued, is not in some remote future but in the present. In the first quarter of the twentieth century, thought "would reach the limit of its possibilities," and the honest historian might logically "treat the history of modern Europe and America as a typical example of energies indicating degradation with 'headlong rapidity' towards 'inevitable death.' " "Already," Adams concluded desperately,

[18] Henry Adams, with an introduction by Brooks Adams, *The Degradation of the Democratic Dogma* (New York, 1919), pp. 137–209.

[19] *Ibid.*, pp. 267–311; *The Education of Henry Adams*, p. 434.

"History and Sociology gasp for breath."[20] We are not concerned, here, with the validity of this argument except in so far
as it constitutes Adams' contribution to the philosophy of history, and Adams himself has furnished us the most pertinent
comment on that contribution. "Historians," he observed,
"have got into far too much trouble by following schools of
theology in their efforts to enlarge their synthesis, that they
should willingly repeat the process in science. For human purposes a point must always be soon reached where larger synthesis
is suicide."[21] In this case, certainly, the larger synthesis was
suicide. Suggestive, provocative, brilliant, and profound the
dynamic theory of history indubitably was; but the most interesting thing about it was that Adams should have advanced it.

But if Adams had damned his formal contributions to history
as insignificant and characterized his historical synthesis as intellectual suicide, we are left with only one alternative. If we
can consider neither the history nor the philosophy, we must fall
back on a consideration of Adams himself. Such an approach
has, fortunately, the warrant of excellent precedent; for it is precisely what Adams himself did in the circumstances. "One
sought," he tells us, "no absolute truth. One sought only a
spool on which to wind the thread of history without breaking
it. Among indefinite possible orbits, one sought the orbit which
would best satisfy the observed movement of the runaway star
Groombridge, 1838, commonly called Henry Adams."[22]

And there is no more convenient spool upon which to wind the
thread of history than Henry Adams. For Adams was not only a
historian: he was himself a historical fact—he was, indeed, to use
a term too often used, a significant fact. Of Adams alone, among
the major historians, can it be said that what he was is more significant than what he wrote. Of Adams alone can it be said that,
given a choice between what he wrote and what he was, we
should inevitably choose the latter. For it is no merely capricious
judgment that has preferred the *Mont Saint Michel and Chartres*[23]

[20] *The Degradation of Democratic Dogma*, pp. 243, 261. See also pp. 142, 154, 308.
[21] *The Education of Henry Adams*, pp. 401–2.
[22] *Ibid.*, p. 472.   [23] Washington, 1904.

and the *Education* to the "History" or the biographies; and as for Adams' philosophical speculations, the most thoughtful of American historians has justly observed that "Adams was worth a wilderness of philosophies."[24]

It is an exaggeration, of course, to suggest that we can interpret the whole of American history in the person of Henry Adams, but it is no very shocking exaggeration to insist that to the student of American history the contemplation of Adams is the beginning of wisdom. For whether we confine ourselves to the mere outward aspects of Adams' career or embrace the history of the entire family which he recapitulated, or penetrate to his own intellectual and psychological reactions to his generation, we will find that Adams illuminates, better than any of his contemporaries, the course of American history.

He explains for us the shift in political power from New England to the West, from agriculture to industry, from the individual to the mass, and the change in the nature of political power from intelligence to instinct, from reason to force. He reveals the decline of the intellectually aristocratic tradition and of the family tradition, the futility of intellectual discipline, the impotence of moral integrity, and the irrelevance of fastidiousness, in politics. He emphasizes what Brooks Adams called the "degradation of the democratic dogma" and the failure of eighteenth-century concepts of democracy to effect a compromise with nineteenth-century society. Intellectually he represents the transition from transcendental faith to pragmatic acquiescence, from evolutionary optimism to mechanistic pessimism, from unity to multiplicity, from order to chaos. He illustrates the rejection of the Victorian idea of progress for the idea of entropy, the rejection of a teleological universe for a mechanistic universe, the substitution of science for philosophy, of the machine for man, of force for faith, of the dynamo for the Virgin, and, at the same time, the convulsive effort to discover a philosophy that would satisfy the requirements of both instinct and reason. And he was never unaware of his significance as a symbol and as an experiment,

---

[24] Carl L. Becker, *Everyman His Own Historian: Essays on History and Politics* (New York, 1935), p. 156.

never unconscious of the larger meaning that could be read out of his intellectual and spiritual biography, and never unwilling to undertake himself the task of interpretation.

No one who has ever turned the leaves of the *Education* will forget Adams' description of the Grant administration;[25] no one who has ever read the scintillating pages of *Democracy* will fail to remember the picture of political corruption in the Washington of the seventies.[26] Anonymity could not conceal, or objectiveness disguise, the intensely personal character of these reflections. But it is a singular distinction of Adams that where he was most personal he was most general. The failure of Henry Adams to adjust himself to the politics of the Grant administration illustrated the failure of eighteenth-century democracy, of the democracy of Gallatin and John Quincy Adams, to effect such an adjustment. The indifference of the politicians of post-war America to the talents and the ideals of Adams represented the indifference of a new, industrialized America to the discipline and the ideals of the past. Adams was at pains, here, to account for his own failure; but had that been the whole of the matter, he would have dismissed the experience as cavalierly as he had dismissed Harvard College or the *North American Review*. It was because he understood the pertinence of his own experience to the experience of the American people, because he appreciated the moral implicit in his story, that he dignified this episode in his life with elaborate analysis and interpretation. So, too, with *Democracy*, that sprightly commentary on American politics and society in the gilded age. As a novel it is thin, and as an analysis of the forces behind American political corruption it is thinner still; but even its brittle thinness, its dilettantism and exoticism, may be taken to reflect certain qualities in the American mind.

Adams himself furnished the best criticism of *Democracy*. The authorship of the book had been well concealed, and it amused

[25] *The Education of Henry Adams*, chaps. xvii and xviii.

[26] *Democracy, an American Novel, passim.*

Adams to impute it to his friend John Hay. He wrote to the long-suffering Hay:

I repeat that your novel . . . . is a failure because it undertook to describe the workings of a power in this city, and spoiled a great tragic subject such as Aeschylus might have made what it should be. . . . . The tragic element, if accepted as real, is bigger here than ever on this earth before. I hate to see it mangled à la Daudet, in a tame-cat way. Men don't know tragedy when they see it.[27]

Could anything better illustrate the futile liberalism of the post-war years than this confession that a great tragic subject had been treated, deliberately, as a joke, or, what was worse, as an essay in cynicism? It is suggestive that the author of the *Gallatin*, of the *Jefferson and Madison Administrations*, should also be the author of *Democracy;* suggestive that the historian of democratic idealism should be the critic of the degradation of the democratic dogma. It is even more suggestive that that mind which had celebrated so magnanimously the idealism of Jefferson should be reduced by Blaine and Conkling to a cynicism that was frivolous and a satire that was frustrated. It was personal perhaps, but no one who recalls the impotence of the genteel tradition as represented by Godkin and Gilder and Curtis can doubt that it was more than personal.

Yet, it would be unjust to imply that Adams and his generation of liberals were defeated by the political pigmies who strut and fret their way through the pages of the *Education* or *Democracy*. Nothing as trivial as a phalanx of Blaines, Conklings, Camerons, and Butlers could account for the failure of an Adams. These men, after all, were the proper objects of satire and, where they did not render even satire ridiculous, could be disposed of easily enough. Nor was it even the more powerful Goulds and Vanderbilts and Whitneys and Morgans who made the existence of Adams irrelevant, if not impertinent. These were but the instruments of larger forces—objects, as Adams showed, of scientific study, not of moral indignation. What silenced Adams

[27] *Letters of Henry Adams*, Mar. 4, 1883, p. 348.

was precisely the realization that "modern politics is, at bottom, a struggle not of men but of forces. The men become every year more and more creatures of force, massed about central power-houses. The conflict is no longer between the men, but between the motors that drive the men, and men tend to succumb to their own motive forces."[28] It took, after all, cosmic forces to account for the tragedy of John and John Quincy Adams, and the indifference of a modern world to the existence of a Henry Adams was less humiliating when it was seen to be the inevitable consequence of scientific forces over whose operation man exercised no control. The failure of Henry Adams to achieve his education was indeed a failure of so cataclysmic a character that it was necessary to invoke the whole of science and philosophy in order to explain it.

But here, again, the experience of Adams was the experience of his generation, though Adams alone seemed to appreciate it. For when Adams began that long pilgrimage which was to end, so curiously, before the altar of Chartres, he had no need of faith other than faith in the beneficent workings of the laws of the universe. Darwin and Lyell had taught him evolution, and every one knew that evolution meant progress. Science and sociology joined hands to justify the findings of the historian; and it was clear that the dreams of Rousseau and Condorcet, of Jefferson and Gallatin, fell short of realities, and that the intuitive truths of transcendentalism were to be justified by the experimental truths of the laboratory. "Then he had entered gaily the door of the glacial epoch, and had surveyed a universe of unities and uniformities."[29] But science was a slut, and treated Adams as shamefully as she had treated his grandfather, John Quincy Adams. Parrington says:

In the nineties the clouds drew over the brilliant Victorian skies. With the substitution of physics for biology came a more somber mood that was to put away the genial romanticism of Victorian evolution, substitute a mechanistic conception for the earlier teleological prog-

---

[28] *The Education of Henry Adams*, pp. 421–22.   [29] *Ibid.*, p. 400.

ress, and reshape its philosophy in harmony with a deterministic pessimism that denied purpose or plan in the changing universe of matter.[30]

Of all Americans, Adams most fully comprehended the change, and he most fully illustrated it. Not for him the heavenly vision of truth that was revealed to John Fiske in his youth: "When we have come to a true philosophy, and make *that* our standpoint, all things become clear. We know what things to learn, and what, in the infinite mass of things to leave unlearned—and then the Universe becomes clear and harmonious."[31] Alas for Adams, his true philosophy taught him only infinite confusion and chaos and left him naked and defenseless in a world that had "neither joy, nor love, nor light, nor certitude, nor peace, nor help for pain."

It would be misleading, of course, to interpret this tragedy as intellectual merely. Indeed, it might almost be said that the whole of Adams' intellectual career was an effort to find some impersonal meaning in the tragedy that had shattered his life. For when he returned home that bleak December morning to find Marian Hooper dead, he entered the waste lands; and for twenty years he walked in desolation until at last he had convinced himself that the universe was but desolation.

To an intimate, he might reveal his anguish; and to Elizabeth Cameron he confessed: "The light has gone out. I am not to blame. As long as I could make life work, I stood by it, and swore by it as though it was my God, as indeed it was."[32] But in his more formal writing he preserved his immaculate impersonality:

The child born in 1900 . . . . found himself in a land where no one had ever penetrated before; where order was an accidental relation obnoxious to nature; artificial compulsion imposed on motion; against which every free energy of the universe revolted; and which, being

[30] V. L. Parrington, *The Beginnings of Critical Realism in America* (New York, 1930), pp. 190–91.

[31] Quoted by John S. Clark in his *The Life and Letters of John Fiske* (2 vols.; Boston and New York, 1917), I, 255.

[32] *Letters of Henry Adams*, Jan. 2, 1891, p. 458.

merely occasional, resolved itself back into anarchy at last. He could not deny that the law of the new universe explained much that had been most obscure, especially the persistently fiendish treatment of man by man; the perpetual effort of society to establish law, and the perpetual revolt of society against the law it had established; the perpetual building up of authority by force, and the perpetual appeal to force to overthrow it; the perpetual symbolism of a higher law, and the perpetual relapse to a lower one; the perpetual victory of the principles of freedom, and their perpetual conversion into principles of power; but the staggering problem was the outlook ahead into the despotism of artificial order which nature abhorred. . . . .

All that a historian won was a vehement wish to escape. He saw his education complete, and was sorry he ever began it. As a matter of taste, he greatly preferred his eighteenth-century education when God was a father and nature a mother, and all was for the best in a scientific universe.[33]

Adams was right, of course, in generalizing his own tragedy; that tragedy was more immediate, more catastrophic even, than the tragedy of others who wandered in the waste lands of the new century; but that it was universal, rather than merely personal, no one can doubt. Twentieth-century America was a nation adrift from its moorings, skeptical of its past, uncertain of its future, The old faiths were gone, the muscular Calvinism of the seventeenth century, the enlightened deism of the eighteenth, the romantic and buoyant transcendentalism of the nineteenth. Pragmatism was a sorry substitute for faith, and the drift from Jefferson to Emerson and from Emerson to Dewey was as heartbreaking as the drift from Newton to Darwin and from Darwin to Haeckel.

No one better illustrated this drift than did Adams himself, and no one was more sensitive to its significance. To Jefferson and his followers the destiny of America, the destiny of mankind, was plain, and they did not doubt the ability of man to control that destiny; but Adams knew that he was the creature, the victim, of forces that he but faintly understood and over which he could exercise no control, and he knew that he was

[33] *The Education of Henry Adams*, pp. 457–58.

unique only in the extent to which he understood his impotence. Intellectually Adams recognized the chaos, the multiplicity, of the twentieth century; and he even went so far as to furnish us with the most illuminating study of that multiplicity in our literature. But intellectually he had recognized, too, the inevitable defeat of "his eighteenth century, his Constitution of 1789, his George Washington, his Harvard College, his Quincy, and his Plymouth Pilgrims. . . . . He had hugged his antiquated dislike of bankers and capitalistic society until he had become little better than a crank. . . . . He had known for years that he must accept the régime, but he had known a great many other disagreeable certainties—like age, senility, and death—against which one made what little resistance one could."[34] Recognition and acquiescence were very different matters, and there was rebel blood in the Adams veins. "The soul," he wrote, "has always refused to live in peace with the body. The angels, too, were always in rebellion." As a matter of taste, he had said, he much preferred a philosophy in which "God was a father and nature a mother, and all was for the best in a scientific universe."[35]

His revolt against the chaos of modern science threw him back on the unity of the church. It was not a matter of taste merely. Force for force, as he never tired of observing, the Virgin was as intelligible as the dynamo, and as powerful. So Adams, "happy in the thought that at last he had found a mistress who could see no difference in the age of her lovers,"[36] turned to the adoration of the Virgin. It was in part an emotional reaction, an act of faith; but Adams could not be satisfied with a reaction merely emotional: he had to rationalize his faith in the power and the grace of the Virgin as John Quincy Adams had rationalized his faith in a democracy. He who had lived, passionately, the life of reason, who had inherited from generations of Adams' a reverent respect for reason, made this gesture of faith an exercise in historical logic.

Abélard had been silenced, and St. Thomas had formulated a philosophy which explained the universe as a unity; but Adams

---

[34] *Ibid.*, pp. 343–44.   [35] *Ibid.*, p. 458.   [36] *Ibid.*, p. 470.

found unity not as the conclusion of a syllogism, though he was fascinated by the syllogism, but in the life and thought and emotion of generations of men. He was persuaded not by the *Summa theologiae* but by the Merveille of the cathedral of St. Michel, by the rose window of Chartres, by the *Chanson de Roland*, and by the miracles of the Virgin.

The Virgin was not rational, but she was the most rational thing in an irrational universe. Faith was above law and scorned logic; and Adams, who had discovered that law was chance and logic bankrupt, preferred to take his chances with the Virgin rather than with science.

Mary concentrated in herself the whole rebellion of man against fate; the whole protest against divine law; the whole contempt for human law as its outcome; the whole unutterable fury of human nature beating itself against the walls of its prisonhouse, and suddenly seized by a hope that in the Virgin man had found a door of escape. She was above law; she took feminine pleasure in turning Hell into an ornament; she delighted in trampling on every social distinction in this world and the next. She knew that the universe was as unintelligible to her, on any theory of morals, as it was to her worshippers, and she felt, like them, no sure conviction that it was any more intelligible to the Creator of it.[37]

Uprooted and demoralized, his life a broken arch, his past without meaning and his future without hope, tortured by a restlessness that found no repose in thought and no purpose in action, resigned to the bankruptcy of reason and the futility of knowledge, disillusioned of progress and of evolution, reconciled to the degradation of energy, the exhaustion of society, and the fall of man, lost in a universe that was mechanistic and chaotic, Adams turned in desperation to the one symbol of unity that seemed to have meaning, and found there such solace as he could. "Her pity," he knew, "had no limit";[38] and it was not only Adams but his generation that needed limitless pity.

[37] *Mont Saint Michel and Chartres*, p. 241; see also p. 286.

[38] *Ibid.*, pp. 83, 244.

XI

ALFRED THAYER MAHAN

JULIUS W. PRATT
University of Buffalo

I shared the prepossession, common at that time, that the naval history of the past was wholly past; of no use at all to the present. . . . .
Thus my mind was troubled how to establish relations between yester-
day and to-day; so wholly ignorant was I of the underlying reproduc-
tion of conditions in their essential bearings—a commonplace of military art.

He who seeks, finds, if he does not lose heart; and to me, continuously seeking, came from within the suggestion that control of the sea was
an historic factor which had never been systematically appreciated and
expounded. Once formulated consciously, this thought became the
nucleus of all my writing for twenty years then to come. . . . .[1]

THIS passage from Alfred Thayer Mahan's brief autobiography describes the germination of the idea which,
through repeated exposition and illustration, was to
make him one of America's best known and most widely acclaimed historians.

Of Mahan, if of any great writer, it can be justly said that he
had greatness thrust upon him. At any rate, the opportunity for
achievement came to him fortuitously and without his own seeking. A graduate of the United States Naval Academy in the class
of 1859,[2] he had served with merit in the United States Navy

[1] A. T. Mahan, *From Sail to Steam, Recollections of Naval Life* (New York and London,
1907), pp. 275–76.

[2] Mahan was born on September 27, 1840, at West Point, New York, where his father,
Dennis Hart Mahan, was professor of engineering at the United States Military Academy.

during the Civil War and had passed the twenty years thereafter in the rather wearisome routine characteristic of a naval officer's life in times of peace. No especial distinction had been his; and, in his forty-fourth year there appeared little ahead of him save a continuance of quiet routine service, an honorable retirement, and a respectable old age.

He had, however, undertaken one small piece of historical writing; and this it was, presumably, which now gave to his life a wholly unexpected turn. In 1883 he had published a small volume[3] dealing with naval operations on the Mississippi River and along the Gulf Coast during the Civil War. This book, while exhibiting care and diligence in getting at the facts, showed no special aptitude for critical treatment of military or naval history,[4] and certainly no signs of the philosophic approach which was to characterize Mahan's later writing. Yet officers who wrote history were not numerous in the navy; and it is not surprising that Commodore Stephen B. Luce, president of the newly created Naval War College, at Newport, Rhode Island, should have selected Captain Mahan to deliver a series of lectures on naval history and naval tactics at the new institution. The invitation reached Mahan, then in command of the U.S.S. "Wachusett" on the west coast of South America, about the first of September, 1884.

The elder Mahan was born in the United States, of Irish parentage, and was baptized in the Roman Catholic church. He was brought up as a Protestant, however; and his son, the subject of this sketch, was a member of the Protestant Episcopal church. Alfred Thayer Mahan's mother, Mary Helena Okill, was the daughter of an Englishman and of Mary Jay, a member of the well-known French Huguenot family. Thus the historian had strains of Irish, English, and French-American blood. "Yet, as far as I understand my personality," he remarked, "I think to see in the result the predominance which the English strain has usually asserted for itself over others." *Ibid.*, p. xii. C. C. Taylor, *The Life of Admiral Mahan, Naval Philosopher* (New York, 1920), pp. 1–3. See also Allan Westcott's sketch in *Dictionary of American Biography*, XII (New York, 1933), 206–8. Before entering the Naval Academy, Mahan had spent two years at Columbia College.

[3] *The Gulf and Inland Waters* (New York, 1883). This was the third and last volume in a series, *The Navy in the Civil War*.

[4] It is instructive to compare the simple narrative presentation found in this volume with the critical appraisal of strategy and tactics applied to the same facts in Mahan's *Admiral Farragut* (New York, *ca.* 1892), written nine years later.

Mahan accepted the offer at once, but it was not until a year later that he was relieved of the command of the "Wachusett" and permitted to assume his new duties. In the interval, however, he was giving thought and study to the problem before him. The idea described in his own words at the beginning of this sketch gradually took form. The library of the "Wachusett" contained "little material and less that [was] first-rate";[5] but in the English Club at Lima, Peru, he found Mommsen's *History of Rome*, and, as he read Mommsen's account of Hannibal's invasion of Italy, he received an inspiration. He records:

It suddenly struck me, whether by some chance phrase of the author I do not know, how different things might have been could Hannibal have invaded Italy by sea, as the Romans often had Africa, instead of by the long land route; or could he, after arrival, have been in free communication with Carthage by water. This clew, once laid hold of, I followed up in the particular instance. It and the general theory already conceived threw on each other reciprocal illustration; and between the two my plan was formed by the time I teached home, in September, 1885. I would investigate coincidently the general history and naval history of the past two centuries, with a view to demonstrating the influence of the events of the one upon the other. Original research was not within my scope, nor was it necessary to the scheme thus outlined.[6]

After returning to the United States in September, 1885, Mahan began work in earnest, devoted the months up to the end of the following May to reading, and the summer months to writing, and by September, 1886, as he relates, "had on paper, in lecture form, all of [his] first *Sea Power* book, except the summary of conclusions which constitutes the final chapter."[7]

Rarely has a historian, in so short a time and with so little preparation, composed a book so justly famous as *The Influence of Sea Power upon History*. The key to Mahan's success lay not in the achievement of any great piece of research, in the more recondite sense of the term. "Original research," he said, "was not within my scope." His sources for the facts of naval history were "chiefly histories written long before, supplemented by a

5 Taylor, p. 30.   6 *From Sail to Steam*, p. 277.   7 *Ibid.*, p. 285.

great many scattered papers of more recent date.''[8] Most of these, particularly the older histories—such as the writings of Campbell and James in English and Lapeyrouse-Bonfils in French—were simple narratives, with little studied criticism. For military principles applicable to the naval art he was forced to turn to writers upon land warfare, above all Jomini, from whom, as he says, "I learned the few, very few, leading considerations in military combination; and in these I found the key by which, using the record of sailing navies and the actions of naval leaders, I could elicit, from the naval history upon which I had looked despondingly, instruction still pertinent.''[9] For the general historical background, which should serve as the setting for his story of the operations and influence of navies, Mahan "relied upon the usual accredited histories of the period. . . . . The subject lay so much on the surface that my handling of it could scarcely suffer materially from possible future discoveries.''[10]

Nor did Mahan claim to have made a new discovery in historical interpretation. His thesis had, it is true, developed independently in his own thought. Yet others had preceded him. "Not to mention other predecessors, with the full roll of whose names I am even now unacquainted, Bacon and Raleigh, three centuries before, had epitomized in a few words the theme on which I was to write volumes.''[11] Mahan's opportunity, to use once more his own words, lay in the fact "that no one since those two great Englishmen had undertaken to demonstrate their thesis by an analysis of history, attempting to show from current events, through a long series of years, precisely what influence the command of the sea had had upon definite issues. . . . . This field had been left vacant, yielding me my opportunity.''[12]

That Mahan seized this opportunity; that he demonstrated, with fact piled upon fact and with unceasing emphasis of his main thesis, the determining influence of sea power in modern times; and that he told his story in untechnical language, as in-

[8] *Ibid.*, p. 280.

[9] *Ibid.*, p. 282.   [11] *Ibid.*, p. 276.

[10] *Ibid.*, p. 284.   [12] *Ibid.*

telligible to the statesman, the journalist, and even the man in the street as to the naval expert—this achievement constitutes Mahan's first claim to fame. But fame is a plant which requires nourishing soil as well as fertile seed, and for Mahan's thesis the times were most propitious. Already there was a reawakening to the importance of sea power, not only in Great Britain, which had enjoyed its fruits in the past, but in Germany, Japan, and even the United States. Already there was beginning that renewed competition in navies and in the acquisition of colonial possessions which was to play so conspicuous and so tragic a role in the international relations of the next thirty years, and Mahan's reasoned demonstration that command of the sea was essential to national well-being supplied the justification for policies already adopted or contemplated. His teaching, as one British writer remarked, "was as oil to the flame of 'colonial expansion' everywhere leaping into life."[13] Such a book at such a time could not fail to make its author famous.

But we have anticipated the course of events. The impulse to publish, as Mahan recalled it, came to him as the result of the favorable reception accorded his lectures by the officers at the Naval War College, where they were first delivered in the autumn of 1886. He repeated the course in the two succeeding years, working, at the same time, to perfect his literary style. His besetting anxiety, he says, "was to be exact and lucid"; and he confesses that the effort to achieve these qualities often encumbered his sentences with an accumulation of qualifying clauses, which gained accuracy at the expense of ease and grace.[14]

The Influence of Sea Power upon History, 1660–1783, was published in May, 1890. Its success was immediate, though the reviews, as Mahan admitted uncomplainingly, "were much more explicit

[13] *Blackwood's Edinburgh Magazine*, CLXIII (April, 1898), 564. The effect of Mahan's books and articles in stimulating this international rivalry is discussed with force, but possibly with some exaggeration, by Mr. Louis M. Hacker, in his article "The Incendiary Mahan," *Scribner's Magazine*, XCV (April, 1934), 263–68, 311–20. To the present writer it seems highly probable that that rivalry would have developed in much the same way had Mahan never been heard of.

[14] *From Sail to Steam*, pp. 285–88.

and hearty in Europe, and especially in Great Britain, than in the United States."[15] Yet there was no lack of appreciation on the part of Mahan's own countrymen. Officers of both the army and navy wrote to express enthusiastic opinions, and two young statesmen who were to play leading roles in the upbuilding of American sea power became at once devotees of Mahan's philosophy. Theodore Roosevelt wrote Mahan that he considered the book "very much the clearest and most instructive general work of the kind" with which he was acquainted, adding: "I am greatly in error if it does not become a classic."[16] Henry Cabot Lodge, first in the House of Representatives and later in the Senate, became the leading proponent of sea-power philosophy in the halls of Congress.[17] Both Roosevelt and Lodge found in Mahan's interpretation of history the practical guidance which it was his dearest desire to impart.

Mahan's labors at the Naval War College (of which he had become president in 1886) were interrupted, after the session of 1888, by an unsympathetic administration; and he was sent away on other duty. During the next three years the college itself was in a state of "suspended animation"; but Mahan was permitted by the Navy Department to devote his time to the preparation of his next great work, *The Influence of Sea Power upon the French Revolution and Empire, 1793–1812*, which was published in December, 1892. The exemption from sea duty which made possible the completion of this study was obtained only with some difficulty. The chief of the Bureau of Navigation ruled against it, with the remark, "It is not the business of a naval officer to write books"; and the desired privilege was secured only through an appeal to the Secretary of the Navy, Mr. Benjamin F. Tracy.[18]

The publication of the new work—more substantial, more detailed, and more largely the product of original research than its predecessor—added greatly to Mahan's reputation, both in

[15] *Ibid.*, p. 302.

[16] Taylor, p. 45.

[17] E.g., *Congressional Record*, 51st Cong., 2d sess., p. 1856; 53d Cong., 3d sess., pp. 3082–84.

[18] *From Sail to Steam*, pp. 311–12.

the United States[19] and abroad. His fame in England presently received convincing demonstration. His request that he be permitted to remain ashore until he should be eligible for retirement in 1896, in order that he might carry his study through the War of 1812, was refused by the Navy Department; and he was assigned to command the cruiser "Chicago." This vessel, as it turned out, was ordered to European waters as the flagship of the admiral commanding on that station. In England, Mahan found himself in the rather embarrassing position of being a much more famous man than his commanding officer. Not only was he dined by the queen and the prime minister and entertained as guest of honor by the Royal Navy Club—the first foreigner to have been so honored—but he achieved the perhaps more memorable distinction of receiving within one week the degrees of D.C.L. from Oxford and LL.D. from Cambridge—a cue which was followed by Harvard, Yale, and Columbia after his return to the United States.[20]

Mahan's voluntary retirement in 1896, upon the completion of forty years of naval service,[21] gave him the opportunity, in ample measure, for the preparation of the work published nine years later, *Sea Power in Its Relations to the War of 1812*. This study, with those which had preceded it, completed the task which the author had set himself in 1885—the analysis of the influence of sea power upon history from the middle of the seventeenth century to the close of the Napoleonic wars. It was the last of his formal historical works.[22] In the meantime he had published two biog-

[19] Cf. reviews of the two works in *Harper's New Monthly Magazine*, LXXXVII (November, 1893), 962, and in *Political Science Quarterly*, IX (March, 1894), 171–73, the latter by Theodore Roosevelt.

[20] *From Sail to Steam*, pp. 313–14.

[21] In 1906 Captain Mahan was promoted to the grade of rear admiral on the retired list.

[22] *The Major Operations of the Navies in the War of American Independence* (Boston, 1913) had appeared originally as a chapter in the third volume of Sir William Laird Clowes's *The Royal Navy: A History from the Earliest Times to the Present* (7 vols.; London, 1897–1903). With the exception of the illuminating account of Benedict Arnold's naval campaign on Lake Champlain in 1776, it is an elaboration of the later chapters of *The Influence of Sea Power upon History, 1660–1783* (Boston, 1890).

raphies: *Admiral Farragut*, which may be regarded as a more mature and critical treatment of the theme of *The Gulf and Inland Waters;* and *The Life of Nelson, the Embodiment of the Sea Power of Great Britain* (2 vols.; London, 1897), a major biography in which, while his declared aim was "to realize personality by living with the man,"[23] he nevertheless found ample occasion to elaborate his thesis of the preponderant role of sea power in Great Britain's struggle with France of the Revolution and Napoleon. *Types of Naval Officers, Drawn from the History of the British Navy* (Boston, 1901), was another by-product of his central work. Numerous books were still to come from his pen, but they were not histories. History had yielded to him the lessons which he had sought. His remaining years were spent in urging those lessons upon his countrymen.

Mahan's approach to history had, from the beginning, and by the circumstances of that beginning, been extremely practical. Detailed to lecture on naval history and naval tactics to a group of practical men, he had sought from the first "to impart to the subject of Naval History an aspect which, in this very utilitarian age, should not be open to the ready reproach of having merely archaeological interest, and possessing no practical value for men called upon to use the changed materials of modern naval war."[24] So fully did he succeed in this purpose that he became, through the medium of his interpretation of history, one of the leading propagandists of his generation.

We may suppose that this emphasis upon practicality largely influenced Mahan's conception of the historian's art. Throughout the sea-power books, detailed as they are, all the detail is nevertheless rigidly subordinated to the main thesis. In 1902 Mahan was honored with the presidency of the American Historical Association; and his presidential address, "Subordination in Historical Treatment,"[25] was a plea for an artistic presenta-

---

[23] *From Sail to Steam*, p. 318.

[24] *The Influence of Sea Power upon the French Revolution and Empire, 1793–1812* (14th ed., 2 vols.; Boston, 1918), I, iii. The first edition was published in Boston, 1892.

[25] American Historical Association, *Annual Report, 1902* (Washington, 1903), I, 49–63.

tion which should subordinate details in order to emphasize the most significant trend in any historical period. He deplored the tendency to present facts for their own sake, without pattern, and the habit of searching laboriously for facts which could not be significant if found. "The significance of the whole must be brought out by careful arrangement and exposition, which must not be made to wait too long upon unlimited scrutiny. The passion for certainty may lapse into incapacity for decision—a vice recognized in military life, and which needs recognition elsewhere."[26]

The principle here expressed has evident merit, if also evident dangers. Certainly all great history has sought to reduce details to pattern and to exhibit their central significance. What Mahan seemingly did not realize was the relativity of significance. Every historical event, or series of events, could be made to surrender its true significance. Each might be treated "as a work of art, which has a central feature around which details are to be grouped, but kept ever subordinate to its due development"; and when this should have been done, "each particular incident, and group of incidents, becomes as it were a fully wrought and fashioned piece, prepared for adjustment in its place in the great mosaic, which the history of the race is gradually fashioning under the Divine overruling."[27]

By historians endowed with divine perspicacity history could be thus definitively written. That each human generation might find a new significance in the same historical episode Mahan did not recognize. To him, for example, it was clear that the significance of the sectional conflict in America was "in the long struggle between freedom and slavery, union and disunion."[28] To some historians of the next generation, as intent as Mahan upon finding central significance, other features would be as plainly central.

This simple belief that certitude was attainable was not unrelated to Mahan's religious prepossessions. His faith that human

[26] *Ibid.*, p. 58.   [27] *Ibid.*, p. 61.   [28] *Ibid.*, p. 55.

events marched under "the Divine overruling," which the careful reader will find implicit in much of his history, was expressly avowed in his other writings. The advance of Christianity he identified with the progress of all that was good in civilization.[29] To insure that advance, Providence worked in mysterious ways, leading the great Christian powers to build up armaments which, ostensibly designed against one another, were destined to serve in the defense of Christian civilization against the massed forces of the Orient.[30] One nation above others appeared to have been the recipient of peculiar providential attention and guidance. When one reflects, wrote Mahan, upon the chains of accidents by which Great Britain had taken and held Gibraltar and Jamaica, "one marvels whether incidents so widely separated in time and place, all tending towards one end—the maritime predominance of Great Britain—can be accidents, or are simply the exhibition of a Personal Will, acting through all time, with purpose deliberate and consecutive, to ends not yet discerned."[31]

God chose to work through human instruments, and men and nations who would serve Him must keep their powder dry. "Of the Christian religion the great constituent is power; which in another shape, easily assumed, becomes force. Force is power in action. . . . . Without man's responsive effort, God Himself is —not powerless—but deprived of the instrument through which alone He wills to work."[32] Within the Christian community, however it might be elsewhere, weakness became a sin; power, almost a guaranty of righteousness. The possession of power was "no mere casual attribute, but the indication of qualities which should, as they assuredly will, make their way to the front and to the top in the relations of states."[33] Abuses of power were self-correcting,[34] but for weakness there was no compensa-

[29] "Twentieth Century Christianity," *North American Review*, CXCIX (April, 1914), 589–98.

[30] *The Interest of America in Sea Power, Present and Future* (Boston, 1897), p. 264.

[31] *Ibid.*, pp. 307–8.

[32] *Armaments and Arbitration, or the Place of Force in the International Relations of States* (New York and London, 1912), pp. 116–17.

[33] *Ibid.*, p. 85.   [34] *Ibid.*, p. 86.

tion. Hence one finds in Mahan far less condemnation of the misuse of force, as by Louis XIV and Napoleon, than of the neglect of it, as by Jefferson. Force, in the long run, could be better trusted than law to effect the just settlement of international disputes; for a settlement unimpeachably legal might yet be incompatible with existing conditions and hence insecure; "whereas in the long run the play of natural forces reaches an adjustment corresponding to the fundamental facts of the case."[35]

Such were the assumptions underlying Mahan's writing of history. Of that history—so successfully did he apply the principle of subordinating details to the central tendency—the main thread admits of summary in few words. As has been stated, he undertook to narrate and explain the rise and triumphant progress of British sea power from the middle of the seventeenth century— a starting-point fixed "by the essentially new departure in the history of England and France, connoted by the almost simultaneous accession of Charles II. and Louis XIV."[36]—to the close of the Napoleonic wars.

In the first two sections of his work[37] his theme was the success, both political and economic, which England had achieved through a wise and steady upbuilding of her sea power, contrasted with the disaster which thrice overwhelmed France by reason of her neglect of it.

"The history of sea power," wrote Mahan at the beginning of his first great book, "while embracing in its broad sweep all that tends to make a people great upon the sea or by the sea, is largely a military history."[38] So it is, in his hands; yet Mahan never permits the reader to forget that navies, campaigns, and battles are only means to further ends. Sea power includes not only military navies and their essential bases of operation but merchant shipping and sea-borne trade. A flourishing merchant shipping is essential to the maintenance of a successful navy—that the

[35] *Ibid.*, p. 12.

[36] *From Sail to Steam*, p. 281.

[37] *The Influence of Sea Power upon History, 1660–1783; The Influence of Sea Power upon the French Revolution and Empire, 1793–1812.*

[38] *The Influence of Sea Power upon History*, p. 1.

navy may have a reservoir of skilled seamen in time of war; but the chief debt is in the other direction, for without a navy, merchant shipping, sea-borne trade, and with them national prosperity may all be swept away. Of England's success, the secret was that, possessing all the essential elements of sea power[39]— among them government by a landed aristocracy which adhered to a sound political tradition, was proud of its country's glory, and "comparatively insensible to the sufferings of the community by which that glory is maintained"[40]—she had consistently supported a navy adequate to protect her commerce, strengthening her position by the appropriation of colonies and naval bases as occasion offered, and thus had enjoyed steady prosperity even in time of war. Control of the sea conferred economic power, and the two combined made their possessor the arbiter of world-affairs. Thus England, because she cultivated sea power while her opponents neglected it, was enabled to thwart the overweening schemes of Louis XIV and Napoleon and, as Mahan plainly believed, to rescue civilization from those who would have destroyed it.[41]

In emphatic contrast stood France, with material potentialities for the development of sea power not inferior to those of her rival, but lacking, in her government, the steady determination to employ them. Colbert's plans for maritime development were set aside by Louis XIV that he might better devote French resources to the pursuit of territorial and dynastic ambitions on the continent of Europe. Deluded monarch! Deprived of the invigorating support of sea-borne commerce, French resources wasted away and proved unequal to the tasks which Louis had sought to impose upon them. Not Louis's thirst for conquest, but his failure to support it with sea power, receives the historian's pitying rebuke. From the close of the seventeenth century until after the Seven Years' War, French naval power was hopelessly inferior to British. The War of American Independence

[39] The "elements of sea power" are analyzed in *The Influence of Sea Power upon History*, pp. 25–89.

[40] *Ibid.*, p. 66.

[41] *The Influence of Sea Power upon the French Revolution and Empire*, II, 371.

found France at last in possession of a navy which could threaten British supremacy; but its efficiency was soon destroyed by the subversive doctrines of the French Revolution, and Napoleon was never able to restore its morale. His efforts to do so reached their tragic climax at Trafalgar. Thereafter, his hopeless inferiority at sea left him no weapon against England save the Continental System, and this it was which in the end encompassed his downfall.[42]

In the third portion of the narrative, *Sea Power in Its Relations to the War of 1812*, the scene shifts from Europe to the United States; and for Mahan's countrymen, as he remarks in the Preface, "the lesson is rather that of the influence of a negative quantity upon national history."[43] The emphasis which, in the earlier volumes, had been placed upon the success of Great Britain, through command of sea power, is here upon the failure of the United States through lack of it.

The causes of the War of 1812 Mahan found wholly upon the sea. The local grievances and ambitions of the westerners he did not recognize. The measures which the British government employed in overthrowing Napoleon, and thus saving civilization,[44] says Mahan, "grievously injured the United States; by international law grievously wronged her also." They were "invasions of just rights, to which the United States should not have submitted." But since England, had she attempted to square her practice with international law, would have been overwhelmed; and since the Britisher's conviction of the rightfulness of his measures was "a compulsive moral force," it is clear that neither party could rightly yield. Both were right, by their honest convictions, and the controversy could be solved

[42] Mahan does not, of course, neglect the sea power of the Spanish, the Dutch, or the Baltic peoples; but all of these played minor roles.

[43] *Sea Power in Its Relations to the War of 1812* (2 vols.; Boston, 1905), I, v.

[44] "The great gain to the cause of stability in human history was made when the spirit of order and law, embodied in the great nation which it had created, rose against the spirit of lawlessness and anarchy, which had now possessed a people who for long years and by nature had been submissively subject to external authority" (*Influence of Sea Power upon the French Revolution and Empire*, II, 371).

only by arms; for "the nation or man is disgraced who shirks an obligation to defend right."[45]

Which was the higher right—the right of Great Britain to employ all needful measures, however illegal, for the destruction of "the spirit of lawlessness and anarchy" incarnate in the French Revolution and Napoleon; or the right of the United States to resist those measures? Such appraisal Mahan did not undertake. Pursuing his reasoning to the end, one must conclude that had the United States prepared the moderate naval force (ten or twelve ships-of-the-line[46]) which would have forced England to square her practice with international law, England would have been "overwhelmed,"[47] and "the spirit of lawlessness and anarchy" would have triumphed over "the spirit of order and law."[48]

Such a paradox, if he was aware of it, did not disturb Mahan. He was intent upon demonstrating the beneficent influence of sea power. Writing of England and Napoleon, he must show that British sea power saved not only England but civilization. Writing, some years later, of England and the United States, he must show that sea power, had she possessed it, would have saved the United States from disaster or disgrace. What if the two happy results were incompatible, mutually exclusive? From each study he had extracted the lesson which he wished.[49]

The lesson for the United States was very plain indeed. Gouverneur Morris had once estimated that the young Republic could, without extravagance, maintain a navy of twenty ships-of-the-line, with the appropriate auxiliary craft.[50] Had this force—or even half of it—been created, the United States would have been in a position to compel England, preoccupied as she

---

[45] *Sea Power in Its Relations to the War of 1812*, I, vii–ix.

[46] *Ibid.*, II, 212.

[47] *Ibid.*, I, ix.

[48] *Influence of Sea Power upon the French Revolution and Empire*, II, 371.

[49] The same tendency to be carried away with enthusiasm for the subject under his hand is seen in the way in which he pictures at one time Pitt, at another Nelson, as the great antagonist of Napoleon. Cf. *The Influence of Sea Power upon the French Revolution and Empire*, II, 404, with *The Life of Nelson*, I, 96–97.

[50] *Sea Power in Its Relations to the War of 1812*, I, 71.

was in Europe, to respect American rights.[51] Lacking such a force, the United States found "an admirable opportunity to write State Papers."[52] The government which must defend its rights by argument without the backing of force, "citing laws and privileges to men who wear swords," was, in Mahan's mind, almost beneath contempt. He penned no passage so full of scorn as that in which he described James Madison, the unfortunate Secretary of State:

. . . . The discussion of principles, the exposure of an adversary's weakness or inconsistencies, the weighty marshalling of uncounted words, were to him the breath of life; and with happy disregard of the need to back phrases with deeds, there now opened before him a career of argumentation, of logical deduction and exposition, constituting a condition of political and personal enjoyment which only the deskman can fully appreciate. It was not, however, an era in which the pen was mightier than the sword; and in the smooth gliding of the current Niagara was forgotten.[53]

Through all Mahan's sea-power volumes, then, runs this precept: Without command of the sea, no nation can attain the fullest measure of internal well-being or of influence in world-affairs. What might follow if this doctrine should win too wide and ready acceptance was perhaps obscured for Mahan himself by his trust in an overruling Providence which would use human power for righteous ends. The dangerous potentialities of his teaching were realized by contemporary critics. *The Influence of Sea Power upon History* seemed, to one British writer, "an admirable book, but the most incendiary of modern times." It should have been published, if at all, in a language intelligible only to Americans and Englishmen, or better still, to Englishmen alone.[54] Its popularity in Germany and Japan[55] was portentous.

[51] *Ibid.*, II, 212.

[52] *Influence of Sea Power upon the French Revolution and Empire*, II, 357.

[53] *Sea Power in Its Relations to the War of 1812*, I, 106.

[54] *Blackwood's Edinburgh Magazine*, CLXIII (April, 1898), 563.

[55] Cf. Taylor, p. 155; *From Sail to Steam*, pp. 302–3.

But while history's deepest lessons concerned national policy, it also had much to teach of strategy and tactics. Mahan went to great pains in analyzing the strategy of campaigns and the tactics of naval engagements, and from these analyses he derived principles as applicable to the navies of steam and steel as to those of wood and sail. Strategically, the great offensive function of a navy was to interrupt the enemy's communications—to destroy his fruitful commerce—not by mere cruiser warfare, which, while annoying, could not be fatal, but by application of that overwhelming force which could seal an enemy's ports and exclude him utterly from the sea.[56]

Of naval tactics, Mahan's ideal exemplar was Nelson, always eager for a fight and never satisfied with less than the annihilation of the enemy's armed forces. Disregarding the slightly hazy line between strategy and tactics, we may say that Mahan's conception of the proper principles of naval war is summarized in three maxims: the first, which he learned from Jomini, that "the organized forces of the enemy are ever the chief objective";[57] the second and third, from Nelson: "Only numbers can annihilate"; and, "Now, had we taken ten sail, and had allowed the eleventh to escape, when it would have been possible to have got at her, I could never have called it well done."[58] To these may be added Napoleon's "War cannot be waged without running risks" and Farragut's "The *best* protection against the enemy's fire is a well-directed fire from our own guns."[59] After Nelson, the naval commanders who best exemplified this style of warfare were perhaps Farragut, Oliver Hazard Perry, and Admiral Suffren, who, almost alone among French naval officers, had combined a high degree of technical skill with a belief in bringing his opponent to close and decisive action.[60]

That Mahan's history was always propagandist in purpose is

[56] *Influence of Sea Power upon History*, p. 138.

[57] *From Sail to Steam*, p. 283.

[58] *Life of Nelson*, II, 333; I, 169.

[59] *Sea Power in Its Relations to the War of 1812*, II, 99; *Admiral Farragut*, pp. 315–16.

[60] *Influence of Sea Power upon History*, chap. xii.

evident from what has been said. With propaganda in this indirect form he was by no means satisfied. From 1890 until his death in 1914 he was a constant contributor of articles upon current issues to American magazines; and those articles, as eventually published in book form, occupy close to a fifth of the traditional five-foot shelf.[61] Aside from the underlying thesis of the vital importance of sea power in its broadest sense, including foreign trade, merchant marine, navy, and naval bases at strategic points, the chief specific lessons with which Mahan sought to indoctrinate his countrymen were three: the United States must control the future isthmian canal and the approaches to it upon either side; the United States must, in co-operation with the other Teutonic powers, take an aggressive attitude toward Asia; the United States must never commit itself to the substitution of arbitration for force in the settlement of international disputes.

Mahan's influence upon the expansion of the United States in the Caribbean and the eastern Pacific has been treated elsewhere.[62] As to Asia, he looked forward with apprehension to a period when Christian and European civilization should confront an awakened and organized Orient. For the protection of the West it was essential that the United States possess not only a navy and an isthmian canal but military outposts at the enemy's gates. But this was not a mere question of military and naval strategy. As Rome had partially civilized and Christianized the barbarians before their invading hordes broke over her boundaries, thus lessening the shock of their impact, so might the menace of the Orient be largely removed if that land could be imbued with "the corrective and elevating element of the higher ideals, which in Europe have made good their controlling in-

[61] *The Interest of America in Sea Power, Present and Future* (Boston, 1897); *Lessons of the War with Spain and Other Articles* (Boston, 1899); *The Problem of Asia, and Its Effect upon International Policies* (Boston, 1900); *Retrospect and Prospect: Studies in International Relations, Naval and Political* (Boston, 1902); *Some Neglected Aspects of War* (Boston, 1907); *Naval Administration and Warfare: Some General Principles, with Other Essays* (Boston, 1908); *The Interest of America in International Conditions* (Boston, 1910); *Armaments and Arbitration: Or the Place of Force in the International Relations of States* (New York and London, 1912).

[62] J. W. Pratt, *Expansionists of 1898* (Baltimore, 1936), *passim*.

fluence over mere physical might."[63] Thus all civilizing contacts, including commerce and missionary enterprise, which should carry these "higher ideals" to the Far East, ought to be sedulously encouraged.

Mahan's belief that force, or diplomacy backed by force, is a more satisfactory solvent for international disputes than the application of legal principles was suggested above.[64] He did not, of course, object to the employment of arbitration in specific cases where circumstances justified it; but he was opposed to the making of any general arbitration treaties which might obligate the United States to arbitrate "moral questions," and any universal system of arbitration seemed to him not only impossible but undesirable. Arbitration must be based upon law; and law is static while conditions change. The legal and the just may be incompatible.[65] But Mahan did not stop there. To eliminate force (armaments) from Christian civilization would, he believed, threaten the health, if not the very existence, of that civilization.

Eliminate, if you can, the competition between the several nationalities, so as to suppress the armaments; substitute for these the artificial system of compulsory arbitration, and disarmament; and you will have realized a socialistic community of states, in which the powers of individual initiative, of nations and of men, the great achievement of our civilization so far, will gradually be atrophied. The result may be that European civilization will not survive, having lost the fighting energy which heretofore has been inherent in its composition.[66]

The armaments of Europe were a guaranty against Asiatic conquest.[67] They were also, it would seem, a form of insurance against both wars and extravagance. "It will be better to depend upon the great armaments, as institutions maintaining peace, which they have done effectually for forty years in Europe itself, and not to demoralize the European peoples by the flood of so-

[63] *The Problem of Asia*, p. 168.

[64] *Supra*, p. 217.

[65] *Armaments and Arbitration*, pp. 111–12.

[66] *Ibid.*, p. 10.

[67] *Supra*, pp. 211, 216, 223.

cialistic measures which will follow upon the release to a bene-
ficiary system of the sums now spent on armament."[68]

Alfred Thayer Mahan was historian, propagandist, and prophet. His permanent rank as a historian will certainly not match
his contemporary fame. As a narrative of events in the limited
sphere to which he chose to confine himself, his work has great
merit. Despite his caution against overindulging the "passion
for certainty," he was a patient and industrious scholar; and if
his first important book was written with a minimum of research, the volumes on the French Revolution and Empire, Nelson, and the War of 1812 exhibit a progressive tendency to rely
less and less upon the work of others and to seek his material
more and more in the original sources. His accounts of campaigns and battles, with the accompanying critical estimates of
strategy and tactics, are still, for the most part, accepted as definitive. His analyses of the commercial prosperity and adversity
that sprang, respectively, from the possession and the lack of
sea power are not seriously disputed. And so consistently,
throughout his historical writing, does he keep his eye upon the
"central significance" of his story that the reader is reminded of
the skilled navigator of Mahan's own profession, tacking to
left and right over a complicated course but never losing sight
of his compass or forgetting the harbor which is his destination.

But unfortunately for Mahan's reputation, the predetermined
course is not that for the scientist. Mahan was no explorer. Intent upon his repeated voyages to the Indies, he never permitted
wind or current to waft him to new lands. He was a man of one
idea. His vision never wandered far enough from the sea to observe, for example, that England's strength, in the Napoleonic

---

[68] *Armaments and Arbitration*, p. 13. It is one of the minor ironies of history that Mahan
was selected as one of the American delegates to the First Hague Conference of 1899, called
for the purpose of considering limitation of armaments. He there informed members of the
British delegation that the United States would not even discuss the question of limiting
naval armaments, and that, because of her interests in China, she would be compelled to
make a considerable increase in her naval forces in the Pacific (G. P. Gooch and H. Tem-
perley, *British Documents on the Origins of the War, 1898–1914* [11 vols.; London, 1926–36],
I, 231).

period, rested as much upon her industrial development as upon her sea power, or that the American West counted for anything in the preliminaries of the War of 1812. Add to this restricted outlook his naïve and sometimes contradictory moral judgments and his confident interpretations of the will of Providence, and it is clear that his place is not among historians of the first rank.

As propagandist, Mahan was singularly successful. When he died, December 1, 1914, his own country had realized most of the program which he had advocated—navy, canal, Caribbean and Pacific bases. In fact, he had been too successful; all the world had for years been engaged in a mad competition for sea power. No one could measure the precise extent to which that competition had contributed to the tragedy of 1914 or the precise degree of Mahan's responsibility for the competition.

As prophet, had he lived until the close of the war which had begun four months before his death, he would have seen his main thesis vindicated, for that war, quite as much as any of which he had written, was won by sea power—that control of the sea which made the United States an available reservoir of materials and men. Yet sea power, triumphant though it seemed, sat now somewhat insecurely on its throne, while of Mahan's other judgments and predictions, few remained intact. European armaments had not preserved the peace. Far from reserving themselves (or being reserved by a higher power) for that Armageddon when West should meet East, they had well-nigh destroyed one another; while the East, still lacking those "higher ideals" attributed to Europe, was relatively far more formidable than ever before. The peace adjustment which, as the result of the "play of natural forces," should, according to Mahan, have corresponded "to the fundamental facts of the case," and should therefore have possessed stability, was to endure but half a generation. The system of international anarchy based on force, which Mahan had acclaimed while others deplored it, had wrought consequences far different from those which he had contemplated. Fortunate, perhaps, that he did not live to witness the full catastrophe.

XII

THEODORE ROOSEVELT

HARRISON JOHN THORNTON
State University of Iowa

LTHOUGH considered "strong" in history during his earlier school years,[1] Theodore Roosevelt made no advanced study of that subject when in college. The law might have won him if he had been "sufficiently fortunate to come under Professor Thayer, of the Harvard Law School." But his brief experience in reading law in the office of his uncle, Robert Roosevelt, convinced him that he disliked legalism. "The *caveat emptor* side of the law, like the *caveat emptor* side of business, seemed to me repellent; it did not make for social fair dealing."[2] His great desire, both before and during his college years, was to become a naturalist, "to be a scientific man of the Audubon, or Wilson, or Baird, or Coues type—a man like Hart Merriam, or Frank Chapman, or Hornaday, to-day." "I fully intended," he recorded, "to make science my life-work." This ambition was frustrated because "at that time Harvard . . . . utterly ignored the possibilities of the faunal naturalist, the outdoor naturalist and observer of nature. They treated biology as purely a science

[1] Lewis Einstein, *Roosevelt: His Mind in Action* (Boston, 1930), p. 10.

[2] William R. Thayer, *Theodore Roosevelt* (New York, 1919), p. 31; Theodore Roosevelt, *An Autobiography* (National ed.; New York, 1926), p. 57. (The National edition of Roosevelt's works is used in this essay unless otherwise indicated.) When, in later years, Roosevelt was confronted with "the tame life of president of the Senate," the law seemed to offer comfort and refuge. He talked of reading law under Justice White (*Dictionary of American Biography* [New York, 1935], XVI, 137).

of the laboratory. . . . ."[3] Nevertheless, the student took honors in natural history as well as in political economy.[4]

It was at Cambridge, however, that Roosevelt not only revived his interest in history[5] but felt a desire to engage in historical writing and evaluation. Reading some accounts of the War of 1812, he judged them to be unsatisfactory. In his club he came upon a copy of *The Naval History of Great Britain* by the English historian, William James. The young student found this "an invaluable work, written with fullness and care"; but it also impressed him as "a piece of special pleading by a bitter and not overscrupulous partisan."[6] His critical and patriotic interests were excited, and he read all he could find on the naval aspects of the second war with England. Then, with the impulsiveness that both in and out of print characterized him all through his mature life, he wrote two chapters of a projected book. "Those chapters were so dry," he afterward confessed, "that they would have made a dictionary seem light reading by comparison."[7] He insisted, however, that they represented serious interest. From this time forward, when committed to do a piece of writing, Roosevelt pressed it to completion with restless energy. Within two years after graduation his book was finished; and at the age of twenty-four, in 1882, he published *The Naval War of 1812.*[8]

[3] Roosevelt, *An Autobiography*, pp. 24–26. Looking back on his years at Cambridge, Roosevelt admitted that Harvard "did me good, but only in the general effect, for there was very little in my actual studies which helped me in after-life." He paid tribute to one of his tutors and to his professor of English, but records: "I saw almost nothing of President Eliot and very little of the professors." Correction of his papers in history "by a skilled older man would have impressed me and have commanded my respectful attention."

[4] C. Guild, Jr., in *Harvard Graduate Magazine;* quoted in John W. Bennett, *Roosevelt and the Republic* (New York, 1908), p. 353.

[5] Albert Shaw, "Theodore Roosevelt as Political Leader," in *The Works of Theodore Roosevelt* (Memorial ed.; New York, 1925), XVI, xii.

[6] Roosevelt, *The Naval War of 1812* (New York, 1926), p. xxiii.

[7] *An Autobiography*, p. 24.

[8] In an appendix Roosevelt notes an occurrence that might have prevented the writing of this book: "After my work was in press I for the first time came across Professor J. Russell Soley's 'Naval Campaign of 1812,' in the 'Proceedings of the United States Naval In-

The work is a descriptive narrative, and in it the young author proved himself extraordinarily competent in the use of nautical terminology and in an understanding of naval strategy. Usually the conflict was between two ships, seldom of mass action; and with verve and skill Roosevelt describes the grim maneuvering of brave antagonists duelling to the death in lonely waters. The work made a great impression on each side of the Atlantic, being both censured and praised.[9] Before long, however, it was accepted as authoritative. Complimentary evidence of this came from England when the publishers of an important work on the British navy invited Roosevelt to contribute the account of the naval war of 1812.[10] In his own country the writer in a few years was Assistant Secretary of the Navy. The late Admiral Sims declared that the book "was listened to by the American people and it profoundly affected the attitude of the nation toward its navy."[11] The study remains important and is accepted as a standard work on the subject.

The success of this first venture might well have been interpreted by the author as a mandate to make historical research and writing his chosen work, especially as a career of scholarship was open to him without the necessity of earning his living.[12] Indeed, he did make history a lifetime interest, but it was merely one among many others. Even before Roosevelt completed *The Naval War*, he had been drawn into the stream of politics and was a member of the New York legislature. Following

---

stitute,' for October 20, 1881. It is apparently the precursor of a more extended history. Had I known that such a writer as Professor Soley was engaged on a work of this kind I certainly should not have attempted it myself" (*The Naval War*, p. 419).

[9] A later printing included an appendix in which answer was made to certain English critics; see the National edition.

[10] William Laird Clowes, *The Royal Navy: A History from the Earliest Times to the Present* (7 vols.; London and Boston, 1897–1903).

[11] William S. Sims, "Roosevelt: Historian and Patriot," in *The Naval War*, p. xiv. In later years the author recognized the favorable background against which his book was set. "At the time I wrote the book, ... the navy had reached its nadir, and we were then utterly incompetent to fight Spain or any other power that had a navy at all" (*An Autobiography*, p. 211).

[12] *An Autobiography*, p. 26.

three terms at Albany, he spent portions of several years ranching in Dakota. But he did not lose contact with the East and politics, and presently he was called to Washington as civil service commissioner, then to New York as head of the board of police commissioners, to Washington again as Assistant Secretary of the Navy, back to New York as governor, then once more to Washington as vice-president and president. Nevertheless, politics did not lessen his interest in the study and writing of history.[13] In 1886 and 1888 were published his *Thomas Hart Benton* and *Gouverneur Morris*, respectively, for the "American Statesmen" series. His *New York* came from the press in 1891, and *Hero Tales from American History* in 1895, this being written in collaboration with Henry Cabot Lodge. The first two volumes of *The Winning of the West* appeared in 1889, and the last two in 1894 and 1896.[14] He closed the century with *Oliver Cromwell*.

Roosevelt's intense political activities during the first decade of the new century checked the flow of historical books. At its close came his lectures at Oxford University on "Biological Analogies in History" and at the University of Berlin on "The World-Movement." Though these were not specifically historical studies, they give evidence of his reflection upon the problems of history. Two years later his address as president of the American Historical Association set forth his vigorous thinking about "History as Literature." It is to be remembered, too, that history alone did not provide sufficient outlet for his busy mind and pen. Through the same years in which he was publishing historical works, and later, he wrote books on hunting and travel, as well as essays, magazine articles, and editorials. These were supplemented by his state papers and an incredible number of letters. All in all, Roosevelt was the author of well over a score of books dealing with history, biography, science, travel, and adventure, besides his collected essays and reviews.

Roosevelt's historical writings are not of uniform merit. *The*

[13] He later wrote: "I did not then believe, and I do not now believe, that any man should ever attempt to make politics his only career" (*ibid.*, p. 58).

[14] Albert Bushnell Hart, "Roosevelt as Pioneer," in Roosevelt, *The Winning of the West* (New York, 1926), I, x.

Naval War had set a creditable standard, though it may be charged with being monotonously descriptive and episodic, too little concerned with an integrated naval policy and insufficiently related to other aspects and problems of the conflict. In preparing to write it, he searched diligently for reliable material. Beginning with William James's *The Naval History of Great Britain*, James Fenimore Cooper's *History of the Navy of the United States of America*, and George F. Emmons' *The Navy of the United States, from the Commencement, 1775 to 1853*, he read also Sir Howard Douglas' *A Treatise on Naval Gunnery* and Admiral E. Jurien de La Gravière's *Guerres maritimes sous la République et l'Empire*. Among other periodicals he studied the files of the *London Naval Chronicle*, and *Niles's Weekly Register*. In the national archives at Washington he "looked over" log books, original contracts, muster rolls, and official letters. The letters he found to be "very complete" in three series: "Captains' Letters," "Masters'-Commandant Letters," and "Officers' Letters." Though often "rather exasperating" and "very incomplete," the log books of individual vessels were quite indispensable to the study. "Whenever it was possible," he declared, "I have referred to printed matter in preference to manuscript, and my authorities can thus, in most cases, be easily consulted."[15]

Thomas Hart Benton is by no means without distinction. Certain parts are written brilliantly and exhibit much understanding of the subject. Yet it was composed hastily (in about four months) during 1886, while the author was in Dakota. He wrote as his arduous ranching labors permitted: often at odd moments, and, when wearied from long hours "on the round-up," "fourteen to sixteen hours every day [in the saddle] . . . . and . . . . pretty sleepy, all the time."[16] When about halfway through the writing, he confided to Henry Cabot Lodge: "If I could work at it without interruption for a fortnight I could send Morse the manuscript; but tomorrow I leave for the roundup, and henceforth

<hr />

[15] *The Naval War*, pp. xxiv–xxv.

[16] Roosevelt to Lodge, June 7, 1886, in Henry Cabot Lodge, *Selections from the Correspondence of Theodore Roosevelt and Henry Cabot Lodge* (2 vols.; New York, 1925), I, 41–42.

I will have to snatch a day or two whenever I can, until the end of June.''[17] The book rests upon a minimum of research and is not fortified with source citations. When it was well advanced, Roosevelt frankly wrote to Lodge from Elkhorn that he had little information about Benton following 1850, and asked his friend to have material sent to him from a biographical dictionary. In the same letter the cowboy-author confessed that he was evolving the book mainly from his "inner consciousness,"[18] and a few days later expressed his hope to make the "skeleton" presentable by "a week's hard work when I get East near the Public Libraries . . . ."[19] The manuscript was sent to John T. Morse, Jr., editor of the "American Statesmen" series, early in August. Being unable to insure it "in the express office," Roosevelt was concerned about its safety; for not for a good deal would he undertake to rewrite it.[20]

With *Benton* behind him, Roosevelt determined that "if I write another historical work of any kind—and my dream is to make one such that will be my *magnum opus*—I shall certainly take more time and do it carefully and thoroughly, ..."[21] This high resolve was made early in 1887, but that same year he wrote *Gouverneur Morris* and did it just as rapidly as he had done *Benton*. Nor was it any better. "The Morrises won't let me see the old gentleman's papers at any price," he told Lodge;[22] but his editor

[17] Roosevelt to Lodge, May 20, 1886, *ibid.*, p. 40.

[18] When Benton "leaves the Senate in 1850 I have nothing whatever to go by; and, being by nature both a timid and, on occasions, by choice a truthful man, I would prefer to have some foundation of fact, no matter how slender, on which to build the airy and arabesque superstructure of my fancy—especially as I am writing a history. Now I hesitate to give him a wholly fictitious date of death and to invent all of the work of his later years. Would it be too infernal a nuisance for you to hire someone on the *Advertiser* (of course at my expense) to look up, in a biographical dictionary or elsewhere, his life after he left the Senate in 1850? He was elected once to Congress; who beat him when he ran the second time? What was the issue? Who beat him, and why, when he ran for Governor of Missouri? and the date of his death? I hate to trouble you . . . . but the Bad Lands have much fewer books than Boston has" (June 7, 1886, *ibid.*, p. 41).

[19] Roosevelt to Lodge, June 19, 1886, *ibid.*, p. 43.

[20] Roosevelt to Lodge, Aug. 20, 1886, *ibid.*, p. 45.

[21] Roosevelt to Lodge, Feb. 15, 1887, *ibid.*, p. 51.

[22] Roosevelt to Lodge, May 15, 1887, *ibid.*, p. 55.

advised him to go ahead anyway. He found Morris an "entertaining scamp," and declined to be drawn away from him to prepare for the series a biography of "dear, dull, respectable old [John] Jay."[23] He read with profit Jared Sparks's life of Morris but found the treatment "drearily platitudinous" and the author "funnily unconscious of his own prolix dullness." Like Sparks, Roosevelt had access to Morris' diary; and he found "ample material" on Morris' "public career" and his "views and writings on public subjects." Sparks included many of Morris' letters and state papers in his biography, and Roosevelt was able to read more letters in the Jay and Pickering manuscripts. Morris' speeches in the Constitutional Convention, summarized by Madison in his *Debates*, were consulted, as well as articles on Morris in *Scribner's*, *Macmillan's*, and the *Atlantic*.[24] The essay by Lodge in the *Atlantic* so impressed Roosevelt that he had a "wild desire" to incorporate about half of it into his book.[25] The enterprise proved to be less congenial to him than the writing of *Benton*, but he allowed himself to believe that he had "struck one or two good ideas." And he found it a joy to lay into his subject "savagely for his conduct in 1812–15."[26]

New York is a less conspicuous production than either *Benton* or *Morris*. At the request of Brander Matthews, then literary adviser to Longmans, Green and Company, it was prepared for a series of "Historic Towns," edited by E. A. Freeman.[27] The author listed his chief sources in his preface but failed to cite them in the text; nor did he attempt to break new ground. He confessed that his aim was "less to collect new facts than to draw from the immense storehouse of facts already collected. . . . ."[28]

[23] Roosevelt to Lodge, June 28, 1887, *ibid.*, p. 57.

[24] Roosevelt, *Gouverneur Morris* ("American Statesmen" series) (Boston, 1888), pp. v–viii. Morris' diary, edited by his granddaughter, Anne Cary Morris, was published in two volumes in 1888.

[25] Roosevelt to Lodge, Aug. 20, 1887, *Selections* (Lodge), I, 58.

[26] Roosevelt to Lodge, Sept. 5, 1887, *ibid.*, p. 59.

[27] Julian Street, "Roosevelt, Citizen of New York," in Roosevelt, *New York* (New York, 1926), p. 347.

[28] *Ibid.*, p. 359.

Brander Matthews recorded that the book did not sell, offering as excuse the fact that in 1890 its author was not yet a celebrity.[29]

Of the twenty-six *Hero Tales*, Roosevelt wrote fourteen and Lodge twelve. The collaborators "did not aim," as Lodge declared, "at novel contributions to history involving original research."[30] The purpose was frankly to present examples of lofty patriotism and to stir admiration for high character and brave deeds in the nation's past. In harmony with his temperament but at odds with the viewpoint of scholarship, Roosevelt, of all his historical writings, indicated a preference for the *Hero Tales*. Referring to a list of readings on American history which his friend Lawrence F. Abbott was preparing for a correspondent, Roosevelt wrote to Abbott: "If you want anything from me, don't take the 'War of 1812,' but take 'Hero Tales from American History,' which Lodge and I wrote together."[31]

When Roosevelt wrote *Oliver Cromwell*, he was, according to Viscount Lee of Fareham, "engaged, and up to his eyes, in work and combats at Albany which would have made it impossible for any other man to dream of, still less to engage in, any kind of literary or extraneous labor."[32] Such conditions permitted only what Roosevelt himself described as a sketch of Cromwell; but the inducement to undertake it was attractive: $5,000 for six instalments in *Scribner's* and 15 per cent on the book sales.[33] Again, as in the case of his *New York*, the author did not essay a new and objective study. Indeed, the subjectivity of the work provoked the criticism "that it was a fine imaginative study of Cromwell's qualifications for the governorship of New York." At the time of the book's preparation, Roosevelt was fresh from the war in Cuba; "and his account of the 'Sixty-seventh Troop,'

[29] Street, *loc. cit.*, p. 347.

[30] Lodge, "The 'Hero Tales,' " in Lodge and Roosevelt, *Hero Tales from American History* (New York, 1926), pp. xiv–xv. This volume was first published in 1895.

[31] Lawrence F. Abbott, *Impressions of Theodore Roosevelt* (New York, 1919), p. 182.

[32] Viscount Lee of Fareham, "Cromwell and Roosevelt," in Roosevelt, *Oliver Cromwell* (New York, 1926), p. 170.

[33] Roosevelt to Lodge, Aug. 10, 1899, *Selections* (Lodge), I, 418.

of which Cromwell was originally captain, might almost be a description of 'Troop K' of the Rough Riders."[34]

The Winning of the West is Theodore Roosevelt's most important and meritorious historical composition. This, it seems fair to suggest, was the *magnum opus* of which he had dreamed at Elkhorn as he reflected dubiously upon his newly completed *Benton*. He found it fascinating from the outset, and it challenged him to his best and most careful effort. In August, 1888, he wrote to Lodge from Sagamore: "I continue greatly absorbed in my new work; but it goes very slowly; I am only half way through the first volume. I shall try my best not to hurry it, nor make it scamp work."[35] Much of the writing was done in the office of its publisher, G. P. Putnam's Sons, of New York City. At his desk there Roosevelt occasionally worked under high pressure. Fresh pages of manuscript were hurried to a floor above, set up in type, printer's proofs drawn, and sent to the author for correction. It was the boast of George Haven Putnam that this "was one of the few books which were in large part written, put into print, bound, and sold under the one roof." Parts of the last volume were prepared in the headquarters of the police department on Mulberry Street.[36]

Roosevelt was one of the best-fitted men of his time to undertake an ambitious work on the American West; Frederick Jackson Turner generously and modestly conceded that probably he was the best equipped.[37] Roosevelt had traveled widely in the western country and had lived and worked among frontier cattlemen and settlers. He was not as completely one of them as he sometimes pictured himself to be, but he had a deep understanding of their temper and way of life and a sincere respect for their character and achievements. He truly loved open spaces, wild

[34] Fareham, *loc. cit.*, pp. 169–72.

[35] Roosevelt to Lodge, Aug. 12, 1888, *Selections* (Lodge), I, 70. He was at work on it while civil service commissioner at Washington, while police commissioner in New York, and while preparing and publishing other books on history, ranching, and hunting.

[36] George Haven Putnam, "Roosevelt: Historian and Statesman," in Theodore Roosevelt, *The Winning of the West*, II, xv.

[37] *American Historical Review*, II, 171–76.

life, and the physical hardships imposed by a rugged environment. As his body was invigorated, so too was his spirit elated, when he essayed the part of ranchman and cowboy. Even his scientific interests were rooted in wilderness places; for they were not those of the laboratory, but of the field, forest, and mountain. Thus, to his competence for historical writing was joined a temperamental fitness for the role of historian of the West. And when the task was done, he declared with feeling that it had been "emphatically a labor of love to write of the great deeds of the border people."[38]

Apart from an opening and a closing chapter that are really prologue and epilogue, the study begins with the Ohio Valley following the defeat of the French, and ends with the purchase of Louisiana and Burr's conspiracy. The scope of the treatment, as first projected, was broader than the actual accomplishment.[39] In agreement with his publisher he originally undertook to treat the regions out of which emerged Kentucky, Tennessee, Ohio, Indiana, Illinois, and "all the territory of the Southwest that came under the domination of the United States."[40] This plan would have involved a discussion of Texas, the war with Mexico, and the acquisitions following the conquest. As it was, he gave the old Northwest a not inconsiderable place in his scheme, and devoted one chapter to "The Explorers of the Far West." But, when Volume IV appeared in 1896, national politics were at flood tide; and Roosevelt was soon drawn into its swirl. Almost at once he was Assistant Secretary of the Navy; a little later a lieutenant colonel of the Rough Riders; and then he moved swiftly toward the vice-presidency by way of the governorship of New York. He did much literary work during the closing years of the century. But history may not be written as rapidly as essays and narratives of adventure—not, at least, by the conscientious—and early in the new century he plaintively reported to his publisher: "I do not see how I am going to be able to complete, according to agreement, those volumes for which you are

---

[38] The Winning of the West, I, xliv.

[39] Hart, loc. cit.   [40] Putnam, loc. cit., p. x.

waiting. You see I am very busy just now."[41] This was in 1902, when he was president of the United States.

Of all his volumes on historical subjects, Roosevelt did the best research for *The Winning of the West*. Like Francis Parkman, he knew from personal contact the country with which he was dealing, having traveled through it, sometimes on horseback.[42] He had a full appreciation of original sources, and found many, in widely scattered places, that had not heretofore been exploited.[43] He read in official records at Washington, including the printed volumes of *American Archives*, *American State Papers*, and scores of volumes of records in manuscript. At Nashville, Tennessee, he states that he "had access to a mass of original matter in the shape of files of old newspapers, of unpublished letters, diaries, reports, and other manuscripts." Much material was also found at Louisville and Lexington, Kentucky, while the historical societies of Wisconsin and New York yielded valuable collections.[44] The Virginia State Papers were, of course, available. From the Canadian archives at Ottawa came copies of the Haldimand Papers. These he regarded as among the most valuable of the hitherto "untouched" manuscripts that he was able to use. "They give, for the first time, the British and Indian side of all the northwestern fighting; including Clark's campaigns, the siege of Boonesborough, the battle of the Blue Licks, Crawford's defeat, etc."[45] He did not neglect the printed histories of the West that preceded his literary incursion into that region; but, for the period with which his own work deals, he found these extremely unreliable. Writings of other travelers proved to be of some service.[46]

[41] *Ibid.*, p. xi.

[42] *Ibid.*, p. xiii.   [43] *American Historical Review*, II, 171–76.

[44] *The Winning of the West*, I, xxxix–xliv. Collections consulted are here listed.

[45] *Ibid.*, p. xliii. A reviewer in the *Atlantic* (LXIV, 698) later reminded him that at least one important document from the Haldimand collection had been published; and Roosevelt had to admit: "I had no idea that any of the Haldimand mss. were in any printed collection of documents . . . ." (Roosevelt to Lodge, Oct. 27, 1889, *Selections* [Lodge], I, 96).

[46] *The Winning of the West*, I, 25, 53, nn.

Roosevelt has been censured for not having personally explored the French, Spanish, and English archives.[47] To have done so would have strengthened his position, of course. Failing this, he gathered a lot of information about the foreign aspects of his subject from his research in the official papers at home and from the private sources studied in Kentucky and Tennessee. There came also into his hands "six bound volumes of MSS., containing the correspondence of the Spanish Minister Gardoqui, copied from the Spanish archives."[48] On the basis of these he grappled boldly with French, Spanish, and English intrigues as these joined with Nature's hazards and Indian hostility to embitter and complicate the western problem.

In dealing with the question of method and form, Roosevelt declared his extreme impatience with "pedestrianism" and openly despised the mere chronicler of occurrences or matters of small consequence. Such topics as the tariff, the currency, and the rise and fall of parties he judged to be of minor importance. The interpreter of American history should concern himself with the conquest of the continent, the struggle between competing groups, the contest over slavery, and the war to preserve the Union.[49] He flouted what he considered to be the tendency to view "a conglomerate narrative history of America . . . . as showing an 'advance' upon Francis Parkman—Heaven save the mark!" To his friend George Otto Trevelyan he declared that in "a very small way" he had been waging war with musty writers of history on this side of the water for a number of years. He accused these pedants of solemnly believing that, if they pooled their collected facts of all kinds and sorts, there would not be any further need for great writers and great thinkers. He regarded them scornfully as of the "day laborer" type. The worth of their work in the field of historical investigation depends en-

[47] *American Historical Review*, II, 174.

[48] *The Winning of the West*, I, xlii. These six volumes are now a part of the Durrett Collection in the University of Chicago Library.

[49] Roosevelt, "Francis Parkman's Histories," in *Literary Essays* (New York, 1926), p. 247.

tirely, he declared, on the arrival of some master-builder to sift their material, and by its aid to erect an edifice of majesty and beauty instinct with truth. A thousand pedants would not begin to add to the wisdom of mankind what another Macaulay or Parkman would add.[50]

Roosevelt was not attacking the scientific method. Indeed, he lost no occasion to declare his allegiance to it. The historians of the future, he urged, should utilize all the facts and methods that science has put at their disposal. We must insist that those who write the history of mankind must accept the scientific spirit and use freely the treasure houses of science. Those "who would fully treat of man must know at least something of biology, ... and especially of that science of evolution which is inseparably connected with the great name of Darwin."[51] Roosevelt was really appealing to historians to be artists. He took the position that no writer of history can be great who lacks dramatic quality. Without imagination and literary grace there can be

[50] Roosevelt to Trevelyan, Jan. 23, 1904, in Joseph Bucklin Bishop, *Theodore Roosevelt and His Time* (New York, 1920), II, 139–41: "In a very small way I have been waging war with their kind (pedants) on this side of the water for a number of years. We have a preposterous little historical organization which, when I was just out of Harvard and very ignorant, I joined. . . . . After a while it dawned on me that all of the conscientious, industrious, painstaking little pedants, who would have been useful people in a rather small way if they had understood their own limitations, had become because of their conceit distinctly noxious. They solemnly believed that if there were only enough of them, and that if they only collected enough facts of all kinds and sorts, there would cease to be any need hereafter for great writers, great thinkers. . . . . Each of them was a good enough day laborer, trundling his barrowful of bricks and worthy of his hire; . . . . They represent what is in itself the excellent revolt against superficiality and lack of research, but they have grown into the opposite and equally noxious belief that research is all in all, that accumulation of facts is everything, and that the ideal history of the future will consist . . . . of a multitude of articles by a multitude of small pedants." Enlightened historians will agree with Roosevelt in this. And to Roosevelt's credit it can be said that he was not without appreciation of those who labored among "dry facts and gray details." "In the field of historical research an immense amount can be done by men who have no literary power whatever. Moreover, the most painstaking and laborious research, covering long periods of years, is necessary in order to accumulate the material for any history worth writing at all. . . . . In particular I pay high honor to the patient and truthful investigator. He does an indispensable work" (Roosevelt, "History as Literature," *Literary Essays*, p. 9).

[51] Roosevelt, "History as Literature," in *Literary Essays*, pp. 28–29.

no good history. Many photographs will not make one Rembrandt.[52] Years before he had touched on this theme in the course of his review of Brander Matthews' book, *An Introduction to the Study of American Literature*.[53] And it was the burden of his address as president of the American Historical Association in 1912. He did not go to Boston that year with pleasant anticipations; for he was not at all hopeful that his thesis would be appreciated or even understood. "I am to deliver a beastly lecture—'History as Literature'—" he wrote to Lodge, "because I am President of the American Historical Association. None of its members, by the way, believe that history is literature. I have spent much care on the lecture, and as far as I now know it won't even be printed anywhere. Even the *Outlook* finds it too tough a morsel to swallow!"[54] Roosevelt had no more respect for the pedagogical abilities of the members of the Association than for their lack of literary appreciation. Years before he had written to Trevelyan of the "small men who do most of the historic teaching in the colleges. They have done much real harm in preventing the developments of students who might have a large grasp of what history should really be."[55] He admitted to the specialists at Boston that the man who uses literary expression as a cloak for his ignorance or misunderstanding of the facts does his reader less than no service.[56] He fully agreed that complete truthfulness

[52] *Ibid.*, p. 7.

[53] "It seems rather odd that it should be necessary to insist upon the fact that the essence of a book is to be readable; but most certainly the average scientific or historical writer needs to have this elementary proposition drilled into his brain. Perhaps if this drilling were once accomplished, we Americans would stand a greater chance of producing an occasional Darwin or Gibbon; though there would necessarily be some havoc in the ranks of those small pedants who with laborious industry produce works which are never read excepting by other small pedants, or else by the rare master who can take the myriad bricks of these myriad little workers and out of them erect one of the great buildings of thought" (*ibid.*, pp. 292–93).

[54] Roosevelt to Lodge, Dec. 26, 1912, in *Selections* (Lodge), II, 427. The *Outlook* did print generous portions of the address in its Vol. CIII (Jan. 11, 1913), pp. 79–84. See also *American Historical Review*, XVIII (April, 1913), 473–89.

[55] Roosevelt to Trevelyan, Jan. 23, 1904, in Bishop, II, 140.

[56] Roosevelt, "History as Literature," in *Literary Essays*, p. 16.

must never be sacrificed to color, but denied the contention that complete truthfulness is not compatible with color. And just as forcibly he denied that sound history, any more than sound science, was called upon to separate itself from literature. History must accept, even gratefully, the assistance of the scientist, of the archeologist, of the anthropologist, and of the paleo-ethnologist, for example. The historian, indeed, must steep himself in such sciences. But to do so should carry no implications of dulness; for it is the mark of a great historian "to take the science of history and turn it into literature." Such a one adds wisdom to knowledge, and the power of expression to the gift of imagination.[57]

Roosevelt regarded as shallow the criticism that the use of the imagination in historical composition leads to inaccuracy. Only the unbalanced imagination is in this danger. What the historian "brings from the charnel-house he must use with such potent wizardry that we shall see the life that was and not the death that is." The point for historians to remember is that "vast and fundamental truths can be discerned and interpreted only by one whose imagination is as lofty as the soul of a Hebrew prophet," and that what they write can live only if it possesses "the deathless quality that inheres in all great literature."[58] Historical works possessing literary quality may be a permanent contribution to the sum of man's wisdom, enjoyment, and inspiration. The solemn "pedagogs" before the lecturer in 1912 were admonished to take note that Macaulay is read by countless thousands who would not otherwise read history, because what he wrote was not only history but also an important contribution to English literature.

Roosevelt harbored no mistaken belief that what he so ardently commended to others he had achieved himself. About his own literary performances he was entirely modest. In one of his letters to Trevelyan, to take an example, he referred to "a book I wrote called 'The Winning of the West.' "[59] From the quick

57 *Ibid.*, pp. 7, 11.
58 *Ibid.*, pp. 7, 18.   59 Roosevelt to Trevelyan, Jan. 1, 1908, in Bishop, II, 168.

succession of his volumes it is obvious that he was a rapid writer. It is obvious, too, that he wrote at high pressure and with many interruptions. He could not wait for leisure or the hour of calm reflection. Having resolved to write, and also to push his interests and energies in so many other directions, he was forced to take time upon the wing and compose amid stress and distraction. He employed the services of amanuenses in his literary undertakings. Indeed, it "was a familiar spectacle to his intimates to find him, whilst being shaved in the morning, dictating to separate stenographers," by turns, the manuscript of a book, replies to letters, and portions of an executive paper.[60] Being thus deprived of the immense advantage of deliberate and prolonged investigation, sustained reflection, and ample time for composition and revision, it was impossible that the harassed author should attain either literary or scientific excellence. Indeed, he gave frequent expression to his genuine doubt of the worth of his historical writing, both as to substance and form. When he commenced his book on Benton, he wrote to Henry Cabot Lodge: "I feel a little appalled over the Benton; I have not the least idea whether I shall make a flat failure of it or not. However I will do my best and trust to luck for the result."[61] When he had finished the first chapter, he again confided his fears to his friend: "Writing is horribly hard work to me. . . . . I have got some good ideas in the first chapter, but I am not sure they are worked up rightly; my style is very rough and I do not like a certain lack of sequitur that I do not seem able to get rid of."[62] Lodge would agree that here at least was a specimen of stylistic clumsiness. Even as Roosevelt dispatched the manuscript to the publisher, he was nervous and distrustful: "I hope it is decent, but lately I have been troubled with dreadful misgivings."[63] It was in only a little more confident frame of mind that a year later he released

[60] Fareham, "Cromwell and Roosevelt," in Roosevelt, *Cromwell*, p. 170.

[61] Roosevelt to Lodge, Feb. 7, 1886, *Selections* (Lodge), I, 37.

[62] Roosevelt to Lodge, Mar. 27, 1886, *ibid.*, p. 38.

[63] Roosevelt to Lodge, Aug. 10, 1886, *ibid.*, p. 45.

Gouverneur Morris. "I don't know whether I have done well or not" was his parting comment.[64]

He returned to the same theme after reading Lodge's *Washington.* "You have now reached what I am still struggling for: a *uniformly* excellent style."[65] One of the few complimentary things he ever said about his own literary ability was to Julian Street, who had asked him if he believed he had genius. "Most certainly not," was the answer. "I'm no orator, and in writing I'm afraid I'm not gifted at all, except perhaps that I have a good instinct and a liking for simplicity and directness."[66] It was his practice to read the printer's proofs of his writing to his wife, and to profit by her criticism. Sometimes, when he failed to do this, some word such as "mutterless" slipped into the published volume, and he had to bear the chiding of both "Cabot and Edith." "I am very sorry," he confessed contritely; "it is a coined word; it seemed to come handy and I used it!"[67] On occasions he was quite absurdly careless. Fort Morgan was "the heaviest of the two forts" in Mobile Bay.[68] "Toward the close of Jackson's administration, slavery for the first time made its permanent appearance in national politics."[69] And at the Battle of King's Mountain the regular army uniform was worn by "probably not a man—especially very few of them."[70]

It has been shown above that Roosevelt was scornful of the mere recorder of historical events. He demanded that the chronicler be also interpreter, and in his efforts to meet his own demand Roosevelt disclosed his philosophy of history either by implication or direct assertion. Deep in *The Winning of the West,*

[64] Roosevelt to Lodge, Sept. 5, 1887, *ibid.*, p. 59.

[65] Roosevelt to Lodge, July 1, 1889, *ibid.*, p. 81.

[66] Street, *loc. cit.*, p. 357.

[67] Roosevelt to Lodge, June 10, 1896, *Selections* (Lodge), I, 222. He was careless in the use of authors' names and the titles of their works; see, for example, the items listed among his sources in *The Naval War*, p. xxiv.

[68] Roosevelt and Lodge, *Hero Tales*, p. 151.

[69] Roosevelt, *Benton*, p. 102.   [70] *The Winning of the West*, I, 494 n.

he paused to remind himself and the reader that the succession of individual incidents is less important than the main current or tendency. "The peculiar circumstances of each case, [of course,] must always be taken into account," but it must also be understood that occurrences are but links in the chain of causation. He warned against too great preoccupation with single events no matter how engrossing, such as the revolt of Texas, the feats of Clark and Austin, and the acquisition of Louisiana. These were merely spectacular and important manifestations of a tendency of prime significance—the certainty of the final absorption of the West by the restless backwoodsmen, and its domination by the people of English speech.[71] He returned to the idea of destiny frequently; in such matters, for instance, as the inevitability of the redman retreating before the whites, and the Mexican before the Americans. Indeed, it was "inevitable, as well as in the highest degree desirable for the good of humanity at large, that the American people should ultimately crowd out the Mexicans from their sparsely populated Northern provinces."[72] Likewise, in the conflict for the Northwest areas, Americans succeeded and British failed because "the British fought against the stars in their courses, while the Americans battled on behalf of the destiny of the race."[73]

Having thus discerned destiny in precise movements, Roosevelt would gladly have penetrated "the causes of the mysteries that surround not only mankind but all life, both in the present and the past." In his Romanes lecture at Oxford University in 1910 he sought for such light as might come from a certain parallelism "between the birth, growth, and death of species in the animal world, and the birth, growth, and death of societies in the world of man." He did not declare for exact parallelism, but detected "strange analogies; it may be . . . . homologies." Roosevelt was careful to keep his socialized inferences of biological processes on a basis of speculation. He stated frankly that his parallels should be applied in only the roughest and most general way, and was unwilling to suggest how far biology could

[71] Ibid., II, 401–2.   [72] Roosevelt, Benton, p. 113.   [73] The Winning of the West, II, 63.

be employed as a clue to the understanding of human history.[74] It was not a matter for dogmatism, certainly, and he denounced those who would carry the biological argument so far into social systems as to assert, for example, the permanence or evanescence of blood strains. He decried as pathetically humorous the simplicity of a half-century ago which accorded a reverential admiration to the terms Aryan and Teuton as if they denoted something ethnologically sacred. Such an attitude was entitled to no more respect than a lineage traced from Odin, or Aeneas, or Noah. In his speculative approach to the larger mysteries of history Roosevelt was reasonable in his expectations. Though we search and peer, we see things but dimly, he granted; only here and there do "we get a ray of clear vision, as we look before and after."[75]

It was easy for Roosevelt to take a moralistic view of the historian's task and to proceed to moral judgments. "The greatest historian should also be a great moralist," he boldly declared before the "pedagogs" in Boston. "It is no proof of impartiality to treat wickedness and goodness as on the same level." He granted, it is true, that "the obsession of purposeful moral teaching" might defeat its own aim, especially when applied to concrete cases.[76] Nevertheless, he did not hesitate to judge John Quincy Adams "not only fantastic, but absolutely wrong" in the nonpartisanship of certain of his appointments, and to assert that the "principles of the Bentonians were right, and those of their opponents wrong," on the currency issue.[77] Slavery he declared to be "ethically abhorrent to all right-minded men"; it is "to be condemned without stint on this ground alone."[78] Writing to congratulate James Ford Rhodes after reading the fifth volume of his history, he took exception to one sentence, "that in which you say that in no quarrel is the right all on one side, and the wrong all on the other. As regards the actual act of seces-

---

[74] Roosevelt, "Biological Analogies in History," in *Literary Essays*, pp. 26, 29.

[75] *Ibid.*, pp. 26, 39–40.

[76] Roosevelt, "History as Literature," in *Literary Essays*, p. 13.

[77] Roosevelt, *Benton*, pp. 54, 218.   [78] *The Winning of the West*, II, 45.

sion, the actual opening of the Civil War, I think the right was exclusively with the Union people and the wrong exclusively with the Secessionists; . . . ."[79] On the other hand, Roosevelt's historical morality was neither invariable in its application nor beyond the reach of expediency. The enslavement of Negroes was a moral iniquity. But the dispossession of the American Indians—that was another thing. Roosevelt was frequently called a preacher by contemporaries, who ridiculed him for having "discovered" the Ten Commandments. He admitted his homiletic propensity, said that he enjoyed it, and found the White House to be "a bully pulpit!"[80] In his mind and feeling were fixed what he conceived to be the ethical and moral fundamentals for the person and the state. They are given expression in his essays, his state papers, and his historical works. They are proclaimed in the *Benton*, the *Morris*, and *The Winning of the West*, as well as in *American Ideals*, *Realizable Ideals*, and *The Strenuous Life*.[81]

It is not possible to assign Roosevelt to any special "school" of historical interpretation. Though he had some definite ideas about the relation of government to private economic enterprise, certainly he was no economic historian. Indeed, his general neglect of economic factors in his historical works is one of their serious defects. Although his interest in politics was intense and he dealt much with political matters in his writings, he cannot be charged with believing history to be merely past politics. His immense regard for forceful leaders, amounting to a virtual hero-worship of a few men of notable achievements in practical affairs, suggests his allegiance to the great-man theory of history; and this was probably as close as he came to selecting a main thread to follow in the search for explanations and understanding of the historic process. He cannot be classed as a social historian, for he makes no conspicuous attempt to grapple with the complex nature of social institutions or to explain their interrelations. It is true that his historical works are not barren of

[79] Bishop, I, 349.   [80] Putnam, *loc. cit.*, II, x.

[81] William Allen White, "Saith the Preacher!" in Roosevelt, *American Ideals* (New York, 1926), pp. xi–xiii.

references to social problems and institutions. There is many a vignette of frontier travel, religion, education, medicine, and literature. Sometimes a larger canvas is used to depict life in Indian villages and pioneer white communities.[82] But Roosevelt's instinct was generally toward episodic narrative, dramatically treated; and in this he invites comparison with Francis Parkman, whom he greatly admired.

Roosevelt found time during his busy years to read broadly in the field of history. Thucydides, Herodotus, Polybius, and Tacitus were well known to him; and the tales of Villehardouin, Joinville, and Froissart gave him much pleasure. Gibbon and Macaulay were deeply established in his esteem. He read them, as he read the works of all other authors, with a critical mind. Thus his personal judgment, based upon knowledge and comparison, was expressed when he informed John Morley in 1904 that "with all their faults Gibbon and Macaulay are the two great English historians, ..."[83] Whenever he returned to Gibbon, he gave thanks that a great writer had been moved to perform a great task.[84] "As you know, I am rather a fanatic about Macaulay," he wrote to George Otto Trevelyan in 1913. "In all the essentials he seems to me more and more as I grow older a *very* great political philosopher and statesman, no less than one of the

[82] Roosevelt's understanding of the function of the social historian broadened with the years. In his American Historical Association address in 1912 he said: "The great historian must be able to paint for us the life of the plain people, the ordinary men and women, of the time of which he writes. He can do this only if he possesses the highest kind of imagination. Collections of figures no more give us a picture of the past than the reading of a tariff report on hides or woolens gives us an idea of the actual lives of the men and women who live on ranches or work in factories. The great historian will in as full measure as possible present to us the every-day life of the men and women of the age which he describes. Nothing that tells of this life will come amiss to him. The instruments of their labor and the weapons of their warfare, the wills that they wrote, the bargains that they made, and the songs that they sang when they feasted and made love: he must use them all. He must tell us of the toil of the ordinary man in ordinary times, and of the play by which that ordinary toil was broken. He must never forget that no event stands out entirely isolated. He must trace from its obscure and humble beginnings each of the movements that in its hour of triumph has shaken the world." (Roosevelt, "History as Literature," in *Literary Essays*, p. 19).

[83] Bishop, I, 269.

[84] Roosevelt, "History as Literature," in *Literary Essays*, p. 18.

two or three very greatest historians."[85] He was not without appreciation of Carlyle; but the more he studied his works the more hearty grew his contempt "for his profound untruthfulness and for his shrieking deification of shams."[86] He had several of Carlyle's and Macaulay's volumes with him in the African jungle; and a comparison of them stimulated a sparkling letter to Trevelyan, a comparison which the latter described as "wonderfully wise and eloquent."[87] Amid the excitements of the political wars, as well as of the chase, he could find in a book on history release from tension and weariness. During the closing tumult of the Republican convention of 1900, with his career in the balance, he was sitting in a quiet room reading Thucydides.[88] Four years later, while campaigning for the presidency, he reread *The American Revolution* and other writings by Trevelyan, Macaulay's *History*, and the first four volumes of James Ford Rhodes's *History of the United States*, together with many of Lincoln's letters and speeches and a good deal of Dickens.[89] And during the years of his presidency when he was ill at ease and sleepless after a day of wrestling with the problems of the Union "and the appointments that must be made of the Fourth-Class postmasters," he confessed that he would "go up-stairs, ... and study out how the empire of Alexander the Great broke to pieces, and into what other empires it developed. . . . ."[90] Scattered through his writings is many a record of his reading of Lecky, Napier, Marbot, Mahan, Oman, Lord Acton, Ferrero, Mommsen, Ranke, and other historians, notable and obscure.[91] The American group, of course, he read widely and often.

[85] Roosevelt to Trevelyan, Mar. 19, 1913, in Bishop, II, 177.

[86] Roosevelt to Trevelyan, Sept. 10, 1909, *ibid.*, p. 173.

[87] *Ibid.*, p. 172. See his polemic against Carlyle, particularly against his *Frederick the Great* (*ibid.*, pp. 173–74).

[88] Jacob A. Riis, *Theodore Roosevelt the Citizen* (New York, 1904), p. 33.

[89] Bishop, I, 349; II, 144. Roosevelt did an immense amount of reading during his first two years in the White House, a partial record of which he included in a letter to Nicholas Murray Butler in November, 1903; see *ibid.*, I, 265–68.

[90] Alexander Lambert, "Roosevelt the Companion," in *Outdoor Pastimes of an American Hunter*, in *The Works of Theodore Roosevelt* (Memorial ed.; New York, 1924), III, xviii.

[91] See, for example, Roosevelt, *A Book-Lover's Holidays in the Open* (New York, 1926), chap. ix, and *An Autobiography*, p. 324.

For certain historians Roosevelt cherished a personal regard. His admiration was so stirred by Ferrero's *The Greatness and Decline of Rome* (which he read in the French translation) that he felt that he must meet and talk with the writer. "I got the author to come to America and stay at the White House," he recorded. He liked Ferrero's work so well that he ordered a copy in the original Italian.[92] For Francis Parkman, Roosevelt's devotion was deep and lasting. In 1888 he wrote to Parkman, asking permission to dedicate to him *The Winning of the West*. The permission was granted, and the dedication made: "To Francis Parkman to whom Americans who feel a pride in the pioneer history of their country are so greatly indebted."[93] Roosevelt entertained a great respect for the writings of the English historian, George Otto Trevelyan, and from them derived unfailing pleasure. Between the two men developed a warm friendship that found expression in delightful correspondence for nearly twenty years.[94] "You are one of the few blessed exceptions to the rule that the readable historian is not truthful," Roosevelt wrote in 1899. He judged Trevelyan's *The American Revolution* as "far and away the best account of the Revolution written by any one. For interest, for delightful humor, for absolute fairmindedness, for exactness of narrative, for profound insight (and for the English!)—why, my dear Sir, no other book on the Revolution so much as approaches it."[95] As an expression of his appreciation of this work Roosevelt joined with Henry Cabot Lodge and Elihu Root in 1907 to send a silver loving-cup to its author.[96]

Roosevelt began publication of *The Winning of the West* before the

[92] Roosevelt, "The Pigskin Library," in *Literary Essays*, p. 339; Bishop, II, 165–66.

[93] See Roosevelt's tribute to Parkman's writings, "Francis Parkman's Histories," in *Literary Essays*, pp. 246–53.

[94] "You know that you are my hero, and always will be," wrote Trevelyan, and rejoiced in the fact "that there is a man in the world who is never wanting in chivalry, humanity, and the dictates of high national duty" (Trevelyan to Roosevelt, May 13, 1915, in Bishop, II, 180.)

[95] Roosevelt to Trevelyan, Jan. 16, 1899, and Dec. 12, 1903, in *ibid.*, p. 139.

[96] *Ibid.*, pp. 166–67. The cup bore the inscription: "To the Historian of the American Revolution from his friends—Theodore Roosevelt, Henry Cabot Lodge, and Elihu Root." In the course of his reply Trevelyan said: "Such an expression from three such men will make it a real heirloom to a coming generation which is well able to appreciate it."

appearance of Frederick Jackson Turner's famous essay on "The Significance of the Frontier in American History." He knew of the essay, however, before completing his study in 1896; yet was moved to no more enthusiastic judgment than that it was "a suggestive pamphlet. . . . ."[97] He was so slightly acquainted with the rising Wisconsin scholar that it was to "Prof. Frederick A. Turner, of the University of Michigan," that he referred with approval for the latter's emphasis on the influence of southern blood in the opening of the West.[98] In reviewing *The Winning of the West*, Professor Turner rebuked Roosevelt for not regarding history as a more jealous mistress and for not devoting to his historical work more time, greater thoroughness of investigation, and more sobriety of judgment.[99] Yet, Turner quoted Roosevelt with appreciation[100] and gave him high praise for his contribution to western historiography, asserting that he had done great service to American history by rescuing a significant phase of American development from the hands of unskilful annalists, that he had made use of original sources widely scattered and not heretofore exploited, and that he was perhaps the best-fitted man of his time to undertake the work.[101] Eventually, Roosevelt and Turner came to know each other very well. Acquaintance broadened into cordial friendship. Letters passed between them; and, like Ferrero, Turner was invited to be a guest at the White House.[102]

When the writings of Theodore Roosevelt are brought to judgment before the strictest canons of historical method and the great models of historiography, it is not difficult to detect their faults. Several of his pieces rest on entirely inadequate research; some, on only the shallowest. Composition was usually hurried,

[97] *The Winning of the West*, II, 181 n.

[98] *Ibid.*, p. 436 n.

[99] *American Historical Review*, II, 176.

[100] F. J. Turner, "The Significance of the Mississippi Valley in American History," in *The Frontier in American History* (New York, 1921), p. 178.

[101] *American Historical Review*, II, 171. Students in Professor Turner's classroom found that *The Winning of the West* was required reading.

[102] The Roosevelt-Turner correspondence is now in the Widener Library at Harvard.

often interrupted, and too little benefited by calm review and revision. Readers are sometimes taken aback by Roosevelt's vigorous projection of himself into his historical pages and by his partisan alignment with one or the other side of conflicting views and policies. His subjectivity of treatment is often far removed from what many hold to be the historian's obligation to treat controversial issues dispassionately. However one may be inclined to judge him in this, there were occasions when his violence of feeling and statement carried him beyond his evidence. For example, he could not prove all the harsh things he wrote of Jefferson; and to call Thomas Paine a "filthy little atheist"[103] indicates that he had not read Paine's declaration in the opening pages of the *Age of Reason:* "I believe in one God, and no more; and I hope for happiness beyond this life." Roosevelt wrote too much on too many subjects and divided his interest and energy far too greatly ever to permit him to become a historian of first eminence.

But in evaluating the work of Theodore Roosevelt in American historiography, it is unfair merely to complain that he did not write superlative history. Rather we should gratefully acknowledge that such a man wrote history at all, and on the whole wrote it so well. It must be borne in mind that he did not recognize the jealous claims of History to be his only intellectual mistress. Other literary jades enticed him, and his passionate writing spirit compelled him to yield to their beguilements. He wrote in youth and vigor, in sorrow, sickness, and age, and under the handicap of defective eyesight. And, with all his writing, he remained a man of action in the full glare of the national and world-spotlight. These things are to be remembered as we pass judgment on his work, and these also: that his public labors carried him to the presidency of the United States and that the historians of America made him president of the American Historical Association.

[103] Theodore Roosevelt, *Morris*, p. 289.

XIII

FREDERICK JACKSON TURNER

AVERY CRAVEN
University of Chicago

✳

FREDERICK JACKSON TURNER wrote less and influenced his own generation more than any other important historian. In his lifetime he published only two books, and one of these was a collection of essays already once printed in periodicals.[1] Since his death two other volumes have appeared: one unfinished, and edited by former students; and the other a second collection of previously published essays.[2] Yet one critic has asserted that for forty years Turner "has so completely dominated American historical writing that hardly a single production of that time has failed to show the marks of his influence."[3] Another has insisted that "American history has been reinterpreted and rewritten because of him."[4]

The explanation is simple. It is found in a wealth of suggestive ideas packed into short essays which interpret rather than narrate, and in a stimulating personality which stirred students to curiosity and inspired them to independent research. Turner was both a "first-class mind" and a great teacher.

[1] *Rise of the New West* ("American Nation Series," Vol. XIV [New York, 1906]); *The Frontier in American History* (New York, 1920). For a bibliography of Turner's work, see Howard W. Odum (ed.), *American Masters of Social Science* (New York, 1927), pp. 310–12, n. 17.

[2] *The United States, 1830–1850* (New York, 1935); *The Significance of Sections in American History* (New York, 1932).

[3] Louis M. Hacker in the *Nation*, July 26, 1933.

[4] Merle E. Curti, in Stuart A. Rice (ed.), *Methods in Social Science* (Chicago, 1931), p. 367.

The thing of first significance in Turner's work was the approach. Until his appearance American historians were, with few exceptions, primarily interested in politics and constitutional problems. Few essayed interpretation. The germ theory of politics, as expounded by Herbert B. Adams, at Johns Hopkins, where Turner went for graduate work, held that American institutions were but a continuation of European beginnings. Economic and social foundations were slighted; geographic factors, largely ignored. American history was a barren waste already sufficiently explored.[5]

Against such attitudes Turner revolted. A Wisconsin background enabled him to take a more penetrating view. He could enter by the back door. Because he had been part of a rapidly changing order, he saw American history as a huge stage on which men, in close contact with raw nature, were ever engaged in the evolution of society from simple beginnings to complex ends. Historians had answered "what" long enough; it was time to inquire as to "how" things came about. America, as it then existed, was the product of the interaction of "economic, political and social forces in contact with peculiar geographic factors."[6] Such an understanding would give a new American history.

These ideas took definite form quite early in Turner's teaching career and reached public expression in a paper presented to the American Historical Association in 1893 on "The Significance of the Frontier in American History." He offered it not as a fixed formula for the interpretation of all that field but as a suggested approach for reinterpretation.[7] He was calling attention to factors which others had neglected. Nor was he dictating results.

---

[5] F. J. Turner to Carl L. Becker, Dec. 16, 1925 (MS).

[6] Turner to Becker, Oct. 3, 1925; Jan. 21, 1911 (MSS).

[7] Turner to Constance L. Skinner, Mar. 18, 1922, *Wisconsin Magazine of History*, XIX (September, 1935), 91–103. Turner, *The Frontier in American History*, p. 3. "This paper makes no attempt to treat the subject exhaustively; its aim is simply to call attention to the frontier as a fertile field for investigation and to suggest some of the problems which arise in connection with it." He had presented his general theses locally before presentation to the American Historical Association.

He was only pointing out the need for research and indicating new approaches which might yield profit. There is nothing dogmatic about any of the conclusions reached. They were tentative. Some of them applied too largely to the middle period of American history, in which he was primarily interested and in which his researches had been carried on, to have universal application. Turner knew this. Yet, because he saw the deeper significance of the process involved, he spoke in broad, general terms. Here "was a huge page in the history of society." The American pioneer was revealing "luminously the course of universal history."[8] Terms from geology crept in naturally; and the purely local history of isolated communities was lifted, for those with imaginations, to the dignity of social evolution. One listener, at least, sensed the fact that "the Monroe Doctrine of American historical writing "was being pronounced.

The basic idea developed in this essay, and repeated in later ones with variations and additions, was that American history, through most of its course, presents a series of recurring social evolutions in diverse geographic areas as a people advance to colonize a continent. The chief characteristic is expansion; the chief peculiarity of institutions, constant readjustment. The areas successively occupied differed in the beginning as greatly from each other in physical makeup and resources as did those in Europe which were separated by national lines. They were all wilderness in character, and each in turn represented "the hinter edge of free land." Into these raw and differing areas men and institutions and ideas poured from older basins, there to return to a more or less primitive state and then to climb slowly back toward complexity along lines fixed by the new environments, the old patterns imported, and the accidents of separate evolution. The process was similar in each case, with some common results but always with "essential differences" due to time and place. The final result, as area after area was occupied from the Atlantic to the Pacific, was the Americanization of both men

[8] *The Frontier in American History*, p. 11.

and institutions in the sense that they were better adjusted to their environments and had altered their original character.

The constant re-exposure of things American to a process of "beginning over again" and developing toward urban-industrial conditions made the great West "the true point of view in the history of this nation."[9] And because the place of most rapid change was on the outer edge, Turner centered attention there. He did not intend to ignore the more advanced stages in the process or to minimize their significance. He objected sharply to being considered "primarily a western historian"; and once, after calling attention to the fact that "urban development has always been one of those processes," he expressed regret that he could not "start all over and investigate more in detail the eastern aspects."[10] But he did realize that the first steps in shifting the interest of the American historian from the "germ theory of politics" to the new approach must be taken by emphasizing the frontier stage. There the interaction of all forces—geographic, economic, and political—appeared in exaggerated form. There the process by which American society had evolved could best be studied. He would bring the frontier into American history as a sober contributing factor, not as merely a series of romantic episodes. He would place the cowboy, the miner, the pioneer farmer, in proper relations with "big business" and city slums.

With the process and its stages briefly described and the importance of the frontier suggested, Turner enlarged upon the general effects of the latter on American institutions and character. He believed that nationalism and democracy were both promoted and given a peculiarly American flavor by the West and that the individual who lived under its influence acquired new intellectual traits. A coarse strength, a masterful grasp of material things, a restless, buoyant individualism—these and other qualities characterized those who had experienced frontier living.

The statement of these effects was in general terms. Turner used the word "frontier" in loose fashion. Sometimes it referred to a place where men were scarce and nature abundant; again it

[9] *Ibid.*, p. 3.   [10] Turner to Becker, May 14, 1927 (MS).

referred to the process itself and included more than one west. He used the terms "democracy" and "nationalism" in equally indefinite fashion. Seldom was he dealing with a specific geographic area. His interest was in the effects of men and environments on each other, and exact definition was not required.

But it was these general effects which appealed to the imagination of most students, and some came to consider them the basic content of the "Turner thesis." They were applied strictly to definite times and places as universal rules. The American experience was unique. Everything about the frontier made for nationalism and democracy. All frontiersmen were rugged individualists, confirmed idealists, and persistent innovators. The all-important matter of the process was forgotten, and the way opened for distortion and misunderstanding. Most of the later criticism of Turner's work has come for such reasons. Hence, because some students, as Turner once sadly remarked, have "apprehended only certain aspects" of his work and have not always seen "them in *relation*," it is necessary to enlarge somewhat upon his own conception of the bearing of the frontier on nationalism and democracy.

As has been said, Turner stated, after describing the American social process, that the frontier promoted the formation of a composite nationality for the American people. Immigrants were Americanized, and dependence on Europe ended by removal to "the edge of civilization." Frontier problems, growing out of the need for land, ways to market, and markets themselves, developed the national government's powers. Men in a wilderness asked for and secured national protection and aid. "The economic and social characteristics of the frontier worked against sectionalism," and "the mobility of population [was] death to localism."[11]

All this seems strangely contradictory to Turner's own later study of sections in American history and his recognition of the fact that they were produced by the steady flow of peoples out of old areas into new physical basins. Here is open conflict of con-

[11] *The Frontier in American History*, p. 30.

clusions, and it would be a simple matter to extract statements regarding the effects of the frontier on nationalism from their settings and to offer them as generalizations easily refuted. In fact, they can be made to appear ridiculous. Yet Turner went on insisting on the nationalizing force of the frontier and describing the thoroughly sectional character of its results.

The matter grows more serious with the second frontier contribution—what it gave to democracy. As described, it was in part individualism, as manifested in opposition to outside oppression or even interference, and in part the greater recognition of individual worth in a wider franchise. But, whatever its character, "it came out of the American forest, and it gained new strength each time it touched a new frontier."[12] Born of contact with free land, it was translated into economic competency and through that into political power. The spoils of office and the right of exploitation for economic advancement were concrete evidence of its immediate application. The pressure put on older sections—even on Europe—by opportunity opened and escape offered, spread the new freedom and the new equality to common men everywhere. The frontier made real that which was elsewhere too often only a theory.

And yet Turner states clearly that "each new tier of states . . . . found in the older ones material for its constitutions." They did not draw them down out of the air. They were not necessarily democratic. Furthermore, the whole social-process idea implied the continuity of the basic elements of American life not only with those on the American seaboard but with those in Europe as well. All things did not begin over again on each frontier in a democratic way. Turner certainly recognized the contributions made to American democracy by the Reformation and by the Puritan revolt at the very moment when he was insisting that it was not carried in the "Susan Constant" to Virginia or in the "Mayflower" to Plymouth. He traced the spread of human slavery from old to new regions, there to become more fixed in a stratified western society, and still talked of a growing de-

[12] *Ibid.*, p. 293.

mocracy. He pointed out the hostility of western men to governmental interference and then told of the tendency among frontiersmen on the plains and in the semiarid regions to call on the
central government to do things for them which did violence to
all laissez faire attitudes. He emphasized the barn-raising, the
husking bee, the logrolling, and the neighborhood roundup as
normal co-operative efforts among those he depicted as extreme
individualists. Everywhere there is contradiction; everywhere
conflicting facts which upset sweeping generalizations.

These seemingly conflicting attitudes have puzzled those who
did not sit as students in Turner's classes. And they have caused
one critic, more clever than wise, to declare "this extraordinary collection of learning . . . . quite worthless"—yes, positively harmful. He has insisted that a mere statement of Turner's
ideas is enough to refute them.[13]

It is not possible to remove completely all these difficulties.
Those who knew the man and his work at first hand were sel-

---

[13] Hacker, *Nation*, CXXXVII, 108–10. Mr. Hacker has been the most rabid and the
least understanding of Turner's critics. His chief complaints are against Turner's insistence
on the uniqueness of America's historical experience and on Turner's failure to view all
American history in terms of a class struggle. Turner was talking about one end of a social
experience; Hacker has his eyes fixed on the other end. The constant exposure of institutions to the influence of free land on a frontier was a unique experience in national history.
The urban-industrial complexity reached at the end of the whole process of evolution from
raw frontier simplicity is not unique. Viewed, say, with the eyes of east side New York
in 1930, American conditions would not appear to differ from those of the Old World. The
class struggle probably would appear to be the chief thing toward which American life
had ever been moving. The farmer would appear only as a much abused victim of capitalistic greed. But there are unique elements in that situation which have come into it
through the process by which it has been reached. The attitudes of all groups differ a bit
from those in other mature social units. The weapons they use and the way they are used
have an American flavor. The rugged individualism of the frontier is still something to
conjure with. The American farmer is still far from a peasant in temper regardless of material conditions. The American millionaire has acted in a rather unique way with his mil-
lions. The democratic dogma is something even yet quite distinct from European democracy as it rises out of the great rural American regions. The average American is still far
more sectionally conscious than he is class conscious. And American history must avoid
a completely urban-industrial viewpoint if it is to remain true to the facts of two centuries
and more of rural dominance. The process by which we reached complexity is still more
significant as a historical fact than the mere conditions reached at the end of that process.
See reviews in *ibid.*, July 26, 1933, and the *New Republic*, June 5, 1935.

dom conscious of contradictions. They are even yet a bit resentful, if not contemptuous, of those who, lacking the memory of a mind which could master detail and then rise far above mere facts to illuminate the whole in universal setting, fail to grasp the real meaning of Turner's work. They forget that something passed with the man—something essential to understanding. Turner dissolved petty contradictions in the very breadth of his grasp. His ceaseless curiosity gave objectivity; his open-mindedness forbade dogmatism. He moved so swiftly from one station to another, that he passed by, though not unconsciously, much that employs lesser minds. He abhorred generalizations, as many a graduate student learned to his sorrow; but he himself wrote the kind of history which required generalizations. It was never a narrative of successive events, but rather Turner's own understanding of the meaning in events. Separated from the man himself and his wider work, or given over for application to students who do not comprehend their full meaning, those generalizations become as weak and as dangerous as generalizations have a reputation of being. It is not strange that there have been both criticism and misunderstanding. Even at the expense of some repetition, a closer examination of Turner's own statements should be made. Limits for their application should be set.

The unity in Turner's work and the key to its real significance, if there is such a key, is found in the approach already noticed. Turner spoke of it as "changes in perspective." He was interested in explaining the United States of his day by its history, as revealed in the "interrelations of economics, politics, sociology, culture in general, with geographic factors." He began with *things as they were* and asked how they came to be *as they were*.[14]

Most historians, as has been said, had answered in terms of old-world germs continuing development in the new. Turner understood the "crossroads society" of the Middle West well enough to realize that men there would not agree. They thought of themselves as unique, and of their experiment in democracy as a sharp departure from all that lay across the Atlantic. And he

[14] Turner to Becker, Oct. 3, 1925 (MS).

agreed in as far as historical perspective permitted. He knew full well the heritage with which America began—men and institutions; hopes, fears, prejudices, and ideals. Most of the social and intellectual patterns had been and still were basically those taken first from Europe and then from older regions in our own East. But something new had crept in. European travelers sensed a new flavor in Boston and Philadelphia and on the farms 'round about. The outlook was different, even the temper. They spoke of more independence in men, of more hope and of more social-economic achievement. The traveler from the American East felt the same difference when he visited the new "Wests." Something American was being added. Changes were being wrought here slowly, there more rapidly. A people on the move, a society fluid in quality, men and institutions thrown in successive waves against the forest and plains, were taking on, in different geographic areas, a *native* tone, if not form.[15]

Turner, in attempting to explain his United States, emphasized these differences—refined out the American qualities and explained their origins in terms of the process by which society had developed in the American physical regions. It was a society of contradictions—the very democratic dogma, which was its boast, was composed of both liberty and equality—things hostile to the point of destroying each other. A raw life fading irregularly back into urban-industrial complexity presented every variety of interest and every stage through which mankind in its long toil up the course of civilization had experienced. Cross-currents of every kind appeared in the stream of national life. Sometimes they ran opposite to the general current. The intense pressure for labor in the conquest of a continent brought slavery into a society fundamentally democratic in practice and profession. The very physical character of the tasks to be done made men, who were at heart idealists, coarse and practical and materially minded. Preoccupation with the pressing work of making a living forced the borrowing of social and political institutions

[15] Joseph Schafer, *Wisconsin Magazine of History*, XVI (June, 1933), 451–69; *ibid.*, XVII (June, 1934), 447–65.

from older states in the East by men prone to innovation, with the consequent restriction of more liberal forms, at least for a time. Every quality manifested had somewhere its opposite. Even the national life seemed often to drift rather than move ahead. There were too many conflicting interests, too many confused demands. And a babel of voices, in a government of majorities, could not command a straight course. Sections differing in age, in physical resources and environments, in origins of settlers, institutions, and values held, could only move forward by compromise. And compromise does not give clear-cut, positive direction.

If, by careful survey and comparison of frontiers and "Wests," Turner found a drift toward "democracy and nationalism," he had reference not to sharp, well-defined, all-inclusive qualities but rather to general tendencies which stood out amid contradictions and variations but which were, nevertheless, easily distinguished and universally recognized. And their importance was enhanced by their very failure to yield to exactness in application. Turner's democracy manifested itself more in the erect head, the stubborn jaw, the buoyant spirit of confidence, the faith in "King Numbers," the sharp dislike of privilege, and the insistence on unrestricted opportunity than in any violent recasting of institutions. These were the things which the traveler noticed. These the things which led to a wider franchise when the settlers "got 'round" to it. In the meantime the democratic dogma might be employed in defending those who had stolen a "quarter section" of land from the government. Such democracy cannot be comprehended by a comparison of western state constitutions with those of the coast, because all American constitutions, of coast and interior alike, have felt the force of the frontier, and because the very process of American institutional development was one of borrowing and later adjusting, not creating. To require a frontier, strictly defined as two persons to the square mile, to make for itself either political or social institutions without reference to habit and origins is absurd. To test the soundness of Turner's belief in the frontier as a democratizing force by such a requirement is even a greater absurdity.[16]

Turner himself adequately revealed the contradictions of frontier nationalism by his work on the sections.[17] But he did not repudiate it. A national outlook of a certain kind among western men was too obvious, even though the crosscurrents ran in quite a different direction. No one would deny that the rising West turned the eyes of Americans inland for several generations, made commerce largely internal instead of foreign, and built lines of communication between distant units to forward that trade. No one could question the fact that internal problems occupied the American statesmen for decades after the War of 1812. Nor could they ignore the larger interest in central government manifested by those who, having left the states of their nativity behind, now looked toward Washington for protection and aid in "advancing civilization." From that angle they could readily agree that the frontier "worked against sectionalism." But they would be blind, indeed, if they did not recognize the fact that the development of distinct and potentially hostile sections might be wrapped up in the very process of westward expansion. Turner pointed this out and made sectionalism the dominant interest of his later studies. He insisted that the occupation of geographic provinces and the evolution of society in them made American history in its later stages largely the record of sectional conflict, sectional combinations, and sectional compromises. When compromise failed, war was a danger and, in one case, a reality. Newer areas demanded peculiar legislation in the treatment of the public domain, the building of internal improvements, the handling of finances, and the encouragement of markets. The older ones required other policies. Northern interests sometimes

[16] See Benjamin F. Wright, Jr., "Political Institutions and the Frontier," in D. R. Fox (ed.), *Sources of Culture in the Middle West* (New York, 1934), pp. 15–38; also *Yale Review*, XX, 349–65.

[17] *Sections in American History, passim; The Rise of the New West; The United States, 1830–1850.* It should be noticed that Turner's two volumes of history are, after all, sectional studies—the national side of the story, which follows sectional analysis, being largely the interplay of sectional forces.

ran counter to those of the South; mining or manufacturing demands often opposed those of agriculture. Even diplomacy had to consider the conflicting claims of different sections. The American statesman, under such conditions, tended to become a sectional spokesman, and "democracy" and "nationalism" were often only emotional stimulants called in to add force to sectional demands. The clash of economic interests closely associated with regional geography gives to American life something of the European international flavor. We are in one sense a federation of "potential nations." The very fact that we have, by discussion and compromise, largely avoided violence, Turner thought, revealed the possibility of "international political parties, international legislative bodies, and international peace."

Nor did Turner neglect the social implications in the evolutionary approach he had taken. Much of the misunderstanding of his work could be avoided by a reading of the essay on "Social Forces in American History" in connection with that on the frontier.[18] The one is a corollary of the other, and almost as important. In this essay Turner faced the problems of American life "when the West was gone" and when urban-industrial complexity predominated. He saw the problems produced by a continuation of the ruthless individualism which the frontier had bred and by the thrusting of frontier attitudes into a new social order which they could neither comprehend nor control. By 1910, when he spoke, "world-wide forces of reorganization incident to the age of steam production and large-scale industry" were writing a new and "wonderful chapter" in American life. The industrial revolution, not the frontier end of the American process, was shaping society. The old isolation was gone. The United States was in world-politics. Natural resources had largely passed into private hands. Foreign labor crowded our shores, and concentrated wealth gave the keeping of the many into the hands of the few. "Self-made . . . . coal barons, steel kings, oil kings, railroad magnates, masters of capital and monarchs of trusts" championed the old pioneer individualism as against the

[18] *The Frontier in American History*, pp. 311–34.

efforts at social control. They arrayed the ideal of freedom in the democratic dogma against its fellow-ideal of equality. A government-of-the-people's struggle for social justice was being thwarted by the continued emphasis on, and worship of, qualities suited only to a pioneer agricultural order. Class conflict was taking the place of geographic sectionalism. American ideals were demanding readjustment to fit the new conditions of a day when the frontier was gone.

Turner concluded that the tangled situation presented could be grasped only by "an understanding of the rise and progress of the forces which . . . . made it . . . . ," and insisted that "we should rework our history from the new points of view afforded by the present." The time had come to place larger stress on that phase of the American social process which lay at the other end from the frontier.[19]

Turner was, of course, a careful, scholarly craftsman in spite of the fact that he undoubtedly viewed history as an art rather than as a science.[20] He laboriously, yet joyously, gathered materials and carefully weighed and analyzed them. His files were filled with countless pages of statistics. The votes of congressmen on measures of all kinds were compiled and plotted on charts and maps. He was never ready for final judgment while sources remained unworked. He was ever ready to forsake the painful task of writing in order to follow up some new clue or to digest some new document. He once said of himself: "I am not philosopher enough to be a 'maker of social sciences'—but I have had a lot of fun exploring, getting lost and getting back, and telling my companions about it."[21] His favorite poem was Kipling's "The Explorer."

The most vital thing in Turner's method was the wide character of materials on which he drew. "Literature and art, politics, economics, sociology, psychology, biology and physiography" all furnished data. He brought all these into larger co-

[19] *Ibid.*

[20] See Curti, *loc. cit.*, pp. 355-62.   [21] Turner to Becker, Feb. 13, 1926 (MS).

operation in his work, and each of these fields is indebted to him for scholarly service. He was a historian both of the oldest and newest schools.

One lasting impression which the student carried away from Turner's classes and from his workshop was that of countless maps, jigsaw in appearance, because they represented the plotting of votes by counties. Such graphic representation revealed sectional interests, the force of habit, the persistence of viewpoint carried by migrants from older areas into newer ones. When thrown against geological survey maps, racial maps, or cultural maps of various kinds, they added something to the American story not to be found elsewhere. Turner gave the United States census maps a new place in the historian's equipment. By his work the character of map materials used in history books was to a degree, at least, altered for the better.

Much attention has been given by writers to the origins of the Turner frontier thesis.[22] He made no claim to priority but insisted on the independent character of his own formulation. To the inquiry of writers he went back to a boyhood in Wisconsin where bits of the old frontier still persisted. He had hunted and fished along rivers where Indian tepees still were to be found. The raftsmen from the pineries sometimes "tied up" at his town. New Englanders, southerners, Germans, Scotchmen, Welshmen, Irishmen, and Scandinavians, mingled together in this "mixing bowl." The local politicians met in his father's newspaper office. He saw democracy painfully at work. And under his very eye Wisconsin left pioneer days behind. At the state university Professor William F. Allen taught him "the ideals of scholarship," and Draper permitted him to work with a rich collection of fur-trader manuscripts. At Johns Hopkins the emphasis on European institutions and the neglect of geographic factors and western influence in American history turned him back to his own experiences as a truer approach to the story.[23] Others had already

[22] H. C. Nixon, "Precursors of Turner in the Interpretation of the American Frontier," *South Atlantic Quarterly*, January, 1929.

[23] Turner to Becker, Dec. 16, 1925 (MS).

caught something of the importance of the frontier factors in American life, but Turner gave them full expression at the time when history study in the United States was ready to incorporate them. There is little point in searching out earlier statements which recognize the social process but which did not take hold to influence the study of American history. But if it is to be done, this terse paragraph from the pen of Thomas Jefferson deserves more attention than it has received:

Let a philosophic observer commence a journey from the savages of the Rocky Mountains, eastwardly toward our seacoast. These [the Indians] he would observe in the earliest stage of association living under no law but that of nature, subsisting and covering themselves with the flesh and skins of wild beasts. He would next find these on our frontiers in the pastoral state, raising domestic animals to supply the defects of hunting. Then succeed to our own semibarbarous citizens, the pioneers of the advance of civilization, and so in his progress he would meet the gradual shades of an improving man until he would reach his, as yet, most improved state in our seaport towns. This, in fact, is equivalent to a survey, in time, of the progress of man from the infancy of creation, to the present day.[24]

In this connection, also, it must be remembered that Turner's protest against the historian's neglect of the West coincided with the Populist's demand for larger political recognition of western interests and with William Jennings Bryan's redefinition of the term ''business man'' so as to include the western farmer. Each of these spokesmen, whether politician or historian, was, in a way, reaffirming faith in the old individualistic democracy which now faced the advancing urban-industrial order. All revealed, in differing degrees, a crusading flavor. All looked backward, rather than forward, for values. All manifested a supreme confidence in the basic soundness of the ''American experiment'' as it had been and an equal distrust of the new forces which moved to dominance. Turner's strength, as well as his weakness—yes, even the appeal his writings made to his own generation—can be

[24] Thomas Jefferson to William Ludlow, Sept. 16, 1824, Official Papers, *Writings*, XVI, 74–75.

understood, in part at least, only by the fact that his work was an expression of the American mind and spirit at "the turn of the century."

The work which came from Turner's own pen is poor measure of his contribution to American scholarship. No other historian of the day inspired in others so much original investigation. Never particularly interested in teaching per se, he thereby became a great teacher. He once begged a former student, who was writing a sketch of him, not to hand him "down to posterity as a teacher." "I had no interest in the 'shooting' of the young idea," he said, "I was interested in history, and in the companionship of men like yourself."[25] And that was exactly what made him "a master." He shared his field with those who had the capacity to appreciate it. He stimulated their interests. His eager mind saw opportunities for new investigation amid the welter of forces which his conception of history implied, and the task was "too big for one investigator and one historian." Students might become companions on his journeys to this frontier. But he would not "rubber-stamp" their minds. He would only point out a great unoccupied land—a wilderness they might pioneer and claim for scholarship, something "tucked away below the foothills where the trail runs out and stops." He had the explorer's instinct, but he also had the good sense to keep out of the way of those "who were willing to blaze trails of their own."[26]

It is therefore not surprising that Turner's students worked in many fields or that they pioneered many lines. Some contributed to economic and social history on subjects that ranged from agriculture to industry, centered on finances or transportation, on primitive Indian tribes, or on the efforts of mature societies to end wars. Some wrote local history—state or regional. Others

[25] Turner to Becker, Nov. 23, 1925 (MS); Turner to A. O. Craven, Nov. 20, 1926 (MS).

[26] Ibid.

dealt with the sections. Diplomatic and political events, well set on their economic foundations, attracted a few. But regardless of the field entered—and they ranged across the whole of America, east and west, north and south, early and late—each believed that he had secured his inspiration and his start from Frederick Jackson Turner.[27]

It is always difficult to write of this man in an impersonal way. He "inspired affection as well as admiration." The rich quality of his voice, the kindly twinkle of his eye, the genuine modesty in regard to achievements, the keen humor of lasting quality— these things and many others have been spoken of by loyal students. But there was something more which Turner possessed and which others caught from him that can be explained only in personal terms. Few who write of him escape the pressure for "personal testimony." I may as well succumb now as later, not for the purpose of telling about myself but to reveal something of Turner which can be conveyed in no other way. I went to Harvard with only the quantity of history I had been unable to resist in a small western college. I left Turner's classes after a year of work, eager and willing to study the history of one county in a rural state. Its hills and valleys had become for me a stage on which a great epic in human history had been written. Its early settlers were part of a great trek; its slow rise from a wilderness to the complexity of general farming about a county seat of four thousand souls was part of a great national and international process. The old buffalo wallows in a prairie stretch and the old abandoned flour mills on its muddy streams were one with the small factories of the town which accepted them as the first steps to industrial importance. The old newspapers and family letters in the attic were social documents. I could be a historian by knowing all about this one area, because local history was hu-

[27] A list of Turner's students who have made real contributions to history is given in Curti, *loc. cit.*, pp. 359–67. It is, however, not complete. Turner influenced fellow-workers in the field of American history also, and gave suggestions which others, who never felt his personal touch, carried out. Few men received more reprints from authors, and no one is mentioned as often in authors' prefaces. Truly he did influence a whole generation of writers.

man history. Of course the outlook changed with greater maturity; but the interest in all social-economic-political matters, the fear of being too certain about things, and the unrest as long as more could be learned, remained as something of an obligation for having "worked with Turner." He did that to most of us.

The historian is the child of his age. New shifts in interests alter values and outlooks. History must be re-written by each generation for itself. It would be asking too much that Turner be to another generation what he was to his own. It is probably fair to say that he generalized too much for the whole West from the Old Northwest which he knew so well. He may have insisted a bit more on the uniqueness of the American experience than the facts warranted, and he may not have stressed the industrial-agricultural class conflicts enough—but this is doubtful. His faith in America's future may have been too great, his hope for democracy too high. These were common faults in his day. But the questions he asked are more or less permanent ones for those who would know how America came to be what it is. His answers may not exactly fit when the pattern is entirely unfolded. He would be among those greatly surprised if they did. I one time asked him why he did not answer a critic who had distorted in order to criticize. He only chuckled and said: "I've always been surprised that there has not been more of criticism." He was too eager for truth to care for praise or blame. He was running down a new clue on Calhoun when death interrupted the eternal urge to "go and look behind the ranges."

NOTE: Frederick Jackson Turner was born at Portage, Wisconsin, November 14, 1861. His ancestors, on both sides, were of New England origin; and his parents had migrated from New York State in pioneer days. Turner graduated from the University of Wisconsin in 1884 and returned to his alma mater as tutor in rhetoric and oratory in the fall of 1885. He held this post until 1888, when he took his Master's degree and went to Johns Hopkins for further graduate study. He received his Ph.D. degree there in 1890, his thesis subject being "The Character and Influence of the Indian Trade in Wisconsin." From 1889 to 1910 he was again at Wisconsin, first as assistant professor of American history, then as professor of history and professor of American history. In the latter year he transferred to Harvard University, where he remained until retirement in 1924. He died on March 14, 1932, in Pasadena, California, while holding the position of research associate at the Huntington Library. For sketches of Turner and his work, see *Publications of the Colonial Society of Massachusetts*, Vol. XXVIII, *Transactions*, pp. 494–502; *Huntington Library Bulletin*, No. 3, pp. 157–64; *Wisconsin Magazine of History*, XVI (June, 1933), 451–69; *ibid.*, XV, 86–103; *ibid.*, XVII (June, 1934), 447–65; *Pacific Historical Review*, II (March, 1933), 34–51; *American Masters of Social Science* (Odum ed.), pp. 273–318; *Methods in Social Science* (Rice ed.), pp. 359–67.

XIV

HERBERT LEVI OSGOOD

E. C. O. BEATTY
Northern Illinois State Teachers College

Denn das Ideal ist immer, die historische
Wahrheit der Welt zu vergegenwärtigen.
—LEOPOLD VON RANKE

OF ENGLISH ancestry, eight generations removed from the mother-country,.Herbert Levi Osgood was born on April 9, 1855, in the farming community of ·Canton, Maine.[1] The parents, Stephen and Joan Staples Osgood, thrifty New Englanders, provided for this, their second, son the best educational advantages available. At the age of eighteen Osgood was admitted to Amherst. There he came under the influence of John W. Burgess, who recognized in his young student ability well worth development.[2] Having completed graduate courses

---

[1] D. R. Fox, *Herbert Levi Osgood—An American Scholar* (New York, 1924), pp. 15 ff. From Dr. Fox's brief but charmingly written biography of his father-in-law most of the biographical facts in this study have been taken. Cited hereafter as "Fox." For other biographical treatments, see Dr. Fox's article on Osgood in *Dictionary of American Biography*, edited by D. Malone, XIV (New York, 1934), 78–79; and *Who's Who in America—A Biographical Dictionary of Notable Living Men and Women of the United States*, edited by A. N. Marquis, X (Chicago, 1918), 1918–19, 2057–58. See also E. Putnam (ed.), *A Genealogy of the Descendants of John, Christopher and William Osgood Who Came from England and Settled in New England Early in the Seventeenth Century*, compiled by the late I. Osgood (Salem, Mass., 1894), p. 1. Here Putnam says that John Osgood, first American progenitor of the historian, arrived in New England "undoubtedly in 1638."

[2] J. W. Burgess, *Reminiscences of an American Scholar: The Beginnings of Columbia University*, with a foreword by N. M. Butler (New York, 1934), p. 159: "I encountered two students in this class [that of 1877 at Amherst] whose interest and success rewarded me for all

at Amherst with Anson D. Morse and at Yale with William Graham Sumner, Osgood followed the advice of Burgess and went to Berlin for a year of further study under Wagner, Schmoller, Gneist, and Treitschke. In Germany he found his model. Earlier he had studied and admired the works of Leopold von Ranke; while abroad he saw the aged scholar. For his own future work he chose deliberately to follow the course laid out by the master, to write history not "to point a moral, or adorn a tale" but "wie es eigentlich gewesen." After some interruption he returned to the student's life and attended Burgess' seminar in the newly founded school of political science at Columbia. In 1889 he published his doctoral dissertation there. To complete his *Lehrjahre* he went with his young wife[3] to England, where he devoted himself to the mastery of English history.

Meanwhile he had taught in various institutions: for two years at Worcester Academy, a term in Professor Morse's place at Amherst, some time at Smith, and six years in the Brooklyn High School. From England he returned in 1890 to accept a chair in the school of political science at Columbia. The association thus begun was continued until the close of his career, twenty-eight years later. In 1891 he began a course at the University on the "Political History of the Colonies and the American Revolution," which developed into a seminar for the researches preliminary to his seven volumes on the American colonies. Though not without interruption, this course was Professor Osgood's main academic preoccupation until death came on September 11, 1918.[4]

the efforts I made to serve Amherst for this year while a professor at Columbia. They were Henry S. Redfield and Herbert L. Osgood, both men of extraordinary intelligence and vast capacity for work. I marked them both for future colleagues. . . . ."

[3] On July 22, 1885, he had married Caroline Augusta Symonds, of Pownal, Vermont, who, in Dr. Fox's words, "with executive gifts and social charm was to smooth the pathway of her scholar-husband until his death" (Fox, p. 29). See also *Who's Who in America*, X, 2057.

[4] Osgood's death was reported in the *New York Times*, Sept. 13, 1918. It called forth two remarkable editorials in appreciation. One of these appeared in the *Nation* (New York), Sept. 21, 1918, pp. 309–10. Unsigned, it was written, says Fox, by R. L. Schuyler. The second was the tribute of W. R. Shepherd, published in the *Columbia University Quarterly*, XXI, No. 1 (January, 1919), 79–81. Both of these are reprinted in Fox, pp. 157–65.

Osgood was never wealthy. His education cost his frugal parents considerable sacrifice. Later, to carry on his extensive researches meant trips to Europe and much secretarial help. At times his family was reduced to careful planning that the work might go on. His income was limited to his salary, never above five thousand dollars, though twice the University granted him a leave of absence at full pay and after 1912 he received a small annual subsidy from the Carnegie Institution. Nevertheless, he was able to provide for the needs of an invalid son, to accumulate an excellent private library, to buy a residence in New York City, and to spend vacations in a summer home. His writings give no indication that personal financial problems or economic status influenced his historical interpretation.

As might have been anticipated from his German training, Osgood was much interested in social and economic theories. During his first sojourn in England he learned to know the Fabian Socialists; but with characteristic singleness of purpose he refused to be diverted from his main end, the mastery of English history. His doctoral thesis, *Socialism and Anarchism*, two articles printed in early volumes of the *Political Science Quarterly*, and numerous book reviews attest his interest in these theories. Yet, except as incidental to the main theme, the development of political institutions, his *magnum opus* deliberately eschews economic and social history.

As an undergraduate at Amherst, Osgood came under strong Puritan influence; but he did not then, or later, accept in any formal sense the Christian theology. Possessed of "the rationalist mind," he found that "orthodoxies wearied him, in politics and religion."[5] Fox says that in the later years of Osgood's life he found pleasure in the sermons of Dr. Merle St. Croix Wright and in discussions with Dr. James H. Hyslop, of the Psychical Research Society. If there were any forces tending to influence his interpretation of historical religious development, they would probably have sprung from his Puritan heritage. A for-

5 Fox, p. 153.

mer student, analyzing his works, has found in them no evidence of bias in favor of the New England Puritans.[6]

Beginning with the fourth number of the *Political Science Quarterly*, of which journal he later served for years as a member of the editorial board, Osgood contributed thirteen major articles and sixty-four reviews to its pages.[7] Excepting three, the articles deal with phases of American colonial history.[8] The reviews reflect his interest in a variety of subjects, including such diverse fields as Marxian economic theory, German medieval and modern economic society, English agricultural and industrial development, the French archives and Revolutionary history, English constitutional and political institutions, American sectional economic history, the general history of the United States, American biography, and the philosophy of history.[9] An active member of the American Historical Association, Osgood contributed three

[6] H. J. Coppock, "Herbert Levi Osgood," *Mississippi Valley Historical Review*, XIX, No. 3 (December, 1932), 400. Mr. Coppock is a former student of Professor Osgood, and the study here cited grew out of a paper read by him in the seminar on American historiography at the University of Chicago conducted by Professor M. W. Jernegan. To check Coppock's opinion see Osgood's two articles on "The Political Ideas of the Puritans," in *Political Science Quarterly*, VI, No. 1 (March, 1891), 1–28, and No. 2 (June, 1891), pp. 201–31. Such passages as that describing Puritan repressiveness in the first volume of the series on the colonies in the seventeenth century substantiate the opinion indicated (Osgood, *The American Colonies in the Seventeenth Century* [New York and London, 1904], I, 218–19).

[7] From 1891 to the year of his death Professor Osgood was a member of the editorial board of the *Quarterly*. In the *Index to Volumes I–XLV—1886–1930*, published as a supplement to the *Polit. Sci. Quart.*, Vol. XLVI, No. 2 (1931), may be found a list of the titles of these articles, as well as references to the volumes and pages where his book reviews are printed (*ibid.*, p. 116). Though the index shows but ten titles for Osgood's articles, he wrote an essay in each of two numbers on one subject and an essay in each of three on a second. In the text, therefore, the total number of these contributions is placed at thirteen.

[8] The three exceptions are: "Scientific Socialism—Rodbertus," *Polit. Sci. Quart.*, I, No. 4 (December, 1886), 560–94; "Scientific Anarchism," *ibid.*, IV, No. 1 (March, 1889), 1–36; "The Prussian Archives," *ibid.*, VIII, No. 3 (September, 1893), 495–525.

[9] Among the writers reviewed are C. Rodbertus-Jagetzow, K. Marx, G. Adler, K. Lamprecht, J. E. Thorold Rogers, A. Sorel, Langlois and Stein, D. J. Medley, J. Macy, H. Taylor, G. T. Lapsley, W. B. Weeden, P. A. Bruce, A. Brown, T. Roosevelt, W. G. Sumner, J. Morley, and R. Flint, in *Polit. Sci. Quart.*, I (1886), 339–41; II (1887), 523–24; III (1888), 172–76, 526–28; VII (1892), 355–57, 731–33; X (1895), 696–97; XII (1897), 543–46; XIV (1899), 147–49; XV (1900), 564–67; V (1890), 722–24; XI (1896), 322–26; VI (1891), 363–65; XIII (1898), 534–36; III, 682–86; VI, 166–68; XIX (1904), 144–48; X, 167–69.

major articles to the *Review* on "The Proprietary Province as a Form of Colonial Government," companion studies to the three published in the *Political Science Quarterly* on "The Corporation as a Form of Colonial Government."[10] As a member of the Public Archives Commission of the Association he was chiefly responsible for the important "Report on the Public Archives of New York."[11] During the years from 1897 to 1913 he published nine reviews in the *American Historical Review*, covering studies by Edward Eggleston, Eleanor Louisa Lord, Evarts B. Greene, Irving B. Richman, and Edward McCrady, and the *Guides* of Charles M. Andrews and of Charles M. Andrews and Frances G. Davenport.[12] Among the papers in the *Annual Reports* is his article entitled "The Classification of Colonial Governments," in which, as in his study of "The Corporation as a Form of Colonial Government,"[13] he attacked Blackstone's threefold classification of the American colonial governments and suggested as more logical a consideration of them under two classes, namely, corporate colonies and provinces, royal and proprietary. Another important article is his "Study of American Colonial History," in which he expressed the view that "the seventy years lying between 1690 and 1760 is to a large extent an unknown period."[14] In the "Report of the Conference on Research in American Colonial and Revolutionary History," Osgood, chairman of the conference, recommended: "a comparative study . . . . of the development of the colonies as institutions of government during

[10] *American Historical Review*, II, No. 4 (July, 1897), 644–64; *ibid.*, III, No. 1 (October, 1897), 31–55; *ibid.*, No. 2 (January, 1898), pp. 244–65. *Polit. Sci. Quart.*, XI, No. 2 (June, 1896), 259–77; *ibid.*, No. 3 (September, 1896), pp. 502–33; *ibid.*, No. 4 (December, 1896), pp. 694–715.

[11] American Historical Association, *Annual Rept.*, *1900* (2 vols.; Washington, 1901), II, 67–250.

[12] *Amer. Hist. Rev.*, II, No. 3 (April, 1897), 528–30; IV, No. 2 (January, 1899), 365–67; IV, No. 3 (April, 1899), 549–50; V, No. 2 (December, 1899), 358–61; VII, No. 1 (October, 1901), 165–67; VIII, No. 3 (April, 1903), 545–46, 557–59; XIV, No. 4 (July, 1909), 829–31; XVIII, No. 3 (April, 1913), 592–93.

[13] Amer. Hist. Assoc., *Annual Rept.*, *1895* (Washington, 1896), pp. 617–27; *Polit. Sci. Quart.*, XI, No. 2 (June, 1896), 259–77.

[14] Amer. Hist. Assoc., *Annual Rept.*, *1898* (Washington, 1899), pp. 63–72.

the early eighteenth century," the investigation of them "as parts of the British imperial system," and "the study by suitably trained men, of the transfer of English law into the American colonies."[15]

In 1901 Osgood printed some minutes of the Society of Dissenters in New York.[16] He shares the credit for the transcription of English public records for the Library of Congress.[17] He was the chief agent in securing the publication of the records of the Virginia Company, for which he wrote the Preface.[18] At his suggestion and under his direction the eight volumes of the *Minutes of the Common Council of the City of New York, 1675–1776* were edited and published.[19] He is the author of the section on the early history of the United States in the eleventh edition of the *Encyclopaedia Britannica*.[20]

The first two volumes of *The American Colonies in the Seventeenth Century* appeared in 1904; the series was completed by the publication of a third in 1907.[21] The work was the fruit of researches which, in Osgood's words, "were undertaken, years ago, at the suggestion of Professor John W. Burgess."[22] Reviewers greeted the contribution with high praise.[23]

[15] *Ibid., 1908* (2 vols.; Washington, 1909), I, 114–15.

[16] Under the title of "The Society of Dissenters Founded at New York in 1769," in "Documents," *Amer. Hist. Rev.*, VI, No. 3 (April, 1901), 498–507.

[17] Fox, p. 123.

[18] *Ibid.*, pp. 123–24. The work in question is Susan M. Kingsbury (ed.), *The Records of the Virginia Company of London—The Court Book, from the Manuscript in the Library of Congress* (4 vols.; Washington, 1906–35).

[19] The "editorial charge of the work" was vested in a committee of the New York Historical Society, composed of H. L. Osgood, F. W. Jackson, R. H. Kelby, and H. Smith (*Minutes of the Common Council of the City of New York, 1675–1776* [8 vols.; New York, n.d.], I, iv–v).

[20] *Encyclopaedia Britannica* (11th ed.; Cambridge and New York, 1911), XXVII, 663–84.

[21] *The American Colonies in the Seventeenth Century*, Vols. I and II; *The Chartered Colonies: Beginnings of Self-Government*, Vol. III: *Imperial Control: Beginnings of the System of Royal Provinces* (New York, 1904 and 1907; pp. xxxii+578; xix+490; xxii+551).

[22] *Amer. Col. in the 17th Cent.*, I, iv.

[23] The most important reviews are those of C. M. Andrews, *Amer. Hist. Rev.*, XI, No. 2 (January, 1906), 397–403, and *ibid.*, XIII, No. 3 (April, 1908), 605–9; D. Schäfer, *Historische Zeitschrift*, XCVI (N.S. LX; 1906), 516–17; St. G. L. Sioussat, *Dial*, XXXVII,

After a brief introduction in Part First,[24] the opening volume begins with a discussion of the early proprietary province. Five chapters are given to the early experiments of Gilbert and Raleigh, to Virginia as a proprietary province, and to the New England Council. Part Second is a discussion in fourteen chapters of the corporate colonies of New England. The second volume, forming Part Third of the fourfold organization of material, treats, in sixteen chapters, of proprietary Maryland, New Netherland and New York, New Jersey, the Carolinas, and Pennsylvania, with five concluding chapters bearing on the judiciary, ecclesiastical relations, the financial system, defense, and Indian relations in the later proprietary provinces. These two volumes, as Osgood put it, "are concerned wholly with the American side of the subject."[25] In the third volume, Part Fourth, he discusses the development of imperial control and the early growth of the system of royal provinces. The entire work brings the account of colonial institutions down to about 1689.[26] A lucidly written

---

No. 437 (Sept. 1, 1904), 107–10; C. Seignobos, *Revue historique*, XCIX (September–October, 1908), 147–49; H. E. Egerton, *English Historical Review*, XXII, No. 88 (October, 1907), 804–7. For other notices see that of an anonymous reviewer in *Nation* (New York), LXXIX, No. 2048 (Sept. 29, 1904), 261–62; that initialed by "P. R." in *Critic*, XLV, No. 4 (October, 1904), 378; those in *Independent* (New York), LVII, No. 2920 (Nov. 17, 1904), 1145–46, and *ibid.*, No. 2925 (Dec. 22, 1904), pp. 1448–49. A brief mention of the appearance of the third volume is printed in the unsigned "Notizen und Nachrichten" in *Hist. Zeit.*, C, 685.

[24] *The American Colonies in the Seventeenth Century* is organized in four parts. These bear the following titles: Part First, "The Proprietary Province in Its Earliest Form"; Part Second, "The Corporate Colonies of New England"; Part Third, "The Proprietary Province in Its Later Forms"; Part Fourth, "Imperial Control. Beginnings of the System of Royal Provinces." Two of these are developed in the first volume, the third in the second, and the fourth in the final volume of the series. Vols. I and III have brief prefaces. Vol. I has an introduction. Vols. II and III have conclusions as separate final chapters. All three have analytical tables of contents, 20 pages in length for the first volume and 15 pages for each of the others. Vol. I has no index; but since Vol. I and Vol. II are in a sense a unit in themselves, the second volume has an index of 47 pages covering both. The third volume has an independent index covering 28 pages. None of the volumes has any bibliographical chapter or list; and none has either map, chart, diagram, or any type of illustration.

[25] *Amer. Col. in the 17th Cent.*, I, iii.

[26] In some cases the account is carried beyond the English Revolution. See, for example, the discussion of the Tuscarora war in the Carolinas, 1711–13 (*ibid.*, II, 429–32).

conclusion at the close of the second volume and a similar chapter at the end of the third summarize "the political and administrative system of the British-American colonies as it was developed during the formative period of their existence";[27] and they point the way to the change in British policy, "imperial rather than particularistic," which induced the slow and gradual transition to the system of royal provinces, "the balanced system which was developed in harmony with the spirit of the English Revolution."[28]

Having completed the three volumes on the seventeenth century, Osgood turned his attention to a field much less thoroughly explored, the study of the American colonies in the eighteenth century.[29] When death came, he had nearly completed his task. With the exception of a few chapters, planned but not written, and some final revision, the volumes on the eighteenth century were ready for the printer. Osgood died, says Dr. Fox, in the belief that the publication of the work had been secured under a contract of long standing. Such, however, was not the case; and for almost four years after the author's death, his heirs sought in vain for a publisher. Studies of such a nature offered too small a prospect of large sales to be tempting to those necessarily concerned with profits. Finally, Dwight W. Morrow, a former student in Osgood's class on early American institutions, contributed the five thousand dollars required to guarantee publication. Prepared for the press by the competent hands of Professor Fox, the four volumes of *The American Colonies in the Eighteenth Century* appeared in 1924 and 1925, six years after the author's death.[30]

In this study of the colonies,[31] as the author says, "an effort

---

[27] *Ibid.*, pp. 433–42.   [28] *Ibid.*, III, 507–21.

[29] In a chapter bearing the suggestive title, "Pioneering in the Eighteenth Century," Fox has described the problems which confronted Osgood in this study and the manner in which he met them (Fox, pp. 84–108).

[30] *The American Colonies in the Eighteenth Century* (4 vols.; New York, 1924–25; pp. xxii+552; xxiv+554; xxviii+580; xxiv+582); Fox, p. 103; Andrews in *Amer. Hist. Rev.*, XXXI, No. 3 (April, 1926), 538.

[31] This series is reviewed by Andrews in *Amer. Hist. Rev.*, XXXI, 533–38, and by H. E. Egerton, in *Eng. Hist. Rev.*, XLI (January, 1926), 132–33.

has been made to trace their development during a period of seventy years,—from 1690 to 1763."[32] The volumes are organized into parts "according to the succession of wars and intervals of peace in the prolonged struggle between the British and the French."[33] Thus, the first volume opens with a chapter on the administrative framework of the British empire after the revolution of 1688–89; and the fourth volume concludes with the capitulation of Vaudreuil at Montreal on September 8, 1760, and the transfer of Canada to British control. With the appearance of this posthumously published work Osgood's major contribution was complete.

In the Preface to the introductory volume of his second series the author wrote: "The history of any nation, at any stage of its development, is a subject of great complexity, far too great to be thrown upon the canvas of a single historical work."[34] Consequently, to present truth effectively as history, Osgood believed that the historian "must choose from among a number of points of view, without denying the equal validity of others, and adhere consistently to his chosen path throughout."[35] For his life-work Osgood chose deliberately to set forth the history of political institutions as it developed in the English colonies within the present limits of the United States. In making this decision he was not ignorant of, or indifferent to, economic, so-

[32] *Amer. Col. in the 18th Cent.*, I, viii.

[33] *Ibid.*, p. ix. There are three parts. Part One, entitled "The Colonies during the First Two Intercolonial Wars, 1690–1714," is treated in the sixteen chapters of the first volume and in eight more in the first part of the second volume. The chapters of each part are numbered consecutively; thus Vol. II opens with chap. xvii of Part One. Part Two bears the title, "The Colonies during the Interval of Peace between the Second and Third Intercolonial Wars, 1714–1740." It begins with chap. i on p. 293 of the second volume, and continues through seven chapters in that volume. Chap. viii of Part Two opens Vol. III, and Part Two runs on through chap. xvii. Chap. i of Part Three, which part is entitled "The Growth of the Spirit of Independence during the Period of the Third and Fourth Intercolonial Wars, 1740–1763," begins on p. 407 of Vol. III and runs through four chapters in that volume. Beginning with chap. v, Part Three is completed in the thirteen chapters of Vol. IV. As in the case of the earlier series, these volumes have neither map, chart, diagram, illustration, nor bibliography.

[34] *Amer. Col. in the 18th Cent.*, I, ix.   [35] *Ibid.*

cial, religious, or even military history; he appreciated the soundness of interpretations other than his own.[36] Though he seems definitely to belong among the political and institutional historians, it is quite evident that he was not willing to assert, in Freeman's classic epigram, that "history is past politics and politics are present history."

He was familiar with the economic interpretation. He had studied Rodbertus and Marx. Though avowing sympathy with the aspirations of the socialistic theorists, he rejected their doctrines as in some respects demonstrable fallacies.[37] His earlier book reviews prove his interest in economic history.[38] The titles of many chapters in the volumes on the colonies show that he saw clearly the import of such factors as land, finance, trade, immigration, naval stores, the land bank, and inflation.[39] His treatment of such matters, however, was centered about their relationship to institutional history; and with reference to his final work, an able critic has expressed the view that the discussion of economic and social factors is inadequate.[40]

Without committing Osgood to a religious interpretation, two of his articles make it clear that he understood the power of spiritual forces in human affairs. Writing on "England and the

[36] E.g., his reviews of G. L. Beer, *The Origins of the British Colonial System, 1578–1660*, in *Polit. Sci. Quart.*, XXIV, No. 1 (March, 1909), 127; of Eleanor L. Lord, *Industrial Experiments in the British Colonies of North America*, in *Amer. Hist. Rev.*, IV, No. 2 (January, 1899), 365–67; of W. B. Weeden, *Economic and Social History of New England*, in *Polit. Sci. Quart.*, V, No. 4 (December, 1890), 722–24; of S. H. Cobb, *The Rise of Religious Liberty in America*, in *Polit. Sci. Quart.*, XVII, No. 4 (December, 1902), 697–99; of L. C. Hatch, *The Administration of the Revolutionary Army*, in *Polit. Sci. Quart.*, XX, No. 1 (March, 1905), 159–61.

[37] H. L. Osgood, "Scientific Socialism—Rodbertus," *Polit. Sci. Quart.*, I, 592–93.

[38] Sixteen of the 64 reviews printed over Osgood's name in the *Political Science Quarterly* deal with books on economic theory, economic history, social and economic conditions. The earlier reviews are almost entirely concerned with works on these matters.

[39] E.g., chapters on the land system, financial system, the acts of trade, the origins of the board of trade, naval stores, immigration, the land bank in Massachusetts, and others (*Amer. Col. in the 17th Cent.*, I, chaps. xi and xii, 424–95; II, chaps. ii and xiv, 16–57 and 347–74; III, chap. vii, 193–241. *Amer. Col. in the 18th Cent.*, I, chaps. iv, vi, vii, and xv, 116–59, 185–227, 228–65, 495–524; II, Part Two, chaps. i and vi, 293–346 and 483–529; III, chap. xvi, 318–62).

[40] Andrews in *Amer. Hist. Rev.*, XXXI, 536; Egerton in *Eng. Hist. Rev.*, XLI, 132.

Colonies," he attributed the overthrow of the charter of Massachusetts in 1685 in part, at least, to religious factors.[41] In a later discussion of "The Political Ideas of the Puritans" he stressed the effects upon the men of early Massachusetts of the fact "that they were the advocates of a definite religious system, which they came to the new world to put into practice."[42] In the same article, using the *Institutes* as his source, he analyzed the religious principles of Calvin. Later he asserted that if the plans of the New York Presbyterians in 1769 had been carried out, "a religious character would have been given to the Revolution."[43] In his books he took occasional opportunity to emphasize the religious motive.[44] Readers of the volumes will no doubt, however, agree with Fox's statement that in Osgood's works "organized religion is often treated, yet as a concern of state, rather than a human interest. . . . . "[45]

Even military history was a field in which Osgood was informed and in which he saw values. Explaining why the West Indian islands were of greater importance to English colonial statesmen than were the continental colonies, he maintained that, aside from economic reasons, military and naval considerations were influential.[46] Reviewing L. C. Hatch, *The Administration of the American Revolutionary Army*, he expressed appreciation of the value in "a study which would show how great an advance on colonial conditions was made during the Revolution, and to what extent those same colonial traditions survived and affected the military system after 1775."[47] In a later review of J. H. Smith, *Our Struggle for the Fourteenth Colony*, Osgood denied that "wars are of little importance and are therefore to be slurred over; for we know the opposite to be true. They are great crises in the body politic, and are always accompanied and followed by

[41] *Polit. Sci. Quart.*, II, No. 3 (September, 1887), 454.

[42] *Ibid.*, VI, No. 1 (March, 1891), 1 ff. The entire article covers pp. 1–28.

[43] *Amer. Hist. Rev.*, VI, 498.

[44] *Amer. Col. in the 17th Cent.*, I, 200, 397; III, 162, 170; *Amer. Col. in the 18th Cent.*, II, 3–48; III, 76–142, 407–90.

[45] Fox, pp. 76–77.

[46] *Amer. Col. in the 17th Cent.*, III, 139 ff.   [47] *Polit. Sci. Quart.*, XX, 160.

results of lasting importance."[48] Osgood wrote institutional history; but, in thus achieving what Dr. Beard would call his "act of faith," he was acutely conscious that he was touching but a single phase of "the totality of history as actuality."

Professor Osgood's books are the fruit of thorough and analytical study of original sources. Surveying Osgood's third volume on the eighteenth century, Coppock found it to refer to original sources in 72 per cent of the total number of citations given. The same student wrote that "perhaps ninety per cent of the seven volumes is based on printed sources."[49] In his review of the first volumes of the work on the seventeenth century, Andrews says that the printed evidence, upon which, "with but a single exception," the book depends, is to be found in the "texts of official documents and records."[50] In the later study, as in the earlier, the original sources are chiefly governmental documents: charters, commissions, instructions to governors and reports from them, statutes, journals of the legislative bodies, rulings of the board of trade, official letters from customs officers, court records, the papers and records of the various colonies, state papers of the British government. Readers of Osgood's article on the history of the English colonies and of the American Revolution in the *Encyclopaedia Britannica* will note the author's emphasis upon such sources.[51] In some of the chapters of his series, notably

[48] *Ibid.*, XXIII, No. 2 (June, 1908), 323.

[49] Andrews in *Amer. Hist. Rev.*, XI, 400; Seignobos in *Rev. hist.*, XCIX, 148; Coppock in *Miss. Valley Hist. Rev.*, XIX, 398–99. Testing a few chapters to prove these conclusions, the present writer examined the first three chapters of the first volume of the second series for specific citations to sources. In these three chapters there were 211 such references. Of these, 136 were to original sources and 75 to secondary works.

[50] *Amer. Hist. Rev.*, XI, 400.

[51] *Encyc. Brit.* (11th ed.), XXVII, 682. Osgood opens his discussion of sources as follows: "The records in which are contained the materials for the internal history of any one of the British colonies are the land papers, the minutes of the executive council, the journals of the upper and lower houses of the legislature, the laws and the correspondence and miscellaneous papers which originated from the intercourse between the colonial authorities—especially the governor—and the home government or other colonies and states. Every one of the original states has published these records in part, in series which are known under the general names of colonial records or archives or documents, or provincial papers."

those on religious institutions and movements, he used, to a relatively small extent, contemporary tracts and pamphlets.[52] Newspapers were not available for the greater part of the first series, and they are used sparingly in the second.[53] Private letters, diaries, and memoirs are occasionally cited.[54] Where French sources, as well as British, might have been used, the nature of Osgood's interpretation explains the marked preference for the latter.[55]

To a much larger degree than may be said of the earlier study, the series on the eighteenth century rests upon manuscripts. In preparation for this work Osgood examined the important collections in the thirteen original states and spent about two years in the study of the documents in the British Museum, the Public Record Office, and other great depositories in Great Britain. He once estimated that he had investigated more than one thousand volumes of manuscript, "a large part of it uncalendared and much hitherto almost unused."[56]

Secondary authorities were not neglected. As Fox remarks, however, Osgood "used them rather as additional help in discovering the sources, as guides to the mines of historical evidence."[57] Occasionally he relied upon the work of others. Thus, in the four chapters of the final volume of *The American Colonies in the Eighteenth Century* which touch the field so competently studied by Francis Parkman, one-eighth of Osgood's references

[52] Two chapters dealing respectively with "The Great Awakening" and "Ecclesiastical Relations at the Middle of the Century" were studied to test this statement. In the former, of a total of 65 references, 18 were to tracts or pamphlets; in the latter, of 95 citations, 12 were to tracts (*Amer. Col. in the 18th Cent.*, III, 407–90).

[53] In the chapter dealing with the Zenger trial, 5 citations out of 202 are to newspapers (*ibid.*, II, 443–82).

[54] Among such sources are the Shirley correspondence, the diary of Samuel Sewall, and George Washington's journal. See especially *ibid.*, III, 540–80 *et passim; ibid.*, I, 293–327; *ibid.*, IV, 334, n. 2.

[55] Studying the citations in the final volume of the second series dealing with the fourth intercolonial war, the writer found 17 citations to French sources out of a total number of 367. Most of the references to the French were to secondary authorities.

[56] Fox, p. 92.   [57] *Ibid.*, p. 101.

to secondary authorities are to the works of that scholar.[58] Discussing the "wild and lawless life of the forest" and the fur trade, Osgood said: "The classic description of this phenomenon is in Chapter 17 of Parkman's 'Old Régime in Canada.' "[59] Referring to Braddock's defeat, Osgood wrote: "As to what happened among the French, see the material cited by Parkman, *Montcalm and Wolfe*, II, App. E."[60]

As Ranke denied to modern historical research any didactic function beyond the mere reporting of truth, so Osgood chose for himself the role of objective historian. Early in his career he noted the unfortunate effect of "national prejudice and partisanship" in the treatment of American colonial history[61] and criticized Bancroft and others for their patriotic bias.[62] In his two series on the colonies, as in most of his printed articles, Osgood is generally cold and dispassionate. Nearly always his research is soberly reported in the form of an expository narrative, descriptive and analytical, but never argumentative. Even though in private conversation he frequently expressed strong feeling with regard to some of the characters whose doings he was recounting, his final written appraisal would almost always be judiciously stated with scrupulous regard for the available evidence.[63] There is nothing to indicate that Osgood considered the historian to be vested with the duties either of moralist or of

[58] In the 128 pages covered by these chapters, there are 449 citations to original sources and 64 to secondary material. Among the latter there are 8 citations to Parkman (*Amer. Col. in the 18th Cent.*, IV, 279–457).

[59] *Ibid.*, p. 281, n. 1.   [60] *Ibid.*, p. 350, n. 1.

[61] H. L. Osgood, "England and the Colonies," *Polit. Sci. Quart.*, II, 440.

[62] H. L. Osgood, "The Study of American Colonial History," Amer. Hist. Assoc., *Annual Rept., 1898*, pp. 70–71; Osgood, "The American Revolution," *Polit. Sci. Quart.*, XIII, No. 1 (March, 1898), 59. See also Osgood's remarks in his review of John Fiske, *The American Revolution*, in *Polit. Sci. Quart.*, VI, No. 4 (December, 1891), 727.

[63] Fox, p. 116. Some noteworthy characterizations, however, which appear largely—if not wholly—incapable of complete substantiation may be observed in Osgood's remarks concerning the following figures: Sir Charles Davenant, Samuel Sewall, James Logan, Charles Gookin, Nicholas Trott, William Pitt and William the Conqueror (*Amer. Col. in the 18th Cent.*, I, 183; II, 147, 255, 267, 356–57; IV, 397). One critic, however, has suggested that to Osgood, "all persons were in a measure, mere automatons which he used as physical apparatus for elucidating principles of institutional development" (*Miss. Valley Hist. Rev.*, XIX, 399).

advocate. If, to use Beard's striking language, Osgood's frame of reference included "things deemed necessary, things deemed possible, and things deemed desirable," if he had made "a deliberate conjecture respecting the nature or direction of the vast movements of ideas and interests called world history,"[64] he wrote, nevertheless, with singular detachment, singular absence of an evident sense of mission. Always well stocked with facts, page after page of his writings may be cited in which the interpretative element is nearly, if not quite, absent.[65] Contrasting him with others, Professor Theodore Clarke Smith has said: "But his tone and manner remained different; where Bancroft or Palfrey had been literary, moralistic, pictorial, Osgood stayed within the realm of the expository, the analytical and, for the most part, the impersonal."[66]

Nevertheless, as Gooch said of Ranke, Osgood's "passionless tone is not the result of indifference. When judgment is pronounced, it is the more weighty from its rarity."[67] In his early writings Osgood occasionally expressed opinions with great vigor. A striking example of such passages appears in his article on "Scientific Anarchism," in which he emphatically denounced the doctrines of the so-called "communistic anarchists."[68] In reviews of books he did not hesitate to pronounce judgments, and in some cases the views stated were sharply critical.[69] In the two series on the colonies, occasional opinions and characteriza-

[64] C. A. Beard, "Written History as an Act of Faith," *Amer. Hist. Rev.*, XXXIX, No. 2 (January, 1934), 227–28.

[65] It is difficult to cite passages particularly typical of the character indicated in the text because Osgood's tone is regularly coldly impartial. For illustrations, however, see chap. ix in *Amer. Col. in the 17th Cent.*, III, 280–308, and *Amer. Col. in the 18th Cent.*, I, 495–524; III, 318–62.

[66] T. C. Smith, "The Writing of American History in America, from 1884 to 1934," *Amer. Hist. Rev.*, XL, No. 3 (April, 1935), 443.

[67] G. P. Gooch, *History and Historians in the Nineteenth Century* (3d impression; London, 1920), p. 78.

[68] *Polit. Sci. Quart.*, IV, 1–36.

[69] For examples see the reviews of the following: J. Fiske, *Dutch and Quaker Colonies;* J. K. Hosmer, *A Short History of Anglo-Saxon Freedom;* E. and A. Porritt, *The Unreformed House of Commons;* Sir G. O. Trevelyan, *The American Revolution,* in *Polit. Sci. Quart.*, XV, No. 1 (March, 1900), 121–22; *ibid.*, VI, No. 1 (March, 1891), 162 ff.; *ibid.*, XIX, No. 2 (June, 1904), 322–23; *ibid.*, No. 3 (September, 1904), pp. 504–5.

tions appear. Such expressions are more common in the later volumes than in the earlier. When stated, Osgood's judgments are usually moderate and judicious, though on rare occasions a touch of irony reveals otherwise hidden feeling.[70]

Some critics have found evidence of unfairness in the works of Osgood. Andrews, for example, regards the treatment of the eighteenth century as an account doing less than full justice to the English side of the controversy; and Coppock thinks Osgood biased against the Quakers.[71] Andrews' charge is perhaps the more serious from the fact that at least at the outset of his career Osgood was plainly aware of the very pitfalls into which his distinguished critic thinks he fell.[72] It is true that passages may be cited to show the historian's disapproval of some phases of the Quakers' activities; but others may be adduced to indicate that he fully appreciated the ideals and services of this remarkable sect.[73] Both in his two series and in his earlier essays on the Puritans there is evidence that with respect to them he can hold the balance quite even.[74]

[70] On one occasion Osgood refers to the "tender treatment" meted out by the Algerines to their captives, William Harris and Seth Sothell (*Amer. Col. in the 18th Cent.*, I, 551). Later Osgood wrote with reference to Cornbury and Fletcher: "It was in harmony with the condition of New York politics in the eighteenth century that the Church had to rely so much for its early progress upon two such brilliant exponents of godliness as were these two governors" (*ibid.*, II, 17).

[71] Andrews says: "Professor Osgood's position of viewing all details of his subject from the standpoint of the colonies tends to create in him a disrelish—I would not call it a prejudice—for the British system and all who upheld it, and to make it difficult for him to understand just what the British outlook was before 1763" (*Amer. Hist. Rev.*, XXXI, 537). Coppock writes: "When Osgood departed from this attitude [i.e., that "all persons were . . . . mere automatons"], as he did occasionally, he held himself open to the charge of bias and prejudice. This weakness is most obvious in his treatment of the Quakers." Then follow citations of passages to illustrate the point, taken from *Amer. Col. in the 17th Cent.*, I, 269, 270, 273, 281; II, 415 (*Miss. Valley Hist. Rev.*, XIX, 400).

[72] *Polit. Sci. Quart.*, II, 440–41.

[73] *Amer. Col. in the 17th Cent.*, II, 252–56; *Amer. Col. in the 18th Cent.*, IV, 48–49, 55–57.

[74] *Miss. Valley Hist. Rev.*, XIX, 400. Cf. Osgood's discussion of "Relations between Church and Commonwealth in Massachusetts," chap. iii of Part Second, *Amer. Col. in the 17th Cent.*, I, 200–223; his discussion of Joseph Dudley, particularly, *Amer. Col. in the 18th Cent.*, II, 142–43; his article on "The Political Ideas of the Puritans," *Polit. Sci. Quart.*, VI, 1–28. Finally, writing of the Quaker attitude toward the exploitation and destruction of

Osgood's style is appropriate to his purpose. His chosen role was to explore, reveal, and enlighten—in no sense, to amuse. Fox has aptly said: "He wished to inform and to explain, and not to thrill; if he was perfectly clear it was not necessary to be melodious."[75] Critics have frequently commented upon the coldness of his prose.[76] The first two volumes of the earlier series Andrews pronounced "severe and unimpassioned . . . . written in a restrained and eminently judicial spirit."[77] The second series the same critic found "neither narrative, description, nor interpretation, but a mingling of all three"; he thought some of the chapters characterized by "seemingly unnecessary minuteness." Describing the work further, he called Osgood's treatment in nowise "exciting, sensational, appealing, or dramatic."[78] Frequently the account runs so evenly that the reader feels a lack of emphasis; and paragraph transitions sometimes are deficient in clarity because of this severe self-restraint.[79] Usually the work is clear; and if the reader has had the proper background, it is

the Indians, Osgood says: "Under the conditions and to the great majority of people in their time, this attitude seemed perverse and purely obstructionist. But to the modern man it appears worthy of all honor as a dim foreshadowing of what human relations should everywhere be. Of the superiority of the Quaker ideal to that of the Calvinist, even when viewed from the standpoint of the New Testament alone, there can be do doubt whatever" (*Amer. Col. in the 18th Cent.*, IV, 49).

[75] Fox, p. 27. That Osgood could appreciate the literary quality in the work of others is shown by his language in a review of J. Morley's *Life of William Ewart Gladstone*, in *Polit. Sci. Quart.*, XIX, No. 1 (March, 1904), 144–48. This work Osgood declared "undoubtedly one of the noblest biographies in the language, a worthy treatment of a great and inspiring theme. . . . ." Of Morley he said: "His mastery of English prose style, his broadly critical temper, the learning and insight which he has shown in his earlier biographical and critical studies, adequately vouch for the literary success of the work."

[76] A former student remarks that his "style resembles certain November days—mostly clear but cold, quite cold—and if one is continuously exposed to the weather they seem quite long" (Coppock, p. 400). Cf. Fox, pp. 114–17; Egerton in *Eng. Hist. Rev.*, XXII, 805; *Critic*, XLV, 378.

[77] *Amer. Hist. Rev.*, XI, 400.

[78] *Ibid.*, XXXI, 535–36.

[79] Fox, p. 115: "He [Osgood] restrained whatever 'literary' impulses he had, for, on the one hand, reckless rhetoric would be foolish and, on the other, too much tooling of a phrase for great force or beauty would take time that should be given to finding out the truth."

not difficult to follow.[80] The first series is somewhat better written than the second. The nature of the later field and the fact that death prevented the author's own final revision with the addition of some useful summarizing chapters may have combined to produce this result.[81]

In some respects—and particularly in the first series—Osgood's technique is unusual. The reference numbers for footnote citations often appear in unexpected places: between an adjective and the noun immediately following, between the definite article and the noun, between the subject and the verb, after a preposition, after a verb but before the verb's object, between the month and the year of a date, and once at the beginning of the sentence rather than at its close.[82] Sometimes the reader is referred in the text to a passage appearing earlier in the volume or in a preceding volume with no citation to locate the item in question.[83] At times, one misses a desirable cross-reference. The absence of an index in four of the seven volumes aggravates the inconvenience of such omissions.[84] Bibliographical lists would have been helpful. Readers not well acquainted with colonial geography would appreciate maps. Both series contain various types of common errors.[85] Usually completely lacking in picturesqueness, Os-

[80] Of the second series Andrews said: "The volumes call for close attention and considerable preliminary preparation, and the incautious and unready reader is likely to lose his way, if he is not careful . . . ." (*Amer. Hist. Rev.*, XXXI, 534–35). "The 'general reader,' " said Sioussat, "may be pardoned some trepidation when he is confronted with the thousand pages that constitute the body of this work [*Amer. Col. in the 17th Cent.*, Vols. I and II], to say nothing of thirty-four pages of 'Contents' and fifty-eight of 'Index' " (*Dial*, XXXVII, 107).

[81] Andrews in *Amer. Hist. Rev.*, XXXI, 534, 538.

[82] An example of each of the cases mentioned in the text follows: *Amer. Col. in the 17th Cent.*, II, 295, l. 6; *ibid.*, p. 290, l. 13; *ibid.*, p. 334, l. 31; *ibid.*, p. 119, l. 22; *ibid.*, p. 122, l. 33; *ibid.*, III, 204, l. 9.

[83] E.g., *ibid.*, III, 280, ll. 6–8; *Amer. Col. in the 18th Cent.*, I, 382, ll. 1–4; *ibid.*, p. 455, ll. 1–5; *ibid.*, III, 199, ll. 31–33.

[84] Vol. I of the first series has no index except as part of the cumulative index appearing in Vol. II. The only index in the second series is the cumulative index at the close of Vol. IV.

[85] Andrews has called attention to some of these in his several reviews: *Amer. Hist. Rev.*, XI, 403; *ibid.*, XIII, 609; and *ibid.*, XXXI, 538.

good's prose is notable for the paucity of adjectives,[86] of emotional words,[87] of exclamation points.[88] Direct quotations are freely employed, often of sufficient length and aptness to make unnecessary much explanatory comment by the author.[89]

With all his attention to minutiae, Osgood possessed the power of clear and forceful generalization.[90] Sometimes his summaries approach eloquence. When he chose to leave his scholarly notes, abandon the details of his study, and draw comprehensive conclusions, he was able to do so in masterly fashion.[91]

[86] Occasionally, however, one reads such passages and phrases as the following: "He [Dongan] proved to be one of the very best of all the colonial governors" (*Amer. Col. in the 17th Cent.*, II, 131). "But the process of development which was begun by its [the Virginia Company's] dissolution was a natural one, though it marked the end of the romantic period of Virginia history and removed from connection with that province some of the most attractive personalities who ever interested themselves in American colonization" (*ibid.*, III, 53). "Its biblical phrases [those of the Massachusetts general court's address to the king] and its exaltation of the royal dignity, its almost fawning humility, might well have befitted a petition from the chosen people, when in exile, to their Persian monarch" (*ibid.*, p. 161). "His [Berkeley's] pique was shown at times by the assumption of an air of mock humility, but more often by stubborn persistence in his chosen course of action" (*ibid.*, p. 286). "He [Edward Randolph] was a partisan of the narrowest mould . . . ." (*ibid.*, p. 380). "It [Leisler's revolt] was a blind and ill-considered movement, led by a fanatical German . . . ." (*ibid.*, p. 448). "He [Lewis Morris] was one of the most prominent aristocrats of his time, the founder of a family, one of the most prejudiced and dogmatic of men, outspoken and energetic, a foe of inefficiency and of dishonesty" (*Amer. Col. in the 18th Cent.*, IV, 5).

[87] Examples of the use of such words are to be observed not only in some of the phrases cited in the preceding note but in expressions like "stupefying monotony and routine," applied to the ceremonies of the church (*Amer. Col. in the 18th Cent.*, II, 4, ll. 30-31).

[88] In reading the seven volumes the present writer noted but two instances of the use of such punctuation. One of these appears in *ibid.*, p. 234, l. 22; the other is to be found in *ibid.*, IV, 400, l. 27.

[89] Two examples are the excerpt from Nathaniel Bacon's "The Declaration of the People," *Amer. Col. in the 17th Cent.*, III, 272-73; and the quotation from the Rev. John Callender, of Newport, on toleration and its effects in Rhode Island, *Amer. Col. in the 18th Cent.*, III, 239-41.

[90] "The highest quality of his style is his power of 'lucid generalization' . . . ." (*Miss. Valley Hist. Rev.*, XIX, 401).

[91] Examples of Osgood's power of generalization and summary may be found in the following passages: his distinction between the realm and the dominions, in *Amer. Col. in the 17th Cent.*, III, 8-9; his important and interesting paragraphs concluding the review of the English commercial policy, in *ibid.*, pp. 239-41; the generalizations introducing his chapter on "The Dominion of New England," in *ibid.*, pp. 378-81; his remarks on war, in

In one of his famous prefaces Ranke declared that historical writing must unite art with science.[92] For Osgood, the admirer of Ranke, however, this requirement was of lesser importance. As Fox has said, he consciously denied himself the devices of the literary historian;[93] his readers clearly recognize that he made no attempt to emulate such artists as Parkman, Macaulay, or Gibbon. Critics have noted that Osgood's works are "written by a specialist, chiefly for specialists"; that he "left to the student the rather heavy task of working out for himself underlying relationships"; that his "work is manifestly designed for serious readers only, professional or otherwise"; that he was "a scholar for scholars, an historian's historian." Readers are reminded that they will "have to work to get the meat of his volumes"; and it has been suggested "that such readers may be few in number. . . . ."[94]

Among scholars Professor Osgood's works have been received with the highest praise. The first two volumes of *The American Colonies in the Seventeenth Century* were welcomed as "a work finely conceived and destined, when completed, to occupy a place of first importance in the literature of American history"; as a "comprehensive and satisfying synthesis of historical investigation and criticism"; as "eine jener eindringenden, stoffreichen Arbeiten zur Geschichte der eigenen Vorzeit, die mehr und mehr charakteristisch werden für amerikanische Geschichtsforschung und Geschichtsdarstellung neuester Zeit." Of the third volume of the series Seignobos declared: "Elle met en lumière et groupe

---

Amer. Col. in the 18th Cent., I, 42 ff.; the introduction to the chapter on "The Outlying Colonies of New England: New Hampshire," in *ibid.*, III, 186–90; and particularly the chapter on "The Great Awakening," in *ibid.*, pp. 407 ff.

[92] L. von Ranke, *Französische Geschichte vornehmlich im Sechzehnten und Siebzehnten Jahrhundert*, V (4th ed., rev., in *Sämmtliche Werke* [3d ed.], Vol. XII; Leipzig, 1877), 5–6: "Die Aufgabe des Historikers . . . . ist zugleich literarisch und gelehrt; die Historie ist zugleich Kunst und Wissenschaft."

[93] Fox, pp. 115–16.

[94] The critics to whom reference is made are Andrews, Coppock, Fox, and Sioussat; see *Amer. Hist. Rev.*, XI, 400; *Miss. Valley Hist. Rev.*, XIX, 398, 403; Fox, p. 117; *Dial*, XXXVII, 107.

une série de faits que les historiens américains, naturellement placés au point de vue des colons, n'avaient jusqu'ici étudiés que d'une façon fragmentaire. ... '' Andrews said that this volume completed ''a study of the colonies in the seventeenth century which may justly be deemed the most important interpretation of our colonial history that has thus far been made.''[95] Later the same scholar described the three volumes on the seventeenth century as ''the most important single contribution to the history of the continental American colonies''[96] and declared that they ''contain the ablest accounts we have of the institutional characteristics of the period.''[97] After the appearance of the third volume of this series, Osgood received the Loubat prize ''for the best work published within the past five years on the early history of the United States.''[98] *The American Colonies in the Eighteenth Century* Andrews called ''a really great work''; and Egerton said that it ''shows a high-water mark of learning and of luminous judgement which will secure for it a place among the classics of American history.''[99]

Since his death in 1918, Osgood's fame has not diminished. Scholars agree in awarding to this quiet, unassuming man a high place in American historiography. Schlesinger termed Osgood's

[95] These opinions were stated by Andrews, Sioussat, Schäfer, Seignobos; see *Amer. Hist. Rev.*, XI, 397; *ibid.*, XIII, 605; *Dial*, XXXVII, 110; *Hist. Zeit.*, XCVI (N.S. LX), 516; *Rev. hist.* XCIX, 148.

[96] In sec. X, "United States" (edited by M. W. Jernegan), *A Guide to Historical Literature* (editors: G. M. Dutcher, H. R. Shipman, S. B. Fay, A. H. Shearer, W. H. Allison; New York, 1931), p. 1013.

[97] C. M. Andrews, *The Fathers of New England: A Chronicle of the Puritan Commonwealths* ("Chronicles of America" series, edited by A. Johnson, Vol. VI [New Haven, 1921]), p. 201.

[98] Fox, p. 83.

[99] *Amer. Hist. Rev.*, XXXI, 538; *Eng. Hist. Rev.*, XLI, 133; *Miss. Valley Hist. Rev.*, XIX, 394. Reviewing the first two volumes of *The American Colonies in the Seventeenth Century*, an anonymous writer adjudged the work to be ''the most substantial and masterful contribution made to the study of American colonial history in recent years'' (*Nation* [New York], LXXIX, No. 2048 [Sept. 29, 1904], 262). Another such writer pronounced these volumes ''the greatest work of the year in American history,'' ''an epoch-making book in the study of colonial political organization'' (*Independent* [New York], No. 2920 [Nov. 17, 1904], pp. 1145–46).

labors and those of Charles M. Andrews "of basic importance" in the modern study of the American Revolution. Bessie L. Pierce assigned to Osgood an important place among those who have revised the traditional notions concerning colonial relations with Great Britain. Bassett declared Osgood's first series "the best work" on the growth of colonial institutions, and the second he described as "highly important upon government particularly." Jernegan characterized both series as "thoroughly scientific and accurate."[100] In several of his writings Harry Elmer Barnes has placed Osgood among the outstanding figures in American historiography, and said of his books that "in America the most extensive contribution to institutional history is to be found in Osgood's history of the English colonies to the Revolution." In another place Barnes declared of Osgood's series that "his monumental seven volume work on the American colonies constitutes the highest point to which exact American scholarship has attained, and is worthy to rank with the writings of Gardiner and Aulard."[101]

If, as student and writer of American institutional history, Osgood holds a place unique among his fellows, his services as teacher are hardly less noteworthy. For many years his seminar was the fruitful school for a remarkable band of disciples, whose work has reflected the spirit and inspiration of the master.[102] Endowed with a personality singularly modest and retiring, un-

[100] A. M. Schlesinger, *New Viewpoints in American History* (New York, 1925), p. 181; Bessie L. Pierce, *Public Opinion and the Teaching of History in the United States* (New York, 1926), p. 206; J. S. Bassett, *A Short History of the United States, 1492–1929* (rev. ed.; New York, 1929), pp. 132, 159; M. W. Jernegan, *The American Colonies, 1492–1750* (in *Epochs of American History*, edited by A. B. Hart [4 vols.; New York, 1931]), p. xxv.

[101] H. E. Barnes, "History, Its Rise and Development," *Encyclopedia Americana* (30 vols.; New York and Chicago, 1934), XIV, 241, 248, 249; Barnes, "History," in H. E. Barnes (ed.) *The History and Prospects of the Social Sciences* (New York, 1925), pp. 29, 49.

[102] As representative of the several generations of Osgood's students, the following are listed by Dr. Fox: G. L. Beer, W. R. Shepherd, A. C. Flick, C. A. Beard, Susan M. Kingsbury, C. R. Lingley, and A. M. Schlesinger (Fox, p. 150). For appreciative tributes from two of these see Beard's review of Schlesinger's *The Colonial Merchants*, in *New Republic*, XIV, No. 179 (Apr. 6, 1918), 301; and Shepherd, "An Historian of the Thirteen Colonies," *Columbia University Quarterly*, XXI, No. 1 (January, 1919), 79–81.

willing to abandon his strict regimen of labor for the distractions which beset the distinguished in academic life, he nevertheless exercised a powerful influence upon the circle of devoted students with whom he came into contact. To few scholars is it given to contribute so solid and enduring a work as Osgood's series have thus far proved themselves to be; to fewer still has come the opportunity to combine with such a contribution the training of so competent and distinguished a group of historians.

Of Ranke, masterly scholar and teacher, Osgood once wrote: "He had also the loftiest conception of the duty of the historian to discover the truth and to state it with absolute impartiality. Again and again in his letters and elsewhere does he rebuke partisanship and insist upon thoroughness in research and objectivity in statement. This is the priceless lesson which his life and work have taught the scientific world."[103] In these words, written twenty-eight years before the completion of his career, Osgood most appropriately described his own great services to American historiography.

[103] *Polit. Sci. Quart.*, VI, No. 3 (September, 1890), 562.

XV

EDWARD CHANNING

RALPH RAY FAHRNEY
Iowa State Teachers College

*

A RECENTLY published bibliography lists forty-nine short articles, six essays, and fourteen books as evidence of the prolific accomplishment and prodigious labor of Edward Channing as an American historian.[1]

His first extensive work, outside the textbook realm, was published in 1896 and surveyed the century between the eve of the American Revolution and the close of the Civil War. Although scarcely more than a rapidly running account of events, based largely upon the work of his old master, Henry Adams, James Ford Rhodes, and others, with "little pretense of originality," it was printed in four languages and furnished Americans, as well as their European critics, a passing glimpse of the American scene.[2]

A decade later Channing contributed *The Jeffersonian System* to a co-operative history that lent renown to the editorial genius of his Harvard colleague, Albert Bushnell Hart. Doubtless its merits and deficiencies were conditioned in part by the plan and scope of the "American Nation" series, which was designed more for the general reader than for the special student. There was a noble effort to utilize primary sources and to quote advantageously from documents; but originality was again somewhat

[1] George W. Robinson (comp.), *Bibliography of Edward Channing* (Cambridge, 1932).

[2] See Edward Channing, *The United States of America, 1765–1865* (New York, 1896), p. vii, for the author's own modest estimate of his effort.

294

lacking as the author leaned once more upon Henry Adams, who had previously combed valuable unexplored sources to present an exhaustive treatment of the Jeffersonian era.[3] The book served the purpose of its design and compared favorably with companion volumes in the series.

But the fame of Edward Channing as a historian rests primarily upon his courageous attempt to write a complete history of the United States from the age of discovery to the close of the nineteenth century. The following appraisal refers almost exclusively to that work. The magnitude of the task was appalling, considering the variety and complexity of sources which modern scholarship had discovered in various hidden recesses. When the embryonic idea seized Channing during his college days, no one had yet realized such a dream. After fifty years of labor Bancroft discontinued his record at 1789; Hildreth did not get beyond 1821; and even McMaster left everything before 1783 and after 1865 to others. That the idea survived in Channing's mind and finally bore much fruit was due to a personal trait of stubborn persistence combined with the farsightedness of President Eliot of Harvard, who lightened committee duties and in other respects paved the way for his ambitious faculty member to concentrate on the great work.[4]

Some knowledge of the family heritage and environmental background of Channing is essential to a critical appraisal of his masterpiece. He was born in Dorchester, Massachusetts, a member of an illustrious old New England family that had contributed some of the most eminent figures in professional life. Handicapped by certain physical deficiencies and an unwillingness to mingle with his fellows, he had a rather dull record of achievement either at study or at play when he squeezed through the entrance examinations at Harvard with six "conditions."[5] After

[3] As a young graduate student at Harvard, Channing had assisted in gathering the data for the first volume of Adams' work.

[4] For this information, as well as for other personal sidelights on Channing's career, I am indebted to Miss Eva G. Moore, formerly his private secretary and research assistant.

[5] Samuel E. Morison, "Edward Channing, a Memoir," *Proceedings of the Massachusetts Historical Society* (Boston, 1932), LXIV, 252, 257.

a rather difficult four years he received his first degree in 1878 from the institution which trained the sons of New England's intellectually élite.[6] Although at first inclined toward the profession of law, he was drawn into the guild of history largely through the influence of Henry Adams, under whom he studied and from whom he acquired much of his later technique both in teaching and research.[7] At the age of twenty-four he completed his work for the doctorate at Harvard. After traveling for a year in Europe and devoting two years in Cambridge to writing articles and book reviews, he finally settled down as an instructor in history at Harvard, where he was destined to labor the rest of his life.

He was obviously a product of attitudes and tendencies which were induced by his surroundings. His entire life, except for brief trips, was spent in the New England environment, from which he seldom strayed. Within the confines of Harvard he resurrected and reconstructed the past, largely immune to counteracting influences from other climes. That such a background should have left an imprint upon the product of his labors was inevitable. Just as his minute description of Elizabethan warships, in which not a demicannon, culverin, or murtherer escaped notice,[8] reflected a typical New Englander's love of the sea, so did certain causal explanations, points of emphasis, and interpretations indicate viewpoints and prejudices traceable to the Atlantic coastline.

Intellectually honest, and naturally disposed to defy tradition and precedent, Channing never intentionally revealed a provincial outlook. He confessed, in the introduction to the first volume of his great work, that "the time and place of one's birth and breeding affect the judgment."[9] Consequently, to avoid the charge of parochialism, he made a special effort to

[6] See the *Report of the Secretary of the Class of 1878*, *Harvard College* (Cambridge, 1892), p. 37.

[7] Letter from Miss Eva G. Moore.

[8] Channing, *History of the United States* (6 vols.; New York, 1905–25), I, 135–37.

[9] *Ibid.*, p. vii.

give "other sections of the country and other points of view than the orthodox New England ones, their proper place." The middle and southern colonies received their full share of recognition in the colonial period, and his last volume was acclaimed by the South and West "as the work of a Yankee come to judgment."[10] Nevertheless, the seclusion of Harvard, where he buried himself in his task, scarcely digressing long enough to attend the meetings of the American Historical Association, and avoiding public lectures and exchange professorships,[11] prevented the infiltration of outside ideas and other influences which might have given a greater breadth of view and detachment to his work.

The element of outright prejudice is most apparent where Channing had occasion to deal with the relations of the colonies to England. Sometimes the colonists who waged a "struggle for justice and then for independence" from the mother-country were portrayed as heroes.[12] The shortsightedness of the English authorities in not permitting colonial governmental institutions and industries to develop in the direction of increasing local autonomy was implied.[13] The Restoration was deemed significant because it marked the beginning of political and social retrogression in England, in contrast with the progressive outlook across the Atlantic, where customs and institutions were reshaped to meet the needs of growing communities in a new

[10] Morison, pp. 278, 283. Critics disagree widely as to what extent Channing kept his writings free from bias. Referring to the relation of England to her colonies, W. L. Grant thinks that "he holds the scales fair, doing justice to Great Britain without falling into the exaggerated imperialism of some recent American authors." Another reviewer is certain that he showed a decided dislike for Charles II and his courtiers, a strong Massachusetts prejudice against the Council for Foreign Plantations, and, in general, an unjustifiable disregard of the English viewpoint in dealing with the outlying parts of the empire. F. H. Hodder concedes that Vol. III at least eliminated "the partisan rancor, the personal prejudice, and the vainglorious boasting of the old books"; while J. S. Bassett and H. E. Egerton agree that Vol. IV, dealing with the Federalist period, is largely devoid of sectional or national bias. D. R. Fox takes a similar view of Vol. V. See the *English Historical Review*, XXIV, 146, and XXXIII, 139; *American Historical Review*, XIV, 364; XXIII, 190; and XXVII, 591; and the *Yale Review*, N.S., III, 407–9, for these reviews.

[11] Morison, pp. 281–82.

[12] Channing, *Hist. of the U.S.*, II, 597.   [13] *Ibid.*, p. 598.

land.[14] The Dominion of New England and the last of the Stuart kings came in for a round of abuse. William of Orange fared no better in a chapter which attacked his colonial policy, emphasized the shortcomings and inefficiency of the Board of Trade, and described the ineptitude of royal governors, for whom Channing exhibited a pronounced dislike.[15]

Although extremely loath, as a rule, to express personal opinions, the author assumed as a general thesis that the Revolution was caused by the avarice of shortsighted Englishmen, ranging downward from the king to his pettiest officeholder overseas.[16] The disadvantages of the mercantile system were stressed, with little reference made to its counterbalancing benefits to the colonies.[17] One finds much about extorting money from America by "Parliamentary fiat." In the discussion of the Grenville policy there is no indication that the writer appreciated better than did most colonists in 1765 the problem of imperial organization confronting the British ministry. The Townshend Acts, according to Channing, were designed chiefly to provide new jobs to satisfy the cupidity of English office-seekers.[18] The concluding sentence of the second volume correctly summarizes his viewpoint of the entire independence movement: "The colonists were patient and long-suffering; only prolonged misgovernment on the part of the rulers of Britain compelled them to declare themselves independent of that empire from which they had sprung."[19]

Despite such criticisms of the English government for colonial mismanagement, Channing at times, however, displayed a decided Anglo-Saxon-mindedness. In the conflict between the English and their Spanish and French rivals in America, the desirability and inevitability of English supremacy were frequently expressed. A "higher power" had reserved the region between Port Royal and St. Augustine for the more patient "Englishman and his kinsfolk from Northern Europe," whose mission it was to "plant a nation in the New World."[20] The claims of Spain to

[14] Ibid., p. 3.
[15] Ibid., chaps. vi and viii.
[16] Ibid., Vol. III, chaps. i–vi.
[17] Ibid., pp. 32, 34; see also II, 8–13, 251–61.
[18] Ibid., III, 81–91.
[19] Ibid., II, 599.   [20] Ibid., I, 110.

the Americas by virtue of various papal decrees were considered "preposterous."[21] A chapter entitled "The Gallic Peril" insisted that former historians erred in assuming that no real danger from French, Indians, and Roman Catholics existed on the eve of the French and Indian wars.[22] Channing deemed it fortunate that the strength of France on both sides of the Atlantic was "distinctly on the wane" as she faced England in the great test for supremacy.[23] While the migration of various "foreigners" and their settlement within the colonies in the eighteenth century received consideration, the influence of non-English racial strains in molding the economic, social, religious, and political life of the backcountry was largely neglected.[24]

Nevertheless, bias of the obvious, positive type is only occasionally conspicuous in the Channing history. It appears more frequently in a subtle form, as a result of omissions, rather than by forthright statements. The critical reader soon surmises that the author lived on the Atlantic seaboard. "Commercialism, the desire for advantage and profit in trade and industry, was at the bottom of the struggle between England and America. . . . . The governing classes of the old country wished to exploit the American colonists for their own use and behoof,"[25] he explained, oblivious to any divergence of sentiment between the eastern seaboard and the backcountry and unaware that a West existed as an important influence on the Revolution. The information to sustain this thesis was derived largely from the pronouncements of prominent eastern leaders, such as Otis and Dickinson, or from pamphlets, tracts, orders in council and statutes of Parliament and the colonial assemblies. In his view, the independence movement reached no farther back than the fall line and involved primarily the articulate element along the coast.

This oversight suggests more than an excessive simplification of the causes of the Revolution. Channing was disposed at all times to underrate, or entirely disregard, sectionalism as a force

[21] *Ibid.*, p. 117.   [23] *Ibid.*, p. 585.

[22] *Ibid.*, II, 131.   [24] *Ibid.*, Vol. II, chap. xiv.

[25] *Ibid.*, III, 1; see Egerton's criticism in the *Eng. Hist. Rev.*, XXVIII, 170-71.

in American history. Apparently, he did not realize that the outstanding events and problems of the "Critical Period" were connected with the formation of political factions, financial difficulties, economic and social insurrections, and the establishment of the Constitution—that all of these had a sectional aspect based upon the opposing demands of rival interests within and between the states under the Articles of Confederation.[26] Even later in history, where he was forced at least to admit the existence of a West, his treatment of it was superficial. An entire chapter on the "Westward March" consists of nothing more than an account of western migration, with valuable space extravagantly spent in order to trace the successive moves of individual families from one part of the country to another.[27] The author appreciated that the West was a geographical area infiltrated with the discontented from the East and Europe, but he ignored it as a positive force in the molding of those ideals and institutions which have contributed to the growth of American civilization. The frontier thesis of his Harvard colleague, Frederick Jackson Turner, was buried in three brief footnote references and a bibliographical comment.[28]

Because Channing disregarded western influences, certain parts of his history present an incomplete and distorted picture. The quit-rent controversies, Shays's Rebellion, and the Whiskey Insurrection are all handled in a superficial manner and with little appreciation of their significance in influencing the general trend of events.[29] Struggles between classes and sections held little interest for Channing. Sometimes the scope of his history is neither broader than New England nor deeper than the dominant class of which the author was a member. Even in the decades preceding the Civil War, when sectionalism furnished the dominant

[26] See Channing, *Hist. of the U.S.*, Vol. III, chaps. xv and xvi, and a review in the *Nation*, XCV, 483.

[27] Channing, *Hist. of the U.S.*, V, 37 ff.

[28] *Ibid.*, III, 32 n., 303 n.; V, 3 n., 67.

[29] *Ibid.*, III, 483–85, 532; IV, 139–40; see the opinion of C. H. Van Tyne in the *Amer. Hist. Rev.*, XVIII, 604.

note, he persistently refused to admit that it was basic to an understanding of the march of events.

The logical result of his disregard of sectionalism was his tendency in his earlier volumes to neglect the operation of social, economic, religious, and intellectual forces, while unduly stressing political and constitutional developments. So pronounced was this defect that one learned reviewer felt obliged to mention Channing's "astonishing blindness to social forces."[30] Channing apparently recognized the validity of this criticism and, in a short essay on historical writing, conceded the necessity of observing "the inter-action of economic forces."[31] Subsequent volumes of his great work often reflected the effort to prevent political and military events from monopolizing the stage. An increasingly larger proportion of non-political matter appeared, reaching a climax with the fifth volume, which embraced no less than ten chapters of such material and discussed most of the important activities of human endeavor, including literature, art, and historiography. In Volume VI, however, on the years from 1850 to 1865, he largely reverted to his first fancy.

The resolve of the author to conform in his fifth volume to a relatively recent trend in American historiography was commendable. And yet, there was still evident a "blindness to social forces," principally because the new material was not sufficiently well correlated with the dynamic elements of the general theme. The "inter-action of economic forces" was lacking. Whole chapters, sandwiched in here and there, represented a digression from the main narrative and failed to clarify the underlying forces at work. Religious conditions and changes in colonial America were discussed without any reference to those attitudes, grievances, beliefs, and theories which had a definite bearing upon sectionalism and the independence movement.[32] A

[30] Van Tyne, *loc. cit.*

[31] Quoted by Morison, pp. 280–81, from Channing's essay entitled, "The Present State of Historical Writing in America," in *Proceedings of the American Antiquarian Society*, N.S., XX (1909–10), 427–34.

[32] Channing, *Hist. of the U.S.*, Vol. II, chap. xv.

chapter dealing with "Economic Adjustments" bridged the gap between "Independence and Peace" and "The States and the Confederation," without so much as hinting that economic problems were in any way related to the movement for a constitutional convention.[33] Such ineffective handling of nonpolitical material caused the disconcerting feeling, as another able critic remarked, "of reading two books in one."[34]

This lack of correlation is partially attributable to a commendable effort to be as objective as possible. When the historian essays an analysis of social forces as they affect human behavior in its larger aspects, he confronts certain imponderables from which the subjective element cannot be entirely excluded. No doubt conscious of the pitfall which lay ahead on such a course, Channing, for the most part, rejected tendencies, theories, abstractions, and large generalizations. He presented the facts, and others might run the hazard of interpreting them. He failed to realize that every historian abandons objectivity as soon as he selects facts for presentation.

This intense devotion to objectivity was likely abetted by an attitude of defiant independence, which led Channing to glory in upsetting tradition at every opportunity. He so delighted in shocking his classes at Harvard by demolishing ingrained prejudices that the college comic paper frequently portrayed him as a rampant crusader with hatchet poised to smash another popular fetish.[35] The ancient and revered New England tradition of Plymouth Rock became the special object of his investigations, and subsequently suffered loss of prestige in the face of new his-

[33] *Ibid.*, Vol. III, chap. xiii; Bassett, *Amer. Hist. Rev.*, XXIII, 192.

[34] D. S. Muzzey, *Political Science Quarterly*, XXXVII, 310–11. Channing appears to have been ever on the alert to avoid the pitfall of unjustifiably according some political development to social and economic forces. The increased railroad-building of the fifties which linked the Northwest to the Northeast, was too obvious to escape his notice, and yet he questioned whether it materially changed the outlook of the Northwest. There is not in his pages the slightest hint that it may have had anything to do with the outcome of the Civil War. See Channing, *Hist. of the U.S.*, VI, 382–83.

[35] Morison, p. 269; A. Lawrence Lowell, *Edward Channing* (commemorative tribute published by the American Academy of Arts and Letters, New York, 1932), p. 75.

torical evidence. It was this trait of character which fostered his admiration for Henry Adams back in his undergraduate days and which shocked Henry Cabot Lodge, whose dogmatism and reverence for ancestors Channing never learned to appreciate. In breaking through the crust of tradition and exposing unsavory reminders of hypocrisy and intrigue, he refused to spare even the honored of his own distinguished family merely because of their affiliation with a commendable reform movement.[36]

In spite of Channing's effort to take "nations, congresses, and generals" as he found them,[37] he did have some viewpoints; and he was not altogether immune to theories and abstractions. The one hypothesis to which he clung throughout the entire sweep of his history assumed the inexorable march of events toward national unity. The preface of his great work frankly affirmed his faith in progress, which led him "to see in the annals of the past the story of living forces, always struggling onward and upward toward that which is better and higher in human conception." He observed, furthermore, that "the most important single fact in our development has been the victory of the forces of union over those of particularism."[38]

Occasionally, as the author proceeded with the narrative, he paused to reaffirm his belief in this "greatest fact of American history."[39] Whether fact or fiction, it reflected the intensely nationalistic spirit which pervaded American life at the turn of the century. And the continuous support Channing accorded the thesis, through the devices of selection, emphasis, and interpretation, certified the formula to be more than a passing whim.

Apparently, this favorite assumption of Channing led him, at times, to simplify the narrative by neglecting vital factors which would have detracted from his general theme. It was easy to consider the framing of the Constitution as merely an additional advance toward national unity, unmindful of the economic and social forces which precipitated a sectional struggle over its ratification. "We, the people" as the author of the Constitution,

[36] Morison, pp. 260, 279.
[37] *Eng. Hist. Rev.* XXVIII, 171.
[38] Channing, *Hist. of the U.S.*, I, v–vi.
[39] *Ibid.*, p. 511.

in contrast with the sovereign states which fathered the "Articles," was emphasized at the expense of historical accuracy concerning the origin of the preamble's opening phrase. The authority and supremacy of the United States Supreme Court in reviewing legislation were unquestioned. The failure duly to recognize the clash of interests in the period of intense sectionalism preceding the Civil War may have resulted from his reluctance to confess that the steady upward march toward national unity had been interrupted.[40]

The Channing thesis concerning the causes of the American Revolution has already received mention. Again, he wrote in his preface: "I have considered the colonies as parts of the English empire, as having sprung from that political fabric, and as having simply pursued a course of institutional evolution unlike that of the branch of the English race which remained behind in the old homeland across the Atlantic."[41] He saw the third George as "no mere tyrant, no misguided monarch, but an instrument of a benign providence bringing, through pain and misery, benefit to the human race."[42] In a later period he summarized the secession episode with the observation: "The motives and reasons that led the men and women of the South into secession are as inscrutable now as they were in 1860 and 1861."[43] And yet, in the preceding chapters and on twelve subsequent pages, he expounded at length a number of very definite motives and reasons for the action.

On at least one occasion, Channing was content frankly to state his thesis, leave it suspended in midair, and hastily return to safer ground. Upon the rejection of Professor Turner's view of sectionalism and the West as "mainsprings of our national development," he substituted "the mobility of men and of things" as the most significant cause of national progress.[44] Content with a brief explanation, the generalization was pushed no farther, and it was associated with virtually no subsequent developments.

---

[40] *Ibid.*, Vol. VI, chaps. i–vii.   [43] *Ibid.*, VI, 256.

[41] *Ibid.*, I, v.   [44] *Ibid.*, V, 3.

[42] *Ibid.*, III, 30–31.

Channing conceived of history as denoting, in its larger sense, more than "merely the annals of the past," and announced his intention of tracing the growth of the nation "as one continuous development from the political, military, institutional, industrial, and social points of view."[45] But realization of that aim was frequently thwarted by assembling a ponderous conglomeration of facts, poorly organized and integrated, and contributing to no particular theme. Consequently, the reader wanders through the forest in dire peril of becoming lost among the trees. He searches in vain for some thread running through the discussion by which he may steer his way through the labyrinth of detail. The evolution of ideas and tendencies is conspicuously absent. There is no main current; and, as one critic expresses it, the narrative lacks purpose and depth and does not move "forward to any culmination."[46] The author failed adequately to synthesize his materials and arrange the picture.[47] One wonders if he did not, as Professor Frank H. Hodder averred, sometimes simply pour "new wine into old bottles," without making any real contribution to an understanding of the mainsprings of American life.[48]

In the matter of proportion and emphasis, Channing threw precedents to the winds. No doubt he preferred to deal more exhaustively with certain subjects which his predecessors had neglected. Perhaps his course was only another manifestation of his independence. Perhaps he was an unconscious victim of the dangers against which he warned others when he wrote: "The historical writer must be a master of perspective . . . . he is likely to come upon new material relating to some one part of his studies that no one else has ever seen. . . . . The temptation is great to apportion his space according to the importance of his materials, not according to the importance of the events or the men."[49]

[45] *Ibid.*, I, v.

[46] *Amer. Hist. Rev.*, XIV, 365.

[47] See Fox, *Amer. Hist. Rev.*, XXVII, 590.

[48] *Yale Rev.*, N.S., III, 409.

[49] Channing, "Present State of Historical Writing in America," *Proc. Amer. Antiq. Soc.*, N.S. XX (1909–10), 431.

At any rate, some of his contractions and expansions are "a bit breath-taking."[50] Only the allure of the interesting and the bizarre could have led him to allot five pages to locating the national capital,[51] three to lotteries,[52] and eight to office-seeking during the Jeffersonian regime.[53] An extensive discussion of drinking habits and the treatment of disease in 1789 enlivens the narrative but fails to contribute appreciably to an understanding of the period.[54] One doubts the importance of knowing that President Jackson smoked his tobacco instead of chewing it, according to the usual custom;[55] and the fact that "Mrs. Polly Goodwin visited Mr. Bolles's and bought tea, coffee, chocolate, and sugar, all of which were charged on one bill," lacks even the element of interest.[56] General Scott hardly deserves ten times more consideration than John Marshall; nor does Eric Janson merit more attention than President Tyler.[57] Seven pages on the "Monitor" and "Merrimac," including elaborate details of their construction and trivial incidents of the battle, in comparison with seventeen lines on one of the bloodiest and most critical engagements of the Civil War, again reflect the author's love of the sea.[58]

While Channing was shedding new and more abundant light upon some of the neglected phases of American history, and occasionally indulging his special interests in a less meritorious fashion, some important episodes, personalities, and incidents were obviously slighted. Subjects such as foreign alliances, armed neutrality, and political conditions in England during the Revolutionary epoch were passed over lightly.[59] The sectional

[50] J. Viles, *Mississippi Valley Historical Review*, XII, 414.

[51] Channing, *Hist. of the U.S.*, IV, 74–79.

[52] *Ibid.*, pp. 24–27.   [54] *Ibid.*, pp. 16–24.

[53] *Ibid.*, pp. 250–59.   [55] *Ibid.*, V, 388.

[56] *Ibid.*, III, 403; Muzzey, *Polit. Sci. Quart.*, XXXVII, 311; H. R. Spencer, *ibid.*, XXI, 346.

[57] See Fox, *Amer. Hist. Rev.*, XXVII, 591.

[58] Channing, *Hist. of the U.S.*, VI, 473–74, 496–503; Muzzey, *Polit. Sci. Quart.*, XL, 622.

[59] See S. F. Bemis, "Professor Channing and the West," *Washington Historical Quarterly*, XIV, 39.

struggle in Congress on the eve of the Compromise of 1850 was completely disregarded. Admittedly, the problem of judicious balance, while attempting a new and comprehensive presentation, is baffling; and the author probably did not adjust his emphasis with any particular motive in mind. Nevertheless, omission of essential events tends to distort the picture and renders the work too compact at some points for the general reader.[60]

Perhaps the greatest weakness of Channing is his faulty organization of material and technique of presentation. From the outset, his failure adequately to correlate the social, economic, and political phases of the narrative rendered a logical arrangement difficult. The problem was the more serious because he usually declined to trace long-range developments and trends, thereby precluding general themes around which he might have woven the various threads of the story.

At times Channing did not adhere to any systematic order, either topical or chronological. A discussion of religious freedom, antislavery agitation, and other social manifestations in the Confederation period follows the framing of the Constitution by two chapters.[61] Such noncontiguous chapters in Volume V as ''The Plantation System and Abolitionism'' and ''South Carolina and Nullification'' contain essentially similar subject matter with variations in detail and emphasis. Sundry phases of the Jackson administrations are spread over two chapters in widely separated portions of the book. ''The Mormons'' serves twice as a headline more than two hundred pages apart.[62]

Unfortunately, the author apparently gave even less attention to the problem of synthesis in his later volumes than in his earlier work. In Volume VI paragraphs often appear to serve no more useful purpose than as a convenient means of breaking the monot-

[60] Van Tyne, *Amer. Hist. Rev.*, XVIII, 604; Hodder, *Yale Rev.*, N.S., III, 407–8. Not all of Channing's critics have been impressed with the lack of proportion. Egerton is warm in his praise of the balance maintained, while Bassett thinks ''he has used his space with a great deal of care.'' See Bassett, *Amer. Hist. Rev.*, XXIII, 190; Egerton, *Eng. Hist. Rev.*, XXVIII, 170.

[61] Channing, *Hist. of the U.S.*, Vol. III, chap. xviii.

[62] *Ibid.*, V, 237, 493; Muzzey, *Polit. Sci. Quart.*, XXXVII, 310–11.

ony of a solidly printed page. Totally different and unrelated topics are thrown together with careless abandon. In some instances a single idea is pursued almost to the end of a paragraph, only to be unceremoniously discarded in favor of an unrelated concluding sentence.[63]

The discussion of the "Election of 1864" illustrates the chaos which frequently prevails within a chapter. Beginning with a brief statement about the military situation in 1864, the author digresses to consider agricultural and industrial enterprise in the North; then reverts to a contrast between the war methods of 1861 and 1918; then to the Homestead Bill of 1862. After the reader is enlightened upon immigration in 1863 and western expansion, he is carried ahead to the political situation in 1864; and thence to the end of the chapter he is obliged to oscillate between 1862 and 1864, as Vallandigham and the Copperhead movement, southern propaganda, and, finally, the Niagara episode pass in review. Whatever may be the main theme of the chapter, it can hardly be the "Election of 1864." Chronology and scenes shift with a frequency which bewilders the general reader and proves somewhat disconcerting even to an advanced student who is less in need of mature guidance.[64]

Channing was probably not aware of any deficiency in this free and easy method of presentation. As a teacher he always manifested a decided contempt for the "finished lecturer" and recoiled from the prospect of spoon-feeding his students with history "in predigested form."[65] He cast his notes aside while lecturing, on the assumption that unnecessary and burdensome details would thereby elude his memory and leave a residue of important information. In presenting class reports, his students were encouraged to emulate this procedure.

Similar notions carried over into his writing and obviously affected the orderliness of his presentation. Unfortunately, while writing and re-writing one of his earliest books in longhand, he developed writer's cramp, which forced him to dictate the mate-

[63] See, e.g., Channing, *Hist. of the U.S.*, VI, 616.

[64] *Ibid.*, chap. xix.   [65] Morison, p. 270.

rial for the remainder of his works, perhaps to the disadvantage of his style.[66] His private secretary states that, when Channing was ready to write, he threw aside his notes and, with his mind saturated with the subject, walked about the study for two or three hours at a stretch, dictating the narrative "directly to the typewriter." This procedure was followed by many rereadings and re-writings of the manuscript. Citations were then inserted, all facts and quotations verified, and the narrative read aloud "to get the swing and rhythm of the words and sentences."[67]

This method of composition might readily be criticized as wasteful and inefficient; and yet it was the Channing way, and, in his hands, probably contributed to the merits of his writings. His disdain for notes may have adversely affected the organization of his material; but it enabled him, as he believed, to use a freer and more expressive flow of words while dictating. His style merits neither high praise nor sharp criticism. It is not breezy and journalistic, for Channing had "no knack of vivid narrative or description";[68] and he declined to popularize history by dressing it up in attractive literary form.[69] Occasionally, his vocabulary seems limited and his expressions slightly crude. To have the figure of Sebastian Cabot loom "larger and more large" does not suggest the polish of a literary genius. Nevertheless, simple and unadorned as the narrative may be, the meaning is always clear.

A cursory examination suggests that the sources upon which Channing based his narrative were fully adequate, both in number and variety. Footnote references appear in profusion. Bibliographical comments cover a wide range of material, including official records, contemporary periodical literature, and statistical tables. Manuscript collections and foreign archives were occasionally ransacked for new and authentic information with which to wreck traditional viewpoints.

Nevertheless, Channing neglected one of the most valuable

[66] *Ibid.*, p. 274.

[67] Letter from Miss Eva G. Moore.

[68] Morison, p. 280.   [69] Lowell, pp. 80–81.

sources at the command of historians—the newspaper.[70] He relied comparatively little upon manuscript material; but monographs and doctoral dissertations received much consideration,
and many graduate students were "embalmed in his footnotes."
An analysis of the footnote references on 100 pages of Volume V
reveals a total of 224 citations, of which more than 30 are to
monographs, approximately 70 embrace other secondary works,
only 4 refer to unprinted materials, and the remainder cite original printed sources.[71] His unusual reliance upon monographs,
coupled with a tendency to use the sources "by way of cor-
roboration and illustration" instead of appealing directly to
them,[72] has led some critics to aver that his work is largely
based upon a foundation laid by other scholars. One eminent reviewer comments, in a vein not wholly devoid of sarcasm, that,
if one would know what doctors of philosophy think of the
Civil War era, he should consult the Harvard pedagogue's last
volume.[73]

In the selection of sources Channing did not always take care
to use the most unprejudiced and reliable for the particular subject under investigation. He was prone to unearth materials of a
curious type and to attach importance to them because they had
hitherto been unexplored. Occasionally the narrative suffered
from this deficiency in evaluation as it proceeded upon a line
marked out by a rather miscellaneous collection of data assembled
without much discrimination. In consequence the Lincoln-Douglas campaign of 1858 received inadequate treatment.[74] The neglect of the newspapers largely explains the failure to recognize
and analyze the successive changes in northern public opinion on

[70] Professor Morison ascribes this neglect to the fact that J. B. McMaster had depended
greatly upon newspapers in his voluminous work, which did not rank very high in Channing's estimation (Morison, pp. 279–80).

[71] Channing, *Hist. of the U.S.*, V, 351–451. As to sources, see the reviews of Van Tyne,
Amer. Hist. Rev., XVIII, 603; Muzzey, *Polit. Sci. Quart.*, XL, 621; Fox, *Amer. Hist. Rev.*,
XXVII, 591–92, and XXXI, 152.

[72] Spencer, *Polit. Sci. Quart.*, XXI, 348.

[73] Charles A. Beard, *New Republic*, XLIV, 310 ff.

[74] Channing, *Hist of the U.S.*, VI, 229–30.

the secession issue between the election of 1860 and the fall of Fort Sumter.[75] Surely no one could have given serious attention to the sources and concluded that "it seems reasonably clear that at no time in the year 1864 was the re-election of Abraham Lincoln within the realm of doubt."[76]

After the most critically minded have had their innings dissecting and analyzing the Channing history with the avowed purpose of unveiling all of its deficiencies, there still remains a bountiful measure of praise to be awarded to the one American historian of the twentieth century who had the courage to attempt a task so colossal. If other historians managed to escape some of the snares into which Channing stumbled, it was in large part because they limited their endeavors and trod upon safer ground. The increasing complexity and variety of sources and the modern trend toward the co-operative efforts of specialists suggest that American historiography has reached a stage which precludes another individual effort of such dimensions.

However, the significance of the work of Channing lies in much more than a mere display of courage. His six volumes will always represent certain qualities of coherence and uniformity of judgment, which, as a recent critic explains, constitute the chief claim of works by a single writer to superiority over co-operative histories.[77] Channing contributed the fruits of an immense amount of research. His tireless effort marshaled an imposing array of new facts and assembled them into a pattern which has greatly enlarged our understanding of the growth of the American nation. His judicious use of the sources for purposes of illustration and his abundant bibliographical comments provide assurances of his scientific method and give an authoritative air to his production. While not always objective, he never consciously veered far from his goal; and few historians ever came nearer reaching it.

While Channing belongs primarily to the old school of narra-

---

[75] *Ibid.*, pp. 289–96.   [76] *Ibid.*, p. 605.

[77] Theodore C. Smith, "The Writing of American History in America, from 1884 to 1934," *Amer. Hist. Rev.*, XL, 444.

tive historians, in a sense he marks a transition to the new "scientific" group which followed in their wake. He was disposed to moralize and mete out praise and blame with an air of impartiality, much as Henry Adams and other of his contemporaries had done. And yet, he became more sparing of such personal judgments as his work advanced, and strove with considerable success to produce a scientific masterpiece of objectivity. Again, like the historians of the old school, he was inclined at the beginning of his task to treat history largely as "past politics"; but gradually he made concessions to the new fashion by including more nonpolitical matter in his narrative. In this particular respect he advanced very little beyond the old orthodoxy because he neglected to fuse the new material with the old in such a way as to display the influence of social and economic forces upon the unfolding of political events.

Of a certainty, Channing did not reach ahead to that newest phenomenon in American historiography which frankly rejects true objectivity as neither existent nor desirable and strives for a "grand philosophy," around which historians, with the scientific method serving rather than dictating, may weave the facts of history into a pattern designed to hasten civilization forward to some desired end. Avowedly, Channing wove much of his narrative around the theme of steady progress toward national unity, but his hypothesis was the product of scientific investigation and was neither the effusion of a "grand philosophy" nor "an act of faith."[78]

[78] The quotations are taken from Beard, "Written History as an Act of Faith," *Amer. Hist. Rev.*, XXXIX, 227, 229. Several paragraphs in this essay on Channing follow rather closely the author's "Edward Channing," *Miss. Valley Hist. Rev.*, XVIII, No. 1 (June, 1931), 53–59, and are used here with permission.

XVI

GEORGE LOUIS BEER

ARTHUR P. SCOTT

University of Chicago

*

EORGE LOUIS BEER was born July 26, 1872, on Staten
Island, New York, the second son of Julius and Sophia
(Walter) Beer.[1] Julius Beer was a member of a German-
Jewish family and had come as a young man from Hamburg to
engage (successfully) in the tobacco business.

It is briefly recorded that George Louis was educated in New
York schools, where it is safe to presume that his textbook of
American history informed him in substance that "England
treated the settlers as an inferior class of people. Her intention
was to make and keep the colonies dependent. The laws were
framed to favor the English manufacturer and merchant at the
expense of the colonist. The Navigation Acts compelled the
American farmer to send his products across the ocean to England
and to buy his goods in British markets." He was also given to
understand that the direct cause of the Revolutionary struggle
"was an attempt to tax the colonies in order to defray the ex-
penses of the recent war. As the colonists were not represented
in Parliament, they resisted this measure, declaring that TAXA-
TION WITHOUT REPRESENTATION IS TYRANNY."[2]

At Columbia University, where George Beer received his A.B.

---

[1] The biographical material in this essay is drawn largely from the memorial volume,
*George Louis Beer: A Tribute to His Life and Work in the Making of History and the Moulding of
Public Opinion* (New York, 1924). Hereafter cited as *George Louis Beer*.

[2] Albert S. Barnes & Co., *A Brief History of the United States* (New York, 1885).

degree in 1892 and his M.A. in 1893, he was introduced to a more critical view of politics, economics, and history by Professors Burgess, Seligman, and Osgood. It was the latter, then but recently embarked on his pioneer reinterpretations of American colonial history, who suggested to Beer the topic of his Master's thesis, *The Commercial Policy of England toward the American Colonies.*[3] This work of one hundred and fifty pages was the first complete study of this highly important subject. It is an unusually mature and competent piece of scholarship for a student not yet twenty-one years of age, one of the very rare Masters' theses of any lasting general value. Its definitiveness was naturally limited by the fact that it had to be based on printed sources, but its scope and its suggestiveness have given it value to all later students of the colonial period.

It is not surprising that an alert student at Columbia should have adopted the ideal of objectivity which the American universities had taken over, largely from the German seminars. "For the historian," declares Beer, "the only true method is to critically examine and to impartially describe the facts, to place them in logical order, and then, if he deems it necessary, to draw the inevitable conclusion. Induction, not deduction, is the historical method."[4] A little later in his introduction he announces another guiding principle: "In view of the prevalent philosophy of evolution, we should before condemning the policy of any age look not at its absolute, but at its relative, efficiency. No institution can be condemned from the historical standpoint, if it is really in advance of that which preceded."[5]

Beer was convinced that the spirit of impartial study of all the facts had "rarely been characteristic of American historians, when treating of the relations of England and her colonies. They start with the idea that England consciously pursued an egotistic and tyrannical policy. By making the facts conform to this preconception, they have produced books that are notably unjust to

[3] "Columbia College Studies in History, Economics and Public Law," Vol. III, Part II (New York, 1893).

[4] *Ibid.*, p. 7.   [5] *Ibid.*, p. 8.

England."[6] By proceeding to present the English point of view, Beer not only filled an important gap in the historical picture but supplied a wholesome corrective to the traditional ultrapatriotic American views. More specifically he presented the constructive side of mercantilism, and he showed in detail its significance in British colonial policy.

Beer found the essentials of mercantilism foreshadowed in the methods used by the early Stuarts to regulate the tobacco trade; but in spite of his belief in evolution, he underemphasized the importance of the changes in mercantilistic theory and practice in the course of succeeding generations.[7]

Beer was not entirely consistent in following his own principle of relativity; for, while he described mercantilism objectively enough, and explained it in terms of its seventeenth- and eighteenth-century background, he showed the free trade and laissez faire orthodoxy of nineteenth-century economics in his verdict that mercantilism "was a policy of unconscious ignorance, not of conscious malice. History teaches that ignorance disguised in the garments of truth has, quite as often as malice, caused the adoption of erroneous policies."[8]

One of the most unexpected of Beer's conclusions was that the economic aspects of Britain's colonial policy had little or nothing to do with bringing on the American Revolution:

Up to 1763 England acted consistently on a false, but historically justifiable, economic principle. She had developed a rounded colonial system, based on economic principles, and but slightly influenced by political considerations. . . . . After 1763 the economic interest largely disappears, and the *raison d'être* of the acts passed after this date, appears only when studied in close relation with political events. Economic motives are subordinated to political principles.[9]

This preliminary study of Britain's "old" colonial empire fixed the particular scholarly field to which Beer later returned. For

[6] *Ibid.*, p. 7.   [7] *George Louis Beer*, pp. 34–39.

[8] Such passages give color to the friendly and quite incidental criticism of C. M. Andrews that Beer's thesis is "academic and a little oracular" (*George Louis Beer*, p. 15).

[9] *Commercial Policy of England toward the American Colonies*, p. 144.

the next ten years, however, his interests were divided. He engaged actively in the tobacco-importing business, but he found some time to lecture on history at Columbia (1897). Meanwhile, in 1896, he married Edith C. Hellman, a niece of Professor E. R. A. Seligman.

Beer was distinctly successful as a business man and not particularly outstanding as a teacher, but his real interest lay in scholarship. In 1902 appeared a study of "Cromwell's Policy in Its Economic Aspects."[10] This is an interesting survey of the diplomacy of the Commonwealth as it was related to commercial and colonial rivalry with the Dutch and Spanish. Beer was convinced that Cromwell played a very important part in developing the British empire, but the evidence which he advanced to show that his "plans were in advance of his times and were prophetic of future developments" is not entirely convincing.

In 1903 Beer found himself financially able to retire from active business and strongly inclined to carry on the scholarly work which so deeply interested him. Accordingly, he went to London and for over a year buried himself in the Public Record Office, studying all sorts of documents connected with the old British empire which had "been virtually undisturbed since they were filed away a century and a half ago in the course of departmental routine."[11]

His plan was the ambitious and comprehensive one of describing the origin and development of the British colonial empire from the days of the Tudors to the eve of the American Revolution. As he saw the movement, it was fundamentally an economic one; but he recognized the impossibility of treating economic developments without reference to political, administrative, social, and psychological factors.[12] He always took into

---

[10] *Political Science Quarterly*, Vol. XVI, No. 4 (1901), and Vol. XVII, No. 1 (1902).

[11] Beer, *British Colonial Policy, 1754-1765* (New York, 1907), p. vi.

[12] "History . . . . is to a great extent based on social psychology, and in studying the dynamic effects of any policy on the relations of two social groups, it is frequently far more important to know what people at the time thought were the results, rather than what these actually were" (*ibid.*, p. 201).

consideration that men had significant noneconomic wants and that "as civilization advances, economic forces work in the main silently in the background, while man's interpretation of his wants, both economic and other, accelerate and retard that work and sometimes even deform it."[13]

While holding steadily to the point of view of English officials and men of business, he was prepared to consider also related economic developments in the colonies and the fashion in which plans devised in England were perforce modified in operation by local conditions.

On his return to New York, Beer found himself best prepared to discuss the later years of his period; and in 1907 he published his *British Colonial Policy, 1754–1765.* This admirably documented volume attracted wide attention for the new material which it presented and the conclusions which it reached. Never before had the administrative shortcomings of the old imperial system been so clearly and convincingly shown, or the inevitability of some such reform measures as those which the British authorities attempted after the experiences of the Seven Years' War been made so patent. Four conclusions, all of them seriously modifying generally accepted views, stand out: (1) that before 1763, the colonies in general acquiesced in the laws of trade, while criticizing some of their specific provisions;[14] (2) that "it would be difficult to estimate whether colony or metropolis was called upon to bear a greater proportion of the sacrifice demanded by the prevailing ideal of a self-sufficient commercial Empire;"[15] (3) that most of the purely commercial regulations of 1764–65 aimed at encouraging, rather than restricting, colonial industry;[16] (4) that not mercantilism but "imperial defence was the rock upon which the old Empire shattered itself."[17]

A sympathetic understanding of the British position did not

[13] *The English Speaking Peoples, Their Future Relations and Joint International Obligations* (New York, 1917), p. 204.

[14] *British Colonial Policy, 1754–1765*, p. 210.

[15] *Ibid.*, p. 201.   [16] *Ibid.*, p. 226.   [17] *Ibid.*, p. 3.

draw Beer into a condemnation of the American attitude. His philosophy of history led him to view the British-American struggle as a clash between the two underlying tendencies in modern historical evolution—nationalism and imperialism.[18]

The volume closes with an unexpected observation that significantly foreshadowed Beer's attitude in 1914. It is too early, he says, to decide whether the break-up of the old empire meant "progress or reaction, or merely a temporary regression necessary to a further step in advance. It is easily conceivable, and not at all improbable that the political evolution of the next centuries may take such a course that the American Revolution will lose the great significance that is now attached to it, and will appear merely as the temporary separation of two kindred peoples whose inherent similarity was obscured by superficial differences, resulting from dissimilar economic and social conditions."[19]

Turning to a chronological treatment of his theme, Beer next worked on *The Origins of the British Colonial System, 1578–1660*, which appeared in 1908. Four years later were published the two volumes covering *The Old Colonial System, 1660–1688*. These volumes are not easy reading, but they are invaluable to the serious student of the period. The style is clear and concise, with little ornamentation and no lighter touches. The treatment of the material tends toward the topical, and the whole rather narrowly escapes being a collection of exhaustive and heavily documented essays on various topics. Their importance, however, well merited the award to them in 1913 of the Loubat Prize for the best work in English of the preceding five years on American history, geography, or archeology.

As Beer's plan unfolded, its scale widened; and he hoped to devote four volumes to the period from 1688 to 1754, and to this end further months were spent in research in the English archives and quantities of notes were amassed. But the great work was fated never to reach completion; the war intervened, and turned all Beer's activities into new channels.

[18] *Ibid.*, p. 315.   [19] *Ibid.*, p. 316.

Despite his German affiliations, his sympathies were very decidedly with the Allies, and particularly with the British empire, and he threw himself wholeheartedly into the task of explaining to his fellow-Americans the underlying issues of the conflict as he saw them. Articles from his pen appeared in the *New York Times*, the *Forum*, the *Political Science Quarterly*, and the *New Republic*. By 1915 he was invited by the British editors of the *Round Table* to interpret to the small but influential group of its readers the changing currents of American opinion.

Whether writing for American or British readers, Beer showed the grasp of facts and principles and the prevailing fair-mindedness which characterized him as a historian. No longer, however, was he content with analysis. He was convinced that the human values in which he believed would best be safeguarded by an Allied victory, and he favored American intervention from an early date. In June of 1917 he enlarged and added to the material which had appeared in scattered periodical form, and published *The English Speaking Peoples, Their Future Relations and Joint International Obligations*. In his preface he recalled his earlier query[20] whether time might bring a reunion of the British and American peoples. He deprecated forcing the issue, but he frankly advocated "a co-operative democratic alliance" of the two English-speaking groups.

His analysis of international anarchy led to a condemnation of the ultranationalism of the existing sovereign states. The United States must bear at least a negative blame for its isolationism and its refusal to assume a share of responsibility in world-affairs. Beer understood that the essential equality of status of the dominions and the mother-country must be recognized within the British commonwealth. On the constructive side he hoped and expected that the war would result in the end of American isolation and in the closest co-operation between Great Britain and the United States in economic reconstruction. The British commonwealth he regarded as proving the possibility of some League

[20] *Supra*, p. 318.

of Nations in which "law and justice rule over a congeries of widely scattered peoples to each one of which is assured the free and full development of its own ideals."[21]

When, in the fall of 1917, Colonel House organized the group of experts to study the various questions which a peace conference would have to settle, Beer was appointed to report on colonial matters; and he accompanied the American delegation to Paris as chief of the colonial division. On various commissions for drafting settlements of a number of colonial issues Beer served conscientiously and effectively. His most important work, however, was in connection with the mandatory plan for German colonies and the areas detached from the Turkish empire. Beer's personality inspired confidence and readily won the friendly respect of his associates. Though on the basis of his published works he had at first been regarded by some of his colleagues as unduly pro-British in sympathy, it was not long before his mastery of the historical background, his breadth and fairness of vision, and his analytical power gave his opinions unusual weight.

While it is impossible to assign to him any specific proportion of the credit for originating the mandatory plan, those closely associated with him at Paris agree that his share was considerable and that it was genuinely significant. On the mandate commission set up by the Treaty of Versailles he sat as alternate to Colonel House; and when the secretariat of the League of Nations was being organized, he was asked to head its mandates division. Against all his personal inclinations he would have accepted the responsibility, but the failure of the United States to join the League of Nations changed everything.

Beer's work as a publicist and statesman in connection with the World War and the peace settlement was to prove his last; for he died within a few months of his return to New York, March 15, 1920.

The reports on colonial issues which he prepared for the Amer-

[21] *English Speaking Peoples*, p. 271.

ican delegation at Paris were edited and published in 1923, with the title *African Questions at the Paris Peace Conference, with Papers on Egypt, Mesopotamia, and the Colonial Settlement*.[22] Condensed as they are, and written for an immediate practical purpose, they are of more than passing interest; for they not only embody a philosophy of colonial responsibility ("in the settlement of the colonial questions, the primary consideration must be the welfare of the native populations,"[23]) but they are also full of temperate, practical suggestions for carrying it out under the varying conditions of the mandated areas. Beer's sense of historical realities made him prefer, for colonial problems, fairly good solutions which had a chance of being adopted rather than better ones which would not, under existing circumstances, be seriously considered.

George Louis Beer impressed his friends and associates as a person of unusual ability, high purpose, and unassuming modesty. In each field of activity in which he engaged—as business man, as interpreter and guide of public opinion, as participant in the peace negotiations—he was successful. But though he was willing to throw himself into worth-while practical activities, his primary interests were in scholarship; and it is as the historian of the old British empire that he will be longest remembered.

His great study was never completed. Even the periods which he did cover were not treated with the breadth which he himself originally planned. Occasionally the general movement threatens to be lost in details, and the interconnections are not always clear. With each rereading of any part of Beer's work, however, the regret deepens that he was not able to complete it. If, thereafter, on the basis of his accumulated knowledge of fact, and in the full maturity of his understanding of historical causation, he had reviewed the whole field and given in briefer compass his final interpretation of the old British colonial system, the contribution would have been of greater value.

[22] Edited by Louis Herbert Gray (New York, 1923).
[23] *African Questions*, p. 431.

As it is, he has done much basic work which need not be repeated; and he has drawn a picture which in its main outlines is likely to hold the field for a long time to come.[24] By reinterpreting British colonial history he necessarily pointed the way to a reinterpretation of the American colonial period. By presenting a juster view of the British position and by depicting the colonies in a truer, if less ultrapatriotic, light, he contributed both to the cause of scholarship and to a better understanding between the two great branches of the English-speaking peoples.

[24] For a criticism of several of Beer's conclusions, see "The Place of Markets in the Old Colonial System," by Curtis Nettels, in *New England Quarterly*, VI, No. 3 (September, 1933), 491–512.

XVII

CLARENCE WALWORTH ALVORD

MARION DARGAN, JR.
University of New Mexico

TO CLARENCE ALVORD it appeared strange that Fate should have chosen a child of the Berkshire hills as editor of a history of the prairie land of Illinois. Yet he reflected that, though it was late when he "followed the well-worn trail over steel tracks in a Pullman car," still he belonged to the vast multitude who had carried their lares and penates from western Massachusetts to build new homes on the prairie.[1] Although never able to forget that he was a "Massachusetts Yankee," this adopted son of the Middle West continually protested against the overemphasis of New England in our national history. This, he thought, should be woven around the westward movement. He declared:

Undoubtedly the blood of the pilgrims and the puritans has added greatly to the growth of the American nation; but the real cradle of the nation was not east of the Hudson river, not even east of the Appalachians, but in the heart of the continent, the Mississippi basin where were gathered the sons of all peoples—New Englanders, New Yorkers, Pennsylvanians, southerners, Germans, Irish, Scandinavians, children of the north and south, the east and west of both hemispheres; and here these diverse bloods have mingled to make the American people.[2]

[1] C. W. Alvord, *The Illinois Country, 1673–1818* (Vol. I of *The Centennial History of Illinois*) (Springfield, Ill., 1920)., p. i.

[2] Review of F. J. Turner, *The Frontier in American History*, by Alvord in *Mississippi Valley Historical Review*, VII, 406.

Alvord was born in Greenfield, Massachusetts, in 1868, of an old New England family, his father being a lawyer who had been active in the antislavery agitation.[3] His youth was spent on the banks of the Connecticut River. Graduating from Williams College at the age of twenty-three, he broke away from the New England scene by making a tour of Great Britain and by spending two years of study at the University of Berlin. After two quarters at the newly founded University of Chicago, he accepted an appointment at the University of Illinois, where he taught four years in the preparatory department before he was given a position in the university proper. At the age of thirty-seven, he was still an instructor; the path to promotion and worth-while achievement seemed blocked. Without a Doctor's degree, he was burdened by many hours of teaching; the university had an inadequate library; and his small salary did not permit him to go away for study or research.

At the opening of the twentieth century, Illinois was a laggard in the historical field, but the situation was ripe for a real renascence. Edmund J. James, a native son who had taken his Doctor's degree in Germany and who was full of enthusiasm for German scholarship, soon became president of the university and head of the State Historical Library. James possessed faith in the future of the university, desired that it make a reputation for productive scholarship, and had the ability to get funds from the legislature. In the summer of 1905, the year after James came to Urbana, Alvord was sent by the State Historical Library on two trips to southern Illinois, where he discovered a great mass of documents relating to the early history of that region. Having been appointed general editor of the "Collections" of the Illinois State Historical Library, Alvord inaugurated a comprehensive

---

[3] The chief sources used in this study regarding the facts of Alvord's life and personality are as follows: S. J. Buck, "Clarence Walworth Alvord, Historian," in *Miss. Valley Hist. Rev.*, XV, 309–20; Alvord Papers in the Library of the Minnesota Historical Society at St. Paul; letters from, and interviews with, former colleagues, students, and secretaries of Alvord. Several of Alvord's articles contain biographical information. For a bibliography of his writings, see *Miss. Valley Hist. Rev.*, XV, 385–90.

program, as a result of which fourteen volumes were published in as many years.

In 1913 the Illinois Centennial Commission was established, with the duty of preparing a five-volume history of the state; and Alvord was appointed general editor of this work. The next year he became the editor of the *Mississippi Valley Historical Review*, which he founded in order that young historians might secure publication of worthy articles. He edited the *Review* for nine years. Alvord was thus triply an editor; nevertheless, he found time to write a number of scholarly articles in addition to three books. *The First Explorations of the Trans-Allegheny Region by the Virginians, 1650–1674*, was published in 1912 in collaboration with Lee Bidgood. One-third of this volume is a brilliant essay on "The Discovery of the Ohio Waters," written jointly by the two authors, while the remainder is devoted to source material. In 1917, Alvord published *The Mississippi Valley in British Politics: A Study of the Trade, Land Speculation, and Experiments in Imperialism Culminating in the American Revolution*, a two-volume work which won the Loubat Prize of one thousand dollars for the best book on the "history, geography, archaeology, ethnology, philology, or numismatics of North America . . . . published in the English language for the five year period" since January 1, 1913. *The Illinois Country, 1673–1818*, the first volume of the *Centennial History*, appeared in 1920.

During Alvord's last years at the University of Illinois, the meagerness of his salary but faintly reflected the quality of his services. Most of his time was given to the State Historical Library, his compensation being fixed by law, and President James's successor being unwilling to add to it. Consequently, Alvord resigned his positions in 1920 and accepted a professorship in the University of Minnesota. After three years he gave up this appointment also, as well as the editorship of the *Mississippi Valley Historical Review*, in order to go abroad. He wished to write a sequel of *The Mississippi Valley in British Politics* and felt that it was essential that he have access to material in the foreign archives. Accordingly, the last five years of his life were spent mostly in London, Paris, and on the Italian Riviera. He was recognized in England as an outstanding American historian. In 1925 he delivered the annual Raleigh Lecture on history before the British Academy, speaking on "Lord Shelburne and the Founding of British-American Goodwill." The next year he gave the Creighton Lecture at the University of London, being the first American to have received this honor. His time seems to have been largely occupied with these activities, with meetings with friends, old and new, and with the preparation of popular articles for publication in the *Contemporary Review*, the *Quarterly Review*, the *Nineteenth Century*, the *American Mercury*, and the *Landmark*. Little progress was made on his book dealing with the American Revolution, in which he hoped to emphasize the role played by the Virginians. He did begin work on several chapters on the Revolution for the *Cambridge History of the British Empire;* but these were unfinished at the time of his death, at Diano Marina in December, 1928.

His students and colleagues at Illinois and Minnesota remember Clarence Alvord as a man of slender build with a fair complexion and a van Dyke beard. He had a brilliant mind, a genial personality, and a childlike conceit. Among his many friends were some of the ablest men of America and Europe. Passionately fond of research, he neglected physical exercise, smoked incessantly, and not infrequently, after a gay party, retired to his study with a pot of black coffee to write for hours on an article or lecture. In later years he was always in frail health, suffered several breakdowns, and no longer held himself erect. A man of varying moods, sometimes dejected and sometimes in exuberant spirits, he was admired by his friends for his "smiling cheerfulness" through it all. Never a good organizer of his time, he was rather dependent upon others. With complete devotion his second wife looked after him both in sickness and in health. Such a source of strength was also his physician and friend, Dr. Otto Schmidt, who gave financial assistance on several occasions when Alvord was forced by illness to go to a sanitarium or to a milder climate. Dr. Schmidt's generosity enabled the historian to spend his last years in Europe.

During most of the twenty-seven years of his scholarly career Alvord was a part-time instructor who devoted the greater part of his energy to editorial duties and research. He seems to have lost interest in undergraduates, but his growing reputation as a productive scholar drew advanced students to his seminars. These found him a stimulating and suggestive teacher, who lectured fluently without notes. He liked to upset fixed ideas, and the members of his classes were spurred to thought when he led a discussion. Students never found him too busy to give them help or wise counsel, and he knew how to call forth the best that was in them. One of his outstanding students wrote Mrs. Alvord after the death of her husband: "I think I owed more to his inspiration than to that of all my other instructors combined";[4] while another states in the preface of his dissertation that Alvord "carefully and painstakingly went over all the material with me, and gave me his time to discuss and analyze every point," making many valuable suggestions and helpful criticisms.[5]

Alvord readily indorsed the tendencies which were making themselves felt in American historiography during the first quarter of the twentieth century. He did not attempt a narrative history on a national scale, but became a specialist whose work was narrowly limited in space and time. Frederick Jackson Turner had only recently called attention to the importance of sectionalism in American history; so Alvord chose Illinois and the Old Northwest from 1763 to 1790 as his field of research. He was, however, never a local historian. George L. Beer and Charles M. Andrews were beginning to study the seaboard colonies not from the standpoint of local history but as parts of the British empire. Following their example, Alvord passed over deeds of frontier prowess and sought to discover how British

4 C. E. Carter to Mrs. Alvord, Jan. 5, 1929.

5 P. C. Phillips, *The West in the Diplomacy of the American Revolution* (Urbana, Ill., 1913), p. 4.

statesmen had grappled with the problem of the West acquired by treaty in 1763. He reflected also the wider scope of the "new history." He had a vision of "a history of Illinois that would be one of the greatest contributions to the knowledge of humanity ever produced," which, in a word, "would explain human society as developed on prairie land."[6] *The Centennial History of Illinois* gives much less space to politics than did the older state histories. Social and economic factors, however, receive still more attention in *The Mississippi Valley in British Politics*.

Having achieved success by the discovery and editing of documents, Alvord followed up his early achievements by directing an almost world-wide search for manuscript material. Thus he edited the *Kaskaskia Records, 1778–1790*, which includes not only the Kaskaskia manuscripts and Menard papers discovered by him but also documents which he had copied from the collections in the British Museum, the Library of Congress, the State Historical Library of Wisconsin, the Canadian archives, the archiepiscopal archives of Quebec, and elsewhere. To facilitate the assembling of source material, the Illinois Historical Survey was established in the University of Illinois graduate school in 1909, with Alvord as its director. Bibliographies were compiled, surveys were made of material throughout the country and abroad, newspaper files were borrowed from all over the state, and copies were prepared of items which threw light on the history of Illinois. With such a laboratory of state history under his direction, it is obvious that Alvord relied much upon co-operative effort. In fact, few equaled him as an organizer and director of research.

As general editor of the "Collections" of the State Historical Library, Alvord did not assume the responsibility for the contents of all the volumes planned, as had Reuben Gold Thwaites of the State Historical Society of Wisconsin, but called upon scholars such as Evarts B. Greene, James A. James, and Clarence E. Carter to edit certain volumes or to collaborate with him. *The Centennial History* was a notable example of co-opera-

[6] Alvord, *The Illinois Country*, p. ii.

tion, its five volumes having been written by eight different professors of the University of Illinois, with the help of a dozen research assistants and a staff of typists. Their method of work was described by Alvord in a letter to Albert J. Beveridge on November 24, 1922:

When we were writing the Illinois Centennial History, [Arthur C.] Cole carried out my ideas of the proper method of procedure very completely. For several years there were two or three well trained graduate students reading under Cole's direction the contemporary newspapers of Illinois. We had an arrangement by which we borrowed these papers from all over the state. The readers checked items of interest, naturally checking everything about Lincoln that was found. I had in the office about half a dozen expert typists under the direction of my stenographer, a very capable girl. These checked items were copied and carefully collated so that they are as good as the originals practically. The result was that Cole, when he came to write the book, had an immense amount of material such as no historian of the period had ever had before.[7]

In the preface to *The Illinois Country*, Alvord acknowledged the faithful work his office force did on the *Centennial History*. Probably his chief assistant on this volume was Dr. Louise Phelps Kellogg, whom he persuaded to help him for several months and who made digests of masses of material from the Paris archives. However, two other assistants prepared "rough drafts" for eight of the twenty-one chapters. *The Mississippi Valley in British Politics* was more exclusively Alvord's own book, but in compiling the special bibliography on "The Pamphlet Warfare, 1759–1763," he was assisted by two other scholars and a class of graduate students, who found the titles of many pamphlets and established the chronology of the bibliography.[8]

An adherent of the objective school of history, Alvord denied that the science of history offered any means of determining whether the United States is better off as an independent nation than as a part of the British empire, or whether the world is the

---

[7] See also *New York Times*, July 14, 1918.

[8] Alvord, *The Mississippi Valley in British Politics* (2 vols.; Cleveland, 1917), II, 253 n.

gainer because the Allies won the World War rather than the Germans. He pronounced the war guilt controversy "a seductive Chinese puzzle," "perhaps as useful to society as English fox hunting," and declared that to pass judgment upon men who have influenced social movements was altogether unscientific and resembled the naïve view of the fisherman who regarded the cod as a glorious creature, the shark as damnable. He cited opinions of history about Washington, Benedict Arnold, Hamilton, and Burr as illustrating this fallacious cod-shark formula. The biologist has the truly scientific attitude of mind, since no question of morals affects his conclusions. Alvord declared that he was "by education a philosophical determinist"[9] and that he could not believe "that there is any escape from a deterministic view of evolving society, provided there is to exist a science of history."[10] Referring to the beginning of the World War, he continued: "In those days, it was not the living but the all-powerful generations of the dead who acted. The leaders and the generation which so blindly followed them were mere pawns in the hands of the social-psychic environment evolved by the past."

Alvord rejected any teleological explanation of history emanating from the New England group of historians, and criticized H. G. Wells because he started out with a thesis and then discovered its justification throughout the whole history of humanity. Alvord declared, however, that "historical reasoning is fundamentally teleological," and that "western expansion" must be its basis. Historians living in the Mississippi Valley have been charged with being materialistic, and Alvord himself said: "At times the Westerners are almost economic determinists." He clearly emphasized economic factors in his volumes.[11] Thus in *The Mississippi Valley in British Politics*, to furnish background for the attempts of successive cabinets to work

[9] Alvord, "Politics in the Revolution," *American Mercury*, V, No. 17 (June, 1925), 175.

[10] Alvord, "Historical Science and the War Guilt," *ibid.*, XI, No. 43 (July, 1927), 326.

[11] Alvord, "Francis Parkman," *Nation*, CXVII, 394.

out a Western policy, he pictured the rivalry of fur-traders
and land-speculators and the maneuvering of each group for
the right to exploit the West. Furthermore, he conveyed the
impression that the Virginians went into the Revolution because
of the check given to their land speculations by the crown, and
that the Scottish fur-traders exercised an almost controlling influence on British policy toward Canada for over fifty years.

While he believed that history was dominated by social forces,
Alvord, to at least one friend, seemed interested "in the striking
individuals more than in blind currents."[12] Ten years later he
wrote further: "I find that my attitude toward the history problem is undergoing considerable change. I am becoming more and
more an adherent of the psychological school of historians. I am
not a follower of James Harvey Robinson; yet I am more in sympathy with his viewpoint than I ever expected to be."[13] Later in
the *American Mercury* he stated that he would like to psycho-
analyze George III but that he lacked enough "intimate materials."[14]

Scheffer-Boichorst, the medievalist in whose seminar Alvord
studied at Berlin, was an able critic and editor of historical documents. His apt American student profited greatly by his training.
Alvord's dissertation on "The County of Illinois" is a brilliant
interpretation of his early discoveries in the southern part of the
state, while his paper on "The Proclamation of 1763," in the
opinion of H. E. Egerton, "first gave a satisfactory explanation
to that puzzling document."[15]

A painstaking editor of the sources, Alvord thus acquired an
intimate mastery of detail regarding many of the topics upon
which he wrote later. He made considerable use of manuscript
material, much of which had not been previously exploited,
especially the Lansdowne and Dartmouth manuscripts. His
work, however, was based principally upon printed sources.

---

[12] P. E. More to Alvord, Apr. 10, 1912.

[13] Alvord to A. J. Beveridge, Nov. 24, 1922.

[14] Alvord, "Politics in the Revolution," *American Mercury*, V, No. 17 (June, 1925), 176.

[15] *English Historical Review*, XXXII, 299.

Thus approximately half of the citations in chapters vi and x of
The Illinois Country are to printed sources, one-fourth to manuscripts, and one-fourth to secondary works. Approximately five-
eighths of the citations in chapters vi and xii of the first volume
of *The Mississippi Valley in British Politics* are to printed sources,
over one-fourth to manuscript material, and over one-seventh to
secondary works. An analysis of the types of sources used in
these chapters suggests a preference for official documents, personal papers, and biographical material.

In spite of his wide research, important items were sometimes
omitted from Alvord's bibliographies.[16] His work is fully documented, but he fails to show his authority for the statement that
Patrick Henry shared the opinion of Lords Camden and York in
regard to the sovereign right of the Indians.[17] Usually generous
in giving credit to others, Alvord occasionally failed to do so.
Thus, in the preface to *The Settlement of Illinois, 1778–1830*, Arthur
C. Boggess states that his unpublished manuscript was borrowed
by Alvord "to use in the preparation of his article on the County
of Illinois." Shortly after this, Alvord elaborated upon the ideas
contained in Boggess' work in an article on "The Conquest of
St. Joseph, Michigan, by the Spaniards in 1781,"[18] but he made
no mention of the Boggess study. In their joint work Alvord
and Bidgood acknowledged their indebtedness, for the one
new source given in the book, to Miss Agnes C. Laut, who
furnished them with a transcript made in London from the
Shaftesbury papers in the Public Record Office.[19] They might
also have pointed out that the rest of the study parallels the
first volume of Draper's manuscript life of Boone, which both
had consulted freely.

[16] Thus the bibliography of *The Illinois Country* fails to cite both A. C. McLaughlin's
study of the "The Western Posts and the British Debts," American Historical Association
Annual Report, 1894 (Washington, 1895), pp. 413–44, and *The Transition in Illinois from
British to American Government* (New York, 1909), by R. L. Schuyler.

[17] Alvord (ed.), *The Illinois-Wabash Land Company Manuscript* (Chicago, 1915), p. 15.

[18] *Missouri Historical Review* (Columbia, Mo.), II (April, 1908), 195–210.

[19] Alvord and Bidgood, *The First Explorations of the Trans-Allegheny Region by the Vir-
inians, 1650–1674* (Cleveland, 1912), p. 210 n.

Alvord read rapidly, analyzing and summarizing important documents. He did not take a great many notes but depended upon his unusually retentive memory. He early acquired the mental habit of breaking his historical research into problems to be considered and solved in the light of the evidence. His office looked like an enlarged wastepaper basket. Around him as he wrote were notes scratched down hurriedly on slips of paper, and many open books and magazines. The appearance was disorderly, but Alvord could instantly find the information he wanted. During periods of ill health he employed a stenographer or used a dictaphone while composing. He dictated easily and concisely, seldom repeating or contradicting himself. A typewritten manuscript was then prepared with triple spaces and wide margins, and this served as a basis for revision. Several manuscripts were sometimes used in making successive emendations of chapter or article. Alvord was unusually receptive to criticism, and many suggestions from friends went into the making of the copy which was finally sent to the publisher.

Alvord's principal characteristics as a historian, according to Professor Solon J. Buck, were "imagination, thoroughness, the critical attitude, objectivity, and literary skill."[20] When he became interested in a line of investigation, he was tireless; and day or night seemed to make little difference to him. Surrounded by his books and manuscripts, he proceeded to live in the period and among the people with whom he was concerned. Thus, he would talk about Lord Shelburne and Lord Hillsborough and the whole coterie of eighteenth-century English statesmen and politicians as though he knew them personally. Furthermore, he early acquired the habit of seeking historical trends so that he could interpret his assembled data. In some cases where he did not have all the facts, his hypotheses have later proved to be valid ones. An example was his surmise that Thomas Bentley aided George Rogers Clark.[21] In other instances he was forced

[20] *Miss. Valley Hist. Rev.*, XV, 319.

[21] Alvord, *Cahokia Records, 1778–1790* (Springfield, Ill., 1907), pp. xxxii–xxxv, xcvi; *The Illinois Country*, pp. 322 ff.

by new sources to revise his assumptions.[22] Alvord was a careful scholar, but his conclusions were not always well grounded. Thus, he was unduly suspicious of the account of the Spanish attack on St. Joseph, Michigan, in 1781 in the *Gaceta de Madrid*, and based his version of this affair on a letter which had been recently discovered.[23]

While he strove for objectivity, Alvord realized that the elimination of all subjective elements was impossible. Certainly he left the imprint of his personality upon his work. He was an iconoclast who liked to shock people, an egotist inclined to overemphasize the importance of his conclusions, a liberal who delighted in his freedom from chauvinism, a warm-blooded person who could not write about John Dodge or Lord Shelburne as though they were mere automatons. In the preface to *The Mississippi Valley in British Politics* he chuckled over the rashness of a son of Massachusetts "in writing a drama of the pre-revolutionary era with several well known Hamlets omitted." He was amused to think that the reader would regard his omission of the Boston massacre and the famous Tea Party as revolutionary. Something of the same spirit is seen when, in announcing a projected work to be called "Imperial Muddlers and the American Revolution, or the Jolly Game of Politics and Propaganda," he stated that he did not hope for the approval of historical critics but for the condemnation of the Ku Klux Klan. Men who were viewed with great reverence in the West aroused his iconoclastic spirit. Thus he seldom lost an opportunity to criticize George Rogers Clark[24] or Daniel Boone, "whom fickle tradition has chosen to apotheosize as the prototype of western state makers of all generations."[25] "Few names are dearer to Americans than

[22] Alvord, *The Genesis of the Proclamation of 1763* (Michigan Pioneer and Historical Society, "Collections," Vol. XXXVI) (Lansing, Mich., 1908), pp. 20–52; *The Mississippi Valley in British Politics*, I, 168 n.

[23] Alvord, "The Conquest of St. Joseph, Michigan, by the Spaniards in 1781," *Mo. Hist. Rev.*, II, 195–210.

[24] See Alvord's review of Temple Bodley's "George Rogers Clark," in *Nation*, CXXIV, 403.

[25] Alvord, *Mississippi Valley in British Politics*, II, 206.

that of Daniel Boone," he wrote in the *American Mercury*,[26] but "research offers no support for his fame, which is a myth, like that of William Tell, conceived in caprice, reared by uncritical history, and perpetuated by popular sentimentality." Bolder still was his "Critical Analysis of the Work of Reuben Gold Thwaites."[27] This paper appeared on the program of the Mississippi Valley Historical Association seven months after the death of Thwaites; but it was not actually read, "owing to the lateness of the hour."[28] Frederick J. Turner, speaking before a popular audience, had confined himself to an appreciation of Thwaites's good points, but Alvord boldly passed on to a criticism which impressed some as sound but shocked others.

Alvord condemned chauvinism and bent over backward to prove himself free from it. Thus, in *The Illinois Country* he clears Canadian officials of the charge of inciting the Indians to warfare against the United States in the period from 1784 to 1795,[29] although other historians are convinced of their guilt. His partiality for the British may be seen in his admiration for Lord Shelburne, who had a reserved and difficult personality and a reputation for insincerity. Feeling that Shelburne had been given less than justice, Alvord pictured him as a young liberal who "conscientiously studied the problem of the West and presented a solution which might have won the hearts of the colonists for the mother country."[30] The evidence for Shelburne's ideas in 1763 is scanty, but Alvord reasoned backward from the liberalism of the statesman in his later years. After asserting that Shelburne was better informed on colonial affairs than any other minister of the eighteenth century, he in the same volume ranked

[26] VIII, No. 31 (July, 1920), 266. Alvord's attack probably had no effect on popular opinion, and a recent historian maintains that Boone's fame was not undeserved. See "The Fame of Daniel Boone," by Louise P. Kellogg, *Report* of the Daniel Boone Bicentennial Commission (Lexington, Ky., 1936), pp. 49–62.

[27] Mississippi Valley Historical Association, *Proceedings*, VII (Cedar Rapids, Iowa, 1914), 321–33.

[28] *Ibid.*, p. 22.

[29] Alvord, *The Illinois Country*, pp. 401–2.

[30] Alvord, *The Mississippi Valley in British Politics*, II, 250.

him as second in this respect to Lord Halifax.[31] Alvord's conclusion is that Shelburne was responsible for the merits but not for the defects of the Proclamation of 1763.[32] As a matter of fact, there is little evidence that Shelburne was more farsighted in 1763 than his colleagues, and it is improbable that he would have avoided their blunders had he remained with the Board of Trade.[33] Alvord's favorite thesis was that the cession of the Northwest to the United States in 1783 did not result from the "conquest" by George Rogers Clark but from Shelburne's vision and love of humanity.[34] While recent research seems to confirm the first part of this conclusion,[35] there is still room for a difference of opinion about Shelburne's benevolence.[36] Although Alvord himself described Shelburne as "one of the most enigmatic of men," he was confident that he had fathomed the reasons for his policy. This was characteristic of him. While he realized that the "prejudice" he had acquired in favor of Shelburne in his earlier studies might lead him to misjudge his motives in 1782 and 1783, in the end he felt certain that he had avoided the blind spots which had blurred the vision of his predecessors.

The chief fault of Alvord's presentation is that his main thesis is obscured by the fulness of the narrative. This is especially true of *The Mississippi Valley in British Politics*.[37] This work is not without literary merit, but the style is monographic and too heavy for continuous reading. Probably the author expected that

[31] *Ibid.*, I, 279, 323.

[32] *Ibid.*, p. 157.

[33] See R. A. Humphreys, "Lord Shelburne and the Proclamation of 1763," *Eng. Hist. Rev.*, XLIX, 257–58.

[34] See Alvord, "Virginia and the West: An Interpretation," *Miss. Valley Hist. Rev.*, III, 19–38; "When Minnesota Was a Pawn of International Politics," *Minnesota History Bulletin*, IV (1921–22), 309–30; *Lord Shelburne and the Founding of British-American Goodwill*, Raleigh Lecture on history (London, 1926), pp. 1–27; "Lord Shelburne and the American Revolution," *Landmark* (London), IX, No. 2 (February, 1927), 79–82.

[35] Samuel Flagg Bemis, *The Diplomacy of the American Revolution* (New York, 1935), p. 219 n.

[36] Louise P. Kellogg, *The British Régime in Wisconsin and the Northwest* (Madison, Wis., 1935), p. 188.

[37] *American Historical Review*, XXII (April, 1919), 672.

the volume would appeal only to scholars. *The Illinois Country*, on the other hand, was prepared for the general reader; and its "sentences are instinct with imagination and literary charm."[38] Alvord wrote more for a popular audience in the last years of his life, but he still liked to employ unusual words.

The most serious limitation upon Alvord's work arises from the fact that he did not have the opportunity of visiting European archives until his health had almost completely failed. He had to depend upon extracts and transcripts selected for him by others, and these sometimes misled him. Then, too, his intense specialization warped his sense of proportion. The West appeared unduly important to him, because he neglected the seaboard. As a result of his concentration upon a few years of history he designated as new certain practices and policies which, in fact, had been fairly well established in the years preceding the period engaging his attention.[39] Too much consideration was given to individual statesmen and too little to the traditions of offices and departments. Alvord's lack of proportion is illustrated by *The Illinois Country, 1673–1818*. Almost one-half of the book, which covers a period of one hundred and forty-five years, is devoted to the first seventy-five years, and more than one-third to the period from 1748 to 1790.

Alvord's distinctive contributions were as follows: he opened up a new field to historical research through the discovery of a mass of manuscript material relating to the early history of Illinois and the Old Northwest; he did much to facilitate further investigation by editing these manuscripts and others from foreign archives; he placed the Old Northwest in the larger field of British expansion and sought to discover its influence in shaping the relations between Great Britain and her colonies in the years preceding the American Revolution; he modified the usual interpretation of the Revolution by showing that the check given by the crown to land speculation was an important cause; he promoted the foundation of the Mississippi Valley Historical As-

[38] M. M. Quaife in *Miss. Valley Hist. Rev.*, VIII, 389.
[39] O. M. Dickerson in *Political Science Quarterly*, XXXII, 497.

sociation and helped to make it a society of individuals "interested in the study of Mississippi Valley history" rather than a federation of agencies; he founded the *Mississippi Valley Historical Review*, edited it for nine years, and made it a success; and, more than any other one person, he was responsible for the production of *The Centennial History of Illinois*, which "was generally recognized as setting a new standard for state histories,"[40] and which was pronounced at the time the most important co-operative work since the appearance of the "American Nation" series.[41]

Without doubt, Alvord has been given a modest, rather than a prominent, place in American historiography because he was the historian of a state and a section. Yet his theme "was worthy of a great performance," as Dixon Ryan Fox has pointed out. He says: "Illinois in a century and a half has developed from a group of trading posts to one of the great states of the Union, ... so typical in its rich variety of interests that its history seems indeed a vertical section of the nation's history, if not a microcosm of the western world."[42] As long as the frontier is regarded as a dominant factor in shaping American life, Alvord will be remembered as one who did pioneer work in a distinctive American field. Probably he will be remembered longest, however, as the founder of the *Mississippi Valley Historical Review*. He was, perhaps, the author of the leading work of scholarship produced by the school of western historians. Certainly he was the first to show the relation between British mismanagement in the West and the American Revolution and to rescue "the study of the beginnings of that conflict from the octopus of Boston Harbor."[43]

[40] S. J. Buck in *Miss. Valley Hist. Rev.*, XV, 312.

[41] Louise P. Kellogg in *Canadian Historical Review*, II, 275.

[42] D. R. Fox, "State History II," *Polit. Sci. Quart.*, XXXVII, 99.

[43] H. E. Barnes in *Encyclopedia Americana* (Chicago, 1925), XIV, 249.

XVIII

CLAUDE HALSTEAD VAN TYNE

PHILIP G. DAVIDSON
Agnes Scott College

*

THE spectacle of the American Revolution had been paraded down to the twentieth century by military and naval historians, by students of politics, and by eulogistic biographers; it had served the orators and pandered to the chauvinism of English and Americans alike. But no one, thought Claude Halstead Van Tyne, had as yet achieved an impartial view or a true view, one in which both England and America had received justice and in which the multiplicity of factors had been recognized. To make a detached study and to inculcate in educated Americans right attitudes toward the Revolution, this was his purpose.

This man, with this purpose, was the product of a little middle-western town of the 1860's, Tecumseh, Michigan, and was reared in what must have been an atmosphere of intense nationalism. He was, furthermore, well started upon a typically American business career as cashier of the Iosco County Savings Bank. Yet out of this background came a historian of the Revolution known on both continents for his impartiality. His qualities and training enabled him to overcome the effects of a limited environment, and his intellectual zeal led him to give up his position in the bank and, though nearly twenty-three years old, to enter the University of Michigan. Within ten years after his graduation in 1896, he had studied a year abroad, obtained a doctorate, published four books, and was back at the University as professor of history. A career so energetically begun brought him unique opportunities and ended in real distinction.

His formal training, first at the University of Michigan and continued at Heidelberg, Leipzic, and Paris, was completed at the University of Pennsylvania in 1900. He remained there for three years as senior fellow in history. During that time he published his doctoral dissertation, *The Loyalists of the American Revolution*, and edited a volume of Daniel Webster's letters.[1] A large part of the year 1903 was spent in Washington with Dr. Waldo G. Leland in the co-operative preparation of a guide to the federal archives.[2] After this work was well under way, he returned to the University of Michigan as assistant professor of history. He was selected to write the volume on the Revolution for the "American Nation" series, and thus in 1905 he published *The American Revolution, 1776–1783*.[3] The next year he succeeded Andrew C. McLaughlin as head of the department of American history, and five years later he was made head of the entire department of history, then united for the first time. Throughout his association with the University he was active in its affairs and was one of its great teachers. His students still bear testimony to his warm personality and his tactful, though rigorous, criticism. But he did not allow his academic duties to stifle his enthusiasm for his own work; he was a constant contributor to historical magazines and to encyclopedias, and for five years he was on the editorial board of the *American Historical Review*. He published in 1911, with Professor McLaughlin, the *History of the United States for Schools*,[4] a book which, in common with

[1] *The Letters of Daniel Webster* (New York, 1902), from documents owned principally by the New Hampshire Historical Society. *The Loyalists of the American Revolution* was first published by the Macmillan Co., in 1902 and reprinted in 1929 by Peter Smith.

[2] C. H. Van Tyne and W. G. Leland, *Guide to the Archives of the Government of the United States in Washington* (Carnegie Institute, Washington, 1904).

[3] This is Vol. IX of *The American Nation: A History*, a series of twenty-six volumes, edited by A. B. Hart and published by Harper & Bros. between 1904 and 1907.

[4] New York and Chicago, 1911.

other good texts, was condemned in 1923 for its alleged unpatriotic statements.

His activities brought him increasing prominence in his own field. La Fondation Harvard pour les Relations avec les Universités francais invited him to lecture in French provincial universities in 1913, and this gave him the opportunity of working in the French archives. For the next seven years he was principally engaged in the preparation of his comprehensive history of the Revolution, originally planned in three volumes. The first of these, *The Causes of the War of Independence*, was completed in 1921.[5] Just as he was getting it ready for the press, he was given another unique privilege. He was intensely interested, as was the whole country, in the new Government of India Act; and on the invitation of Sir Frederick Whyte, first president of the Legislative Assembly, he decided to observe the experiment at first hand. A group of Michigan alumni contributed the necessary funds, and Professor Van Tyne, specialist in the American Revolution, sailed for India to report on the situation. With no knowledge of the country, and with nothing, as he said, "but merely a mind trained to a study of the social sciences and to observe political activities past and present,"[6] he spent five months in careful investigation. His views were first published in two articles in the *Atlantic Monthly*[7] and subsequently in the book, *India in Ferment*. Friends of Indian self-government criticized him severely for his honest doubts as to the probable success of the plan and for his apparent lack of sympathy with Indian demands and even with Indian culture. He could not overcome, he agreed, his Western prejudices in favor of "cleanliness, sanitation, hygiene, universal education, and the necessity of training for political fitness." "I found myself," he added, "not so sympathetic with superstition, religious fanaticism, and the mystic Indian philosophy as the old English residents in India. . . . ."[8]

[5] (Boston and New York, 1922). The three volumes were to have as their general title, *The Founding of the American Republic*.

[6] *India in Ferment* (New York, 1923), p. x.

[7] *Atlantic Monthly*, July, September, 1922.   [8] *India in Ferment*, p. xi.

His planned study was again interrupted because he was obliged to fight the "heresy hunters," or what he termed that "aspirated trinity, Hearst, Hirschfield, and Hylan." He and Professor McLaughlin had endeavored to present in their school history a balanced and impartial view. For its alleged pro-English bias it was attacked in 1923 from California to New York and banned from school after school. Van Tyne defended the text resolutely and made only minor changes in the edition of 1923.[9] This controversy served to make his liberal views known to many people who had never heard of his textbook.

Foreign acknowledgement of his scholarship came once more when he was asked, in 1927, to accept the Sir George Watson Chair of American History, Institutions, and Literature. That year he spent lecturing at British universities—Birmingham, Glasgow, London, Cambridge, and Oxford. These lectures were published in 1927 and reprinted two years later under the title *England and America, Rivals in the American Revolution.*[10]

He returned from this interlude with renewed enthusiasm for the work on which he had been so industriously engaged; and within two years he had completed the second, and last, of his major volumes on the Revolution, *The War of Independence.*[11] The final recognition of his contributions came fittingly not only from his fellow-scholars but also from the Pulitzer Prize Committee, which reflected in its decisions the opinion of intelligent lay readers of history. News of the award was published in May, 1930, but Van Tyne did not live to know the full success of his book; seriously ill since the summer of 1929, he had died in March.

Van Tyne's best work was done in the field of the American Revolution, and it is by this that he must be judged as a historian. An evaluation of his contributions may properly begin

---

[9] See particularly the *New York Times*, Apr. 1, 1923, p. 20; June 4, 1923, p. 1; July 24, 1925, p. 12. A list of the changes made in the edition of 1923 is in H. K. Beale, *Are American Teachers Free?* (New York, 1936), pp. 282–83.

[10] New York and Cambridge, 1927.

[11] *The War of Independence: American Phase* (Boston and New York, 1929).

with a quick survey of the character and content of his individual writings on the subject. His important contributions were made in four articles in the *American Historical Review* and in five books. The articles contain some of his most careful research. The first of these, "Sovereignty in the American Revolution," in the April, 1907, issue, grew out of his early interests in constitutional and legal history, an interest engendered no doubt by Professor McLaughlin. In this essay Van Tyne presented the facts which demonstrated to him that the states were sovereign during and after the Revolution. This view he had first advanced in his *American Revolution, 1776–1783;* and the essay, he believed, gave substantive proof of what he had said. He recognized that there might be a metaphysical truth in the view that there was an essential unity underlying the surface diversities, but with metaphysics he was not concerned.

This interest in constitutional history did not develop, however, and in his next article he dealt with the social forces in the Revolution. These were one of his most lasting interests. He had said in 1901 that the primary motives which divided Whig and Tory were not religious or social but economic in character. "Even those who appear as religious champions," he said, "were influenced by economic considerations."[12] The more he studied the sources, however, the more convinced he became that economic issues were subordinate to others; and by 1913 he had changed his earlier position almost completely. In October of that year he published the paper, "Influence of the Clergy, and of Religious and Sectarian Forces, on the American Revolution," which contained the positive views on religious issues amplified in his later work.

The last two articles treat of foreign relations. One of them, entitled "Influences which Determined the French Government To Make the Treaty with America, 1778," and published in April, 1916, developed an idea which he had first presented in his *American Revolution, 1776–1783*. There he had recounted the con-

---

[12] This statement was made in Van Tyne's review of A. C. Flick's "Loyalism in New York," in *American Historical Review*, VII, 168.

versation of Beaumarchais and Arthur Lee wherein Lee argued that France would be drawn into the war in any case; for, unless she joined with America, the revolting colonies would accept peace with England and turn upon the French islands in the West Indies. "Improbable and illogical as was the argument showing that war was inevitable," wrote Van Tyne in 1905, "it doubtless had great weight with the king and some members of his cabinet."[13] But the force of the argument grew upon him the more he studied the French documents during his year abroad, and in 1916 he offered this view as the dominant motive affecting the French government:

> We may therefore accept, with as much confidence as historical evidence ever grants us as to the motives of men, the assertion of Vergennes in 1782, that France entered into alliance with the United States in the spring of 1778, because the king and his ministry were convinced that France was doomed to a war with Great Britain whether she formed the American alliance or not, but that it was the better policy to join with America and thus win her support rather than to wait for England to make peace with America, and then make war in company with her upon the House of Bourbon whose insular possessions would lie so completely at their mercy.[14]

The last article, "French Aid before the Alliance of 1778," printed in October, 1925, was a by-product of some work done by himself and his students; it was a straightforward statement of the amount of aid France gave the colonies, and was noncontroversial in character.

Of the five books on the Revolution, four deal with extremely broad aspects. The first alone is on a special phase of the subject; and of the five, it is the least satisfactory. *The Loyalists of the American Revolution* was a doctoral dissertation, characterized by

---

[13] *American Revolution, 1776–1783*, p. 209.

[14] *Amer. Hist. Rev.*, XXI, 541. In the last chapter of his *War of Independence: American Phase*, he reinforced this view with additional contemporary material. Corwin, in a paper published just a few months before Van Tyne's book appeared, dealt with the more fundamental causes of the treaty and doubted that the argument of Vergennes was more than one of the factors contributing to the immediate decision (see E. S. Corwin, "The French Objective in the American Revolution," *Amer. Hist. Rev.*, XXI, 33–61).

one of his colleagues as "over-ambitious but promising."[15] He attempted in this volume a survey of the trials of the loyalists and succeeded admirably in demonstrating the difficulties they faced. He failed to place them adequately in their American setting, and the entire book lacks coherence. It was aptly described at the time as a "loosely arranged group of essays, in texture often rather chatty, without adequate framework, not showing full grasp of the material nor effective synthetic power."[16] In spite of its technical flaws and ineffective style, it did go far, in that early day, toward adjusting the balance of opinion in regard to Whig and Tory, and that had been one of the author's primary aims.

The second book, *The American Revolution, 1776–1783*, was written for the "American Nation" series; and it was necessary for Van Tyne to cover the entire subject in brief form. This he did effectively, in lucid, almost terse, style. There was little opportunity for originality, but he did bring to the book a knowledge of the sources and a fresh and unbiased point of view. He ably summarized a mass of secondary material; and on the whole, the volume was a well-balanced study. When published, it certainly was the best summary available of the scholarly research that had been done on the Revolutionary War.

The third volume was the *Causes of the War of Independence*, the first of a series which was to give to the cultivated world the product of Van Tyne's thought and study. The book begins with the Treaty of 1763 and carries the development of the controversy between the colonists and the English government down to the Battle of Lexington. Nine of the eighteen chapters deal with basic conditions—the economic, political, and social background of the Revolution. Here he developed in detail the view, first stated in the *American Revolution, 1776–1783*, that the conflict was in reality a civil war, a war between liberals in England and America, on the one hand, and conservatives in both countries, on the other. The thesis developed throughout the book is that

[15] A. L. Cross in the *Dictionary of American Biography*, XIX, 217.

[16] Victor Coffin in *Amer. Hist. Rev.*, VIII, 776.

the "freest of peoples were the first to rebel." In support of this contention, he introduced a chapter, unusual in histories of the Revolution, on the imperial practices of other nations which held colonies. The value of the book lies again in its effective summarization of the scholarly work done by others in more limited fields. He relied openly and gratefully upon special treatments: Clarence W. Alvord's *The Mississippi Valley in British Politics*, Arthur M. Schlesinger's *Colonial Merchants and the American Revolution, 1763–1776*, Andrew C. McLaughlin's works on the constitutional aspects of the Revolution, and various monographs dealing with separate colonies. The primary sources used were almost exclusively the printed collections available in the larger libraries—the collected works of the statesmen, Hansard's *Debates*, and the published colonial records. There was only one reference to manuscript material in the United States; only twelve foreign documents were cited, and but three newspapers. Yet the book is not a mere collection of summaries: it is a synthetic whole and gives adequate expression to Van Tyne's firm conviction that the Revolution should be studied from the standpoint of the British empire as a whole and as the product of social and economic forces. Professional historians who reviewed the book complained that there was not much new in it; that it was little more than a summary of others' work. The general reader, however, was told that it was an able synthesis, although he was cautioned that it was clumsily presented and badly written.[17] Between the two the book apparently had little left to recommend it. There was a class, however, for whom it did a real service: the overworked teacher of history, who was attempting to specialize in some other field; the senior-college and graduate student; and the historically minded layman. They found in this book the best available summary of the ten years

[17] See A. M. Schlesinger's review in *ibid.*, XXVIII, 327. The figures given above on the documentation were taken from this critique. The reviewer made some valuable suggestions which Van Tyne followed in his later work. Reviews for the general reader may be found in the *New Republic* for Oct. 25, 1922, XXXII, Suppl., 15, and in the *Nation*, CXV, 416.

preceding the Revolution—and this in readable, though not literary, form.

The fourth volume was the Sir George Watson Lectures. Here Van Tyne stressed again his favorite ideas and attitudes. The first lecture, delivered in the House of Lords, was an explanation of the newer views of the Revolution and attacked those writers who would pervert history for mistakenly patriotic purposes, who would see in the war simply a conflict between "British vandalism, barbarity and cowardice, and American valour, heroism, and undaunted firmness."[18] The remaining five lectures dealt with the rival merchants, preachers, soldiers, and diplomats. In none of these did he have anything strikingly new to say, but in all there was the same insistence upon an unbiased approach and the same demand that forces should be emphasized rather than events or people. Here was a book that made even more popular appeal than the *Causes of the War of Independence:* it was more readable, less burdened with the mechanics of scholarship, and definitely phrased to appeal to the leisured and the cultivated layman.

The final study of the Revolution was the prize-winning *War of Independence.* The William L. Clements Library, of the University of Michigan, with its collection of Shelburne, Germain, Clinton, and Greene papers and the rapid publication of other sources, provided him with such a mass of information that his studies were prolonged and his projected book greatly lengthened. He had originally planned a series of three volumes to cover the period from 1763 to 1787; but this volume, which was to have treated the entire Revolution, carried it down only to the French Treaty of 1778.

This second volume, unlike the first, which was obviously based upon secondary material, bristles with citations to primary sources. Of the twelve-hundred-odd footnotes, at least half refer to manuscripts, newspapers, pamphlets, and printed collections of original documents. So much of the material in this volume

18 *England and America,* p. 5.

was his own that it was said at the time that no history of the Revolution based upon so thorough a knowledge of the sources had as yet been written. The chapters differ considerably in this regard. Carl L. Becker, *The History of Political Parties in the Province of New York, 1760–1776;* Charles H. Lincoln, *The Revolutionary Movement in Pennsylvania, 1760–1776;* and Hamilton J. Eckenrode, *The Revolution in Virginia,* still provided him, as in *The Causes of the War of Independence,* with the material on these states, the only ones to which separate chapters are devoted. Those parts of the book, however, which deal with British and American preparedness, military events, divided opinion in England and America, the development of the spirit of independence, and French relations with the states are based largely upon manuscripts, newspapers, and pamphlets. The manuscript sources relied upon are almost exclusively those to be found in Ann Arbor, London, or Paris; there is almost no reference to the collections in the eastern libraries and historical societies. He made little use of broadsides; but he did cite English newspapers and pamphlets extensively; of the American papers, only one printed in the South is noted, but the Massachusetts and Pennsylvania gazettes are well represented.

So much for the mechanics of the book. In content, like *The Causes of the War of Independence,* it is primarily concerned with conditions. Fourteen of the twenty-three chapters trace the development of ideas, in both England and America, on the rebellion and independence in the light of prevailing conditions, separately treated; three discuss the relations with France and Europe; and six describe the progress of the war. A study over so broad a field, especially in view of the large number of monographs on special aspects of the general subject, cannot be expected to make a contribution on every page; and a large part of *The War of Independence: American Phase,* synthesizes the work of others. The imprint of the author is best seen in those chapters which deal with attitudes and social forces. On military events he had at hand in the Clements Library fresh material of an important character, which provided him with a mass of illustrative detail. On the battles, except perhaps for the Saratoga campaign, he found little to change in what he had written in the *American Revolution, 1776–1783*. The basic explanations are essentially the same in the two books, but his later volume adds much contemporary material. On Saratoga his sources furnished him with new light on the relations of Howe and Clinton and on Burgoyne's difficulties, but he discovered nothing to alter his earlier conclusion that Howe was essentially to blame for Burgoyne's defeat.[19]

In its larger aspects, the book was warmly welcomed. It was generally praised for just those qualities that Van Tyne had conscientiously striven to develop in his writing: a candid detachment and impartial tone, and an engaging literary style.[20] Once more he had ably summarized a great body of research, his own as well as others, and had worked it into a synthetic whole for the use of the student. The result was a "fresh, illuminating, and distinctly readable treatment."[21]

When Van Tyne is surveyed more broadly as a historian, it is evident that he was impelled by the sincere purpose of discovering and making known the truth about the Revolution. It had been obscured in the past by intense national prejudices and a narrow view of historical forces. Van Tyne proposed to reveal the truth by using the detached methods of the scientific investigator, who, without bias, examines the multiplicity of relationships and factors.

In pursuit of this objective, Van Tyne achieved an almost complete detachment from national prejudice. He had a marked distaste for the historical chauvinism of the nineteenth century; and of all the semipopular treatments of the Revolution, there is

[19] Miss Jane Clark, archivist of the William L. Clements Library, read the same papers and arrived at a somewhat different view: to her, Burgoyne was in large measure responsible for his own defeat ("Responsibility for the Failure of the Burgoyne Campaign," *Amer. Hist. Rev.*, XXXV, 542–59). Van Tyne had seen this paper when he wrote his book.

[20] This statement closely paraphrases one made by D. S. Muzzey in a review in the *Political Science Quarterly*, XLV, 120.

[21] A. L. Cross, in the *Dictionary of American Biography*, XIX, 217, thus sums up admirably the general view of the book.

none that surpasses his in its impartiality. He viewed it always in its imperial and European setting and did not allow his own liberal inclinations to blind him to the imperialist's argument. "And, after all," he wrote, "a cynic might ask, was Lord North's purpose different from that of Abraham Lincoln several generations later?"[22] It is true that he never really overcame the deeply rooted attitudes of Western civilization, as he himself found when he came to survey India. But these did not affect his work as much as they would have done had he been studying world-history.

Still in pursuit of the truth, he sought to broaden the view of the Revolution by interpreting it in terms of social and economic forces, the factors most neglected in the past. The military, personal, and political aspects of the Revolution had formerly been emphasized; but he told his students rather of the "mutating systems of land-holding, shifting paths of commerce, the new arteries through which American thought and feeling flowed, and the modified relations of social classes to each other . . . . of the march of social, economic and political principles instead of the march of armed men."[23] That he considered such an interpretation the only correct one is not apparent in his writing. Perhaps he recognized it only as another version, albeit a truer one because it took into account more of the significant interests involved.

His treatment of these problems was expository and descriptive, and for the most part he was content to let facts speak for themselves; only rarely did he indulge in larger historical interpretations. He definitely considered the Revolution to be the inevitable product of impersonal forces, and thought of individuals only as the agencies through which they operated. He wrote in *The Causes of the War of Independence:* "A theory of individual responsibility for the Revolution is very pleasing to the eulogist, but in the larger view it is plain that James Otis was only the

[22] *War of Independence: American Phase*, p. 186.

[23] *England and America*, p. 8. He was referring to teachers of history as a group but clearly included himself.

embodiment of New England's indomitable will to have its own way; just as Patrick Henry was only the frontier product of Virginia's high-strung spirit of liberty."[24] He once said of the motives which led to the division into Whig and Tory: "The rank and file beyond question joined one party or the other only on the spur of the moment, influenced by some trifle, by personal spite, obstinacy, economic interest, or by the influence of friends and family connections; their motives were in the main without roots in the past."[25] But although the rank and file might be swayed by immediate considerations, the attitude of the leaders, he felt, was determined by long-accumulated social pressures: ". . . . there were certain classes," he wrote, apropos of the loyalists, "foreordained by the logic of their place in society and in the political structure to be the leaders of that faction."[26]

To him, diverse conditions predestined the Revolution: "Many things indicate that independence of England was foreordained. . . . . Owing to forces working during the whole colonial period to differentiate America from England, the two countries had come to be unlike in character, ominously opposed in interests."[27] In his own study of these differences, Van Tyne tended to emphasize the social aspects. He recognized the value of detailed economic treatises and incorporated their findings in his writings, but he was not the one to make such studies himself. The freshest view, he felt, would come from an examination of social factors. The most characteristic material in his two major volumes on the Revolution is contained in the chapters on social and intellectual problems, and it was on these points that some

[24] P. 179.

[25] *Amer. Hist. Rev.*, VII, 168. Twenty years later he modified this statement: "There were motives as diverse as the variety of human emotions and interests which made men Loyalists when the hour for decision arrived . . . ." (*Causes of the War of Independence*, p. 449).

[26] *Causes of the War of Independence*, p. 450. In apparent contradiction to his statements on the inevitability of the Revolution, he said in this same volume (p. 273) that George III and Lord North obstinately carried out their policies "at the cost of dismembering the British Empire," but it is evident that Van Tyne was not attempting an explanation of the Revolution in that statement.

[27] *Ibid.*, p. 312.

of his best research was done. Although he believed, in general, that economic necessities dictated the character of political philosophies, he once said flatly that "an outraged logic rather than economic suffering drove the colonists into rebellion."[28] A later statement amplifies this view:

Thus a difference in environment and of methods of living worked changes in certain basic conceptions of political order which threatened the unity of two parts of the empire. Every social and intellectual difference which diverse conditions created between England and America diminished the understanding and sympathy which alone would keep harmony in the empire.[29]

Otis was the product of New England's will to have its own way; Henry was the product of Virginia's spirit of liberty—thus more and more he sought explanations in terms of attitudes. There is an increasing insistence upon ideas as historical forces of deep significance; each volume stresses them more and more. It cannot be shown that he had accepted the full implications of such a theory, but in this emphasis there is at least the germ of a belief in the reality and power of ideas as such.

Van Tyne's purpose in these studies and these views was to discover and make known the truth about the Revolution. The verity he primarily sought was the truth of right attitude, and to discover it was not enough—it must be made known. The ideal expressed by Andrew D. White in his presidential address to the American Historical Association might well have been his own; "While acknowledging the great value of special investigations and contributions to historical knowledge . . . . it is not too much to say that the highest effort and the noblest result toward which these special historical investigations lead is the philosophical synthesis of all special results in a large, truth-loving, justice-loving spirit."[30] Each of his books was, in its time, the best available summary of the prevailing scholarship; and therein lies his real contribution to American historiography. The specialists had the same light as he, but there were many other

---

[28] *Amer. Hist. Rev.*, XVIII, 605.   [29] *Causes of the War of Independence*, p. 314.
[30] American Historical Association, *Papers*, I, 50.

people still in darkness. For them he wrote; for them he sought to make known the truth. He realized the gulf between popular tradition and the results of scholarly research; and he felt impelled, as a trained, detached thinker, to bridge that gulf.[31] It was not to be done by detailed, highly specialized studies, necessary as they were; it was not enough to state the "hard concrete facts of history"—these must be animated by the spirit.[32] But he did not write for the uneducated, and never popularized at the expense of accuracy. Van Tyne, the synthesist, using the technique of the scientific investigator and the attitudes of the scholar, presented to intelligent readers the truth as revealed in his own and others' research. He had sought the truth, and he had fought for it; but its cause would not triumph until "the best educated American citizens would keep abreast of the results of historical research, and join battle to preserve its conquests."[33] To keep them abreast of the truth as it was uncovered—this was his task, and this his contribution.

[31] *England and America*, p. 2.

[32] *Amer. Hist. Rev.*, VII, 169.   [33] *England and America*, p. 26.

XIX

ULRICH BONNELL PHILLIPS

WOOD GRAY

George Washington University

*

LITTLE more than a generation ago the South might well have been called the "dark continent in American historiography." Northern historians exhibited a profound disinterest in the section, perhaps under a vague feeling that it was not quite a respectable subject with its twin iniquities of slavery and secession. And southern writers themselves had accomplished little. Except for some state and community histories, generally marked more by local pride than scholarship, a number of pious biographies and rambling memoirs, and a few monographs of distinct value, there had been little exploitation of the immense possibilities of the field. Most of what had been published bore the imprint of the sword and magnolia cult; the aroma of the "lost cause" lingered in their pages. Even the best of the monographs, such as the studies by Philip Alexander Bruce of the institutions of seventeenth-century Virginia, suffered from a certain provincialism of outlook.

But in the past thirty-five years a veritable revolution in the regional orientation of historical studies in the United States has taken place until no part of the nation has been the subject of more painstaking research and prolific publication than this once neglected section. It has been a work in which a multitude has shared. Professors, graduate students, journalists, and zealous amateurs have all played a part. But it is clear that in this advance three men in particular have, in point of priority and influence, led the van. All three have been teachers in leading universities: William Archibald Dunning, of Columbia; William Edward Dodd, of the University of Chicago; and Ulrich Bonnell Phillips, whose period of greatest productivity coincided with his professorship at the University of Michigan. The careers of Dunning and Phillips are ended, and an evaluation of their completed scholarship is possible. The second has temporarily withdrawn from the writing of history to serve as ambassador to Germany and to take part in the making of history, which most of his colleagues are privileged only to observe.

Ulrich B. Phillips was, as ran an aphorism of the section, a southerner "bawn and bred." Unwittingly, from the moment of his birth he was receiving preparation for his future career and induction into an understanding of the society which he was to mirror. The house in Troup County, Georgia, where he was born —white, two-storied, porticoed, frame structure that it was— could have been endlessly duplicated throughout the eastern Cotton Belt. In his parentage there had been a meeting of the Old South and the New. His mother's family, of Virginia origin, was related to such leaders in secession and the Confederacy as William L. Yancey and Joseph E. Brown and connected with plantation gentry from the Old Dominion to the Gulf Coast. His father was one of that ante-bellum yeomen group that saw in the coming of industrialism to the post-war South a promise of economic redemption for the section and opportunities for their own advancement. At the son's birth, in 1877, the era of war and carpetbag rule was passing from the scene; but bitter memories were still fresh. Tradition has it that an earlier family home had been pillaged by a detachment of Sherman's army and that, of all its furnishings, only a great secretary had been preserved. It was at this desk, with such associations, that Ulrich B. Phillips was to write his histories. And in an atmosphere of still-smoldering wartime emotions it was unlikely that an impressionable growing boy would fail to react to the feelings of his elders. Of this, a youthful incident bears testimony. He had originally been given the name of the doctor, one Ulysses Bonnell, who had presided over his arrival in the world. At the age of twelve the namesake made the appalling discovery that Ulysses was a name as "damnyankee" in association as one could well find. A threatened new secession movement was appeased by parental permission to discard the offending praenomen. Ulrich was selected at random as preserving the original initial.[1]

At about the time when this domestic crisis was averted, the family moved to Milledgeville, where the father entered into a business enterprise, ultimately unsuccessful. At fourteen the boy was sent to the Tulane Preparatory School at New Orleans and thereafter lived with his family only during school vacations. His undergraduate college work was taken at the University of Georgia, where he received his Bachelor's degree in 1897 and his Master's in 1899. While working toward the latter, he served as a tutor in the department of history. For a time he nourished the ambition of becoming a cotton-planter. When, consequently, the effects of eyestrain forced his withdrawal from school one spring during his undergraduate career, he rented a suitable plot of land, plowed it, and planted a crop of cotton. But when harvesting time came, he found that his fingers, stiffened from guiding a plow, made a slow task of harvesting. In disgust he hired a negro woman to finish the job and, with some relief, returned to the university.[2] Though he continued to manifest a keen interest in the situation of the cotton industry in his own time as a student of the section, thereafter he was willing to forego any other direct ventures into the field.

By the time that his Master's degree had been conferred, Phillips had fully determined upon teaching as a career. His former instructors recommended entrance to the graduate school of Columbia University as the wisest course for a young southerner who wished to become a teacher of history. Here Professor Dunning's seminars in southern history had already won wide recog-

[1] Much of the personal information in this sketch is derived from an interview with Mrs. U. B. Phillips, who, with complete helpfulness and without reservation, opened to the writer the papers and recollections at her disposal. See also the *New York Times*, Jan. 22, 1934, p. 15, and the *American Historical Review*, XXXIX (April, 1934), 598-99.

[2] U. B. Phillips, *Life and Labor in the Old South* (Boston, 1929), pp. 123-24.

nition. From Dunning, Phillips received thorough training and the former's abiding interest. But Dunning's primary concern with political and constitutional problems somehow failed to arouse any responsive enthusiasm in his pupil; that came from another source. Before completing his doctorate he had occasion to hear a lecture delivered by Frederick Jackson Turner, of the University of Wisconsin, on the subject of American sectionalism. This lecture was his light on the road to Damascus. It furnished him with the key to the subject with which he had been struggling in his dissertation,[3] and suggested a direction for his further undertakings. To the end of his life Phillips avowed his indebtedness to Turner.

Emerging from Columbia in 1902 as a doctor of philosophy and with the American Historical Association's Justin Winsor Prize awarded to his dissertation, he accepted an instructorship at the University of Wisconsin. Developing under the opportunity thus afforded for intimate association with Turner, he was raised to the rank of assistant professor in 1907; and then in 1908 took a full professorship at Tulane University. Three years later he was called to the University of Michigan as professor of American history, a position he retained until he accepted a similar appointment at Yale in 1929. During his earlier career he taught the wide variety of courses in American history commonly expected of young instructors. While at Wisconsin he even ventured into Continental European and English history fields and, after the World War, for two years presented at Michigan a course on the causes of that conflict. But his main interest lay from the first in southern history. In this field he offered, during his teaching career, courses and seminars on the colonial and ante-bellum South, on race and sectional relations, negro slavery, the slavery problem in federal politics, nullification, the Civil War and Reconstruction, and the plantation system.[4] As a teacher

[3] "Georgia and State Rights: A Study of the Political History of Georgia from the Revolution to the Civil War, with Particular Regard to Federal Relations," American Historical Association, *Annual Report, 1901*, II (Washington, 1902), 5.

[4] Based upon an examination of the catalogues of these universities.

he was a lively and stimulating lecturer to undergraduates but was more effective still in the less formal preserves of graduate study. Here his sympathetic personality and ability to communicate enthusiasm combined with his thorough knowledge to make him an ideal instructor and guide.

But it was as a writer, more than as a teacher, that Ulrich Phillips was to win lasting recognition in his profession. In this respect he differed to an extent from Dunning and Dodd. Both of these men, though making notable additions to the literature of their fields, have made perhaps their most significant contribution to historical scholarship through the development and guidance of younger scholars. That Phillips' work in this regard was less outstanding was no doubt due mainly to differences in opportunity. Although while at Michigan he did train a number of men who were later to achieve rank in the profession, it was not until he went to Yale that he was in a position to devote the greater part of his time to graduate students.

As a writer he was extraordinarily productive. This was particularly true in the earlier part of his career. In a period of thirty-two years there came from his pen five books, four volumes of edited documents, some fifty-five articles, and nearly fifty book reviews contributed to a long list of periodicals and co-operative publications.[5] His writings dealt primarily with three topics: the development and bases of pre–Civil War political parties in the South; the field of southern ante-bellum transportation, principally the subject of railway construction in South Carolina and Georgia; and the administration of the slave plantation, with particular reference to the management of its labor supply.

In the first field, that of politics, Phillips' earliest and most ambitious undertaking was his *Georgia and State Rights*.[6] With the relationship of state interests to federal authority as its focus

[5] For full lists of Phillips' published writings see David M. Potter, Jr. (comp.), "A Bibliography of the Printed Writings of Ulrich Bonnell Phillips," *Georgia Historical Quarterly*, XVIII (September, 1934), 270–82, and Everett E. Edwards (comp.), "A Bibliography of the Writings of Professor Ulrich Bonnell Phillips," *Agricultural History*, VIII (October, 1934), 199–218.

[6] "Georgia and State Rights," Amer. Hist. Assoc., *Annual Report, 1901*, II, 3–224.

this work essays, as indicated by its subtitle, to sketch the political history of Georgia from the end of the War of Independence to the outbreak of the Civil War. It is an epitome of painstaking and thoroughness. In the course of his research the author visited every depository of materials that gave promise of holding pertinent data and was, in addition, indefatigable in running to earth materials in private possession. The first three chapters of the work are severely factual and circumscribed in outlook after the strictest traditions of the "scientific school" of history that was dominant in this country in the latter part of the nineteenth century. They testify to the author's diligence rather than to his insight or literary gifts. Not until there is an opportunity for application of the Turnerian thesis does the work come to life. Then it is established that, regardless of changes in name and leadership, political divisions in the state were, for more than half a century, basically continuous and unaltered. This permanency of division is accounted for on grounds of economic cleavage based primarily upon differences in soil fertility. Other factors, such as the personalities of leaders and local jealousies, are also recognized as having played a part, but not to such an extent as to destroy the essential pattern. Borrowed though the central concept of the work is, the industry and intelligence displayed by the author in its application are of such a nature as to obviate any need for apology on this point. Also revealed is Phillips' understanding of the fact that it was in large part from personal rivalries and local divisions that national political parties in the United States evolved. A particular feature is the series of maps constructed to illustrate the predominant thesis, revealing the correlation between political affiliations and the geographic distribution of wealth. Like Turner, Professor Phillips always found a fascination in such maps, and in succeeding years made many others for different parts of the South.

This study afforded Phillips a strategic redoubt in the very center, geographic and chronological, of southern history. It gave him a key to the types and locations of available records and a comprehension of some of the dominant forces to be reckoned with in any study of the section. In subsequent efforts he extended his lines in the same sector. An article that appeared in the *American Historical Review* in 1909[7] applied the earlier formula to the Federalist party in South Carolina with entire success. The culmination of his political studies appeared in an essay on the southern Whigs included in a volume compiled by former students of Turner.[8] The essence of this group, Phillips here stated, was to be found in those plantation gentry who saw in Andrew Jackson, his followers, and his shibboleths a threat to the privileged political position which their property had theretofore given them. Being in a numerical minority and forced to function in a democratic medium, they had to move mainly by indirection. It was this practical consideration that had driven them into a marriage of convenience with the National Republicans of the North and West, had impelled them to take part in the circus processions that carried military heroes into the White House, and, paradoxically, had made national success something of a liability to them. In this article, which is in the nature of a brief survey of a larger field, more attention is given to specific generalizations than in the previous studies, where the author had been usually content to let his interpretations emerge largely from his marshaling of facts. It marks in this respect his farthest advance as a political historian.

In all these studies the essential achievement is the application of a formula derived from the author's doctoral dissertation and for which he was originally indebted to Turner. His last important venture into the political field was, owing to the absence of any such integrating concept, rather disappointing. This was his *Life of Robert Toombs*,[9] a by-product of his work of editing the correspondence of Toombs, Alexander H. Stephens, and Howell Cobb. In this book the reader seldom feels any sense of intimacy with, or deep understanding of, its central figure; and the result

[7] "The South Carolina Federalists," *Amer. Hist. Rev.*, XIV (April and July, 1909), 529–43, 731–43.

[8] "The Southern Whigs, 1834–1854," in *Essays in American History Dedicated to Frederick Jackson Turner* (New York, 1910), pp. 203–29.

[9] *The Life of Robert Toombs* (New York, 1913).

resembles a portrait made from the viewpoint of the visitors' gallery of the Senate chamber. Although an adequate biography of a type once considered acceptable, it can hardly be said to reveal its author's talents suitably employed. Its best sections are those in which his mastery of the intricacies of Georgia factionalism could be called into play.

The field of ante-bellum transportation in the South occupied a position distinctly secondary in Phillips' interests; but his contribution to the subject is, nevertheless, meritorious. Like so much of his earlier work, it apparently developed from materials unearthed in the research for his first book. His most ambitious undertaking in this quarter was the *History of Transportation in the Eastern Cotton Belt to 1860*.[10] It incorporates the substance of certain earlier articles[11] and is essentially a straightforward factual narrative based upon an impressive quantity and variety of sources. Even so, an intelligent analysis of the southern transportation problem is not omitted. The Old South is considered to have been divided into seven major geographic and industrial provinces having the common problem of getting staple produce to an external market in exchange for manufactures and foodstuffs. By 1860 a transportation network adequate to the ordinary needs of the section had been achieved. This represented a triumph over the obstacles of scattered population, the seasonal nature of staple movements, the absorption of capital, labor, and managerial ability in the plantation system, the lack of an extensive local trade, and the dominant conservatism of the section. Noteworthy was the absence in the financing of the southern railways of the speculation and peculation so common elsewhere in the nation. For the most part, investments in such undertakings were conceived of as a civic responsibility rather than as an opportunity for gain, since cotton and other agricultural staples were the only roads to wealth in which most southerners of the

[10] New York, 1908.

[11] "Transportation in the Ante-Bellum South: An Economic Analysis," *Quarterly Journal of Economics*, XIX (May, 1905), 434–51; "An American State-owned Railroad: The Western and Atlantic," *Yale Review*, XV (November, 1906), 259–82.

time were interested. In Phillips' judgment railway construction was not an unmixed blessing to the South, as it tended to discourage industrial diversification and to bind the section more firmly than ever to staple production, ultimately a source of both economic and political weakness.

But the most abiding and significant interest of Ulrich Phillips lay in the economics of the plantation system. Apparently his first approach to the subject was practical and contemporary rather than academic and historical. In 1903 he joined that earnest group of young southerners which, through the columns of the *South Atlantic Quarterly* and under the aegis of John Spencer Bassett, was attempting to guide its section to industrial and cultural parity in the nation.[12] Being a historian, Phillips sought to get at the bases of the share-crop and cotton-fixation problems of the South by studying their origins. The scope of his investigation steadily broadened and intensified. The first article was followed by many others in various periodicals and culminated in two books. In them he limned with insight, thoroughness, and detail the character of the central institution in the life of the ante-bellum South. The most elaborate summation of this theme appears in his *American Negro Slavery*,[13] a solid, painstaking work of some five hundred pages. About half of this volume is devoted to a tracing of the course by which the institution of African slavery was introduced to America and the manner in which it spread therein. The remainder treats analytically of the system as it existed at its height, particularly in the production of cotton. In this study monographs and a myriad of sources, published and unpublished, are worked exhaustively and to excellent effect. Eleven years afterward appeared his *Life and Labor in the Old South*,[14] covering many of the same lines of investigation and reincorporating a portion of the earlier material. Additional

[12] "The Economics of the Plantation," *South Atlantic Quarterly*, II (July, 1903), 231–36; "Conservatism and Progress in the Cotton Belt," *ibid.*, III (January, 1904), 1–10.

[13] *American Negro Slavery: A Survey of the Supply, Employment and Control of Negro Labor as Determined by the Plantation Régime* (New York and London, 1918).

[14] Boston, 1929.

evidence is herein adduced, and the whole accumulation of facts manipulated with a somewhat lighter touch than that displayed in its predecessor. In certain respects it may be viewed as something of a popularization of the *American Negro Slavery*, with a greater attention to vivacity of tone and deftness of style. Some of the articles in the same field that preceded, accompanied, and followed these books—articles too numerous for any to receive individual attention in so brief a survey as this—contain even clearer vignettes of the subject as a whole.

By pressing them all together, books and essays, and obtaining thus a composite, rather than through finding in any one of them a concise and explicit summary, there can be drawn an integrated picture of the plantation system as it appeared to its most devoted student.[15] In Phillips' conception the southern plantation represented a fusing of three elements: first, there was the plantation itself, simply a large-scale capitalistic agricultural unit devoted primarily to the production of commodities for the market; next, slavery, a system of labor, lodging complete responsibility and authority in the employer; and, finally, the negro, a savage schooled by an environment that was alien to nearly all that American conditions represented. Owing to peculiarities of climate, the fresh lands of the South were in a position to produce crops for which a ready demand existed in Europe. Enterprising men had, in the colonial period, seen in this situation an opportunity for the gaining of wealth; but, as in all new countries, they faced a shortage of labor as an obstacle to their ambitions. Neither compulsion of the sparsely settled and intractable natives nor contractual white servitude was sufficient to their needs. Therefore the forcible importation of Africans was adopted from the Portuguese and Spanish practice. Since these blacks labored unwillingly and because they were taken direct from jun-

---

[15] The nearest approach to an interpretative synthesis of the history of the plantation regime from Phillips' pen can be found in certain of his articles, including the following: "The Economic Cost of Slaveholding," *Political Science Quarterly*, XX (June, 1905), 257–75; "The Origin and Growth of the Southern Black Belts," *Amer. Hist. Rev.*, XI (July, 1906), 798–816; "The Decadence of the Plantation System," *Annals of the American Academy of Political and Social Science*, XXXV (January, 1910), 37–41.

gle savagery, a system of slavery was required to make them economically effective and socially controllable.

Under colonial conditions the supply of such labor had been sufficiently plentiful, and thus low in first cost, to permit the system to yield profits, often very extensive ones. But Phillips was of the opinion, based on a careful charting of available statistics, that after the abolition of the foreign slave trade by Congress in 1807 the margin of profit under even the most favorable circumstances became increasingly doubtful. With the extension of the slave plantation system to new cotton lands in the lower South, an expanding demand for negroes was confronted by a limited supply. Prices for slaves were driven to levels that bore little relationship to the actual value of the laborer's services. Burdened at the outset with a top-heavy capital investment in future labor, the plantation-owner in the nineteenth century suffered from other handicaps as well. The crudity of his working force necessitated its employment in endeavors that permitted simple, year-round routine. This bound him, without hope of escape, to staple production and eventually led to cutthroat competition with other producers caught in a like dilemma. Apart from this fact, the system employed was, Phillips believed, as efficient as could well have been devised for crude labor under compulsion; indeed, under it the mass of negroes in America were far more productive than they have ever been since emancipation.

Phillips held that, even from an ethical point of view, the slave, once past the initial outrage of his enslavement, was, on the whole, not ill used. The relationship of masters and servants was, his extensive studies convinced him, a matter of individual exceptions rather than of widely applicable generalizations; but the average plantation-owner was neither harsh nor unreasonable, if for no better reason than because the slave represented an expensive investment that might suffer through ill health or truancy if improperly treated. The slave, as a matter of fact, needed much cajoling to secure the measure of co-operation needed for profitable employment. Extensive personal contact had a softening influence and made the arrangement under its best conditions patriarchal rather than exploitative. The most striking injustice was to a minority of unusually gifted individuals, often mulattoes, who were intellectually equipped to assume a position of equality in the white man's civilization. Had the slave not been of a different race and, in the mass, of a vastly lower cultural endowment, slavery would doubtless have given way to a more profitable system of indentures and free contract. Because of the prestige that slave ownership conferred upon men of property, serving often to obscure the economic shortcomings of slave labor, and because of apprehension for the stability of the social order, the institution persisted after most of its other reasons for being had ceased to exist. Unfortunately, its abolition came without adequate preparation and in circumstances that brought race relations under the worst possible influences. Though the incubus of slavery was gone, no new institution was prepared for carrying the negro through the needed adjustment to the responsibilities of freedom.

His studies developed in Phillips a fuller appreciation of the commendable, as well as the undesirable, qualities of the plantation regime; and from these considerations he came to cherish the hope that the best features of the plantation might be adapted to the conditions of southern agriculture of his own time. Thus he advocated the general re-establishment of units of agricultural production large enough to justify investment in a full equipment of machinery, careful attention to seed selection and scientific analyses, and the employment of trained and expert management. At the same time he wished the unit to be small enough to entail close personal contact between owner and the working force and, indeed, desired a restoration of the best features of the plantation as it had existed, for instance, in Virginia in the eighteenth century. Both white and negro laborers would operate under long-term labor contracts and would work in groups under close direction. In this manner he believed that greater efficiency and profits for the owner and better care and higher returns to the worker would be obtained. The shiftlessness, poverty, and degradation that, because of the prevalent system of migratory crop-lien tenantry, hung like a millstone about the neck of the South might, under some such a plan, be lifted from the section. As conditions stood, parts of the South that had been among the most productive areas under slavery were held back by their great proportion of undirected negroes and were lagging behind less fertile districts where the percentage of white farmers was higher. Even convict labor had proved itself more efficient than that of negroes without compulsion.[16]

It has already been suggested that it is a marked characteristic of Phillips' writings that he was little given to specific interpretation.[17] Only through a careful reading of all of his many contributions is a clear impression gained of the patterns implicit in his handiwork. He seldom furnished the profession with convenient keys to the mass of his production. Apparently, broad generalizations did not come readily to him; he preferred to build up, with careful and meticulous attention to detail, skilfully laid mosaics. Their clarity and meaning might depend somewhat upon the reader's perspective and previous understanding. Yet it was hardly to be expected that so reverential a Turnerian would be content to leave his work without at least one definitely expressed thesis, and toward the end of his career such a statement appeared.[18] This interpretation commenced with the premise that in the case of a section so indubitably distinct and unique as had been the South, both before and after the Confederate experiment, there must be some central integrating factor. Explanations applicable in other highly self-conscious units, such as racial individuality, a single language, religious uniformity,

[16] "The Economics of the Plantation," *S. Atlantic Quart.*, II, (July, 1903), 231–36; "Making Cotton Pay," *World's Work*, VIII (May, 1904), 4782–92; "The Plantation as a Civilizing Factor," *Sewanee Review*, XII (July, 1904), 257–67; "The Overproduction of Cotton and a Possible Remedy," *S. Atlantic Quart.*, IV (April, 1905), 148–58; "Plantations with Slave Labor and Free," *Amer. Hist. Rev.*, XXX (July, 1925), 738–53.

[17] In this connection see the illuminating review of *Life and Labor* by Avery Craven in the *Polit. Sci. Quart.*, XLV (March, 1930), 135–37.

[18] "The Central Theme of Southern History," *Amer. Hist. Rev.*, XXXIV (October, 1928), 30–43.

consolidation of political views, absorption in a particular industry, and so on, would not fit the facts of southern history. There
remained the negro, the "perennial negro," as the key to the sectional individuality, past and present, of the South. A determination to keep the negro "in his place" in order that the South
might be "a white-man's country" was one to which rich and
poor, ignorant and thoughtful, slaveholder and poor white,
could—and did—rally in unbroken ranks. It explains much of
what is ordinarily incomprehensible in the region to outsiders.

Though subject to qualifications which its author would have
been the first to admit, the interpretation is a peculiarly satisfying one. It embraces the facts of the case, possesses the essential
simplicity of all great generalizations, and has the final attribute
of practical utility to students of the field to which it applies.
One may regret that the progenitor did not more often give himself to such illuminating précis.

One is naturally led to inquire as to just what qualities serve
to raise Phillips' writings to first rank. Most obvious is the attractiveness of literary style that he was able to achieve, a quality more apparent in his later compositions than in his early efforts. It was not, as a matter of fact, one with which he was
naturally endowed; but instead it had been gained laboriously
by conscious effort and cultivation. It was his habit to keep at
hand a dictionary of several volumes to which he constantly referred in search of variety and precision for his vocabulary.[19] He
took careful note, too, of felicities in style and uncommon usages
in the works of others. In some of the best of his passages a close
examination will reveal the striations of careful polishing. In
time the use of deftly turned phrases and well-chosen extracts
from the rich sources which his researches afforded became his
preferred methods of achieving the desired effect. Since he had
found this endowment difficult to acquire, he sometimes tended
to place undue stress upon its desirability in the training of ap-
prenticed historians; but, at any rate, his own success in this re-

[19] See the introduction by Fred Landon to the bibliography of Phillips' writings in
Agric. Hist., VIII (October, 1934), 198.

gard should serve as an encouragement to others who in the beginning lack the attributes of literary proficiency.

But mere attractiveness of style is an insufficient basis for a historical reputation, and it was by no means the chief of Phillips' merits. The real source of his strength lay in his mastery of materials. Perhaps he, more than any other man who has worked in the field of southern history, succeeded in gaining this thorough familiarity with its sources. In this regard a number of special opportunities early came his way. Charged in 1903 and 1904 with preparing reports for the Public Archives Commission of the American Historical Association on the state and local archives of Georgia, he made a painstaking survey that was invaluable to his own scholarship.[20] Many of the sources with which he then became acquainted served him throughout his career. Some years later he undertook a broader project under the auspices of the American Bureau of Industrial Research, headed by Richard T. Ely. The fruit of this investigation was published as the first two volumes of *A Documentary History of American Industrial Society*[21] and served as the core for his *American Negro Slavery*. About the same time he edited the correspondence of Toombs, Stephens, and Cobb, an excellent opportunity to steep himself further in the records of the Old South.[22] And he was forever in pursuit of fugitive papers on his own responsibility. Attics of old southern homes drew him like so many magnets. In his later years he and Herbert A. Kellar, of the McCormick Historical Association, made regular forays into the section in search of undiscovered family and plantation records. He haunted bookshops and vigilantly followed the offerings of auctions.[23] At his

[20] "The Public Archives of Georgia," Amer. Hist. Assoc., *Annual Report, 1903*, I (Washington, 1904), 439–74; "Georgia Local Archives," *ibid.*, *1904*, II (Washington, 1905), 555–96.

[21] *Plantation and Frontier Documents, 1649–1863* (Vols. I and II of *A Documentary History of American Industrial Society*, ed. John R. Commons *et al.*) (Cleveland, 1909).

[22] "The Correspondence of Robert Toombs, Alexander H. Stephens, and Howell Cobb," Amer. Hist. Assoc., *Annual Report, 1911*, Vol. II (Washington, 1913).

[23] Thus he picked up at a New York auction an eighteenth-century plantation record book from the West Indies, an almost unique survival ("A Jamaica Slave Plantation," *Amer. Hist. Rev.*, XIX [April, 1914], 543–58).

death he had accumulated one of the finest private collections of southern materials in existence.[24] In addition he had for years free access to the treasures of an even more ambitious collector than himself, Wymberley Jones DeRenne of Wormsloe, Isle of Hope, Georgia. This paragon among literary hosts was noted not only for the riches of his library but for the excellence of his table and cellar as well. All were available with equal generosity to those who had the good fortune of an invitation to his estate.[25]

Almost from the inception of his research Phillips developed an appreciation of the value of incidental and unconscious records of ordinary folk. These, he felt, might reveal more of the actual operations of a departed order than the statements of public figures. From such materials he was in a position to project a reconstruction of the old plantation regime as it had actually existed rather than as it appeared in the declarations of polemicists, pro or con.

One secret of his remarkable productivity and of the authority with which he could deliver himself was to be found in the twofold economy of effort that he displayed in his work. First of all, he from first to last confined himself to a limited field of study, primarily that of the life of the Cotton Belt before the Civil War. Indeed, it was the even narrower range of the upland area of Georgia that served as the point of departure for most of his studies. Thus he was able to master his subject with a thoroughness that would not have been possible had he broadened his canvas. And second, he was accustomed to work and re-work his materials until almost the last possible bit of utility had been squeezed from them. Choice bits of evidence reappear in his writings to a noteworthy degree. A topic was not infrequently redone from slightly varying points of view as many as three or

[24] After his death this collection was acquired by Yale. A brief description may be found in the *Bulletin of Yale University*, 32d ser., No. 7 (Dec. 15, 1935).

[25] Phillips' review of *Catalogue of the Wymberley Jones DeRenne Georgia Library*, in the *Amer. Hist. Rev.*, XXXVIII (October, 1932), 174-75.

four times, and, repeatedly, whole sections and even articles already published were incorporated with little change in later works. The practice is neither uncommon nor reprehensible, but it does partially explain how he was able to write so much in the midst of a demanding professional career. As a historian he operated strategically upon interior lines.

So long as histories are written by mere mortals, the best of them will have their shortcomings; and from this universal quality Phillips was not exempt. Perhaps the failing most common to historical composition is the tendency for the author's preconceptions and prejudices to show through even the most honestly knitted fabric. Phillips was perhaps less vulnerable in this regard than many other writers because of his practice of relying on interpretation through inference from presented facts rather than essaying explicit generalizations. But occasionally, evidence of southern self-consciousness, never entirely eradicated by northern residence, would appear. Particularly in some of his earlier writings the juxtaposition of statements in which a northern provocation of the sectional struggle would be presented without extenuation while a similar southern act would be softened by a statement of the factors that induced it, evidenced a falling-short of complete objectivity.[26] But in general he was singularly free from this type of bias. Most of his lapses could be easily forgiven as reactions against the lingering abolitionist coloring in many of the standard histories of his time. At least he refought no wars, wept over the graves of no lost causes, and recognized the shibboleth of state sovereignty as a political theory of convenience rather than as a precept to be revered.[27] Even less did his social attitudes intrude upon his writings. Though he sometimes described himself as a "progressive conserva-

[26] "The Slavery Issue in Federal Politics," in *The South in the Building of the Nation* (Richmond, 1909), IV, 382–422; *The Life of Robert Toombs*, pp. 194–95.

[27] "The Literary Movement for Secession," in *Studies in Southern History and Politics, Inscribed to William Archibald Dunning* (New York, 1914), p. 33.

tive,"[28] it would be hard to substantiate such a position from the products of his pen, except perhaps in the fact that he refused to become indignant over the abstract injustices of slavery.[29]

Most serious of his weaknesses was the narrowness of his knowledge. Being content to master a single field had its disadvantages. He obviously never felt at home in any realm of history outside of his chosen preserve; and this sometimes threw his view, even of his own field, out of focus. He was never able to fit the abolitionist movement into its proper niche in the sectional problem because he lacked an adequate understanding of northern trends in the period. In his writings, at least, he failed to distinguish between abolitionist sentiment and opposition in the North to slavery extension in the territories—two very different things indeed.[30] Even his generalizations about the South, when he ventured them, sometimes suggested that the basis of his perceptions of the section was too narrowly construed in terms of the Georgia piedmont. His foundation, though deeply laid, was sometimes overnarrow for the structure that he attempted to erect upon it. But when a balance is struck between his shortcomings and his many commendable qualities, the weight of the latter is hardly shifted to any perceptible degree by the former.

With such wealth of scholarly attributes in his possession, Ulrich Phillips had in 1929 approached the zenith of his career. Recognition came to him in that year from every quarter. Columbia and Yale conferred honorary degrees upon him, and the latter university added him to its staff on terms that promised a broadening of opportunity; Little, Brown and Company had awarded a substantial prize to the manuscript of his *Life and*

[28] "Conservatism and Progress in the Cotton Belt," *S. Atlantic Quart.*, III (January, 1904), 1–10.

[29] For this attitude W. E. B. DuBois rather heatedly criticized him in a review of *American Negro Slavery* in the *American Political Science Review*, XII (November, 1918), 722–26.

[30] *The Life of Robert Toombs*, pp. 50–51.

Labor;[31] the Albert Kahn Foundation granted him a choice fellowship for a year of foreign study of the plantation and the negro.[32] With an imposing array of contributions behind him he seemed destined to proceed to new achievements. His intellectual powers were at full tide; his physical endowment in keeping. A genial personality and rare qualities of good companionship made him a favorite in his profession, while his learning and inherent dignity commanded respect. His generosity with both his time and his rich collection of materials to distinguished scholars and humble students alike was proverbial. He was in this same year chosen, for a second time, as a member of the executive council of the American Historical Association and, as chairman of the Beveridge Memorial Fund, was planning a schedule of important publications on the origins of the War for Southern Independence. His reputation in his field had come to extend far beyond his profession.[33]

But any expectation that he was to have a decade or more of continued productivity and leadership was soon to be blighted. By a tragic co-incidence his trip abroad under the Kahn Fellowship contributed to the sudden termination of his life. Permitting an undiagnosed ailment to forego attention until his return to the United States, he discovered, when examined, that a cancerous growth had progressed too far for treatment. But he refused to surrender until the last sands had run.[34] He took up his teaching assignment at Yale with outstanding success, and, made director of graduate studies in history, inaugurated practices of permanent value. He began work upon the second volume of the trilogy forecast in *Life and Labor*, though the prospect of completing it was all but hopeless. Until within a short time

[31] *New York Times*, Dec. 17, 1928, p. 3.

[32] *Ibid.*, May 4, 1929, p. 11. A description of this tour will be found in the Albert Kahn Foundation for the Foreign Travel of American Teachers, *Reports*, IX (New York, 1930), 11–47.

[33] A letter from Du Bose Heyward of July 25, 1930, expresses the novelist's appreciation of Phillips' work and his own dependence upon it.

[34] For information on this period of Phillips' life I am indebted to Professor Erwin R. Goodenough, of Yale, who was an intimate companion of his last years.

of his death, in January, 1934, he met his classes, and only the day before the end came, wrote to a loved friend, "I am down in body but not in spirit." He voiced no self-pity and insisted that, lying helpless, he could find pleasure in retracing in his mind the road that he had traveled. No soldier of the Old South, which he had loved and helped to raise from historical oblivion, ever met death with more calm fortitude and stoic composure.

That he was removed from the world of men before his pen could glean the acres of his "full-ripened grain" was a tragedy in American historiography. But so much had he already done that his place in it is secure. So long as historians turn to the study of the South, his work will stand as a landmark in the field.

XX

ALBERT J. BEVERIDGE

TRACY E. STREVEY
Northwestern University

✳

IN THE study of a biographer, and especially of one who may be designated as a "biographical historian," the critic is confronted with a double responsibility. Consideration must be given not only to the primary aim of the author, which is to present the life of some individual and his relations to the world in which he lived, but to the method used in handling historical materials, to the arrangement of facts and the various problems involved in the author's interpretation. In dealing with one central character, objectivity seems more difficult of attainment than when one is writing history in the accepted sense of the term. The resulting picture may be hazy and uncertain, or sharp and clear, according to the skill of the author and his adherence to the guiding principle of truth.

In a study of Albert J. Beveridge as a historian, author of *The Life of John Marshall*,[1] in four volumes, and an uncompleted two-volume *Abraham Lincoln*,[2] it is necessary to consider briefly those factors tending to influence his historical writing. Beveridge's father, of Scotch ancestry, came to Ohio as a young man from the piedmont region of Virginia. His mother was the granddaughter of Oliver Ross, a Scotch Presbyterian, who was born in Ireland and was the founder of the New Market settlement in

[1] Boston, 1916–19.

[2] *Abraham Lincoln, 1809–1858* (Boston, 1928).

374

Ohio following his migration to America in 1783.[3] Albert Beveridge was born on an Ohio farm in 1862, the child of a second marriage upon the part of both parents. At that time Beveridge's father and half-brothers were serving in the Union Army, and his earliest memories were of blue-clad soldiers returning from the Civil War.[4] Brought up in the Middle West during the years immediately following this conflict, Beveridge was exposed to Republican politics of the "bloody-shirt" variety. Living in a section of the country where Republicanism and patriotism were viewed as identical, it is little wonder that the youth received as his heritage an aggressive Americanism.

In 1868 the Beveridge family moved to Illinois in an effort to rebuild the family fortune lost through faith misplaced in indorsing the promissory notes of returned soldiers. After the lease of a large farm in Moultrie County, young Beveridge had his share of work and responsibility. From the age of twelve he experienced the life of a ploughboy; and before his sixteenth year he had been railroad laborer, logger, and teamster.[5] Again facing disaster, the family moved to Sullivan, Illinois, where by working at odd jobs Albert finished high school. Claude Bowers portrays the boy reading Plutarch and Emerson, so regaling the illiterate lumberman with stories of the campaigns of Caesar that they called him "historian."[6] During these years Beveridge came into contact with the Granger movement and the dilemma of the farmer. In much the same surroundings Lincoln had spent his youth, and this fact no doubt contributed to Beveridge's later understanding of Lincoln's early life.[7]

Determined to secure a college education, Beveridge wrote letters to several college presidents, explaining that he had no

[3] Claude Bowers, *Beveridge and the Progressive Era* (Boston, 1932), pp. 1–3; James A. Woodburn in *Dictionary of American Biography*, II, 231–33.

[4] Bowers, pp. 3–4.

[5] *Ibid.*, pp. 4–7.

[6] *Ibid.*, p. 8; *Who's Who in America, 1927; American Review of Reviews*, LXXV (June, 1927), 609.

[7] Paul M. Angle, "The Beveridge 'Lincoln,' " Lincoln Centennial Association, *Bulletin*, No. 13 (Dec. 1, 1928), p. 2.

money, no Latin, and no Greek but was anxious to enrol as a
student. Finally a reply came from the head of Asbury College,
later DePauw University, giving the minimum cost for one year.
Thereupon borrowing fifty dollars from a former employer, Beveridge
was soon in Greencastle, Indiana.[8] During his college
years Beveridge joined a fraternity, waited on tables, sold books
during the summer as far west as Iowa, and won the reputation
of being the best orator among the undergraduates. It was in
Iowa that he heard Senator Jonathan P. Dolliver and Robert G.
Ingersoll, and the impressions left by such speakers added to his
zest for public speaking. In 1884 Beveridge ventured forth as a
campaigner in behalf of James G. Blaine and the Republican
cause in Indiana. According to his own account, he "made the
American eagle look like a young robin just thrown from the
nest," and, it must be added, waved the "bloody shirt" with
abandon.[9]

As the winner of the state and interstate oratorical contests,
aside from numerous local victories, Beveridge graduated from
DePauw, assertive, sure of success, and inclined to be impatient
of less brilliant people. True, his only formal training in history
had been secured from a reading course under the direction of
John Clark Ridpath, professor of belles-lettres and history and
the author of several popular histories widely read at that time.[10]
It is doubtful if such a course had any influence on his later interest
in historical writing.

In reality it was from the study and practice of law that Beveridge
developed an abiding enthusiasm for constitutional law and
history. For twelve years after being admitted to the bar in
1887, Beveridge devoted his time to study and to cases usually
involving constitutional issues. According to Bowers, it was
during this period that Beveridge became interested in John
Marshall and determined to write a biography of the great chief
justice,[11] although many years were to elapse before this was begun
and completed. In the meantime Beveridge became a national
figure, subject to new forces and influences.

[8] Bowers, p. 12.   [10] *Dictionary of American Biography*, XV, 599.
[9] *Ibid.*, p. 22.   [11] Bowers, p. 545.

Thrust into politics in 1899, when he was elected to the United State Senate from Indiana, Beveridge served there until he was defeated by his Democratic opponent in 1911. In the following year he bolted the Republican party and served as the key-noter and convention chairman of the Progressive party. Running on the Progressive ticket in 1914, he was again defeated in the senatorial contest; and, following his reaffiliation with the Republican party, Beveridge lost for a third time in 1922. No doubt it was a bitter disappointment to Beveridge that the people of Indiana refused to return him to the Senate, especially in view of his long support of the amendment calling for the direct election of senators.[12]

Through all of these political vicissitudes Beveridge was a peculiar combination of conservative and progressive. In 1900 he was chiefly the former, although more liberal than some of the "old-guard" Republicans in Indiana. When elected to the Senate, Beveridge declared that he would stand "for the business interests of this country, when that means the welfare of all the people."[13] At the same time, being influenced by the prevalent hysteria of that day, he denounced organized labor.[14] While in the Senate, Beveridge advocated reduction of the tariff, conservation of natural resources, direct election of senators, antitrust legislation, pure-food laws, antichild labor laws, and government regulation of public utilities. His support of these measures illustrates his trend toward political liberalism.[15]

By 1912 he was truly progressive, but eight years later he was realigning with the conservative group of his party. During the World War he opposed government regulation of railroads and favored a sales tax because he held it to be less burdensome to business than corporation and income taxes.[16] Writing at this time, Beveridge defined true conservatism as a willingness to advocate whatever changes were made necessary by altered con-

[12] Ibid., pp. 424–25, 452–53, 530–35.

[13] John A. Coffin, "The Senatorial Career of Albert J. Beveridge, "Indiana Magazine of History, XXIV, 165.

[14] Current History, XXXVII (November, 1932), iv.

[15] Woodburn, loc. cit.　　　　　[16] Nation for May 17, 1922, CXIV, 586.

ditions; and he believed that only the Republican party could effect such progress.[17]

His public career was well calculated to affect his later writings. His acquaintance with practical politics, the methods and motives of political leaders, furnished him with a remarkable background for understanding political history. Because of his knowledge of constitutional law and experience in government, Beveridge was in a position to unravel and clarify many of the perplexing problems associated with earlier constitutional struggles in the United States. Furthermore, he was never halted by seemingly insurmountable obstacles.

Fact-finding was Beveridge's passion. Before taking his seat in Congress at the close of the Spanish-American War, he journeyed to the Philippine Islands in order to be prepared with specific information. Incidentally, he expected to receive the chairmanship of the Philippines Committee and a place on the Foreign Relations Committee.[18] In later years he went to the Southwest to investigate conditions in the territories then seeking statehood.[19] Armed with facts secured through hard work and application, Beveridge often felt himself to be better qualified than his colleagues. Henry Cabot Lodge in a letter to Roosevelt applauded the soundness of Beveridge's views and his store of information but believed that he should show more deference for the older senators.[20] Regardless of seniority rules or of "hazing" by his colleagues, Beveridge was delivering set speeches in the Senate within a month after his first admission to that body. The greater the opposition, the more determined he was to be heard.

For some years preceding the appearance of *The Life of John Marshall*, Beveridge was engaged in writing several books and numerous articles on a wide variety of subjects. Many of his vacations were spent abroad; and he recorded his impressions and experiences for *Collier's*, the *Review of Reviews*, and the *Satur-*

[17] "To the Women of America," *Collier's* for June 12, 1920, LXV, 8.

[18] R. V. Oulahan, *Current Hist.*, XXVI (June, 1927), 442.

[19] Coffin, *loc. cit.*, p. 174.   [20] Oulahan, *loc. cit.*, pp. 442–43.

day Evening Post. After returning from a visit to the Far East in 1903 to study the Russo-Japanese struggle, he published *The Russian Advance.* In 1915 he journeyed to Europe and prepared articles on the World War, doing his writing in a neutral nation in order to be removed from influences which might prejudice his point of view.[21]

From his speeches and essays one may learn his opinions on matters of national importance, some of which colored his later works. In an address before the New York City Republican Club on Lincoln's Birthday in 1898, Beveridge said:

We hear of a new Declaration of Independence. I prefer the old Declaration of the fathers. We need no new philosophy of society or of politics to-day. We need only a renaissance of common sense. Let the political philosophy of Abraham Lincoln be our guide.

If you ask me to state that philosophy in a phrase I should answer that his life spells out these two words, patriotic conservatism.[22]

Again we find Beveridge declaring in Boston on Grant's anniversary, April 27, 1898:

Partizanship should only be a method of patriotism. He who is a partizan merely for the sake of spoils is a buccaneer. He who is a partizan merely for the sake of a party name, is a ghost of the past among living events. . . . . But he who is the partizan of principle is a prince of citizenship; and such a partizan was Grant the practical.[23]

Beveridge was an American and proud of it, an imperialist who believed in the destiny of his country. In this role he ventured to reveal God's will, as follows:

And of all our race He has marked the American people as His chosen Nation finally to lead in the regeneration of the world. This is the divine mission of America, and it holds for us all profit, glory, happiness possible to man.[24]

In 1900, Beveridge made an address in Chicago in which he demanded the annexation of Cuba:

I speak for myself alone, but speaking thus, I say that it will be an evil day for Cuba when the Stars and Stripes come down from Morro

[21] *North American Review,* CCI (May, 1915), 655–56.
[22] Beveridge, *The Meaning of the Times and Other Speeches* (Indianapolis, 1908), pp. 28–29.
[23] *Ibid.,* p. 37.　　　　　　　[24] *Ibid.,* p. 85.

Castle. . . . . I say that Porto Rico is ours and ours for ever; the Philippines are ours and ours for ever; and Cuba ought to have been ours, and by the free choice of her people some day will be ours, and ours for ever.[25]

Thus speaking and writing on topics ranging widely from "Grant the Practical" to "The World's Debt to Methodism," Beveridge covered a vast amount of political, social, and economic territory.

This was Beveridge's background when he began his *Life of John Marshall* in 1913. He had little, if any, conception of historical criticism and scholarship. He had a good knowledge of constitutional law and, in the preparation of briefs and speeches, knew the value of citations to sound authorities. But so far as historical training was concerned, Beveridge was an "amateur." Yet his desire to write about Marshall's career had grown with the years. In 1908 he had suggested to the Century Company a one-volume interpretative biography which could be first published serially in some magazine. Rebuffed in this plan, Beveridge dictated four chapters in the summer of 1913, and then, discouraged, dropped his work for the senatorial battle of that year and a subsequent trip to Europe. It was on this voyage, according to Bowers, that "something clicked in his mind" and he saw the real task ahead.[26]

Upon his return to America he began again, this time with no stenographer but with paper and pencil. As he progressed, the project continually grew in scope. In 1916 appeared the first two volumes; and despite the warning of Worthington Ford as to length, Beveridge continued with the same expansiveness. The other volumes were published in 1919, to be followed by

[25] *Ibid.*, pp. 123–24. A brief list of his speeches and writings indicates the material covered. It is noteworthy that many topics bear directly or indirectly on constitutional issues: "America of Today and Tomorrow"; "The Meaning of the Times"; "The Russian Advance"; "The Invisible Government"; "What Is Back of the War"; "Vitality of the American Constitution"; "Lincoln, the Conservative"; "Grant, the Practical"; "Morton, the Nationalist"; "The March of the Flag"; "Trusts, a Development"; "Conservatism, the Spirit of National Restraint."

[26] Bowers, p. 548.

praise and suggestions that he write on Roger B. Taney and the younger William Pitt. Rejecting this advice, Beveridge decided on Lincoln as his next subject.[27]

Beveridge sought another Marshall; and Lincoln, whom he had admired for many years, appealed to him as the statesman around whom the history of the mid-nineteenth century could best be told. He began his new task in 1922, and until his death in 1927 held tenaciously to his original purpose of portraying the great "Emancipator" on the same scale and by the same method as he had dealt with Marshall. Almost ready to submit his first two volumes for criticism and revision, his sudden death interrupted the work near the halfway mark toward his final goal. W. C. Ford, long the friend and adviser of Beveridge, prepared and checked the manuscript for publication, adding a sketch of the period from the Lincoln-Douglas debates to 1861.[28] Thus it was that in July, 1928, Albert Beveridge's two-volume *Abraham Lincoln, 1809–1858*, left the press and took its place alongside his four-volume *Life of John Marshall*.

Upon these two studies Beveridge's reputation as a historian and biographer must rest. It is remarkable that a man trained as a lawyer and orator and leading an active life in politics for fourteen years should convert himself into a notable scholar and author. This Beveridge did, and he confided to his friends that he was thankful he had been forced out of politics.[29]

In considering Beveridge's workmanship, it must be remembered that because he was primarily a historian, not a biographer, he emphasized the times rather than the man in his masterpieces. He wrote in the preface to his *Life of John Marshall:*

In order to make clear the significance of Marshall's public activities, those episodes in American history into which his life was woven have been briefly stated. . . . .

Vitally important in their effect upon the conduct and attitude of

[27] *Ibid.*, pp. 549–61.

[28] *Abraham Lincoln*, I, vi.

[29] Bowers, p. 545; W. E. Barton, "A Noble Fragment: Beveridge's Life of Lincoln," *Mississippi Valley Historical Review*, XV, 497.

Marshall and of the leading characters of his time were the state of the country, the condition of the people, and the tendency of popular thought. Some reconstruction of the period has, therefore, been attempted. Without a background the picture and the figures in it lose much of their significance.[30]

From the outset Beveridge planned to write an account of the social, economic, political, and cultural conditions of the periods in which Marshall and Lincoln lived. He did not believe in placing a halo about the head of his hero. He expressed his own ideas concerning history by stating, "The science and scholarship of today require that the truth be told." In years not long gone by, according to Beveridge, "it was the fashion to write biography and history according to propaganda made plans"; but this old school of history and biography was wrong: it was a "cult of falsehood." These earlier historians had wrongfully assumed that the right had to be made beautiful, the wrong hideous, and that notable leaders had to have "at all times and under all circumstances, sound judgments, high souls, clean minds, fearless hearts." Beveridge insisted that this method, even if it was meant to inspire youthful readers, was bad. "How could anyone be so full of unction as Parson Weems told the people that Washington was from birth to death?"[31]

Beveridge held that the weak, as well as the strong, points of a man's character must be revealed by his biographer. He believed that in a biography the subject should not be isolated from his environment and associates. "What they say and do often give meaning and direction to the whole plot."[32] He felt that the intimate details of a man's life should be portrayed, such as his dress and words, his relations with other men, and his attitude toward women. In short, Beveridge determined that his biographies not only should be truthful and entertaining but should also depict the environment sufficiently at length to make clear its influence upon Marshall and Lincoln.

[30] *Life of John Marshall*, I, vi.

[31] Beveridge, "The Making of a Book," *Saturday Evening Post* for Oct. 23, 1926, CXCIX, 185.

[32] *Ibid.*, p. 182. *Current Hist.*, XXXVII (November, 1932), iv.

This was a large and perilous task. John Spencer Bassett thought it impossible to secure such a treatment without introducing much irrelevant material. Even Beveridge was aware of this difficulty and justified his position by pointing out that he was writing for persons not well informed on the history of the period. Bassett reminded him that, although the reading public does need to have things made plain, they should not be so plain as to be diffuse.[33]

To what extent was Beveridge able to realize this relationship of environment and man in his *Life of John Marshall?* Beginning the first volume with the cry, "The British are beaten!" in referring to Braddock's defeat, it is six pages before Marshall is mentioned. The discussion of Marshall's part in the adoption of the federal Constitution is accompanied by a long treatment of the attitude of the people of the United States toward union. This suggests the difficulties of communication, whereupon Beveridge introduces a chapter of thirty-seven pages on "Community Isolation." In a similar manner, earlier in Volume I, twenty-four pages are devoted to the hardships of the army at Valley Forge, and its seventh chapter deals with social conditions in 1783. In the third volume nearly one-half of the space is devoted to the Burr conspiracy. An analysis of this biography as a whole reveals that about 14 per cent of it is actually devoted to the man, 34 per cent to constitutional history, 32 per cent to political history, and the remainder scattered over miscellaneous topics.

About the same unusual apportionment of space exists in his *Abraham Lincoln.* In its second volume, the first three chapters, totaling over two hundred pages, deal exclusively with the fundamental causes of the Civil War. In fact, Lincoln does not figure prominently until the latter half of this volume.[34] Many pages, however, in both the *Marshall* and *Lincoln*, are devoted to the characteristics, family life, and problems of the two statesmen;

[33] J. S. Bassett in *American Historical Review*, XXII, 666. A. C. McLaughlin in the *American Bar Association Journal*, VII, 231, contends that the *Marshall* is not a balanced history of the period.

[34] Angle, *loc. cit.*, p. 5, notes that only 33 out of 350 published titles in the bibliography are directly concerned with Lincoln.

but this fact does not invalidate the general conclusion that these biographies are historical in scope and even to a large degree in treatment. They are histories built around a central personality. In view of Beveridge's emphasis on environment and general background, he probably did not subscribe to the "greatman" theory of history.

Neither did he believe there was any place for historical interpretation. He looked upon himself at all times as an objective historian and made this clear in the preface of each of his two major works. To him even the term "interpret" meant "something very like indolence, ignorance and egotism." "It means that certain facts are missing; . . . . that the author . . . . tells the reader what he thinks those facts would have meant if they had been as he imagines them to have been."[35] Beveridge believed that facts "justly arranged interpret themselves." Not only that, but interpretation was unnecessary. There is "no time for the author to argue or explain." Charles A. Beard answered Beveridge's statement that facts, properly arranged, eliminated interpretation by contending that "the moment you say arrangement you say interpretation."[36]

A. C. McLaughlin points out that Marshall was Beveridge's hero.[37] On the other hand, Lincoln appeared to Beveridge as an opportunist and "never the apostle of a cause; he was to become the perfect interpreter of public thought and feeling and so the instrument of events."[38] In his *Marshall*, Beveridge paints Jefferson as a self-seeking politician whose sinister course was only halted by the stern nationalist hand of the chief justice. Evidently the author's selection and arrangement of material were not alone responsible for all of his interpretation. At other times, however, the reader is left grasping in mid-air because of the bewildering mass of details with no conclusions. Edward S. Corwin, in his review of the *Life of John Marshall*, feels that Bever-

[35] "The Making of a Book," *Saturday Evening Post* for Oct. 23, 1926, CXCIX, 186.

[36] Quoted by N. W. Stephenson, *Amer. Hist. Rev.*, XXXIV, 616.

[37] McLaughlin, *loc. cit.*   [38] Beveridge, *Abraham Lincoln*, I, 107.

idge in his first volume failed to show "just *how* . . . . environment impinged upon the character of his hero."[39]

Beveridge did not attain his goal of objectivity. Because he endeavored to find place in his biographies for all the forces and factors influencing men and history, his pages sometimes serve only to confuse the reader. By the time he was well along with his writing of *Abraham Lincoln,* he had reached the conclusion that history had a utilitarian value. He believed that statesmanship must be based on a sound knowledge of history and that a true historical perspective weakened intolerance, bigoted partisanship, and fanaticism.[40]

As a layman writing history, he found the methods used in preparing speeches and popular articles no longer adequate. Hence he sought advice from the professional historian. He joined the American Historical Association, the Mississippi Valley Historical Association, the American Antiquarian Society, and various state historical societies.[41] Usually Beveridge attended the meetings of these organizations regularly in order to talk with other writers and discover and study methods of historical research.

Beveridge wrote to W. C. Ford in 1924 that "scholarship cannot compromise with falsehood; and although I am not a scholar, I have got from you and from others, but especially from you, what I hope and believe is the spirit of scholarship." He found that truth-telling brought its penalties, for by so doing he sometimes raised "a storm with the Mid-Victorians."[42]

There is no doubt of Beveridge's diligence in research. After he concluded that he had unearthed all the facts relating to a subject, he carefully arranged them in their apparent proper order. Topic after topic in logical sequence was first handled in this fashion. Thus Beveridge slaved at his task. He went through thousands of records, letters, manuscripts, and newspapers. In

[39] E. S. Corwin, *Miss. Valley Hist. Rev.,* IV, 117.

[40] *Outlook* for May 11, 1927, CXLVI, 44.

[41] *Who's Who in America, 1927.*   [42] Bowers, pp. 566–67.

some cases he used a magnifying glass in order to decipher small print on old, yellowed paper. On one occasion he complained that progress was slow: only five thousand notes had been collected.[43] A false rumor has it that he had a large staff of research assistants. In truth, he did his own work and only used a secretary occasionally to copy from papers he had marked. As a rule Beveridge did even this grinding labor without any aid.

Nor in the actual writing did Beveridge spare himself. To revise and then revise again was the keynote of his work. He thought it best to write the first draft of a chapter with material fresh in mind but without references or footnotes. When finally the narrative ran smoothly, then, as Beveridge wrote, "comes the labor of correcting and enriching this draft by supporting each statement from the mass of data relating to that chapter." So came more revisions as a result of corrections and additions, always holding to the principle of truth. It has been said that one chapter of *Abraham Lincoln* was re-written fifteen times, others even more. Beveridge declared before his death that *Abraham Lincoln* would require a complete revision despite the fact it had already been re-written from eight to fifteen times.[44]

Furthermore, Beveridge sent many of his chapters to leading historians for criticism and correction, and they spared him the embarrassment of many errors. In the preface to both *Marshall* and *Lincoln*, acknowledgments are made to scholars such as J. W. Weik, T. C. Pease, A. C. Cole, U. B. Phillips, C. A. Beard, J. F. Jameson, N. W. Stephenson, J. S. Bassett, F. L. Owsley, E. Channing, W. E. Dodd, C. W. Alvord, W. C. Ford, and many others. At least fifty co-operated with Beveridge by giving him the benefit of their own knowledge and scholarship.

Few works ever published have been so heavily documented as the *Marshall* and *Lincoln*. Many of their pages are a "rivulet of text flowing through a meadow of footnotes." A review of the *Marshall* in the *Nation* declares that it outdoes a Ph.D. thesis in

[43] *Ibid.*, pp. 551, 565.

[44] "The Making of a Book," *Saturday Evening Post* for Oct. 23, 1926, CXCIX, 182, 185, 186; *New York Times*, April 28, 1927.

this respect.[45] In fact, Beveridge used many unnecessary references, although they provide for the scholar a wealth of suggestive material. They sometimes impede rapid reading, but their value makes any adverse criticism of their length seem petty and unconvincing. Corwin concluded that this heavy documentation was due to Beveridge's great desire to show historians that he knew the game.[46] In the first volume of *Lincoln* the opening twenty pages are footnoted ninety-four times, many notes so long as to occupy half a page. In the first volume of *Marshall* the same number of pages have sixty-four footnotes.* All six volumes average approximately three footnotes per page, and each footnote often contains several citations. In the use of footnotes Beveridge was not always judicious . He was prone to accept a fact if a contemporary document could be found. This at times led to error through a lack of proper discrimination. Taking a few footnotes at random and checking them against the sources revealed a high degree of accuracy. Bassett, although critical of the profuse documentation in *Marshall*, praised Beveridge for his devotion to truth.[47]

In all of his writing, Beveridge emphasized the use of primary source material. No doubt because of his legal training, he realized the value of hunting out every clue and authentic source. In this procedure he employed newspapers, periodicals, letters, manuscripts, diaries, memoirs, state and federal papers, and documents. In his "The Making of a Book"[48] he warned writers that newspapers should be used cautiously and only with a due regard to each paper's policy; that reminiscences were often unreliable; and that letters to a wife usually told the truth. Whenever possible, he relied upon manuscripts in preference to secondary works. Information gained from the latter was employed to add color to his narrative, but he preferred to pack his pages with citations from the sources. An examination of both *Marshall*

[45] *Nation* for Apr. 10, 1920, CX, 479. See also, Barton, *loc. cit.*, p. 498.

[46] *Miss. Valley Hist. Rev.*, IV, 117.

[47] *Amer. Hist. Rev.*, XXII, 667.

[48] *Saturday Evening Post* for Oct. 23, 1926, CXCIX, 185.

and *Lincoln* indicates that primary sources were used from 90 to 96 per cent of the time. Regardless of the drudgery, Beveridge ransacked much material passed over by other historians. His industry was rewarded by bringing to light obscure phases of Marshall's and Lincoln's careers, such as Lincoln's record in the Illinois legislature and his early position on slavery. At other times he succeeded in correcting mistaken impressions.

There are, of course, some errors in statement and judgment in his biographies. It is rather preposterous even to suggest that Lincoln was suddenly changed into another and entirely different man by hearing Seward speak for the first time. Beveridge also states that, when Lincoln and Mary Todd were married, the "ring-and-book" form of wedding ceremony was used for the first time in Springfield. Barton says it had been used eight times before in that city by Rev. Charles Dresser. Corwin detected only three misprints in the first two volumes of *Marshall*.[49] Beveridge was a careful workman, and errors of fact in his volumes are hard to find.

Important faults, however, seem to lie in Beveridge's interpretation, although he, like other modern historians, held that true scholars had "no more business with a prejudice or fixed idea than the chemist, the biologist or the astronomer." He pointed out that those who wrote subjectively were "promoters of a legend, nurses of a myth." As to whether a writer should have an opinion, Beveridge frankly stated: "If he wants to give his opinion as the champion of a cause let him say so, and not palm off his views as history or biography. If he means to propagandize, let him do it honestly; let him write a tract or hire a hall."[50]

Nevertheless, Beveridge was unable to live up to his high purpose. He was an ardent nationalist and expansionist. He had opposed the entrance of the United States into the World War and later denounced the League of Nations. He believed that the schools should devote some time each day to the teaching of patriotism, to instruction in the "pricelessness of our institu-

[49] *Abraham Lincoln*, I, 355, 476; Barton, *loc. cit.*, p. 501; Corwin, *loc. cit.*, p. 118.
[50] "The Making of a Book," *Saturday Evening Post* for Oct. 23, 1926, CXCIX, 186.

tions," and "to exhortation that the highest duty of every boy and girl is to live and die for the Republic."[51] He likewise advocated study of the Canadian Constitution in the belief that it provided a strong central government without selfish interests hiding behind the cloak of "State Rights."[52] To Beveridge there was more danger in a decentralized government than in extending federal powers. In this respect he was a Federalist, a Hamiltonian; and he could not rise above his political views.[53]

It is in Beveridge's study of Marshall that his bias becomes distinctly noticeable. Bowers declares: "He was using Jefferson as a foil for Marshall throughout the biography."[54] As a boy he had learned to associate state rights with secession; and Jefferson, largely responsible for the Virginia and the Kentucky Resolutions, was thus chargeable with the growth of disunionism. The facts that Jefferson was an enemy of Hamilton, a friend of the French Revolution, and, as president, was the one who led an attack on the federal judiciary, were enough to condemn him in Beveridge's eyes.

Upon the publication of the Marshall volumes, reviewers agreed that Beveridge was a staunch advocate of a strong central government and made Marshall his hero. Bassett added that, although Beveridge had Federalist leanings, he had tried to escape them.[55] According to Dr. McLaughlin, "We are not furnished a calm portrayal of the great forces of the time," but Jefferson is made the background to "show off the gleaming worth of Marshall's supreme genius."[56] In reading these volumes, one finds Beveridge explaining that, although government meant law and order and the fulfilment of obligations, the people were not interested. He attacked the "monstrous individualism" growing out of this "dank soil" and felt that na-

[51] "School and Nation" in *The Meaning of the Times and Other Speeches*, p. 239.

[52] *Saturday Evening Post* for Sept. 9, 1911; *Rev. of Revs.*, XLIV, 471.

[53] Bowers, p. 555.

[54] *Ibid.*, 554; *Amer. Bar Assoc. Jour.*, VII, 231.

[55] *Amer. Hist. Rev.*, XXII, 668.

[56] *Amer. Bar Assoc. Jour.*, VII, 231; Corwin agrees in *Miss. Valley Hist. Rev.*, IV, 118.

tionalism suffered while "democracy marched arm in arm with State Rights."[57] He further pointed out that, if Marshall should succeed in his purpose, orderly government would be assured and the judiciary placed in its rightful position.[58] In fact, Beveridge was blind to some of the great issues involved in Jeffersonian Republicanism. He did not appreciate the yearning of the small farmers for a share in government.

Possibly Beveridge, who had admired Marshall for years, was so captivated by his extraordinary abilities that he could not or would not see any mistakes in his career. Certainly, W. E. Dodd, J. F. Jameson, Max Farrand, H. J. Eckenrode, and others criticized his treatment of Jefferson while the work was in manuscript. In reply to their advice and warning, Beveridge attacked Jefferson as a "reckless demagogue" and was disgusted to find out what "sort of man he was personally."[59] He was unwilling to change his views and at times slashed into Jefferson without quarter. He pictured Marshall as a brave soldier, but Jefferson as a rich man who did not enlist during the Revolution. Again, Jefferson was shown both as a demagogue and a secretive autocrat, according to need. Channing alone seemed to have accepted Beveridge's estimate of the master of "Monticello."[60]

In some instances Beveridge apparently closed his eyes to material which reflected against Marshall. In his treatment of the Virginia Constitutional Convention of 1829, although he shows Marshall to have been a Conservative, he does not make clear that the Chief Justice played a leading part in maintaining the *status quo* in his native state in order to leave the big planters in control. Nor does he point out that Marshall aided in the defeat of gradual abolition plans in Virginia at a time when other states seemed likely to follow her lead. Marshall is depicted as believing in sending negroes back to Africa, but this imperfectly represents his position on slavery in the Virginia Convention.[61]

[57] *Life of John Marshall*, I, 285; III, 48.

[58] *Ibid.*, III, 113–14.   [59] Bowers, p. 557.

[60] *Ibid.*, pp. 556–57; *Life of John Marshall*, I, 126–27; III, 148–49.

[61] *Life of John Marshall*, IV, 472–508.

Again the biographer has been charged with partisanship in his defense of Marshall and Burr in connection with the Burr treason trial. Bassett blamed Beveridge's partiality for Burr upon his liking for the Chief Justice; for to support the one was to uphold the other.[62] However, Beveridge's thesis that Burr never plotted disunion is borne out by the latest research on the subject. According to Professor I. J. Cox, Mexico was the focus of Burr's "conspiracy."[63]

Beveridge probably wrote the truest account of Lincoln's career to 1859 that has yet appeared. The author gained in tolerance as his research advanced, and in 1926 he admitted that he had been too severe in his treatment of Jefferson.[64] If anything, Beveridge judged Lincoln too critically. This is the more surprising when it is remembered that the author had been nurtured on Lincoln "myths," and as a young Republican had shared in the worship of the "martyred" president.

In the chapter entitled "Seeds of War," Beveridge leans toward the South. He was shocked by the abolitionist literature and its attack upon the Constitution. Thus, while he lets facts speak for themselves, he selected for presentation extreme examples of antislavery propaganda and tactics. Differing from the way he treated Marshall, Beveridge tested critically Lincoln's every act. From this ordeal Lincoln emerges chiefly as a politician, an interpreter of public opinion, and as an "instrument of events." Despite this general criticism, most students will probably agree with William E. Barton's conclusion that "the excellencies so far excel the faults that one could excuse himself from any attempt to point out any of the defects."[65] Because of its objectivity, the *Lincoln* is probably more satisfying to scholars than the *Marshall*. Beveridge showed a capacity for growth as a historian. The lessons of experience and the spur of criticism led

[62] *Amer. Hist. Rev.*, XXV, 516.

[63] *Dictionary of American Biography*, III, 314–21.

[64] Bowers, p. 558; *Outlook* for May 11, 1927, CXLVI, 44.

[65] *Miss. Valley Hist. Rev.*, XV, 508.

him to approach Lincoln with a more scholarly attitude and an improved technique.

Beveridge's prose often has great dramatic power. Yet even his style changed as he gained experience. In the first two *Marshall* volumes the influence of his palmy oratorical days carried over into his writing. Bassett objected to the lavish use of such inept phrases as "Pinckney rode Gerry hard"; Bushrod Washington "had no more political acumen than a turtle"; and "the President grasped by the forelock this possibility for peace."[66] In the last two volumes his manner of writing is more subdued. All of his works are packed with anecdotes, picturesque incidents, and interesting details. His narrative usually is forward-moving, and at times it is brilliantly told. As a rule, Beveridge was markedly successful in handling masses of facts and details in such a way as to hold the attention of his readers.

Beveridge ranks as one of the great biographers and historians of recent times. His faults were those of a sincere but opinionated man, and he overcame most of these before he began his later work. He proposed to write for the layman as well as the historian. How well he succeeded is shown by the many favorable reviews of his books and the deep regret expressed that he did not live to complete his *Lincoln*. The wide sale and use of the biographies further illustrate his success as an author.

Professor McLaughlin, although refusing to overlook its faults, wrote that this generation or the next is not likely to see another such skilful biography of John Marshall.[67] Bassett felt that Beveridge deserved high esteem as a historian who was able to reach the reading public.[68] Nathaniel W. Stephenson wrote of Beveridge's *Abraham Lincoln* that, in spite of certain peculiarities of method, "the book remains an invaluable contribution."[69] Other critics, including Claude Bowers, W. E. Barton, Rupert Hughes, R. V. Oulahan, W. C. Ford, and E. S. Corwin,

[66] *Amer. Hist. Rev.*, XXII, 669.

[67] *Amer. Bar Assoc. Jour.*, VII, 233.

[68] *Amer. Hist. Rev.*, XXV, 517.   [69] *Ibid.*, XXXIV, 619.

tempered their criticism with praise for the man and his work.[70] Even before his death, full recognition came to Beveridge. Honorary degrees, the Pulitzer Prize, and the Roosevelt Foundation Prize for his *Life of John Marshall* all evidenced the admiration of his colleagues.

Beveridge lifted the writing of historical biography in the United States to a high level of achievement, both as to style and content. His synthesis of history about the life of one man, his amazing research, and his unusual degree of accuracy set an example that few have equaled. Rejected by his constituents in political life, Beveridge carved out a new and distinguished career as a historian and biographer.

[70] See Corwin, *Miss. Valley Hist. Rev.*, VI, 583; Ford, *Amer. Hist. Rev.*, XXXVIII, 350; Oulahan, *loc. cit.*, p. 444; Barton, *loc. cit.*, p. 510.

XXI

VERNON LOUIS PARRINGTON

WILLIAM T. UTTER

Denison University

KANSAS in the heyday of the Populist movement may not have been the blissful heaven of which the poet once wrote; but to be young in Emporia while Mrs. Mary Lease and the "Sockless" Jerry Simpson were on the hustings might well give one's political thinking a twist to the left, and that permanently. Vernon Louis Parrington's father, judge of probate in Emporia, was much concerned over the avowed Populism of his son. Two years at Harvard had not given him immunity against the radicalism which was now reaching alarming proportions in Kansas. The effects of this early exposure to Populism were still observable in Parrington when, thirty years later, he published the first history of American thought to be written in the liberal tradition. His liberalism by that time would be described as Jeffersonianism, yet lacking still that full respectability which several generations of readers had come to expect in the viewpoint of those who surveyed American letters.

The career of Parrington in those thirty years was not greatly different from that of many another successful college teacher. Graduating from Harvard in 1893, he became an instructor in English and French at the College of Emporia, the Presbyterian school where he had studied before entering Harvard. He left Emporia in 1897 to accept a professorship at the University of Oklahoma, where he remained until he lost his position as the result of a political upheaval in 1908. From that date until his death in 1929 he was associated with the University of Washington, in Seattle. In 1903–4 he made an extended visit to England and France, and again in 1923 he was in Europe. Members of his own guild may have noted, with or without comment, that he had never experienced the accolade of the Ph.D. and that he had received his Master's degree from the College of Emporia while he was teaching there.

His friendships among his faculty associates were not extensive. His closest friend was his neighbor, J. Allen Smith, the political scientist, whose work, *The Spirit of American Government*, was such a devastating criticism of the established conception of the American constitutional system that it became something of a Bible for the rising Progressive movement. Daily association with this stimulating neighbor was of inestimable importance in the shaping of Parrington's ideas in the fields of politics and economics.[1]

Of Parrington's extraordinary skill as a teacher there is abundant testimony. His manner before his classes was informal and kindly, although he had the bearing and appearance of a natural aristocrat. He developed a notable series of courses in the history of American literature and thought and in the English literature of the nineteenth century. A "class with Parrington" was thought by the more intellectual students to be a necessary part of their college regimen. His interest in English literature as evidenced in his teaching centered in John Ruskin, Matthew Arnold, and William Morris. In them he saw the combination of cultural and politico-economic interests to which he had given his own sympathies and which his own writings were to exemplify.[2]

[1] Parrington dedicated his work to J. Allen Smith. He wrote an introduction to Smith's *The Growth and Decadence of Constitutional Government* (New York, 1930). Both works are invaluable in studying Parrington's viewpoints on political theory.

[2] Biographical sketches of Parrington appear in *Who's Who in America, 1928–1929;* in the *Dictionary of American Biography;* and in J. B. Harrison, *Vernon Louis Parrington, American Scholar* ("University of Washington Chapbooks," No. 31 [Seattle, 1929]). E. H. Eby writes appreciatively of him in the foreword to Parrington's third volume. See also Russell

It must have been apparent to all who knew him that Parrington was essentially an artist. To all classes it was shown in the care, almost meticulous, with which he polished his phrases, the search in his interpretations for harmonious balance and proportion, as if it were a structure of stone, rather than of ideas, which he was erecting. Those who knew him intimately were aware of his interest in architecture and painting; that he had studied in those fields during his first European residence; that he had even considered entering them professionally. He had more than ordinary ability as a poet, according to his friends, although his own judgment did not permit of publication. In his writing, this artistic temperament was to be demonstrated not only in his constant effort to attain unity but also in the care with which each phrase was turned—care which brings to mind the artistry of the eighteenth-century conversationalist.

It was characteristic of the man that he chose to work in silence on his comprehensive study of liberal thought in America. It would have been more typical of the craft to which he belonged to have published chapters of his study as it progressed in the form of monographs, thereby apprising the scholarly world of his endeavors. When, in 1927, he had reached the climactic date of 1860 in the course of his work, he released his first two volumes. The plan for his third and final volume was roughed in, awaiting only the finishing touch. But death intervened before its completion. The tragedy of his death was the more poignant because he left the rafters of his structure unsheathed and the scaffold yet standing.[3]

Blankenship, "Vernon L. Parrington," in the *Nation* for Aug. 7, 1929, CXXIX, 141–42. The writer of this essay is also indebted to Professor J. B. Harrison, of the University of Washington, for information courteously furnished by correspondence.

[3] The three volumes collectively comprise *Main Currents in American Thought: An Interpretation of American Literature from the Beginnings to 1920*, Vol. I: *The Colonial Mind, 1620–1800* (New York, 1927); Vol. II: *The Romantic Revolution in America, 1800–1860* (New York, 1927); Vol. III: *The Beginnings of Critical Realism in America, 1860–1920* (New York, 1930). The third volume, completed to 1900 only, includes reprints of "The Incomparable Mr. Cabell," which originally appeared in the *Pacific Review*, December, 1921, and "Sinclair Lewis: Our Own Diogenes," which appeared as No. 5 of the "University of Washington Chapbooks" (Seattle, 1927). Parrington contributed articles on "Nathaniel Hawthorne"

That the author of *Main Currents in American Thought* is entitled to consideration in a volume of essays on historiography is made clear by the comparison of his work with the achievements of earlier writers in the field. *The Cambridge History of American Literature*, to which Parrington had contributed a chapter on "The Puritan Divines," was the only satisfactory survey of the whole field of American writing. Despite its unquestioned value, critics agreed on the unevenness of the chapters and the lack of unity inevitable in a co-operative work; they mildly condemned the body of the work by giving higher praise to the bibliographies. Of the making of textbooks in the field, there had been no end; but these followed so stereotyped a pattern that one disgusted authority declared that he could dictate a text after the accepted style in three days.[4]

The first systematic study was that of Charles Francis Richardson, whose two-volume *History of American Literature* (1886–88) was written while he was pioneering in the teaching of the subject at Dartmouth. His work was painstakingly done, but he was too exclusively concerned with the rank which American writers merited in comparison with their European contemporaries, and failed largely either to describe or appreciate the historical background against which their writing was done. He, like Barrett Wendell, whose volume, *A Literary History of America*, appeared in 1900, has been roundly accused of doing more than justice to writers from New England. Professor Wendell, indeed, has been described as suffering from nearsightedness induced by the environment of Harvard. Thirty-four pages out of more than five hundred sufficed for the two chapters in which Wendell com-

and "American Literature to the End of the Nineteenth Century" to the *Encyclopaedia Britannica* (14th ed., 1929). He also wrote an article on "Brook Farm" for the *Encyclopaedia of Social Sciences*. He wrote a chapter on "The Development of Realism" in *The Reinterpretation of American Literature*, ed. Norman Foerster (New York, 1928). He edited, and wrote the introduction to, *The Connecticut Wits* ("American Authors" series [New York, 1926]). He contributed reviews to such periodicals as the *Nation*, the *New Republic*, and the *Saturday Review of Literature*.

4 Particularly valuable essays on the problems of the writing of the history of American literature are those of Fred L. Pattee, Arthur M. Schlesinger, and Harry H. Clark, which appear in *The Reinterpretation of American Literature*, ed. Norman Foerster (New York, 1928).

mented on the literature of the West and South. He was much
concerned with English writers and English historical conditions, endeavoring seriously to discover the factors which lay
behind the deviation of the colonists from the pattern set by
their contemporaries in the motherland. The usefulness of the
work of these two scholars has declined much more rapidly than
has that of Moses Coit Tyler, whose volumes, *A History of
American Literature during the Colonial Period* and *The Literary History of the American Revolution*,[5] were published between the years
1880 and 1909. This work, because of its fairness, scholarly discrimination, and the thoroughness with which it is documented,
has not as yet been superseded. In discussing his aim and method,
he wrote:

> In the composition of a work of this kind, it is a very grave judicial
> responsibility that the author is forced to assume, it is also a very sacred
> responsibility. . . . . I have studied, as I believe, every American writer
> of the colonial time, in his extant writings . . . . . Upon no topic of
> literary estimation have I formed an opinion at second hand. In every
> instance, I have examined for myself the work under consideration.[6]

That Professor Tyler worked faithfully under the burden of his
"very sacred responsibility" is apparent to all who read his
books. His work is not vitiated, at any rate, by dependence upon
ephemeral secondhand estimates.

It is not to be inferred that the impetus which compelled Parrington to make a fresh attack on the subject was in the shortcomings of his predecessors. He himself attributed much of his
inspiration to the reading of Taine's *History of English Literature*.
One may conjecture that Parrington's admiration for Taine's
work was based on his agreement with its method and scope. In
concluding the introduction to his voluminous study, he writes:

> The question as now stated is this: given a literature, a philosophy,
> a society, an art, or a certain group of arts, what is the moral state of

5 M. C. Tyler, *A History of American Literature during the Colonial Period, 1607–1765* (2 vols.;
New York, 1880–1909); *The Literary History of the American Revolution, 1763–1783* (2 vols.;
New York, 1897, 1905).

6 Tyler, *History of American Literature during the Colonial Period*, I, vii.

things which produce it? And what are the conditions of race, epoch and environment the best adapted to produce this moral state? I intend to write the history of a literature, and to seek in it for the psychology of a people.[7]

More important than Taine, save possibly for the kindling of some initial enthusiasm, was the inspiration which came to Parrington from the work of contemporary American historians. A friend wrote:

In American scholarship, he discovered the most stimulating development in the field of history. A new method worthy of description was being developed in history. Until students of literature should come to view literary facts as historians were coming to view historical facts the interpretation of American literature would remain lifeless, a meager display of volumes opened at illuminated pages like medieval manuscripts under a glass in a museum.[8]

In particular Parrington's work expressed his own rather ungenerous revolt against the "Ph.D. tradition," which in his opinion dominated the scholarly work being done in the leading American universities. To him, much of the product of research in American literature in the graduate schools was the unimaginative assembling of trivial facts. He felt that American scholarship in this field was still burdened by what Santayana once called the "heavy handicap of the genteel tradition." With Parrington the adjective "belletristic" was a favorite term of opprobrium. Not that the aesthetic element in literature was lacking in appeal to him—quite the contrary! But in attempting to formulate the method and approach from which American literature could be studied profitably, he was well aware that the aesthetic test would yield a scanty harvest. A study of American writing as an expression of American thought, on the other hand, would leave the writer untrammeled, free to use the methods which in his opinion had been so productive in the field of American historiography.

[7] Hippolyte A. Taine, *History of English Literature* (tr. by H. Van Laun; 2 vols.; New York, 1896), I, xxiii. Taine is generally conceded to be the first author to attempt a general interpretation of English literature.

[8] Harrison, *Vernon Louis Parrington, American Scholar*, p. 13.

The most sacred canon in the code of the "scientific" historian is that he shall withhold the conclusions both from the reader and himself until the "evidence" is thoroughly sifted and the facts properly arranged. The conclusion must, in some way, virtually write itself. It is doubtful if any great amount of writing has been done in perfect conformity with the rule; yet it remains a test of orthodoxy. Parrington was willing to be branded as a heretic. In the foreword to his first volume he states frankly:

The point of view from which I have endeavored to evaluate the materials, is liberal rather than conservative, Jeffersonian rather than Federalistic; and very likely in my search I have found what I went forth to find, as others have discovered what they were seeking. Unfortunately the *mens aequa et clara* is the rarest of attributes, and dead partisanships have a disconcerting way of coming to life again in the pages of their historians. That the vigorous passions and prejudices of the times I have dealt with may have found an echo in my judgments is, perhaps, to be expected; whether they have distorted my interpretation and vitiated my analysis is not for me to determine.[9]

One who was well acquainted with his methods of writing states that he "habitually began with his thesis—a phrase, a sentence, or a revealing figure. . . . . So imperious was the habit of this procedure that his ability to write would be blocked until he had in mind a perfectly crystallized concept expressible at the maximum in one sentence."[10] It is, of course, to be assumed that this intellectual neatness was achieved by Parrington only after a long period spent in the assimilation of his facts.

It has been stated that Parrington followed the study of architecture as a hobby. One might almost deduce this fact from the symmetry of the tables of contents of his three volumes, for each is divided into three books, which in turn are separated into parts, each with its orderly subdivisions. No better evidence will be found of the precision of Parrington's mind.

The outline having been drafted, the sections were completed as circumstance or mood permitted. Each section was then altered in emphasis to fit with its neighbors. "As many as twelve

[9] *The Colonial Mind*, p. i.   [10] *The Beginnings of Critical Realism*, p. vi.

times he rewrote a single section in this complex and delicate effort for harmonious adjustment."[11] The third volume, published in its unfinished state, gives almost complete evidence of his method. The outline was virtually complete, his intentions are fairly clear, his conclusions may be inferred; yet the writing was scarcely half-done. Because of these habits of thought and of method, one may attempt in a paragraph to summarize the complete work.

The theme is: "Give some account of the genesis and development in American letters of certain germinal ideas that have come to be reckoned traditionally American—how they came into being here, how they were opposed, and what influence they have exerted in determining the form and scope of our characteristic ideals and institutions."[12] In the period from the first settlement to the triumph of Jeffersonianism the main interest is in the transplanting into the New World of Old World liberalisms: English independency, French romantic theory, supplemented by contributions of English Whiggery. The resulting doctrine of natural rights became entangled in New England with an absolutist theology, a struggle dominating the first century. With the influx of new immigrants came diverse political philosophies, French romantic theories, spreading widely in the up-country, which produced a native agrarianism, while English liberalism with its laissez faire doctrines dominated the commercial centers. With the triumph of Jefferson is ushered in a period of romance and rapid economic change in which one witnesses the rivalry of the varied sectional philosophies: the English laissez faire, French equalitarianism, physiocratic agrarianism, and the strange counter-philosophy of Greek democracy based on slavery. The romantic optimism of the ante-bellum decades passed into a period of slow decay after the Civil War, succumbing to the three forces: the stratification of the economic system, the rise of a mechanistic science, and the spread of a spirit of skepticism. This skepticism arose in part from the writings of European intellectuals but more directly from the industrialization of

[11] Ibid., p. vii.   [12] The Colonial Mind, p. iii.

the country and the teachings of the physical scientists. One ends the study with a feeling of pessimism, doubting whether the American middle class has been a trustworthy custodian of the American tradition of liberalism.

An appraisal of the works of Parrington in detail would be an arduous task. One is compelled, in an essay of limited scope, to use the "sample method," with its limitations and possible injustices. It is safe, at the outset, to bestow high praise upon his prose style. More erudite scholars may or may not have written on American letters; but few, if any, have shown the facility of expression, the variety and pungency of phrasing, or the wealth of vocabulary which Parrington displayed. Whether writing on "The Puritan Heritage," "The Skepticism of the House of Adams," or on the felicity of Cabell's style, his versatility is not exhausted. It may be that he was at times betrayed by his own resourcefulness, for he leans toward polysyllables and is tempted into the use of descriptive titles for sections of his study, such as "The Passing of the Tie-Wig School" and "The Authentic Brahmin," which carry a sting along with their cleverness.[13]

His greatest skill is displayed in the blending of each personality with the social and intellectual background in which he moved. Take, for example, this passage in his treatment of Nathaniel Ward, "Elizabethan Puritan":

The most caustic pen of early New England was wielded by the lawyer-minister and wit, Nathaniel Ward of Ipswich, author of the crotchety little book *The Simple Cobbler of Aggawam*, and chief compiler of the celebrated *Body of Liberties*. He is a strange figure to encounter in the raw little settlements. To come into his presence is to feel oneself carried back to an earlier age, when the courtly wits were weaving their silken terms into gorgeous tapestries. . . . . Far more strikingly than any of his emigrant brethren he belonged in taste and tempera-

---

[13] Particularly valuable reviews are: Charles A. Beard, "Fresh Air in American Letters," *Nation* for May 18, 1927, CXXIV, 560; Percy H. Boynton, *New Republic* for July 6, 1927, LI, 181; Kenneth B. Murdock, *Yale Review*, XVII (January, 1928), 382; T. Vernor Smith, *International Journal of Ethics*, XXXVIII (October, 1927), 112; Henry S. Canby, *Saturday Rev. of Lit.* for June 25, 1927, III, 925; Morris Cohan, *New Republic* for Jan. 28, 1931, LXV, 303; T. V. Smith, *Intl. Jour. of Ethics*, XLI (April, 1931), 386.

ment to the later Elizabethan world, which lingered on into the reigns of James and Charles, zealously cultivating its quaint garden of letters, playing with inkhorn terms, and easing its cares with clever conceits.[14]

Thus, in a short paragraph is laid the foundation for a brilliant essay of appraisal. Parrington greets Ward with enthusiasm, for his work comes as an oasis in the arid writings of his contemporaries.

The paragraph introducing William Gilmore Simms, "Charleston Romancer," illustrates Parrington's ability to compress ideas without sacrificing ease of expression:

From the background of Old Charleston emerged, about the year 1825, the figure of Gilmore Simms, lately a drug clerk but now come to the dignity of admission to the bar; a tall, vigorous young fellow, with little formal schooling, no Latin or Greek, without land or slaves, but heavily involved in Byronic odes and like unprofitable investments; a social nobody soon to be married at the age of twenty to a girl of no better station than his own, who offered himself as candidate for the poet laureateship of the South. A somewhat presumptuous proceeding on the part of a plebeian quite outside the cultivated circle of the Petigrus and Grimkés and Hugers and Legarés, who were the accepted custodians of Charleston culture and who did not take kindly to ambitious newcomers. They regarded literature as a polite art that could flourish only in polite circles, and they turned a cold shoulder upon a young man whose ways suggested the Carolina buckra.[15]

The very readability of Parrington's prose might lead the critic to assume subconsciously that thoughts so well expressed must, of course, be well founded in historical fact. If one's skepticism should be awakened, it is often impossible to check the sources of his statements, for, aside from appended bibliographies, one has only occasional citations to guide him. In an ungenerous chapter on John Marshall, for example, the reader is casually referred to Beveridge's biography.[16] The lack of thorough documentation, which may have been the policy of the publisher, makes it difficult likewise to judge the extent to which Parring-

[14] *The Colonial Mind*, p. 76.

[15] *The Romantic Revolution in America*, p. 125.   [16] *Ibid.*, p. 475.

ton was dependent on secondary sources. He evidently took no oath, as did Moses Coit Tyler, to form "no estimates at second-hand," for to have read all the works which he cites would manifestly have been impossible.

The more serious misstatements of fact which various reviewers have brought to light have involved, as well, an element of misinterpretation. Two examples may be given here in some detail. In the opening chapter of his first volume Parrington contrasts the political implications of Calvinism and Lutheranism. Calvinism he holds to have been the foe of democratic liberalism. In contrast: "The teachings of Luther, erected on the major principle of justification by faith, conducted straight to political liberty, and he refused to compromise or turn away from pursuing the direct path."[17] In carrying out the argument, Parrington associates Lutheran origins with the thinking of Roger Williams and the Separatists generally, which accounts in part for their long struggle with the Calvinistic Puritans. One may attack both the fundamental assumption as to the political implications of the two systems of thought and also the supposition that the opponents of the Puritans were in any great degree dominated by Lutheran theology.[18]

Another example of error in interpretation may be seen in his discussion of Thomas Jefferson's political philosophy, which, according to Parrington, was "an amalgam of English and French liberalisms, supplemented by the conscious influence of the American frontier. That fusion early took place in his mind."[19] As instances of the influence of French humanitarianism he submits Jefferson's advocacy in 1769 of a bill in the Virginia assembly which would permit owners to manumit slaves, and that famous phrase "the pursuit of happiness" in the Declaration of Independence which is interpreted by Parrington as

[17] *The Colonial Mind*, p. 11.

[18] See the critical article by Esther E. Burch, "The Sources of New England Democracy . . . .," in *American Literature*, I (March, 1929), 11 ff., where this controversial interpretation of Parrington's is first brought to notice. Her mild conclusion is that the first chapter should have been more thoroughly documented.

[19] *The Colonial Mind*, pp. 343 ff.

marking a departure from Locke and the substitution of the broader French conception.[20] Much has been written on the source of Jefferson's political philosophy, the best conclusion being that of Carl Becker, who writes that the question as to where Jefferson got his ideas is not so important as where he could have gone to have got away from them.[21] Although Jefferson may have known of Rousseau's theories, the probabilities are against his having read the works of any French writer other than Montesquieu prior to the writing of the Declaration.[22]

Parrington's faults of omission, as noted by critical reviewers, arise from their disagreement with the author as to the scope of a work containing the phrase "Main Currents" in its title. One writer regrets the neglect of the natural sciences, particularly as influencing theology and politics; whereas another shows that Parrington has stated that science changed the outlook of American writers but fails to show how. Henry Seidel Canby praises the first two volumes highly but finds that Parrington is so busy fighting Calvinists that he overlooks John Woolman and other unobtrusive Quakers. In the uncompleted third volume no place is given for the treatment of religious leaders or movements; nor does it provide for the discussion of American magazines. The fields of intellectual endeavor which Parrington left virtually unexplored include drama, music, art, architecture, and law. Here the quarrel quite clearly is with Parrington's right to his title. Historiography is nowhere treated at length, although historians figure prominently in the bibliographies. Most surprising is the disregard of Frederick Jackson Turner, whom Parrington must have considered a potent force in the field of American thought. Here, again, the incompleteness of the third volume bars finality of judgment.

The most persistent criticism of Parrington's work is that he

[20] *Ibid.*, p. 344.

[21] *The Declaration of Independence: A Study in the History of Political Ideas* (New York, 1922), p. 27.

[22] *Ibid.*, p. 28; Gilbert Chinard, *Thomas Jefferson the Apostle of Americanism* (Boston, 1929), p. 85. Chinard emphasizes the importance of a pamphlet by James Wilson on the political theory behind the Declaration of Independence.

schematically developed a thesis. That he was aware of his own prejudices is shown by the confession in the foreword of his first volume, already quoted. A respected authority in the field of American literature, in commenting on Parrington recently, wrote: "In the study of the evolving American character there is no more reason for a historian's taking sides with the characters, groups, or regions than there is for a chemist's showing an emotional partiality for one of the elements."[23] Such sublime objectivity could never have been Parrington's, however well others may have succeeded in attaining it.

The list of biases with which he has been charged is appalling: he had the insularity of a Far-Westerner; he disliked all New Englanders save the rebels; he was not kindly disposed toward his alma mater; there was no balm for him in Calvinism; all theologians come to a bad end save the rebellious Theodore Parker; and, most "damnworthy" of all, he cut the cloth to fit his pattern of economic determinism.

Many of the criticisms which are listed above with cumulative distortion appeared during his lifetime. His mild reply is in the foreword of his third volume:

It ought not to be necessary to add that in these volumes I have not essayed to write a history of American literature—that rather difficult task for which no scholar is as yet equipped. But I have suffered so many gentle reproofs for failing to do what I did not set out to do, that it may be well to repeat what I said in the Foreword to Volume I, that I have been concerned in the present study with the total pattern of American thought—the broad drift of major ideas—and not with vagrant currents or casual variations. In particular I have been repeatedly taken to task for a seeming slight put upon certain of our artists, and it has been inferred that I slighted them because I chose to ignore whatever did not fit into a rigid scheme of economic determinism. Let me say in rebuttal that I hold no brief for a rigid scheme of economic determinism. I recognize the rich culture potentialities that inhere in individual variation from type, and I realize that the arts are likely to receive their noblest gifts from men who should be classed biologically as cultural sports or variations from the cultural type. But in such a

[23] Boynton, *Literature and American Life* (Boston, 1936), p. 540.

study as I have undertaken, individual variation is significant not for its own sake, but rather for the help it may offer in determining the type.[24]

The most ardent partisan of Parrington would find it impossible to deny all charges of prejudice and partiality. That he was unjust in his estimate of the Mathers, Thomas Hutchinson, Jonathan Edwards, and John Marshall, among other Puritans and conservatives, seems to be established. His essay on John Marshall is particularly malevolent:

An easy-going nature, he was wholly wanting in intellectual interests. Strangely ill-read in the law, he was even more ignorant of history and economics and political theory. . . . . Of social and humanitarian interests he was utterly devoid. One might as well look for the sap of idealism in a last year's stump as in John Marshall. . . . . The narrowness of his outlook intensified the rigidity with which he held to his fixed opinions; and his extraordinary courage coupled with a dominant personality clothed his strategic position as Chief Justice with fateful influence on the later institutional development of America.[25]

Here is a Jeffersonian with a vengeance! He does not even admit the strength of Marshall's position from the standpoint of legal reasoning. In the discussion of the case of *Fletcher* v. *Peck*, Parrington says that in plain language the decision meant: "A legislative contract is sacred no matter how corruptly got."[26] He adds that this was a curious decision for one to make who professed a veneration for the common law. That Marshall may have had a higher veneration for the Constitution, which contains a clause forbidding a state to impair the obligation of contracts, is neither asserted nor implied.

An elaboration upon the prejudices of Parrington would serve no purpose here; let the reader make his own list in the light of his own preconceptions. The apparent biases of the author have vitiated his conclusions for many scholars. To what extent this unfavorable reaction is due to unfamiliarity with his viewpoint it is difficult to conjecture.

[24] *The Beginnings of Critical Realism*, p. xx.
[25] *The Romantic Revolution*, pp. 21 ff.   [26] *Ibid.*, p. 26.

There remains the question as to the distinction between so-called "prejudice" and "interpretation." Parrington, it is only fair to say, felt that he was within his proper bounds as a writer on the liberal tradition when he "took sides," thereby enabling all who followed after to distinguish friend from foe. The limitations of his work may derive largely from the limitations of economic determinism, although that approach to the writing of political history has received wide approbation in the most respectable circles.

He worked hard at the task he had set for himself until death overtook him. In simplest terms he may be said to have written an account of the important economic, political, and social theories as reflected in the works of certain American men of letters; or, more generously, that his work, in spite of its fragmentary end, stands as the most comprehensive study of American thought written, fortunately or unfortunately, from the point of view which had proved fruitful in the wider field of American historiography. It is the most eloquent defense of American democracy which has appeared thus far in the twentieth century.

INDEX

Adams, Charles F.: judgment of Rhodes by, 182, 184; quoted, 23

Adams, Henry: character of, 191, 198, 199, 201, 203, 205, 206; democracy and, 199–201, 205; Harvard and, 148, 191, 192, 200, 205; Hildreth and, 41–42; the *History* of, 192–96, 198, 199, 201, 294–95; importance of, 191, 192, 195, 198, 199, 203–5; influence on Channing, 294, 295 n., 296, 303; literary technique of, 191, 194, 195; objectivity of, 191, 195, 311; philosophy of, 191–206; Parkman praised by, 57; quoted, 57, 191–98, 201–6; religion and, 202–6; teaching of, 191–93, 195, 294; views of history of, 196–98, 201–3. *See also* Adams, J. Q.; American Historical Association; Becker, C.; Channing, E.; Darwin, C.; Gallatin, A.; Grant, U. S.; History; Jackson, A.; Jefferson, T.; *North American Review;* Randolph, J.; Washington, G.

Adams, James T.: judgment of Bancroft by, 18; mentioned, 195 n.

Adams, John: Hildreth on, 36 n., 37; Schouler's use of works of, 91, 99 n.; mentioned, 4, 76, 97, 194, 202, 402

Adams, John Quincy: H. Adams and, 194, 200, 202, 205; Fiske's view of, 160; Roosevelt's view of, 245; Wilson's view of, 109; mentioned, 76

Alvord, Clarence W.: adverse criticism of, 333–37; appearance and character of, 326–27, 333–36; attitude toward New England of, 323, 329, 333, 337; as author, 325–38; Beveridge and, 386; early life of, 323–24; economic factors stressed by, 330–31, 337; as editor, 324–25, 328–29, 331, 337–38; importance of, 337–38; literary technique of, 328–29, 332–33, 336–37; objectivity of, 329–30, 334–36; Parkman criticized by, 57, 59; pro-English views of, 325–26, 329, 335–36; quoted, 323, 328–31, 334–36; residence abroad of, 323–25, 327, 331; as teacher, 324–27; Van Tyne and, 345; views of history of, 323, 327–31, 334–38. *See also* American Revolution; Barnes, H. E.; Footnotes; History; Lincoln, A.; Local history; Loubat Prize; Mississippi Valley Historical Association; News-

papers; South in history; Thwaites, R. G.; Turner, F. J.; University of Chicago; West in History; World War

American Historical Association: H. Adams and, 196; Beveridge and, 385; Channing and, 297; McMaster and, 129, 130 n., 143 n.; Mahan and, 214, 215, 218, 219; Phillips and, 357, 360, 368, 372; Roosevelt and, 239–41, 247 n., 251; Schouler and, 92; Turner and, 253; Van Tyne and, 340, 343, 352

American Revolution: Alvord and, 326, 329, 331, 334–38; Bancroft and, 11, 16–21, 23; Beer and, 313, 315–18; Beveridge and, 379, 383, 390; Channing and, 19, 297–99, 301–2, 304, 306; Fiske and, 149–50, 153–55, 166–67; Hildreth and, 27, 34–35; von Holst and, 70, 82–83; Mahan and, 213 n., 218–19; Osgood and, 272, 281, 284 n., 291–92; Parrington and, 404–5; Rhodes and, 179; Roosevelt and, 243–44, 248–49; Schouler and, 88–90, 100 n.; Van Tyne and, 339–52; Wilson and, 111–12, 115–16; mentioned, 128 n., 141, 294, 359

Andrews, Charles M.: Beer's work judged by, 315 n.; Osgood's work judged by, 276 n., 278 n., 280 n., 286–87, 288 nn., 290 n., 291; mentioned, 275, 292, 327

Bancroft, George: accuracy of, 17, 19–21, 23, 28; biography by, 12; character of, 1, 2, 6, 7, 9, 10, 12, 17, 23; children of, 4 n.; democracy of, 4, 8, 9, 12, 17, 22, 23, 49; education of, 2; Fiske's judgment of, 166; friends of, 2, 3, 7; Hildreth's judgment of, 28; the *History* of, 4, 5, 7, 8 n., 9–24, 294; importance of, 1, 12, 23, 24; literary methods of, 12–16, 20; literary style of, 9, 13, 16, 17, 20–23; McMaster and, 123, 126, 135; marriage of, 3, 4, 9; objectivity of, 4, 12–15, 17–20, 22, 23, 28; orations of, 4, 6–9; Osgood's judgment of, 284; parents of, 1; Parkman's judgment of, 57; philosophy of, 7–9, 13, 16–18; poetry of, 3, 9, 10, 12; popularity of, 11, 12, 19, 28; quoted, 2, 3 n., 4–10, 12–14, 17–20, 22, 23; religion and, 2, 3, 7–9, 16–18; research of, 7, 13–15, 20, 21; residence abroad of, 2, 3, 7,

409